LEBANON VALLEY COLLEGE:

A Centennial History

1866-1966

LEBANON VALLEY COLLEGE:

A Centennial History

by Paul A. W. Wallace

*Published
by the College
1966*

DEDICATED
To all who have taken part
in this
"glorious venture in faith"

A wise man will hear, and will increase learning; and a man of under-standing shall attain unto wise counsels.

—Proverbs, 1:5

Happy is the man that findeth wisdom, and the man that getteth under-standing.

—Proverbs, 3:13

She is a tree of life to them that lay hold upon her; and happy is every one that retaineth her.

The Lord by wisdom hath founded the earth; by understanding hath he established the heavens.

By his knowledge the depths are broken up, and the clouds drop down the dew.

—Proverbs, 3:18–20

Yea, if thou criest after knowledge, and liftest up thy voice for understand-ing;

If thou seekest her as silver, and searchest for her as for hid treasures;

Then shalt thou understand the fear of the Lord, and find the knowledge of God.

—Proverbs, 2:3–5

And wisdom and knowledge shall be the stability of thy times.

—Isaiah, 33:6

On such an occasion it is well to pause, as you do now, and review the story of the past; to linger with pardonable pride over difficulties manfully faced and overcome, to point out the steps of progress and take pains to show the measure of advance, to state the present problems (for problems there must always be in every human movement that has life), and take courage for a new and ever more inspiring future.

—Judge J. B. McPherson, at the Twenty-Fifth Anniversary of Lebanon Valley College, June 15, 1892.

The Lebanon Valley College Centennial Seal was one of 23 designs submitted by staff members, alumni, and students of the college. It is the creation of Mr. Peter Bugda, formerly an instructor at the Annville-Cleona High School and an instructor in art at L. V. C.

The Centennial Theme—one of 28 ideas submitted for consideration —is "The Discriminating Mind and the Understanding Heart." It was suggested by Dr. George G. Struble, Chairman of the Department of English and Secretary of the Faculty.

Foreword

LIKE A WRITER for the Elizabethan stage, the author of a denominational college history must address an audience which, though small, embraces a wide variety of people. There are, to begin with, the alumni, who expect to be reminded in these pages of their undergraduate days, with the help of screened anecdotes and personalities. There are the professors and the administrative staff, who desire to know, in more general terms, how the College came into existence and why current traditions got such a hold. Members of the supporting conferences desire to know how well the original purpose of a Christian Liberal Arts College has been fulfilled. Parents wish to see (if they are not themselves graduates) what manner of institution it is to which they have sent their sons and daughters. It should be added that all of the prospective readers will expect to learn something of the struggle, of which they may have heard rumors, out of which the College has emerged into maturity.

The writer of a centennial history is confronted with still another problem. All the readers mentioned above want their history, in addition to everything else, to be a reference library: a compendium of all the information contained in a hundred college catalogs and a hundred thousand separate minutes kept by the Faculty, the Administration, and every campus organization since its inception.

The attempt to fulfill even a modicum of these demands in the present book would have failed if it had not been for the generous help given by friends of the College and especially by alumni and members of the present college staff. It is impossible to thank them all by name, but a few must be singled out for special acknowledgment.

The author owes much to President Frederic K. Miller for his advice and encouragement, and for his patience under interview; to Dr. Carl Y. Ehrhart, Dean of the College, who has not only thrown light on present student-faculty relations (as seen in quoted interviews), but has read the manuscript and offered valuable suggestions; to Dr. Samuel O. Grimm, who helped to set the writer on a true course at the outset of this study, and contributed a wealth of information about events in which he had participated; to the Rev. Bruce Souders, Director of Public Relations and Historian of the Eastern Conference of the E. U. B. Church, for a variety of aids—providing information, setting up interviews, and seeing this book through the press; to Dr. Ralph S. Shay, Associate Professor of History and President of the Lebanon County Historical Society, for instant help in research whenever the need arose and for making available his history majors' senior papers dealing with various segments of the College's past. The writer's acknowledgments to Miss Gladys M. Fencil, who typed the manuscript and whose wide knowledge of the College, past and present, was frequently called upon, is more fully extended in Chapter 27. Without the assistance of Mrs. D. Clark Carmean, Executive Secretary of the Centennial Committee, it would have been impossible to complete the present work within the allotted time. She typed many transcripts from the Lebanon *Courier,* the Lebanon *Daily News,* and the conference minutes. She collected pictures, prepared Appendices B, C, and D, and made available a rich file of notes and correspondence dealing with the college history. To Dr. Donald E. Fields, Librarian, and Mrs. Fields, Cataloging Librarian, particular thanks are due for the collection of *L. V. C. Memorabilia* which they had organized and which provided indispensable tools for such an undertaking as this.

Special thanks are due to Dr. Harold Bennett who, having seen service on the L. V. C. Faculty during the crucial 1920's, now contributes an appraisal of President Gossard and Dr. Paul Wagner.

I am deeply indebted to Dr. John H. Ness, Jr., the Curator of the Evangelical and United Brethren Historical Society at Dayton, Ohio, and to his staff; to Mrs. J. Balmer Showers of Dayton, for her generous sharing of information about her father, President Lorenz, and for her permission to quote from his manuscript autobiography; to Mr. and Mrs. Ray E. Kiefer of Scottdale, for family reminiscences about Mrs. Kiefer's grandfather, President Keister, and for copies of his letters, books, and other publications; to the Rev. Dr. J. Bruce Behney, Vice President of United Theological Seminary, and to the Rev. Dr. Calvin H. Reber, Professor of Missions at the same institution, for sharing with the writer reminiscences of an earlier time at L. V. C.; to Mrs. Laura Reider Muth of the class of 1892, and to former Professor Albert H. Gerberich of the class of 1888 for reminiscences of their student days.

With the help of these and others, the author has attempted to write what might be called a biography of Lebanon Valley College. The College is here presented, not from the faculty angle alone nor exclusively from that of the students and alumni. Both these and other elements that have contributed to the College's Life have been kept in view. It is hoped that there will emerge in the reader's mind the impression, not of a college with a split personality, but of one which, though complex, is well integrated in character and also distinctive.

To put the author's aim in simplest terms, he has tried to do three things: first, to make the story of the College's struggle for recognition sufficiently intimate to be recognized by the alumni; second, to show the significance of that struggle when viewed against the background of the Church that gave it birth and in the light of the democratic process of which it is a prime example; third, to explain the successful outcome of the struggle in today's sound and forward-looking College of Liberal Arts at Annville, Pennsylvania.

Paul A. W. Wallace
Annville, Pennsylvania
January 1, 1966

Contents

Illustrations

CHAPTER ONE

"Say Not the Struggle Nought Availeth"

WHEN LEBANON VALLEY COLLEGE first opened its doors on that Monday morning, May 7, 1866, the founders had a vision of what a Christian Liberal Arts College could be: a place where the minds of young people, under Christian influence, might be trained to the greatest efficiency, so that these young men and women, freed from the drag-chains of ignorance, superstition, and prejudice, might the more fully realize themselves in the service of God and man.

That vision, both in its aim and in the method of its attainment, is neatly summed up in the College's motto, *Libertas per Veritatem*: "The Truth shall make you Free."* Its fruits are expressed in the special motto chosen for this Centennial: "The discriminating mind and the understanding heart."

The exultation of the founders on that opening day was tempered by awareness of a struggle around them and ahead of them. Already the College was at the vortex of a fierce debate over the wisdom of allowing the Church to provide higher education for its young people. It is true that in 1845 the General Conference of the Church of the United Brethren in Christ had gone on record as favoring the establishment of a denominational institution of learning, and that as a consequence Otterbein University (now Otterbein College) had been founded at Westerville, Ohio, in 1847, and Mount Pleasant College in Westmoreland County, Pennsylvania, in 1850. But opposition to higher education was nevertheless outspoken and well-entrenched among the United Brethren. It was based in part on the practical fear of incurring "irredeemable debts" (as the General Conference minutes noted), but chiefly on the more basic fear of spoiling candidates for an effective ministry among the pioneer settlements of America.

In order to understand the depth of this latter fear and the sincere, if mistaken, attacks it precipitated against the College, one must understand the strange elements that went into the making of the United Brethren Church. It is to the eternal glory of the Church that these discordant elements should

---

* L. V. C.'s first motto was, "Knowledge is Power." It was not until 1906 that the present motto, together with a new seal, was adopted.

have been brought together at all; but no one should be surprised at the resulting paradox: that the church founded by the learned Philip William Otterbein (son of the "Very Reverend and Very Learned" John Daniel Otterbein, rector of a Latin school at Dillensburg in Germany), should have inherited, as it did, a tradition of indifference and even hostility to higher education.

A glance at the Church's origins will explain the paradox. It was born of an evangelistic movement in America, sometimes known as the Second Great Awakening. The name, United Brethren, came from an incident at a revival meeting held in Long's barn, near Lancaster, in or about 1767. A sermon delivered on that occasion by a Mennonite preacher, Martin Boehm, awakening men to the vision of Jesus, the Christ, so stirred the Reverend Philip William Otterbein of the German Reformed Church, who was present, that he embraced the speaker and exclaimed, *Wir sind Brüder,* "We are brethren."

Out of that meeting of opposites came informal gatherings of Mennonites—plainest of the "Plain Folk"—with members of the liturgical Reformed Church and of other communions in an effort to break down denominational barriers and come to the heart of Christianity. Interest in this embryonic ecumenical movement, with its heart-warming fellowship, grew. Under the leadership of Otterbein, with the powerful aid of Martin Boehm (who in the meantime had been expelled from the Mennonite Church), meetings were attended by High-Churchmen and low, German Reformed and Lutherans, Methodists, Mennonites, and Dunkards, and by some Moravians, who had long been preaching religious fraternity. Otterbein and Boehm worked closely with Bishop Asbury of the Methodist Church, and Christian Newcomer led a strong movement for union with the Methodists. It was largely a matter of language that kept the two churches apart.

These United Brethren beginnings are beautifully summarized in the minutes of the Fifteenth General Conference of the U. B. Church, held in 1869:

"The United Brethren in Christ sprang from diverse, yet converging elements. A devout Reformed and a holy Mennonite cast aside all that was formal, all that was not purely of Christ, in their respective churches. They came together, and congenial souls clustered about them."

There was no thought at that time of creating a new church, only a desire to revitalize the old ones. But, to accomplish their aims, the leaders found a tighter organization was necessary. Accordingly, on September 25, 1800, at the home of Frederick and Peter Kemp near the city of Frederick, Maryland, a general meeting of "United Brethren" was held at which reports were received, plans were laid for regular annual conferences, and the name, United Brethren in Christ, was adopted.

This may be said, writes Dr. Edwin H. Sponseller in *Crusade for Education,* "to have been the first formal session of the original conference of the church," the Pennsylvania Conference. Fifteen years later, as the work of the

Rev. Philip William Otterbein
Courtesy of The Eastern Pennsylvania Historical Society

United Brethren expanded across the Allegheny Mountains, the first General Conference was held at Mount Pleasant in Westmoreland County.

At first it was exclusively a German language church, entirely rural, and small in numbers. But the influx of English-speaking people into the country created a demand for English-speaking ministers. These were provided. Many of them (like John Russel) moved with the immigrants into the West. The number of adherents rapidly grew. According to the estimate of the Reverend Abram P. Funkhouser (President of Lebanon Valley College, 1906–1907), from a low of about nine thousand in 1820, the church membership had risen by 1850 to forty thousand and by 1860 to ninety-four thousand.

In its earliest years, during the lifetime of Philip William Otterbein, ministers of the German Reformed Church played the leading role in the United Brethren movement. But after his death the flow of adherents from the Reformed Church dwindled, while that from the Mennonites continued. Small, semi-independent bodies of Mennonites (who have a tendency to fragmentation) drifted into the movement and became absorbed in the Church

3

of the United Brethren in Christ. So it was that, despite the influx of new members from other denominations and of many without previous church connections, the Reformed Church yielded in numbers and influence to the Mennonite.

In those days, the Mennonite tradition, in contrast with that of the Reformed, was against higher education. The simplicities of farm life, especially in a day when schooling was not at all general, predisposed most of the Plain People to be suspicious of learning. They feared that schooling beyond the three R's would draw their young people away from the two things they believed most essential to the good life: the plow and the Bible. The Mennonites were against high schools and colleges as tending to "worldliness."

Even Philip William Otterbein (as Dr. J. Bruce Behney, '28, writes in "Sanctified Education"), "as he labored among people of the frontier . . . believed their primary need was for the preaching of the gospel in very simple terms and with considerable evangelistic emphasis, and that any attempt . . . to develop an interest in advanced education was superfluous."

So it came about that the church founded by one of the most learned men in Pennsylvania was slow in providing college education for its young people, and, once it had established colleges, nurtured a strong minority devoted to their destruction.

This is not the place to discuss the pros and cons of the Church's doubts about higher education. It is enough at this point to observe that, while most young colleges are slow to take root, Lebanon Valley College suffered more than her share of hindrances to growth. When the complexion of the soil in which she was planted is considered, her success in the end seems all the more remarkable. It was reported in 1955 that, out of thirty-four colleges, seminaries, and academies founded by the United Brethren Church, only four survived. These were Otterbein University, Lebanon Valley College, Shenandoah Collegiate Institute, and Indiana Central College.

But there is more in the story of Lebanon Valley College than the issue of a church controversy. Her history is heartening to all who wish well to democracy. If the price of liberty is eternal vigilance, and if (as is certainly the case) vigilance without the discriminating mind is ineffectual, it follows that the long struggle from which Lebanon Valley emerged triumphantly is a victory for the democratic process.

She was not founded by an industrial tycoon who took this humanitarian way of preserving his name. She was not founded by an historic church with a great educational tradition behind it. She was created by a body of devout but unlearned people (not one member of the Conference that established her was a college graduate) who shared a vision of the good life and took the best way they could think of to preserve it for their children and their children's children.

4

CHAPTER TWO

"An Institution of Learning of High Grade"

A RESOLUTION APPROVING the establishment of a college was passed by the General Conference of the Church of the United Brethren in Christ on May 22, 1845.

"*Resolved*," it ran, "That proper measures be adopted to establish an Institution of learning."

But who was to take the initiative, and where was the financial burden to lie? Those questions were immediately answered.

"*Resolved*, therefore," continued the conference record, "that it be recommended to the attention of the annual Conferences, etc., avoiding *irredeemable debts*. (Approved 19-5)."

The initiative having been thus passed to the local conferences, several of them quickly responded. The first to do so was the Miami Conference of Ohio, which proposed to co-operate in such a project with the St. Joseph Conference and others; but nothing came of it. The Scioto Conference next entered the lists, and in 1847 succeeded—against strong opposition—in establishing Otterbein University at Westerville, Ohio. Allegheny Conference followed with the opening of Mount Pleasant College in Westmoreland County, Pennsylvania, in 1850. Things did not go well with it, and in 1858 it disappeared, being united with and absorbed by Otterbein.

Nine other United Brethren Colleges were founded before Lebanon Valley opened its doors in 1866, but none of them lived long. These were Hartsville University, Indiana, founded in 1850; Evergreen Seminary, Ohio, 1851; Blandinsville Seminary, Illinois, 1851; Western (Leander Clark) College, Iowa, 1856; Sublimity College, Oregon, 1858; Michigan Collegiate Institute, 1859; Westfield College, Illinois, 1861; Bourbon Seminary, Indiana, 1861; Lane University, Kansas, 1865. The death rate was appalling. Seventeen other United Brethren Colleges, founded before the century was over, failed to reach maturity.

It is not known precisely when the Pennsylvania and East Pennsylvania conferences, which at first had given support to Otterbein, began to think of venturing to establish a college for themselves, but it is known that things were coming to a head as early as 1860.

The Rev. G. W. Miles Rigor was mistaken when, in a brief paper which constitutes the earliest known history of Lebanon Valley College, he said: "It was during the closing years of the Civil War that the cause of higher education and the founding of a college among the United Brethren of Eastern Pennsylvania began to be seriously agitated." Rigor's memory of East Pennsylvania Conference proceedings went back only to 1862, for that was the year in which he was transferred from the Allegheny Conference to East Pennsylvania.

He apparently knew nothing of the action which had been taken by the East Pennsylvania Conference on January 17, the 4th day of the proceedings in 1860. It is thus recorded:

> In a reference to our cooperation with the Otterbein University, the following preamble and resolution were presented viz.
>
> Whereas we do not find it to our advantage longer to remain in cooperation with Otterbein University, therefore, Resolved, that we withdraw our cooperation with said institution, with a view of establishing an institution of learning in Pennsylvania as soon as possible. Adopted.

It would appear that the movement to establish a college in Eastern Pennsylvania was pretty well advanced before the Civil War. Probably the lengthening shadow of war and then the conflict itself, delayed action; but, after Gettysburg and Vicksburg, the discussion was resumed at the point at which it had been broken off four years earlier.

Be that as it may, it is certain that, on March 1, 1864, a report was presented to the East Pennsylvania Conference by the Committee on Education (consisting of Lewis W. Craumer, Jacob Erb, Daniel M. Kauffman, Henry Hilbish, and Daniel S. Early) which, after recommending continued support of Otterbein, went off on another tack altogether and submitted the following resolution:

> That we will not lose sight of our former resolution, that we erect an institution of learning in the bounds of this Conference, hoping that the Pennsylvania Annual Conference will co-operate with us in this glorious enterprise; yet not losing sight of Otterbein University, hoping from it to receive a benefit of professors and teachers for our own institution of learning.

That the opposition to higher education (led by the Rev. William Rhinehart, first editor of *The Religious Telescope*, and by the redoubtable Bishop John Russel, of whom more hereafter), was awake and determined, is made clear by the preamble to the above resolution. It finds it necessary to assure the Conference that higher education is not out of harmony with God's purposes for man:

JOHN H. KINPORTS, 1821–1893
(popularly known as Judge Kinports).
Clerk of the Orphans and Quarter Sessions
Court, Lebanon, and one of the founders of
the Annville National Bank, of which
he was the first president.

RUDOLPH HERR, 1827–1914.
Farmer, lumber dealer, member
of the first Board of Trustees
of Lebanon Valley College.

REV. LEWIS WENTZ CRAUMER, 1827–1889.
Presiding Elder of the East Pennsylvania
Conference of the United
Brethren Church.

HON. GEORGE W. HOVERTER, 1824–1894.
Dealer in coal, lumber, and grain,
member of the Pennsylvania House of
Representatives, 1879–1880.

REV. GEORGE A. MARK, 1826–1887.
Presiding Elder of the East Pennsylvania
Conference, Trustee of Lebanon Valley
College and of Trinity United
Brethren Church of Lebanon.

7

> Believing that God gave to man, in His creation, a Capacity to acquire a knowl-
> edge of Himself—His will & works—and implanted in the human mind a desire
> for knowledge, & that He did not endow him with such Capacities to know, with
> a view to their never being improved . . . but, on the Contrary, desires & demands
> an improvement of the faculties given . . .; also, that a Sanctified education is
> necessary to fully qualify man for the proper discharge of the duties growing out
> of the varied relations of life, and will the more fully fit him for that life which
> is to come; therefore—*Resolved*. . . .

The disappearance of Mount Pleasant College put two strong arguments into the hands of those in favor of a United Brethren college for the East. The first of these touched the pocketbook, the second, denominational pride. It was expensive for families in Eastern Pennsylvania to send their young people to Otterbein University at Westerville, Ohio. On the other hand, if they sent them to the already-established colleges nearer at hand (such as Dickinson or Franklin and Marshall), United Brethren parents risked the loss of their sons and daughters to other denominations.

Opinion among the United Brethren in Eastern Pennsylvania swung into line with the movement to establish a local college.

Accordingly, on February 24, 1865, the Committee on Educational Interests of the East Pennsylvania Conference, after noting that "all history proves conclusively that the influence & power of scientific & literary culture, bear with greater weight upon the moral status of a people than any other natural means or agency"; and, after recommending continued aid to Otterbein, went on to propose that, in order "to subserve educational interests of a more local character," the East Pennsylvania Conference should "Co-operate with the Pennsylvania Conference in building up a Seminary of learning somewhere within the limits of the Conference in mention."

The East Pennsylvania Conference thereupon appointed a "Board of five Trustees" to confer with a similar Board of Trustees appointed by the Pennsylvania Conference "upon the place of the School's location." The East Pennsylvania "Trustees of the contemplated High School" were three ministers and two laymen: the Revs. Daniel S. Early, G. W. Miles Rigor, W. S. H. Keys, and Messrs. John B. Stehman and Abraham Sherk. The Pennsylvania Conference appointed four ministers and one layman: former Bishop Jacob Erb, the Revs. Daniel Eberly, A.M., John Dickson, William B. Raber, and Mr. Joseph B. Hursh.

The joint committee, which met at Mechanicsburg, July 11, 1865, elected former Bishop Jacob Erb chairman and Miles Rigor secretary.

Various sites were considered: York, Chambersburg, and Newville, west of the Susquehanna; and, east of the River, Lebanon, Mount Joy and Annville.

The two conferences drifted apart when Jacob Erb and Daniel Eberly purchased Cottage Hill College, and the Pennsylvania Conference prepared to send its daughters to this "female" institution. For a time, East Pennsylvania Conference found itself alone in its plans to establish a co-educational college. The Conference suffered some doubts and fears, but it managed to carry on.

In one respect at least, the temporary defection of the conference across the river cleared the way. It settled the question on which side of the Susquehanna the proposed institution should be established. By midsummer, 1865, the selection of a site was approaching a decision. The Lebanon *Courier* broadly hinted as much. In its issue of August 3, it reported: "We understand that the United Brethren organization have in contemplation the establishment of a college in Annville."

The report, however, was premature. The choice of site had been narrowed to two, Lebanon and Annville, but it was not certain which of the two would be chosen.

On Thursday afternoon, September 28, 1865 a public meeting was held in the Birch Woods, Lebanon, to arouse public interest and find a solution. Annville sent a delegation. Miles Rigor, vigorous and forward-looking (he was soon to be appointed to a new English-language mission, later Trinity Church in Lebanon) addressed the meeting, giving, according to the *Courier,* "reasons why the contemplated school should be located in Lebanon Valley and at Lebanon."

The Rev. Ezekial Light brought the meeting down to fiscal realities. Since the college would be located in whichever town made the best financial offer (as had happened with Susquehanna University in 1858 when it chose Selinsgrove), he wanted a committee appointed by Lebanon to look into the matter and see what that city could raise. The delegation from Annville claimed a similar privilege. Their committee was composed of Rudolph Herr, George A. Mark, Jr., the Rev. L. W. Craumer, John H. Kinports, and George W. Hoverter.

Those five men proceeded to carve niches for themselves in the local Hall of Fame among the Founding Fathers of Lebanon Valley College, by purchasing a well-built school in their town, the Annville Academy, for $4,500, and donating it to the East Pennsylvania Conference "on condition," as the College Charter states, "that they would establish and maintain forever an institution of learning of high grade. . . ."

In February, 1866, at Columbia, the East Pennsylvania Conference, on the advice of its Committee on Educational Interests, adopted the report of the "Board of Trustees" which it had appointed to confer with its sister conference about a suitable college site. The report was to the effect that:

> Inasmuch as the United Brethren of Annville, Pa. propose purchasing the Academy located at that place, and to donate it to the East Pennsylvania Conference of the Church of the United Brethren in Christ, upon the condition that it be for ever

9

retained and conducted as a classical School of the U.B. Church; Therefore

We respectfully recommend to the Conference the propriety of cheerfully and thankfully accepting the said Academy at Annville on the terms proposed.

Respectfully submitted, D. S. Early
G. W. Miles Rigor
W. S. H. Keys
John H. Stehman
A. Sherk

The first LVC seal reflects the origins of the United Brethren Church.

CHAPTER THREE

Annville

WHEN LEBANON VALLEY COLLEGE was founded, Annville was already known in its neighborhood as something of an educational center.

Before 1800, Squire David Stroh is said to have conducted a school there, though where the schoolhouse stood is not known. In 1804, there was organized a "Church School," to which Lutherans and Reformed alike contributed, at the corner of Queen and White Oak Streets. Its first teacher is said to have eked out his modest income by serving as a grave-digger and a soloist at funerals.

In time the Church School became so well patronized that it had to seek larger quarters. These were found in a wing of a blacksmith's shop. It may be said that Annville boys and girls for some years conned their lessons to the rhythm of an authentic Anvil Chorus.

In later years, the town came to take its greatest pride in the Annville Academy, which had been established in 1834 and incorporated in 1840. That excellent institution soon attracted teachers and students from other states. By 1866 it had risen high in both physical and academic stature. It now occupied a handsome three-story brick building on Main Street, erected in 1857 and 1858 by Professor Daniel Balsbaugh—the structure to be known in college days as Ladies Hall and later as South Hall.

On its purchase by Balsbaugh in 1855, he renamed it the Lebanon Valley Institute. In 1860 it changed hands again, being purchased by some local investors. Though the official name remained the Lebanon Valley Institute, the older name, Annville Academy, clung to it.

It was more than the fiscal enterprise of her citizens that drew the College to Annville. The church fathers approved of the community on other grounds as well. It was a quiet village, "far from the madding crowd," and suitable, in the thought of the time, for a student's life of undisturbed study and contemplation. There were few distractions and therefore, according to the psychology of that day, there was little occasion for young people to go wrong.

The Lebanon *News* elaborated on that theme in its issue of April 29, 1876:

> Annville is truly a most promising town, as it is blest with a great number of churches and few hotels and its people are law-abiding citizens. The town, which is the second largest in the county, has but three taverns and they are doing a poor business, and of saloons, or what are commonly called restaurants, the town possesses none. We doubt whether it can be surpassed for orderlyness and quietude.

An air of innocence pervaded its tree-shaded streets and the small, neat homes, many of them clapboarded log houses, whose porches (on some streets) ran flush with the sidewalk. The more ambitious residences had overhead water spouts projecting dizzily from the eaves and in rainy weather discharging cataracts of water directly on to the road—or the heads of unwary pedestrians.

The Annville housewife made it a point of pride to occupy a rocking chair on the porch by 7:30 a.m., *after completing her morning chores.* On Mondays, competition to be first to hang out the wash saw many clothes lines filled before sunrise. On Saturdays, sidewalks in front of the houses were swept and scrubbed in preparation for the Lord's Day.

The people of Annville were sober, industrious, and friendly. Careful of their pennies but lavish in hospitality, reserved with strangers but hilarious among themselves, always active, emotionally responsive, proud of their racial inheritance yet interested in the world outside, they were a fair representation of the town-bred Pennsylvania German a hundred years ago.

Their leaders were men of substance, with cash in the bank and pride in the town. Annville had no race problem, no underworld, no radicalism. The Lebanon *Daily News* hailed it as "The Eden of Lebanon Valley."

Main Street (before the hurricane) was lined with tall magnificent trees. The town as a whole had an intimate air and was pleasant to look at. Its environs were entrancing. Beyond the woods and fields—green, yellow, and brown as the season advanced—lay the hills. Eight miles north of town were the Blue Mountains, stretched straight across the horizon like a seascape. What lay behind them? The question was always alluring.

Mud roads penetrated these mountain fastnesses (the Indians called them the Endless Mountains) at Indiantown Gap, Manada Gap, and Swatara Gap. But in the nineteenth century most Anvillians preferred to satisfy their curiosity with a trip on the Tremont Branch of the Reading Railroad to Pine Grove and Tower City in the anthracite country

Oiled wagon roads led out from Annville in all directions: to Lebanon, Schaefferstown, the Cornwall Mines, Campbelltown, Derry Church (now Hershey), Bellegrove, Mt. Ararat, Ebenezer. It used to be said that from Annville a spring wagon could take you *anywhere.* By 1866 this progressive town had acquired a railroad station. The recently completed Lebanon Valley Railroad (now part of the Reading) gave Annville rail connections with

From an early painting.

Harrisburg and the developing West, as well as with Reading, New York, and Philadelphia.

South of Annville rose the South Mountains, an older range than the Blue Mountains, its more ancient heritage (part igneous) being seen in the rounded contours of its heights and the unexpectedness of its hidden valleys.

Immediately west of the town, Quittapahilla Creek, coming from Lebanon, made a right-hand turn to the north on its way to join Swatara Creek. The "Quittie," as it came to be known by collegians, served many uses. Among others, it provided water for grist mills, immersion for German Baptists, canoeing for students of both sexes, and a good dousing for losers in the Annual Freshman-Sophomore Tug-of-War.

Annville was happy in the possession of an uneventful history. The bend in the Quittapahilla had been settled first by Scotch-Irish squatters, whom Surveyor General John Taylor found here in 1735 when he surveyed land nearby for Michael Baughman (Bachman). After the Germans moved in—the Bachmans, Raiguels, and Millers—Andrew Miller laid out the town, allowing the original Scotch-Irish to remain on payment of a ground rent.

The place was early known as Millerstown, but the name was subsequently changed to Annville, there being another Millerstown in Perry County. There is some debate about the origin of the later name. The town is commonly supposed to have been "named for Ann Miller, wife of the founder." The late H. Lenich Meyer, a graduate of the College in the class of '94 and at one time "Professor of Natural Science and Political Economy," assured the present writer that, in his opinion, it had been named in honor of Queen Anne, who in 1709 had given emigrants from the German Palatinate a haven in the British Isles and Pennsylvania.

War has never ravaged this countryside. There is no historical record here of atrocities committed during the French and Indian War. Legend is the source of some stories of Indian raids, but these have never been authenticated. George Washington passed this way during the Whisky Rebellion. That was about as close as the town ever came—until the Civil War took its sons away—to touching the mainsteam of national history.

Its population growth has been steady but not spectacular. When John Heckewelder, the Moravian missionary, passed through "Millerstown" in 1789, he reported thirty-five houses—fifteen more than Hummelstown. In another fifty years—by 1839—Annville's count had risen to 114 houses. In 1866 the friends of Lebanon Valley College were able to boast that their town had "over one thousand inhabitants."

The Rev. C. P. Croll, in *Ancient and Historic Landmarks in the Lebanon Valley,* had this to say of it: "Like a sparkling diamond upon the bosom of a king, so the neat little aggregation of houses, and schools and churches and workshops, and business houses, known as Annville, formerly as Millerstown, begems the bosom of this Quittapahilla Valley."

It was a small town, but as Daniel Webster might have said, there were those who loved it.

CHAPTER FOUR

Organization

THE ANNUAL SESSION of the East Pennsylvania Conference which on February 23, 1866, accepted the offer of the Annville Academy, proceeded to organize the new institution, with a view to opening it the same spring.

If this action seems precipitate—at least to those today who know something of the time it normally takes to find a president, gather a faculty, devise a curriculum, collect a student body, and procure an endowment—it should be remembered that among these conference members there was little academic experience. Not a man of them had a college degree, let alone administrative experience in the academic field.

But the old evangelism of the United Brethren was not dead, and it now expressed itself among a majority of conference members in eagerness for an institution of higher learning where their children might have a "Sanctified Education" without traveling too far from home. Accordingly, these followers of Philip William Otterbein and Martin Boehm took a long step, with faith, into the unknown.

It was a faith that had a good underpinning in wordly wisdom. "He who hesitates is lost." No doubt that thought was in the minds of those who understood the strength of the opposition to the college project. It would be well to have the new institution in operation before the forces of reaction had time to gather full head.

So it came about that the East Pennsylvania Conference in February, 1866, adopted the report submitted by its "Committee on Educational Interests":

> *Whereas,* This Conference has accepted the proffered donation by the people of Annville, Lebanon County, Pa., & vicinity, of the Academy buildings located at that place; therefore
>
> *Resolved,* That we recommend to this Conference—
>
> 1st, That a Board of 12 Trustees, consisting of an equal number of Ministers and Laymen in this Conference be appointed, whose duty it shall be to consummate the contract entered into by this Conference with the people of Annville, Pa.
>
> 2nd, That said Board of Trustees call a meeting not later than the third tuesday in March, 1866, for the purpose of starting the school according to the provisions of the contract made by this Conference with the donors of the property.

3rd, That said Board of Trustees lease the buildings to a responsible party, competent to conduct the school in the name of the Church of the United Brethren in Christ, and subject to visitation and supervision of the Board of Trustees, and upon the most favorable terms practicable, without incurring to the Conference, in its projection and operation till next annual Session of Conference a greater cost than one thousand (1000) dollars.

4th, That at the first meeting of the Board of Trustees they shall, before their final adjournment, appoint an Executive Committee to act in the interim of their meetings.

5th, That in establishing a Classical School in our midst, we do not contemplate interfering with the interests of *"Otterbein University,"* but hope thereby rather to promote its interests by arousing our people to the importance of Education, and in preparing Students for graduation in the regular College Course in said Otterbein University.

Respectfully submitted, E. Light
      G. W. Miles Rigor
      L. Peters
       Committee

The following members were elected to the first Board of Trustees: Rev. D. S. Early, John B. Stehman, Rev. G. A. Mark, Jr., John H. Kinports, Rev. G. W. Miles Rigor, Abraham Sherk, Rev. J. B. Dougherty, Rudolph Herr, Rev. L. W. Craumer, H. H. Crider [Kreider], Rev. D. Hoffman, Samuel Walmer.

It is apparent from the minutes quoted above that conference members were not unaware of some at least of the difficulties ahead. Two points in particular are to be noted.

Section 5, with its attempt to relieve the Conference of the charge of disloyalty to Otterbein, noted that the new institution was in the nature of a preparatory school, such as had long been in operation in the Annville Academy. Lebanon Valley College, in fact, was not starting "from scratch." It was continuing the old Academy, adding—bit by bit—some college departments, putting in, this coming year, a few courses for freshmen. It was anticipated that the bulk of registrants would be pupils of school age. That this was actually the case will be seen from a glance at the curriculum of the first year with its courses in reading, writing, spelling, and arithmetic, and from an examination of the list of students.

In the first college *Catalogue,* 1866-1867, President Vickroy's sons are listed as students: Willie R. Vickroy (born in 1859) and S. Percy Vickroy (born in 1861). Before Vickroy left Annville in 1871, his daughter Florence (born in 1864) was, according to her own statement, attending classes with her brothers at L. V. C.

As late as 1874, President Hammond announced: "The total number of students in attendance this year up to date [February] has been one hundred

16

and twenty-one. Of this number twenty-eight are in the College classes. Seven belong to the senior class and expect to graduate at the next commencement in June."

Section 3 of the Education Committee's report to conference in February, 1866, was the crucial one, instructing the Board of Trustees not to enter directly into the labyrinth of college finances, but to *lease* the whole operation (under conference supervision) to some competent person who would assume all the risks as well as "the rights and privileges" appertaining to the adjustment and collection of college fees. When the Lebanon Valley College Articles of Incorporation were recorded, January 7, 1868*, Article 5, under the heading "Trustee's Powers and Duties," held this proviso: "that the said Board of Trustees shall do no act conflicting with a lease held by G. W. Miles Rigor and Prof. T. R. Vickroy."

There was nothing unusual, at that time, in the leasing of young fresh water colleges to competent individuals. Nevertheless, the difficulties that lay ahead of L. V. C. were all but insuperable. The more honor, therefore, to the men whose faith carried them forward, and in particular to the leader whom the hour drew forth: the young, tall, handsome, and unbeatable George Washington Miles Rigor.

Miles Rigor (1831–1906) was born on a farm near Mount Pleasant and Scottdale in Westmoreland County. The Rigor (Reager, Reuger) family has been traced back to Spain in the fifteenth century. During the Spanish Inquisition, they fled to Bohemia and later to Alsace, France. Under continued persecution, they moved into Switzerland; and there in 1713 Burckhart Reagor, first of the family to come to America, was born. Burckhart settled in Berkley County, West Virginia, near Shepherdstown. His son, Henry, during the Revolutionary War, served in Light Horse Harry Lee's cavalry. Henry's son, David, who had a farm near Scottdale, changed his name to Rigor.

David's son, Miles (George Washington Miles) Rigor, grew up on the farm. As a result of a deeply emotional religious experience in 1850, he joined the church of the United Brethren in Christ. A man of great mental as well as physical vigor, he had a vision of what a college education might do for him, and in 1852 enrolled in nearby Mount Pleasant College, which the United Brethren had established two years before. He planned to enter the ministry. In his freshman year he received a license to preach, and in the middle of his junior year, he accepted a call from the Allegheny Conference to enter the active ministry. He left college—to his later regret—and began his labors in the Altoona and Tyrone circuit. Later he served at Johnstown, Springfield, Liverpool, and Perrysville, all then in the Allegheny Conference. He threw himself into this work with full abandon, and learned to respect

---

* Recorder of Deeds Office, Lebanon, Miscellaneous Index Book F-723.

Rev. G. W. Miles Rigor
Courtesy the Rigor Family

his own power of concentration. On the Liverpool circuit he had a round of thirty appointments—a four-weeks tour of 250 miles. He was formally ordained at Greensburg on January 26, 1860.

In 1862 he was transferred to the Pennsylvania Conference. It was here that he became interested in the possibility of establishing a local U. B. college, and was more and more drawn into the negotiations toward that end. He was secretary of the joint committee in the preparatory stages, and he was a member of the Board of Trustees appointed by the East Pennsylvania Conference to bring the movement to a head.

The Board made immediate search for a qualified man in the East Pennsylvania Conference to serve as Principal of the new college. There being no one in the Conference who had a college degree, they looked abroad. Daniel Eberly, of the Pennsylvania Conference had a degree, but he was already engaged as head of the college for girls his own conference was in process of establishing at York, Pennsylvania. They went still farther afield, and invited men from other conferences who had college degrees, but all declined.

When the Board of Trustees met on the third Tuesday in March, 1866, they—with the optimistic spirit of the hour—agreed upon three things: (1) to name the institution Lebanon Valley College; (2) to lease it for five years to a responsible person who would organize it and take the financial risk off the shoulders of the Conference; and (3) to open it on May 7, that is, in seven weeks.

The rest of the episode is best told in the words of Miles Rigor in his history of Lebanon Valley College:

> But when the reports of those who had been canvassing for a lessee came in, they revealed the sad fact that no one had been found who was willing to lease the School, as it involved considerable expense and responsibility. Correspondence with about all the available graduates of Otterbein University had failed to get a single favorable response. It was a trying hour. The opening of the School less than Seven weeks distant and no lessee and none in sight. What was the Board to do was the uppermost question just then.
>
> While in this dilemma, one of the youngest members of the Board, who had been active in promoting the interests of the school, came to the rescue. He had spent over 3 years at Mount Pleasant College [he tells elsewhere that he still had a year and a half to go] . . . and for 12 years had been in the active work to which he had devoted his life. But, in this crisis, he declared that if there was no other way out he was willing to risk his all, take the lease, open the School at the appointed time and conduct it in the manner prescribed. It is needless to say that his offer was most gladly accepted.
>
> This young man was G. W. Miles Rigor, who had just been assigned by the recent Conference to open a Mission and organize an English church in Lebanon.
>
> He still resided in Columbia, the place of his former pastorate, but was preparing to remove to Lebanon. He now hastened home to Columbia to prepare to remove to Annville. God ordered it otherwise. His next door neighbor was Rev. Thomas Rees Vickroy, A.M.,* a local preacher of the Methodist Church and holding a responsible position in the First National Bank of Columbia. Mr. Vickroy was a ripe Scholar and an experienced teacher in conducting boarding Schools. The lessee of the contemplated college called upon Mr. Vickroy to gather some information in regard to conducting a boarding School, etc.—After the situation had been talked over fully & the necessary information obtained, Mr. Vickroy said to R., "You should not quit preaching. Now teaching is my profession & you had better let me have that lease and you remain in the ministry." "Yes," said R., "but you are not a United Brethren which is a necessary requirement for a lessee, but I think I can take you in as a partner." This was finally agreed upon by the Board and all concerned, and V. was made principal of the School & R. was made Gen'l Agent, to keep a general oversight over the School and solicit students. . . .

The following is the contract between Rigor and Vickroy by which Lebanon Valley College was brought into being:

> This agreement made and concluded this twenty-third day of March Anno Domine One Thousand eight hundred and sixty-six, between Rev. Geo. W. Miles Rigor, of Lebanon, in the County of Lebanon and State of Pennsylvania, and Thos. Rees Vickroy, of the Borough of Columbia, County of Lancaster and State of aforesaid, witnesseth as follows viz.
>
> That for a valuable consideration, the receipt whereof is hereby acknowledged, the said parties agreed to associate themselves for the purpose of leasing the Lebanon Valley College until July fifteenth, A.D. one thousand eight hundred

---

* He received this degree from Dickinson College a few weeks after L. V. C. opened.

This agreement made and concluded this twenty-third day of March,
Anna Domine One thousand eight
hundred and sixty-six, between
Rev. Geo. W. Miles Rigor, of Lebanon,
in the County of Lebanon and State
of Pennsylvania and Thos Reed
Vickroy, of the Borough of Columbia County of Lancaster and State
aforesaid, witnesseth as follows, viz:
  That for a valuable consideration, the
receipt whereof is hereby acknowledged
the said parties agree to associate
themselves for the purpose of leasing
the Lebanon Valley College until July
fifteenth, A.D., one thousand eight hundred and seventy-one, and conducting
the same as a classical school of
high grade.
  It is further agreed between the said
parties that each shall furnish one-
half of the sum of money that may be
necessary to carry on said school,
  And it is further agreed between
the said parties that said Rigor shall
use his best efforts to secure pupils and influence
the public in favor of the said school.
  And that said Vickroy shall also use his
best efforts to secure students and take

Agreement between G. W. Miles Rigor and Thomas R. Vickroy

charge of the Classical department of said school, teaching the ancient and modern languages, mathematics, natural sciences, higher English, &c, and in connection with his wife, to take charge of the boarding department, attend to the business, keep the books, and exercise a general government over the school; and, in consideration of these extra services on the part of himself and wife, he is to receive one thousand dollars per annum, with boarding and lodging for himself and family, without charge.

And it is further agreed between the said parties that they will employ whatever assistance in instructing &c that may be necessary, and that whatever net profits remain over the one thousand dollars per annum mentioned above shall be equally divided between the said Rigor and Pickroy.

In testimony whereof we have hereunto set our hands and seals, the day and year first above written. The words "to secure pupils," in 5th line underlined before signing; also the words "per annum"

Signed, sealed and delivered G. N. Miles Rigor (Seal)

in presence of

T. Suffling Theo Rees Pickroy (Seal)

Edward E. Davis

From the Lebanon Valley College Memorabilia

and seventy-one, and conducting the same as a classical school of high grade.

It is further agreed between the said parties that each shall furnish one-half of the sum of money that may be necessary to carry on said school.

And it is further agreed between the said parties that said Rigor shall use his best efforts *to secure pupils* and influence the public in favor of the said school.

And that said Vickroy shall also use his best efforts to secure students, and take charge of the classical department of said school, teaching the ancient and modern languages, mathematics, natural science, higher English &c, and in connection with his wife, to take charge of the boarding department, attend to the business, Keep the Books, and exercise a general government over the school; and, in consideration of the extra services on the part of himself and his wife, he is to receive one thousand dollars *per annum* with boarding and lodging for himself and family *without charge*.

And it is further agreed between the said parties that they will employ whatever assistance in instructing, &c, that may be necessary, but that whatever net profits remain over one thousand dollars per annum mentioned above shall be equally divided between the said Rigor and Vickroy.

In testimony whereof we have hereunto set our hands and seals, the day and year first above written, the words "to secure pupils" in 25th line underlined before signing; also the words "per annum."

Signed, sealed and delivered	G. W. Miles Rigor (Seal)
in the presence of	Thos. Rees Vickroy (Seal)
Z. Supplee	
Edward E. Davis	

These two young men had embarked on what must have seemed to most persons "in the know" a foolhardy adventure. They trusted their own strength, trusted each other, and possessed the faith that moves mountains—not by physical miracles but by the wonders of human energy. As a story of loyal and successful partnership, it is unsurpassed.

A printed sheet was issued, showing a picture of the Annville Academy and giving particulars regarding Instruction, Religious Services, the School Calendar, and Expenses. It announced:

"This Institution, under the patronage and visitation of the East Pennsylvania Conference of the Church of the United Brethren in Christ, will be opened for the reception of Students on Monday, May 7, 1866."

It was subscribed: Rev. G. W. Miles Rigor

General Agent, at Lebanon, Pa.

Rev. T. R. Vickroy, A.B.

Principal at Annville, Pa.

CHAPTER FIVE

Transition from Academy to College

MINERVA, Goddess of wisdom, sprang fully grown from the brain of Jupiter. Lebanon Valley College, though an institution of learning, came into being quite another way. She underwent a slow metamorphosis from the Annville Academy to a College of Liberal Arts.

The Board of Trustees appointed by the East Pennsylvania Conference allowed the lessees of the projected college, Rigor and Vickroy, seven weeks in which to get the institution under way. They had to prepare the building for its new purposes, appoint a teaching staff, enroll students and start classes. What the friends of the college were about to witness was as competent a piece of practical statesmanship as could be imagined.

Rigor and Vickroy had a building to start with, the Annville Academy. What they wisely proposed to do was to take advantage also of the Academy's goodwill. They would continue the old school classes from primary to "prep school," merely adding such courses of college grade as advanced students might call for.

That the Annville Academy (as the Lebanon Valley Institute was still popularly called) was a going concern as late as December, 1863, is evidenced by a copy of the *Student's Monthly*, of that date, "Edited and Printed in the Lebanon Valley Institute" and now preserved in the L. V. C. archives. That issue of the *Monthly,* moreover, advertises a continuance of the current session into 1864, with no hint of a coming suspension.

Whether the old school building had been lying idle and the old course of studies interrupted for a few months, is not known. Professor H. H. Shenk, historian of the Annville Academy, could not say, although he had been in touch with those best able to inform him. Dr. S. O. Grimm who often talked about this matter with Dr. Shenk before his death, has this to say: "My guess would be that the Academy was turned over to the College as a going venture. If it was dead, it had not been dead long enough to be completely washed up."

The two founders of Lebanon Valley College set out to make the transition from school to college so smooth that the public would scarcely notice the change, and would continue to send up their children as they had been accustomed to do. In that way the financial undergirding of the college would be insured.

Evidence that this was the deliberate policy, is found in the *First Annual Catalogue,* 1866–1867. The frontispiece (see page 26) shows the familiar Annville Academy in its three-storied glory with cupola, overlooking the street where a coach, a carriage, a horseman, and pedestrians are passing, ladies in crinolines on the sidewalk or mounting the steps. Underneath is the caption, MODEL SCHOOL of LEBANON VALLEY COLLEGE, as though the old school had merely changed its name.

It was to be well over half a century before the College's metamorphosis was complete and the primary and secondary school program had been completely discontinued.

The College opened officially on Monday morning, May 7, 1866. It is not known what students were enrolled on that day, nor whether ceremonies of any kind marked the occasion. It is questionable if any students were registered so early for courses in what was called the "Collegiate Department."

A few months after the opening, a *Confidential Circular* was distributed among the members of the East Pennsylvania Conference. It provides the most intimate account to be found of the College's first days. It is a very human document, showing as it does the natural self-congratulation of promoters who had brought their infant charge so far along the way without serious mishap. It shows also their anxious search for students, and their shrewd appraisal of the best means to win the support of the clergy in the matter of student solicitation.

> We, the Trustees appointed by the East Pennsylvania Conference of the Church of the United Brethren in Christ, which met in February last, to receive and control the School property donated to the Conference by the citizens of Annville and vicinity, beg to inform you that the property has been thoroughly refitted and elegantly furnished, and that the school is now fully organized and in successful operation, with nearly fifty students. We would further state that we have leased the property to responsible parties who are sparing no pains to make the School one of the best in the land.
>
> The School is now under the Principalship of Prof. T. R. Vickroy, a graduate of Dickinson College,* a fine scholar and a christian gentleman, who is now assisted by Miss E. A. Stetson, a graduate of the State Normal School at Millersville, a very excellent and successful teacher, and a superior Elocutionist. Additional teachers of superior qualifications will be employed as the school increases.
>
> We have witnessed the manner in which the school is conducted, and take

---

* Thomas Rhys Vickroy (who preferred to spell his middle name the Welsh way) attended Dickinson College, but he left without finishing his work for a degree. Subsequently, however, he received the degree of A.B., having completed the required work at home. On June 28, 1866, a few weeks after he was appointed to the principalship of Lebanon Valley College, Dickinson awarded him, at his request, the further degree of Master of Arts *in cursu.* He was a highly educated man, as the list of his forty-eight copyrighted books (some of them second editions) in the Library of Congress bears witness.

pleasure in declaring to you the deep satisfaction the recitations and exercises afforded us. For the brief period the College has been in operation, the progress is marked—unsurpassed—, and we beg to express to you our implicit confidence in the Principal, Prof. Vickroy, and Miss Stetson, as teachers possessed of superior qualifications and unusual tact. One peculiarity of this school and one that should commend it to all, is that, besides all the ordinary studies pursued, all the students of this institution are daily exercised in vocal music, elocution, penmanship and drawing, and this, too, without extra charge.

The building has been re-painted, the rooms are entirely furnished and neatly carpeted, and everything wears the appearance of a pleasant home. The students are well pleased both with the instruction given and the boarding furnished, and we assure you that you are perfectly safe in recommending Lebanon Valley College to all your friends and neighbors as possessed of every desirable feature.

As the College belongs to the Conference, and as we have leased it in such a way that each additional boarding pupil will bring a revenue to the Conference of from $9 to $17 per annum, we trust you will put forth every effort, and diligently use your personal influence to secure students for the school. This we esteem to be your bounden duty, be you preacher or layman, for thus you may help on the advancement of the Church, and promote the Glory of God. Will you not be an earnest co-laborer with us in the building up of this as a first class institution of learning?

The Fall Session of 18 weeks will commence on the third Monday (20th day) of August, and it is desirable that the school be filled with students. Can you not influence at least five?

The charges for session of 18 weeks, comprising boarding, furnished room, light, fuel, washing and tuition in all branches except instrumental music and painting, is $88.50, one-half payable in advance; the balance at the middle of the session.

Please report the students whom you secure to the Principal, who will give any desired information. Trusting that you may duly appreciate the importance of this matter, and that you may aid us all you can, we beg to subscribe ourselves. . . .

A few months later, as the academic year of three sessions was closing, there appeared the *General Circular and First Annual Catalogue of the Officers and Students of LEBANON VALLEY COLLEGE for the Academic Year 1866–67* (Columbia, Spy Steam Power Press Printing Office, 1867).

This encouraged the general public to see what a successful year the College had had. It listed the names of 153 "Students," alphabetized and segregated according to sex. There was, however, no indication which among these hordes were college students and which elementary school pupils. Here is the general "Summary" of attendance:

Females,	49
Males,	104
Total,	153
Instrumental Music,	42
Drawing—Penciling,	66
Drawing—Crayoning,	8
Preparatory, or Model School,	100

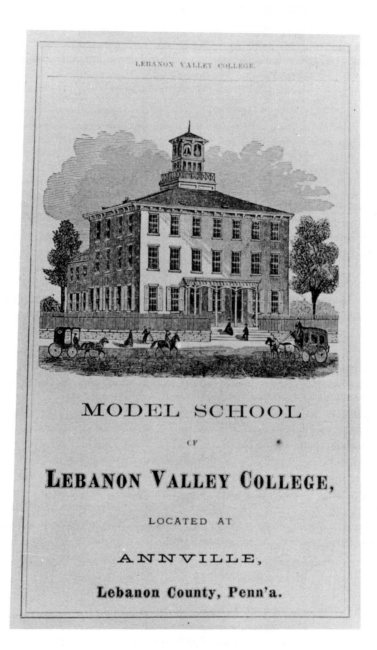

From the first Catalogue

Commercial Department, ...	17
Normal Department, ...	18
Collegiate Department, ...	53

It is not known how many of the 53 listed in the Collegiate Department were *bona fide* college students headed for a degree. It is known, however, that at the end of four years the first list of "Graduates" contained the names of only three students, and that not one of these was the recipient of a degree!

In *The College Forum* for April, 1888, it was stated that: "During the 22 years of its [the College's] existence 1500 ladies and gentlemen have been in attendance. 121 have graduated in the Collegiate department. . . ." Those figures would mean a yearly average of six graduates during the College's first twenty-two years.

That such figures were not abnormal for fledgling colleges is apparent from a glance at the history of a sister college, Otterbein. The Rev. Lewis Davis had this to say about the opening of Otterbein in 1847:

"We had one full teacher and others who helped. I taught some. Professor Griffith was our chief teacher. We struggled ten years before we could graduate anyone."

By the end of Lebanon Valley College's first academic year, the original number of faculty members had been quadrupled, being now eight. That only a portion of faculty time went into the more advanced courses may be seen from the positions they held:

Rev. T. R. Vickroy, A.M., President of the College; Professor of Philosophy and the Greek Language and Literature;

John S. Krumbine, Professor of Mathematics and Mechanical Philosophy;

E. Benj. Bierman, Professor of the Normal Branches, and Principal of the Model School;

Henry Houck, County Sup't, Theory and Practice of Teaching;

John Wesley Etter, Teacher of Penmanship and Book-Keeping;

Mrs. E. S. Vickroy, Preceptress;

Miss Ella L. Walker, M.A., Music and Drawing;

Miss Lizzie M. Rigler, Music, Painting and Ornamental Branches.

Blanks in the list (for names "To be Supplied") drew attention to four other positions in search of incumbents:

Professor of Ancient and Modern Languages and Literature;

Professor of Natural Science;

Professor of the English Language and Literature;

Elocution, Primary English and Object Lessons.

The art of Public Relations was not so well developed in those days as it has since become, but by August, 1866, the newspapers were aware of Lebanon Valley College. In its issue of August 9, the Lebanon *Courier* ran a report

Sketch of the New College, as it appeared in the 1867–1868 Catalogue

on "The closing exercise of the first session," which had taken place the preceding Thursday, August 2.

Principal Vickroy on that occasion had conducted the oral examinations, which were open to the public and were to be a feature of college life for many years. Miss Stetson performed "as an elocutionist and vocalist."

> Prof. and Mde. Castro were also there [continued the report],—in all their glory—and 'softly touched the guitar' to the gratification and praise of all present. We are glad to chronicle the fact that the Lebanon Valley College, under its present judicious, energetic, and well-skilled management, bids fair to become a permanent institution, and a blessing, an honor, an ornament to our beautiful valley.

Miss Stetson, though her name does not appear in the first Catalogue, seems to have been for a time the College's chief asset in publicity.

> Miss E. A. Stetson, teacher of elocution in the Lebanon Valley College at Annville [reported the *Courier* of August 18, 1866] gave an elocutionary entertainment in that place on Saturday evening last. The reading consisted of extracts of prose and poetry from various authors. The reading was entertaining—some parts highly amusing—and elicited the admiration of every one present, proving her to be a perfect master of the art she teaches. We understand that efforts will be made to induce her to give an entertainment of the kind in Lebanon.

A few weeks later, the *Courier* announced her forthcoming appearance at the Court House in Lebanon, at which time she would read "Enoch Arden, selections from the Bedott Papers, Sheridan's Ride, Mrs. Caudle's Lectures, and The Stripes and Stars."

The formal lease of the college property to Vickroy and Rigor was executed on July 15, 1866. The original document has not been found, but some of its most interesting terms are contained in the report of the Board of Trustees to the Conference in February, 1867. How little the members of conference understood college finance may be judged from their evident hope that the institution would be a money-maker for them.

> According to your instructions we leased the property to Rev. Thomas Rees Vickroy, A.M., and G. W. Miles Rigor, for the term of five years from the 15th day of July 1866, on the following conditions, viz:—that they pay into the Treasury of the board
>
> | | |
> |---|---:|
> | For each day pupil .... | 5 cents per week. |
> | For 20 or less boarding Students, ... | each 20 cents per week. |
> | For over 20 or less than 45 Students, ... | each 25 cents per week. |
> | For over 45 or less than 70 Students, ... | each 30 cents per week. |
> | For over 70 or less than 100 Students, ... | each 35 cents per week. |
> | and for all over 100 Students, ... | each 40 cents per week. |
> | So that 50 day pupils at 5 cts. per week, would amount to .... | $107.50 |
> | 20 boarding Students each at 20 cents per week .... | 172.00 |
> | 25 additional boarders at 25 cents per week .... | 268.75 |
> | 25 additional boarders at 30 cents per week .... | 322.50 |
> | 30 additional boarders at 35 cents per week .... | 420.00 |
> | 50 additional boarders at 40 cents per week .... | 860.00 |
> | Making a total income of .... | $2,150.75 |
>
> per year for 50 day and 150 boarding Students.

Next year the Board reported to the Conference: "The amount of rent received from the lessees was $497.85. The building was too small to accommodate the school, so much so, that we were compelled to rent accommodations outside."

The Conference, accordingly, authorized purchase of more land and the erection of a new building to meet this emergency.

Article IV. The said Corporators and their successors shall forever be one body politic and corporate in deed and in law, to all in and purposes whatsoever, and the name, style and title of Lebanon Valley College, and shall be competent and capa in law and in equity, to take to themselves and their succe for the benefit of said Colleg any estate, in any messuages, tenements, hereditaments, goo chattels, moneys or effects, b the gift, grant, bargain, sal conveyance, assurance, will devise or bequest of any pe or persons whatsoever, and the same property or effect sell, rent, or dispose of as oc sion may require for the use o said College, in such manne as to the said trustees or majority of them, at a lega

An article from The College Charter as recorded by the
Lebanon County court in 1867.

30

CHAPTER SIX

The College Charter

ON RECOMMENDATION of the Board of Trustees of the College, the East Pennsylvania Conference, in February, 1867, adopted terms for a charter to be applied for from the State Legislature. On April 5, the Charter was granted by the Commonwealth of Pennsylvania.

The document (as reprinted by the College in 1959 from the *Laws of the General Assembly of the State of Pennsylvania Passed at the Session of 1867*) contained five introductory *Whereases* which summarized the steps taken to establish Lebanon Valley College.

1. The purchase of the Annville Academy by citizens of Annville, who "presented the same to the East Pennsylvania Conference of the Church of the United Brethren in Christ, on condition that they would establish and maintain forever, an institution of learning of high grade. . . ."

In later years, when the removal of the College to some other community was seriously considered, this item in the Charter was widely quoted. Those opposed to the removal reminded their opponents that the Academy building had been donated on condition that the East Pennsylvania Conference maintain there "forever, an institution of learning of high grade." The original deed of property (the Academy and its grounds) dated February 18, 1868, stated explicitly that, "as soon as such classical school is abandoned then this present conveyance shall become of non effect and the property hereby conveyed shall revert to the grantors and their heirs. . . ." The College could not move away without losing this valuable property.

2. That "Said conference accepted said gift, and appointed a board of trustees to receive and control the same."

3. That the Board of Trustees "leased said property, with all additional buildings to be erected, to George W. Miles Rigor and Thomas Rees Vickroy, until the fifteenth day of July, one thousand eight hundred and seventy-one, said parties having obligated themselves to provide instruction in the elements, the sciences, ancient and modern languages and literature, the ornamental branches, and biblical literature and exegesis, with the privilege of teaching such other branches, as are usually taught in universities."

4. That "Said parties have successfully organized said institution, having invested their own means, and gathered a number of students from different sections of the country, the said school being under the principalship of Professor Thomas Rees Vickroy."

5. That "The said conference have appropriated twenty-five thousand dollars for the purpose of purchasing additional grounds, and erecting thereon suitable buildings: therefore,

Section 1. Be it enacted by the Senate and House of Representatives of the Commonwealth of Pennsylvania in General Assembly met, and it is hereby enacted by the authority of the same, That there be and is hereby erected and established, at the village of Annville, in Lebanon county, in this commonwealth, a college for the education of persons of both sexes, the name, style and title of which shall be Lebanon Valley College.

The clauses that followed dealt with the Board of Trustees, their election, terms of office, powers and privileges; the duties of the "head or chief master, . . . [who] shall be called and styled the president of the college"; and the duties of the "masters of the college [who] shall be styled professors, and their assistants, tutors."

The "first trustees of said college," as listed in Section 4 of the Charter, were the following:

J. J. Glossbrenner, of Augusta county, Virginia; John B. Stehman, of Lancaster county; George A. Mark, Jr., John H. Kinports, Ezekiel Light and L. W. Craumer, of Lebanon county; Joseph Hill, of Philadelphia; D. S. Early and Benjamin Riegel,

Bishop J. J. Glossbrenner
Courtesy of The Eastern Conference Historical Society

of Dauphin county; John Young, Rudolph Herr and Samuel Groh, of Lebanon county; I. L. Kephart, P. J. Riland, Joseph Young, Samuel Walmer and W. S. H. Keys, of Dauphin county, and Levi Hoover, of Lancaster county; David Hoffman, of Lehigh county; Michael Sherk, of Dauphin county; J. B. Daugherty and John Shultz, of Schuylkill county; D. M. Kauffman of Philadelphia; Lewis Peters, of Berks county; Benneville Kremer, of Snyder county, and Abraham Sherk and N. Steigerwald, of Lebanon county. . . ."

Several other particulars in the Charter are of special interest today. The first is that Lebanon Valley College was to be co-educational: "a college for the education of persons of both sexes." In this it was decidedly advanced. While not the first college in Pennsylvania to be co-educational, it was first among its degree conferring competitors in Eastern Pennsylvania. Swarthmore though it received its Charter in 1864 did not open until 1869. The University of Pennsylvania did not become co-educational until 1877.

A second interesting item was the granting to the faculty of the unusual privilege of being "ex-officio members of the board of trustees. . . ." During the first year of the College's existence, when the faculty was in process of growth from a start of two members, the complications that might ensue seem to have been missed by the Conference. Later, as faculty numbers increased, adjustments had to be made to save the Board from becoming unwieldly and its conference members from being swamped. It was then decided that the privilege of faculty membership be accorded only to full professors.

A further item of interest is that the Charter gave the College broad degree-conferring powers: the privilege "of granting and conferring, by and with the consent and approbation of the board of trustees, signified by their mandamus, such degrees in the liberal arts and sciences . . . as are usually conferred and granted in other colleges of the United States. . . ." The College has shown restraint in not abusing that privilege.

Before leaving the subject of the Charter, it is well to note that the Board of Trustees, in proposing the terms of the Charter to the East Pennsylvania Conference in February, 1867, had a concluding recommendation. It was this:

"That if the Trustees of Lebanon Valley College, shall at any time involve the Institution in a debt exceeding $10,000, the Board be personally responsible for the indebtedness exceeding the amount in mention."

Adopted as it was by the Conference, this hobble rope explains in part the reluctance of the Board in early days to undertake needed expansion programs.

Bishop John Russel

Taken from *History of the Pennsylvania Conference of the United Brethren in Christ*,
by Paul E. Holdcraft

CHAPTER SEVEN

The Debate over Higher Education

OPPOSITION TO HIGHER education among many members of the United Brethren in Christ was for a long time emotional and occasionally savage. It cannot be denied that there was some foundation for that opposition, although unfortunately those who voiced it were not, in general, the most articulate members of the Church.

The defenders of higher education, being on the whole better educated and with more dispassionate minds, were able to present their arguments more lucidly and forcibly. Nevertheless, they did not always go to the root of the matter, and they sometimes confused the issue. Seeing in their opponents only ignorance and prejudice, they tended to over-simplify the whole problem.

It was easy to show that higher education did not necessarily, as some claimed, make men "proud" or "rogues," or "backsliders"; that it did not "spoil" girls and make them "lazy"; that studies did not commonly ruin a student physically; that "playful recreation" did not have to be of "an immoral tendency"; and that what in 1847 Bishop John Russel called "preacher factories" did not inevitably turn out "poor, puny, debilitated creatures," as a man who signed himself Pharus described college graduates in the *Religious Telescope* for May 12, 1847.

The opponents of higher education were by no means all ignorant or unintelligent. They did, it is true, look backward rather than forward, being unable to think of the church as operating successfully in any but the pioneer communities they themselves had known. But some of these conservatives were more clear-sighted than their opponents. They saw sharply the dilemma hidden in the very idea of a "Christian Liberal Education."

If the purpose of a Liberal Education is, as the term suggests, to *free* the mind, to render it inquiring, discriminating, and susceptible to beauty as well as truth; and if, on the other hand, the Christian be one who seeks to reject all thought and experience that does not immediately "instigate to prayer"— then, assuredly, there would appear to be no such thing as a Christian Liberal Education.

Cardinal John Henry Newman, in his classic work, *The Idea of a Univers-*

ity, met the dilemma head on, and came to the conclusion that "Liberal Education makes not the Christian . . . but the gentleman," the latter being one with "a candid, equitable, dispassionate mind." Newman saw too far into the problem to be deceived by the apparent paradox. What he saw was that the habit of mind developed by a Liberal Education made better human beings and therefore better Christians: men and women more alive to God's world— its grandeur, its beauty, its dangers, its needs—and so better prepared to play a responsible part in bringing (as they prayed) God's Kingdom to earth.

Such a habit of mind is surely what the *Book of Proverbs* extols as Wisdom: "for whoso findeth me findeth life, and shall obtain the favor of the Lord."

If the definition of "Christian" be broad enough to include those whose fullness of life, irradiated by the spirit of Jesus who found a blessedness in the unselfconsciousness of children, enables them the better to understand and help their fellowmen, then there need be no contradiction in the term Christian Liberal Education. That is surely what the General Conference had in mind in 1845 when it passed its memorable resolution on behalf of "sanctified education."

To look back for a moment, it has been seen that some members of the Church of the United Brethren in Christ were, for a time, hesitant about allowing the Church to provide higher education for its young people. When Otterbein University and Mount Pleasant College were founded, the opposition to them was vehement and cruel. Otterbein barely survived. Mount Pleasant disappeared.

The founding of Lebanon Valley College seemed at first to mark a change. A writer in the *Religious Telescope* for July 18, 1866—only a few weeks after the Annville institution had opened its doors—congratulated the Church on its progressiveness and looked back with some amusement on what had been the prevailing attitude less than a score of years before:

> The friends of those early schools were compelled to fight their way at every step. The general sentiment was seemingly irreconciliably opposed to any advance in this direction. A large majority of the ministers shared this opposition. It was not an unusual thing for some of them, in the pulpit, to thank God that *"they had never rubbed their backs against college walls."* We distinctly recollect with what admiration we used to contemplate these exhibitions of pluck . . . ."
>
> But how is it now? Where is the man who would now give expression to such foolish utterance?

Where was the man? Not as far to seek as the writer supposed. The man was the Rev. John Russel, former Bishop, who now in his retirement was still an evangelical knight errant wielding as good a spear as he had used in 1845, when he tried to prevent the Rev. Lewis Davis from speaking on behalf of Otterbein University-to-be.

"Father" Russel, as he came to be known, was revered by all, loved by most, and feared by those who disagreed with him. He was earnest, resourceful, brave, and uncompromising in attack on anything he took to be evil. "Whatever he thought and believed he told the world, and when he got through saying it he left no doubt in anybody's mind what he meant." So Dr. Paul E. Holdcraft, historian of the Pennsylvania Conference, has described him.

Bishop Russel in his prime seemed to possess all good qualities except two: the discriminating mind and the understanding heart.

He was a product of pioneer life, and gloried in that fact. Born in 1799 on Pipe Creek in Maryland, he began his adult life as a blacksmith apprentice. His father helped him to set up his own shop, buying him a negro slave "to blow and strike."

John Russel early impressed himself on his neighbors. Tall, with good carriage, a powerful mind, and the muscular strength of a giant, he rejoiced also in possession of a voice deep-toned and resonant, commensurate with his magnificent physique.

In 1818 he received "license to exhort." Freeing his slave and moving west, he was received into the Scioto Conference. Thereafter his adventures with men and animals, as he pushed on west through Ohio and Indiana into Iowa, tested and confirmed his courage, faith, and wit.

"He was the open enemy of everything he believed to be wrong," said the Rev. C. T. Stearn, at one time his pastor, "and upon wrong he was ready to make war."

Quick on the trigger when he encountered what he called "the old serpent, who goes about like Roreing lion," he involved himself in many an uncertain contest. Witches he abhorred, wherever he found them, in the city of Baltimore or out in the country. One of the many adventures that liven his "Recollections" was his contest with a male witch or "conjurer" in a German Reformed congregation to which he had been invited as temporary pastor:

> . . . here I allmost found my match, there was an old fortune teller among them who gave out that [he] could Cure any purson or beast that was bewiched, find anything that was lost   this man stood high in estimation of the people, I felt my duty to teach them otherwise, undertook it in a mild way, in my sermon   after meetin, he made it his Bost by precenting a little ½ oz wheight bag. if that is hung around the neck of man or Beast no wich nor Bullet can harm   I asked "will it protect a Chicken? o yes any thing living." by permission I ask the Boys to get Ruster all the Congregation stood in the yard,   the Ruster was tied fast, the gun loaded the Bag put on, How far must I stand off? go as Close as you please said the cungerer, now I said to the Peopel if I dont kill that Ruster Il believe his doctrin, if I kill, I shall oppose it with all my might, stood off about 10 steps shott him dead; this on the Sabouth, done more good than any Sermon, in a few months wichera was done for. . . ."

In the same spirit, Father Russel opposed any venturing by his church into the abyss of higher education. Harking back to what, as an itinerant preacher, he had learned of the church's redeeming power in frontier communities, he thought that ministers should be trained solely for such service, and he loaded his gun against those who thought otherwise.

He lost one fight in 1845 when Otterbein was founded. He lost a battle in 1866 when Lebanon Valley appeared. But Father Russel was not a quitter. He resorted to guerrilla warfare in what he believed to be the Lord's service. In 1867 he made a raid on the new College that nearly wiped it out. E. Benjamin Bierman, who was then a professor at the College, thus described the incident in reminiscences published twenty-five years later.

> At about this time opposition to the school by an element in the church became very manifest. Members of the local church, who had been active in religious work, absented themselves from the stated meetings and the pastor in charge, under mistaken views of collegiate training, sympathized with the dissatisfied ones and invited an ex-bishop into his pulpit who, taking for his text Paul's saying: "Knowledge puffeth up" and without the edifying charity, spent an hour on Sunday morning, June 30*, in hurling his fallacious arguments at the heads of astonished friends and complacently regaling the deluded enemies of the progressive movement. President Vickroy says in his report to the conference, "The attendance of students was reduced from one hundred to seventy-five and the cause of this diminution was persistent opposition to the school on the part of certain brethren."

Vickroy, on February 20, 1868, ended his report to conference on the same incident with these words:

> However, the fury of the storm seems to be past, and the hope is entertained that the brethren who were instrumental in inflicting so much injury without any compensating good, will see wherein they have erred, and make suitable efforts to repair the damage they have done. The highest considerations of duty require this at their hands.

Russel had fired his shot, but this time the "Ruster" did not die. The College, instead, received a certain benefit from the incident, since it had made the issue clear-cut, narrowed to one particular. It was no longer an ideological question, whether institutions of learning were good or bad. It was an immediate question of life or death for a living organism, Lebanon Valley College.

It was also a question of conference honor. In founding the College, the East Pennsylvania Conference had committed to its support a number of people, members of the college staff, students, and their parents. Should they now be sacrificed and driven out, it would be a betrayal, weakening public confidence in the Church's integrity.

The issue was joined. The Conference stood firm. Enrolment at the College increased. Pastor Hoffman was dropped from the Conference. He left the

---

* There has been some question about the year in which this occurred. It is to be noted that in 1867 June 30 did fall on a Sunday.

United Brethren and founded the United Christian Church (also known as the Hoffmanites).

There is a tradition, strongly adhered to in some quarters, that John Russel underwent a change of heart and endowed the College to the amount of $10,000. It is worth examining.

To begin with, it must be understood that he was not opposed to education as such. But he had an aversion to the kind of tenderfoot minister he supposed an academic institution would foist upon the pioneer world he knew best.

He made a bequest of ten thousand dollars to the East Pennsylvania Conference, another ten thousand to the Pennsylvania Conference, and five thousand to the Virginia Conference, the interest on which was to be applied to assisting "young men of limited means to prepare for the ministry . . . by gaining sufficient knowledge of the Holy Scriptures."

Rules to govern what he called his "Biblical Chair" were announced in the *Religious Telescope* for July 7, 1868, page 346. It was there stipulated that the teacher was to have but one student, that the teacher was to be paid not less than $100 nor more than $120 a year, and that the rest of the interest on the money was to go to the student, if poor. In selecting the recipients of these scholarships, no distinction was to be made "on account of COLOR, or of the GERMAN AND ENGLISH LANGUAGES." No student, however, was to be admitted "who belongs to a SECRET SOCIETY, and is not of INDUSTRIOUS HABITS, OR WHO USES TOBACCO."

The crux of the matter was that the student was to live on a farm while studying (Bishop Russel conducted classes of this sort on his own farm) and avoid the contamination of college surroundings:

> The student shall labor with his hands (Eph. 4:28) not less than two hours per day, nor more than three. He shall be allowed, in addition to the above, three weeks to labor during hay-making and harvest; but he is not to overexert himself at any time in any way. All the proceeds of his labor shall go to the benefit of the teacher, except what he may earn in hay-making and harvest, which shall be his own . . . .
>
> The biblical chair shall, for the following named reasons, be kept separate and apart from any institution of learning.
>
> A—It requires an experienced itinerant minister to occupy the chair.
>
> B—Important things need to be impressed upon the student, in relation to an itinerant life.
>
> C—Manual labor is all-important to be connected with the chair, for health and vigor of mind which is not in the schools. . . .

But that was not Father Russel's last word on the subject. The tradition in some quarters that he changed his mind about college education has its roots in a strange, self-contradictory document which he signed a few months before his death:

> March the 21, 1870
>
> The regulations of the Biblical Chair as they are now printed in the Religious

Tel. July 7, 1869 whole Number 1520 shall be carried out to the letter by East Pa. Anual Conference, also the Pa. anual Conference, and the Va. Anual Conference, with this addition that each Anual Conference above named shall have power for the improvement and convenience sak to change aney part of the above Rules provided the Spirit intend and meaning of the same is not changed

John Russel

Attest
J. Erb
Ephraim Geeting

This amendment, despite its preliminary statement that the original regulations "shall be carried out to the letter," was understood at the time by some persons close to Russel to give large discretion to the conference beneficiaries. The Rev. C. T. Stearn, Father Russel's pastor, informed the Virginia Conference (as recorded in the *Religious Telescope,* March 9, 1870) that Russel had authorized the conference "to change the conditions of instruction if the conference so desire in the future."

There is, however, no record at the College nor in conference minutes of a direct bequest by Father Russel to Lebanon Valley. No documentary evidence has been found that any part of his bequest to the conferences ever reached this institution.

Whether or not Russel himself mellowed towards the end, it is certain that warriors of a kind he had at one time encouraged continued after his death to harass the College. When the ideological motivation of the conflict had subsided—the need of higher education having become almost universally accepted—a *tradition* of hostility to the College remained to imperil its life. It exhausted the energies of many presidents and took the lives of several of them.

CHAPTER EIGHT

President Thomas Rhys Vickroy

THOMAS RHYS VICKROY, first President of Lebanon Valley College, was a remarkable man from whatever angle he be approached: whether as an administrator who obtained a charter for the College, set up its rules and regulations,
established its curriculum, helped it to survive an attack by the formidable
John Russel, and gave diplomas to its first two graduating classes; as a
scholar who published, while at Annville, three separate treatises on English
Grammar; or as the descendant of an interesting set of ancestors who made
a splash on the Seven Seas and lands adjacent thereto.

His grandson, Thomas Vickroy Balch of Cleveland, Ohio, in 1963 compiled a "Genealogy: Thomas Rhys Vickroy," containing family traditions
which, while not all authenticated, may help to account for the taste for adventure which President Vickroy managed to blend so happily with his devotion to teaching.

On his father's side, he believed himself to be descended from a crusader,
whose name (Avé Croix or L'Croix, as the Vickroys liked to think) marked
him a follower of the Holy Cross. One of the crusader's French descendants
came to Scotland in the train of Mary, Queen of Scots. In a later generation,
the family is said to have had some connection with the devout but liberty-
loving freebooter, Rob Roy. Mr. Balch surmises that the Vickroy name may
possibly derive from the Highland *Vich Roy* or Black Roy.

Hugh Vickroy, from whom the President's line is more clearly traced,
was a Scottish sea captain who brought his family to America and settled it
in Cecil County, Maryland, he himself returning to his ship, to be later lost
at sea.

Hugh's son, Thomas (grandfather of T. R. V.) moved to Bedford, Pennsylvania, in 1772. During the Revolutionary War, we are told, he became
Commissary under George Rogers Clark, and in 1780 held the two block-
houses at Cincinnati while General Clark made his successful raid on the
British at Vincennes. Returning to Pennsylvania, he is said to have built Shade
Furnace—the first iron furnace in what is now Somerset County and now
one of the County's most romantic ruins. It stands in the woods on the bank

Rev. Thomas Rhys Vickroy, M.A.
President, 1866-1871

of Shade Creek, which was named for the forest through which it flowed, so dense that it was at one time known as "the Shades of Death." In 1793, Thomas Vickroy is said to have laid out the city of Pittsburgh—unfortunately with a "Surveyor's Pole" an inch too long—with some interesting consequences.

Thomas's son, Charles Vickroy, was born in Bedford, January 20, 1814. He married Nancy Rees in 1833, but died a few months later of yellow fever in Illinois.

Thomas Rees (Rhys) Vickroy, Charles Vickroy's posthumous child, was born at Stoystown in Shade Township, Somerset County, on December 27, 1833. His mother remarrying, he was brought up by his grandmother, Mary Trent Rees.

From his mother he drew several interesting strains. One was from William Trent (friend of George Washington) who in 1754, while building for Virginia the first fort at the Forks of the Ohio (Pittsburgh), was interrupted by a French expedition that destroyed his work and erected Fort Duquesne. William Trent's descendants, nevertheless, like to think of him as the founder of Pittsburgh.

Another interesting strain in President Vickroy's blood was from the Welsh family of Rees (originally Rhys, a spelling that our Vickroy took legal steps to adopt). The Rhys line has been traced back to Meredyd ap Rhys (1440);

to Madoc, who is traditionally said to have discovered America in 1170 or 1172; and to King Edward I of England who conquered Wales and Scotland. Certain branches of the Rhys family are thought to reach back to the earls of Hereford and Northumberland (the Percy family, which included, as students of Shakespeare will remember, Harry Hotspur).

Thomas Rhys Vickroy, who as a boy worked in a print shop, never lost his love of the printed page. Mr. Balch records a family tradition that "he walked twenty-five miles to buy his first volume of Shakespeare."

From the Cassville Seminary in 1855 he went up to Dickinson College at Carlisle. At the beginning of his Junior year, he married Ettie Stahl and left college, planning to take up a career in the Methodist ministry. In 1860, after completing his college work at home (as he wrote in a letter of June 12, 1866 to President H. M. Johnson of Dickinson), he received from that institution the degree of A.B. On June 28, 1866, in response to a request made in that same letter, he received from Dickinson the further degree of "M.A. *in cursu.*"

Meanwhile he had taken a position with the First National Bank at Columbia, Pennsylvania. While there, he was approached by his friend, Miles Rigor, with a story about a U. B. college struggling for birth in the small town of Annville; and being of an adventurous heritage and disposition, our Methodist preacher-banker volunteered his services.

When this tall, slender young man, with piercing grey eyes and black hair that set off the unusual whiteness of his skin, arrived in Annville, he made friends at once in the town, and the college students (when they came) adored him. He was a good talker, with a youthful warmth, clear-headed, informative, and courteous. It was seen at once that he was a hard worker: organizing the college, soliciting students, preaching, teaching, looking well after his wife and family, and, during his five years at the College, publishing three separate treatises on English Grammar.

Best of all, considering the wolf pack at his heels, he had courage and stamina no less than John Russel's. He had no hesitation in telling "Father" Russel where his duty lay.

In his Valedictory Address, delivered at the College Commencement, June 22, 1871 (the Board having failed to re-elect him on termination of his five-year trusteeship), he spoke frankly and prophetically.

> To-day I live not in hope but in memory. My thoughts wander over the past. For more than five years I have devoted my life and my energies to the interests of this institution. From a few primary pupils, I have seen it grow to collegiate proportions, I have seen it when it existed only in thought, when it was the latest bud hid beneath the bark of the trunk, when it was a child sick unto death and needed the fostering care of a father, when its friends were few and disheartened, and its enemies were bold and boisterous, when some who now are prominent were too fearful to sustain it by open advocacy, and who, Joseph and Nicodemus-like, would have embalmed it and laid it in the tomb. But the sentiment is changing, the opposition has expended its force, and, like a spent arrow, it lies harmless

Mrs. Vickroy, the first preceptress
Courtesy Mrs. Florence Vickroy Brewer

in the dust. A new spirit has been aroused, and though I shall not see it, nor reap its benefits, the College will long enjoy the things for which I have toiled and suffered.

In considering Vickroy's contribution to Lebanon Valley College, it is useless to compare what he produced during its first five years with what his successors have accomplished in the twentieth century. Vickroy began, as the saying is "from scratch." To put it, as he did, in more Biblical language, "It was like making brick without straw."

> Had there been [he continued] a nucleus of college classes with which to begin, the work would have been accomplished with comparative ease. There was then no taste for liberal learning. The great work was to create a thirst for knowledge...
> To train all the powers of body and mind has been my earnest aim. In music and art, as in science and literature, much has been accomplished.

A good businessman, he saw that the College could not indefinitely support itself. From the start he called for an endowment; and, to his great joy, in 1867 and 1868 he superintended the first expansion of the College's physical plant.

The Annual East Pennsylvania Conference in March, 1867, apprised of the shortage of rooms for boarding students, authorized the Board of Trustees to purchase additional grounds and to erect thereon a new building to contain a dining room, chapel, offices, and student residences. Eleven acres were purchased from John D. Beaver, C. Carmany, and Peter Graybill.

Benjamin B. Lehman, an architect of Lebanon, was engaged to draw up plans. A Building Committee consisting of President Vickroy, George A. Mark, and Rudolph Herr let the contract to Rudolph Herr for a three-story building: dining room and kitchen on the ground floor; chapel, president's

44

office and reception room, and four classrooms on the first floor; and with dormitories on the second and third floors

Ground was broken, May 28, in the presence of the Building Committee, the Rev. E. Light, and Professor E. Benjamin Bierman. An onlooker was a lad of fifteen named John Evans Lehman, who will be much heard of in this history.

While there had been no special celebration marking the opening of the College on May 7, 1866, a year later the laying of the cornerstone for the new building provided occasion for what Professor Bierman, who was present, described as:

> impressive ceremonies, in the presence of the Faculty and students of the college and many other interested spectators. The Rev. William S. H. Keys, pastor of the United Brethren church at Harrisburg, officiated, placed the contents into a tin lined box in the stone, and offered the prayer. After these exercises the large concourse of students, teachers, ministers and friends formed into line and marched to the United Brethren church in town where interesting and eloquent addresses on the educational work of the State and in the United Brethren church were delivered by Hon. J. P. Wickersham, LL.D., State Superintendent of Public Instruction, and Rev. Ezekiel Light, P. E., of Lebanon. This occasion was graced with the presence of a distinguished visitor to this country at the time in the interest of general education in the person of Senor Sarmiento, minister plenipotentiary of the Argentine Confederation, South America, to our government at Washington . . . .

It was over a year before Rudolph Herr, contractor, was ready to hand over the building. Meanwhile Herr had himself supplied the lumber and John N. Smith, the brick. Abraham Kauffman took charge of the carpentry work, while Israel Gruber attended to the brick work. Joel Boltz was the "boss plasterer." Students and professors lent a hand on occasion, helping to carry the large timbers and place them in position. A young Annville citizen, John Lehman, helped carry mortar.

No building program since then has more greatly stirred the imagination of the community than did the erection of this structure at a total cost of $31,000.

The progress of construction was eagerly watched. Occupation of the building followed closely on the heels of carpenters and plasterers. As parts of the building became habitable, they were immediately made use of. The chapel was early in demand. December 19, 1867, it was the scene of what was called "a public oratorical exhibition." In June, 1868, the College's closing exercises were held in it. On Sunday, June 14, the Rev. William S. H. Keys preached the first sermon in it, and on the 16th John H. Weiss, Esq. (later President Judge of the Dauphin County Courts) addressed the Philokosmian Literary Society there.

In August, President Vickroy, with his lovely wife and their growing family of children, left their rooms in the old Academy and moved into quarters

Mrs. Florence Vickroy Brewer
Courtesy Mrs. Brewer

in the "New College." Before the opening of the fall term, the building was completed, accepted by the Building Committee, and at once taken over by professors and students. Affectionately, the latter named it "Penitentiary Hall."

It is fitting to close this chapter with reminiscences from President Vickroy's only surviving child, Mrs. Silas Herbert Brewer (Florence Vickroy, listed in the 1870–1871 *Catalogue*), who, as this is written, has passed her one-hundredth birthday. Two letters of hers—February 6, 1962 and March 5, 1965—written to Mrs. D. Clark Carmean, are here interwoven:

. . . We went to Annville when I was nearly two years old. I had to be carried on a pillow as there was some serious trouble in my right leg. We lived in the "old College": which was the "Academy"—My Mother had a large bed room on the second floor, over the parlour. The boys room was across the hall. All I remember of this was the big front porch where I was taken to see a Circus Parade and my first sight of an elephant. We moved into the New College in August, 1868, and my sister Clara Estelle was born Aug. 26, 1868.

My Aunt came to be with us about that time (my grandfather had died and she was alone) so I was taken up to her room to make room in Mother's room for the new baby Clara. I was 4 years old at the time C. was born, but a lonely child as I had no one to play with out on the campus when the boys were in school but they played with me when out of school. I went to the Academy several terms, but did not like it and was not made to go to school until we got to St. Louis.

. . . One could not help being educated with a Father like mine. I kept up my music, went to many lectures, listened to my Father's conversation and got my love of reading which I never gave up. . . . As to my lovely Mother, she was lovely in person and a very charming woman. My mother was the Housekeeper and had to oversee any food served but I was too young to notice any special foods prepared at the College. I do remember one time when a Panorama was shown in one of the class rooms that my Mother sent in when the show was over several large trays of doughnuts all hot and sugary.

I do remember Annville with much pleasure and wanted to go there five years ago when we went to Boston to my Grandson's Wedding. All my memories are most pleasant. I remember Miss Ella Walker and Miss Bella Strawinski, her Father a Polish nobleman. Also I remember Mrs. Trump and her daughter, who had a good voice; a student Mr. Fischer too, those are all I remember.

Sincerely,
Florence Vickroy Brewer

CHAPTER NINE

The First Curriculum

PRESIDENT VICKROY and his teaching staff, sensitive to winds of change in the academic world, were resolved to have an up-to-date curriculum. But first they prepared solid ground. Quoting John Locke on *sensation* and *experience* as the basis of sound education, Vickroy announced in the *First Annual Catalogue* the ambitious structure he intended to raise:

"Upon such a beginning as a foundation, we propose erecting an educational structure symmetrical in its proportions, and towering to the regions of pure thought and holy aspiration."

It was only to be expected that the President, who had received his academic training at Dickinson College where progressive views on higher education were entertained, should be receptive to new ideas. He was aware that the dominance of the Classics, Latin and Greek, in colleges of Liberal Arts was being challenged, and that a movement was being pressed to admit subjects more immediate to the students' interests: Modern Languages, English Literature, Music, and the Natural Sciences.

Aware also of the hostility persisting in some circles to such innovations, Vickroy was careful to treat the Classics as still the mainstay of the curriculum, and to put such a subject as Music (which he was advanced enough to introduce) under a common heading with the Ornamental Branches.

"The course in this department [Music and Ornamental Branches]," announced the *Catalogue,* "is extended and thorough. It embraces Vocal and Instrumental Music; Pencil, Linear, Crayon and Perspective Drawing; Antique, Pastel, Water and Oil Painting; Worsted Flowers, Wax Flowers and Fruit, &c., &c."

It is to be noted that, being a practical educational statesman whose first business was to draw students to college from a constituency in which, as he said, "There was then no taste for liberal learning," he was far from undervaluing the Ornamental Branches. In the first *Catalogue,* while professorships in Ancient and Modern Languages and Literature, Natural Science, and the English Language and Literature were listed as vacant, there were *two* teachers in Music and the Fine Arts: Miss Ella L. Walker, M.A., who taught Music and Drawing, and Miss Lizzie M. Rigler, who taught "Music, Painting and Ornamental Branches."

Vickroy is to be honored for having given Music a good start at Lebanon Valley and for building a tradition that in time led to the establishment of a separate Department of Music in 1879 and finally to the high reputation the College's Conservatory (Department) of Music enjoys today.

Though the chairs of Modern Languages and English were, in 1866-1867, without incumbents, the curriculum provided storage places for these subjects against such time as they could be brought out and put to use. Even in the revered "Collegiate Department" (i.e., the conventional college courses), Vickroy found a way to introduce the Modern Languages. They were not listed among the requirements for the four-year Classical Course, which alone prepared students for the A.B. degree; but French and English were allowed a place on the distaff side of the College. Both subjects were listed among the requirements for the three-year Ladies' Course, which led to the degree of Mistress of Arts.

The Scientific Course, like the Ladies' Course, was a convenient hide-out for these radical elements. The chief difference of the Scientific Course from the Classical Course was that it was shorter and substituted French and German for Latin and Greek. In place of the traditional Freshman, Sophomore, Junior, and Senior years of the Classical Course, it was divided into Junior, Middle, and Senior.

Science, as understood today, scarcely showed its head. In the so-called Scientific Course, the first or Junior year offered courses in German, French, Mathematics, and English. The next year (Middle) continued these four and added Philosophy—which, when broken down, was found to consist of Logic and Rhetoric. In the final or Senior year, Mathematics and Philosophy were continued, the former subdivided into Calculus, Astronomy, Analytical Mechanics; and the latter into Mental Science, Moral Science, Elements of Criticism, Political Economy, and Political Philosophy. In this last year of the Scientific Course, "Natural Science" was at last introduced in the form of Geology, Chemistry, and Natural Philosophy. A *science graduate* of those days might well ask, "What's in a name?"

In the first two *Catalogues*, there was listed a four-year "Biblical Course," solid in substance, as appeared by its description, but apparently without any takers. It disappeared from the 1868-69 *Catalogue* and did not reappear. Like the Classical Course, it followed the Freshman to Senior time-scheme, offering "Biblical" studies (Theology, Exegesis, etc.), New Testament Greek, Hebrew, Mathematics, and English. There was also a touch of Hebrew, a taste of Philosophy (Logic and Rhetoric again), and a good deal of history, including the history of the United States.

In that adventurous first *Catalogue,* there was advertised a Business or "Commercial Course." It offered instruction in Book-Keeping, Commercial

Arithmetic, Commercial Correspondence, Commercial Law, and Partnership Settlements. If desired, instruction could be had also in Business Penmanship (three months for $10.00), Ornamental Penmanship (three months for $10.00), Card Writing ($5.00), and Phonography (Shorthand, $15.00). But Commerce was then regarded, in academic circles, as a second class citizen. The course did not lead to a degree but merely to what was described as "the Diploma or Certificate of the Institution."

No less than six degrees were offered. The undergraduate degrees were these:

On completing the Normal Course, Bachelor of Elements.
On completing the Scientific Course, Bachelor of Science.
On completing the Ladies' Course, Mistress of Arts.
On completing the Classical Course, Bachelor of Arts.
On completing the Biblical Course, Bachelor of Biblical Science.

The Master of Arts was an honorary degree given to graduates on terms similar to those that prevailed in other institutions of the day, such as, for instance, Dickinson whence President Vickroy had derived his. This was the announcement concerning the M.A. degree in the first L. V. C. *Catalogue*:

"Alumni of the College will receive the Master's degree in three years after graduating, provided they sustain a good moral character, and engage in literary or professional pursuits. The fee for each Diploma will be $5.00."

The most radical departure from the old-fashioned curriculum was announced towards the end of the *Catalogue,* following "Courses of Instruction," "Requirements for Admission," "The Best Mode of Preparation," "Fuller Explanation of the Studies," "Miscellaneous Information," and "General Remarks." In three lines, under the heading "Eclectic Studies," it made hay of all the course requirements painstakingly listed in the preceding thirty pages of the *Catalogue*. This is how it ran:

"The laws of the College provide that students of any Course may elect to pursue an equivalent study in any other course, with the consent of the Faculty."

Even progressive Dickinson did not take so strong a stand for the elective system until the next year, 1868, when the president of that institution informed his Board of Trustees: "No college can long maintain its hold in the feelings and interests of the people that does not fall away somewhat from the old classical curriculum and fall in with the drift of modern culture and modern needs toward the Scientific & Literary Studies."

It is not known how fully this elective system was allowed to operate at the College. The note concerning Eclectic Studies was omitted from later *Catalogues*. Nevertheless, the inclusion of that bold statement in its first *Catalogue,* 1866-67, is something to be proud of. It shows that Lebanon Valley College, with all its initial handicaps, was strong enough to march with the times and in the front ranks. It cannot be said that this College was the first to adopt the elective principle, for "optional courses" had been introduced by some other institutions a few years earlier. Nevertheless, Dr. Saul Sack, whose recent *History of Higher Education in Pennsylvania* is a landmark in its field, writes, "I think it safe to say that of the institutions emerging after the mid-point of the 19th century, Lebanon Valley College was among the earliest to adopt the elective principle."

To sum up, the first curriculum was a product of fear and hope: fear of offending either side in the debate over truly liberalizing Liberal Arts, hope that by taking a somewhat ambivalent stand on the question the College might win over both parties in the dispute.

Undoubtedly Vickroy was looking forward to a time when the Liberal Arts could be more closely adjusted to modern life, without, however, sacrificing either the mental or the moral training which some advocates of the established order claimed to be the exclusive prerogative of the Classical Course. He believed not only that such a change would draw more young people to take advantage of college training, but also that it would better enable them after graduating to discharge their responsibilities in the world in which they found themselves.

If one understand's Vickroy's problem and his vision, one will be less inclined to find the College's first *Catalogue* primitive. Miles Rigor and Thomas Vickroy, the two "lessees," were confronted with what a business man today might call a "hard-boiled proposition." They were attempting, in a period of change within the academic world, to start a new Liberal Arts college without having (as Vickroy said) even the nucleus of a student body to work with. They were starting it, too, in a constituency that not only had no academic tradition to guide its thinking but, on the contrary, had a strong tradition against institutions of learning.

If the first curriculum which the College offered (but failed to put fully into operation because of a lack of students and professors) now appears naive, the circumstances under which it was drawn up should be recalled.

Give honor where honor is due: to Thomas Vickroy and Miles Rigor, the lessees, who had put their bank accounts and their professional lives at stake on the successful issue of Lebanon Valley College.

CHAPTER TEN

"To Collegiate Proportions"

CURRICULUM CHANGES

PRESIDENT VICKROY'S first curriculum, like William Penn's First Frame of Government, was pre-conceived: that is, it was planned in advance of any contact with those whom it was intended to serve. At the time the plans were prepared, Penn had not seen his province and Lebanon Valley College was without students—except those in the so-called "Preparatory" stages. As Penn is praised for his ability to adjust his plans to the needs of the colonists; so Vickroy may be commended for continuously adapting his curriculum to the needs of students as they appeared.

The Model School Department, advertised in the first *Catalogue,* was dropped after one year. The Normal Department lasted only two. Even the Collegiate Department underwent a quick transformation. In the *Third Annual Catalogue,* 1868–1869, the name was dropped and in its place two courses were listed independently: the Classical Course and the Scientific Course. In the next *Catalogue,* 1869–1870 a two years "Class in the Modern Languages" was advertised. That the Modern Languages were becoming aggressive is seen in the fact that the requirements for the degree of Bachelor of Science now permitted the substitution of a modern language for Latin.

The 1869–1870 *Catalogue* continued to announce the Ornamental Department, with courses in Music, Vocal and Instrumental (Piano, Organ, and Guitar), as well as Drawing and Painting.

The Ladies Course by this time had been dropped. The degree of Mistress of Arts, however, was still conferred as the *Catalogue* announced, "upon any female student who shall complete the Classical Course, omitting some of the Higher Mathematics and Greek and substituting German and French."

To the graduate degree of Master of Arts, there was now added a Master of Science, under the same conditions as applied to the former: a graduate's good conduct for three years, and the payment of five dollars.

Lebanon Valley Business College was opened, August 3, 1868, "the good will and fixtures of Bryant, Stratton & Francisco's Business College" of Harrisburg having been purchased and transferred to Annville. Though not integrated with the academic courses, the new Business College was much advertised. In the old Academy (South Hall), various model stores, offices, and even a bank were set up for the student's practical training. As advertised in the 1869–1870 *Catalogue,* "Nothing is FEIGNED, all is REAL." The time required to complete the course was "from four to eight months." The fees were not excessive. What was called a "Life Scholarship [i.e., tuition fees] for full course" was $40.00. Text books "with full set of blanks" cost an additional $20.00. "Boarding, Washing, Light, Fuel and Room-rent, *per week*" came to $4.00.

During Vickroy's presidency, there was a rapid advance in the faculty. In the 1869–1870 *Catalogue,* Lucian H. Hammond appears as "Professor of the Greek and Latin Languages and Literature." Vickroy's professorship is now that of "Belles-Lettres and Philosophy." Krumbine has dropped out and Bierman has changed from "the Normal Branches" to "English and German Languages and Literature." The Ornamental Branches have dwindled, having now only one instructor, Miss B. O. Strawinski, M.A., who taught "Music, French and the Ornamental Branches."

The Lebanon *Courier,* in its issue of December 3, 1868, put in a strong "plug" for the College, especially its Commercial School, "where Stratton and Bryant's system is taught, with all the appliances to afford a perfect practical knowledge of the science. The rooms are handsomely fitted up, with a banking department, insurance company, notary's office, commercial houses, telegraph office, post office, &c. Through these departments the student is carried as if he were in actual business."

THE FIGHT FOR CO-EDUCATION

During Vickroy's presidency, the principle of co-education, on which Lebanon Valley College and indeed the Church as a whole prided itself, underwent an attack from an unexpected quarter. It will be remembered that at York (within the area of the Pennsylvania Conference, whose support the College most urgently desired) Cottage Hill College had been established as an exclusively female institution.

At the annual meeting of the Pennsylvania Conference in January, 1867, the following proposal was adopted: "That it would meet with our approbation if the proprietor of Cottage Hill College and the managers of Lebanon Valley College make such arrangements as would enable them to conduct the one as a male and the other as a female school."

Cottage Hill did constitute itself a "female school," but Lebanon Valley remained co-educational and took the consequences of educating the sexes "on the mixed system," as the Pennsylvania Conference expressed it. The latter, in reply to an invitation from Lebanon Valley College to send a Visiting Committee to see whether or not it would be proper to co-operate, replied stiffly in January, 1868, that "no proposition looking to co-operation with said 'Lebanon Valley College,' can be entertained until the authorities of the same shall manifest a disposition to transfer their female department to 'Cottage Hill Female College'. . . ."

Next year the Virginia Conference made friendly advances towards Lebanon Valley College. During its February session, 1869, after recommending Cottage Hill Female College "for the education of our daughters," it added that "we are also pleased with the Ma[na]gement and advantages of Lebanon Valley College and recommend it as the proper place for the education of our Sons."

That the struggling College almost succumbed to the temptation offered by these two conferences, whose support it so desperately needed, is evident from the resolution which, in February, 1869, its Board of Trustees recommended to the East Pennsylvania Conference:

> Whereas, we are informed on good authority, that the Allegheny and Pennsylvania Conferences are willing to Cooperate with Lebanon Valley College, on the condition that Said College receive as boarders only male Students.
>
> Therefore, Resolved, That the condition mentioned shall be accepted by this Conference, and that said Conference, together with the Virginia and Parkersburg Conferences, be invited to elect three Trustees and enter into said Co-operation, whereupon Lebanon Valley College shall receive among its female students none but day scholars.

But the tide was turning. The East German Conference, founded in 1869 (though its first annual conference was not held until 1871) supported Lebanon Valley College from the start.

In 1870, the Pennsylvania Conference adopted a resolution recommending that their people send their sons to Lebanon Valley. Within two years the Pennsylvania Conference, and within three years the Virginia Conference (as will be seen in the following chapter), had elected trustees and were in full co-operation with the East Pennsylvania Conference in sponsoring a co-educational Lebanon Valley College.

STUDENT DISCIPLINE

Most of the students at the College came from Pennsylvania Dutch homes where paternal discipline was proverbially strict. Modern psychology was as yet unheard of on the campus, and the problems of frustration and release were not under discussion. It was demanded by parents that disciplinary control be unremitting, especially in an institution where males and females attended the same classes. There was no student government, and very little in the way of extra-curricular activities.

The best way to understand the social atmosphere of the time is to study page 32 of the 1869-1870 *Catalogue*:

The Government of the College is *strict,* but *parental.*

The object of the Institution is to afford a home, where parents or guardians may place their children and wards with safety and profit, and where young men and young ladies may be fitted for usefulness under influences calculated to refine their tastes, ennoble their aspirations, discipline their intellectual powers, and develop a high Christian character.

1. Things Required.

1. Registry of names before taking recitations.
2. Settlement of bill according to the terms.
3. Strict observance of the study hours.
4. Full employment of time in study and recitation.
5. Promptness in the duties of speaking, reading, and writing.
6. Strict observance of the Sabbath.
7. Attendance of public worship twice on the Sabbath.
8. Attendance of morning prayers in the Chapel.
9. Strict obedience of temporary prudential rules.
10. Free access of any teacher to the room of any student.

2. Things Prohibited

1. Unpermitted association of students of either sex.
2. Games of chance; the use of intoxicating drinks.
3. Profane or obscene language; using tobacco on the premises.
4. Visiting on the Sabbath or during study hours.
5. Clamorous noise in or about the buildings.
6. Absence from the examinations or other required exercises.
7. Leaving the College without permission.
8. Frequenting bar-rooms, groceries or other public places.
9. Unpermitted absence from room after evening signal for study.
10. Unpermitted societies among the students.
11. Croaking, backbiting, and all evil speaking.

3. Penalties

Every unexcused absence, failure, or misdemeanor, is reported to the faculty, and a record made of the same.

Three demerit marks will subject a student to private reproof; six, to public reproof; nine, notice to parent or guardian; and twelve, to dismission.

The Faculty may, on evidence of reformation, restore a dismissed student.

For graver offences, the punishments are reproof, loss of privilege, confinement, dismission and expulsion.

EMBRYO LIBRARY

The foundation of any institution of learning today is a good library. Lebanon Valley College began its career with virtually none at all.

The need of one was formally recognized in January, 1867, when, "At a public meeting of the teachers and students," as Professor Bierman was later to write, a committee of three was named "for the purpose of devising ways and means to establish a library:" Cyrus A. Loose, David W. Crider, and Sallie M. Rigler. Three months later the committee was able to report that they had raised the sum of $86.39 and collected about a hundred books. Professor Bierman notes that the Rev. Daniel S. Early had donated *Josephus' Works* in six volumes; the Rev. G. W. Miles Rigor, Clark's *Commentary* in four volumes; the Rev. Adam Steigerwald, D'Aubigny's *History of the Reformation;* George W. Hoverter, Greeley's *Great Conflict;* and President Vickroy, Bancroft's *History of the United States.*

From these small beginnings, the growth at first was slow. It was not until 1874, under President Hammond, that the first real library appeared at the College.

THE FIRST LITERARY SOCIETY

In most colleges of the United States during the nineteenth century, the Literary Societies were not only important elements in the students' social life; they contributed something essential to the intellectual atmosphere, supplementing the formal college curriculum by introducing a wide range of intellectual interests not directly handled in college classes.

Literary societies helped the curriculum in other ways as well. Addresses delivered by the students at monthly meetings afforded training in public speaking and in parliamentary procedure.

It was in April, 1867, that a movement was started to organize a literary society at L. V. C. A committee appointed to draw up a constitution presented its report on May 3, 1867, and the Philokosmian Literary Society (the name having been suggested by President Vickroy) came into being with the following officers: David Wilson Crider, President; John Wesley Etter, Secretary.

These were the founders, as listed in the Philokosmian Membership Book:

Crider, David Wilson	York
Loose, Cyrus A.	Myerstown
Etter, John Wesley	Powell's Valley
Burgner, Peter Bohn	Pinegrove
Driver, William H.	Altoona
Light, Joseph Horst	Avon
Reider, Abraham Henry	Elizabethtown
Moyer, Henry Peter	Annville
Meiley, Cornelius Seltzer	Lebanon
Bomgardner, David E.	Grantville
Stauffer, Harry	Union Deposit
Graybill, John Henry	Annville
Henry, Christian Calvin	Lebanon
Seibert, William Henry	Progress
Gipple, Samuel R.	Millersburg
Light, Nathaniel Brinton	Lebanon

Members of Philokosmian Literary Society 1870

Outer circle, clockwise, beginning lower left: *Austin Best, J. H. Graybill, '72, Charles Wood, John N. Riland, Robert Perry, M. P. Sanders, '77, J. G. Stehman, John E. Lehman, '74, John Piper, John R. Wright, '76, Allen W. Tate, John G. Dissinger, S. P. Johns.*

Inner circle, clockwise, beginning lower left: *Z. S. Light, '74, H. B. Stehman, '73, C. S. Meiley (Tutor in English), J. Wesley Etter, '72, C. S. Daniels, '73, John K. Fisher, '72.* Center: *Professor E. Benjamin Bierman.*

Bolton, John J. ....Linglestown
Bickel, A. Stoner ....Jonestown
Kremer, Henry J. ....McKees Half Falls
McAlister, Joseph Calvin ....New Buffalo
Best, Joseph Houser ....Eberly's Mills
Sheesley, Samuel ....Progress
Bierman, E Benjamin ....Annville

On March 29, 1872, the motto, *Esse quam Videre*, was adopted.

The First "Commencement"

The closing exercises of the College in June, 1867—advertised as "Commencement," although there were no graduates and no degrees were conferred—made a good impression on the public. The examinations were oral and were a part of the public exhibition enjoyed on the occasion. Examinations for many years remained oral and public. There is a suspicion that they were sometimes rehearsed in advance by professors and students—with unfortunate results in future years. A tradition grew up that oral examinations were a public show in which professor and student worked together as a team. Even written examinations came to be looked upon by students (and some professors) as tests not so much of individual merit as of co-operative skill.

Be that as it may, the July 4, 1867, issue of the Lebanon *Courier* commended the new institution for having put on a good show: "The examinations and exhibitions throughout, on Monday, Tuesday, Wednesday, and Thursday evinced training in the various departments, and reflected much credit on the labors of President Vickroy and his corps of assistants—Profs. Houck, Bierman and Grumbine, and Misses Walker and Rigler."

Continuing, the *Courier* noted the beginning of one of the most popular items in the L. V. C. tradition: the President's reception to the students.

"The future of the College," said the *Courier* in an expansive moment, "is very promising, and no efforts will be spared by its friends to make it not only a point of interest and an ornament, but a blessing to Lebanon Valley College and to the whole world."

The First Graduates

The week of what the *Courier* called "the 4th Anniversary" (i.e., the first Commencement, properly so called) at the College was opened on Sunday, June 12, 1870, by Bishop Jonathan Weaver of Baltimore with a sermon on "The Logic of Christianity." On Monday, J. H. Jacobs, Esq., of Reading delivered an "Oration" before the Philokosmian Literary Society on "Our Land and Her Politicians." On Tuesday night the Annual Address was given by Prof. S. D. Heilman of Dickinson College on "Man the Fighter or the Laws of Anteposition as an Element of Human Progress." On Wednesday evening the "Oratorical Exercises" of the undergraduates were held.

On Thursday came the "Commencement Proper," at which the three graduates spoke their pieces. Mr. William B. Bodenhorn dwelt on "Man's Aspirations after the Unknown." Miss Mary A. Weiss read an essay on the subject, "Rest, but not Here." Mr. Albert C. Rigler, gave the Valedictory address: "The Past and the Present."

So it was that President Vickroy could say, in his last report to the East Pennsylvania Conference in March, 1871, that he had built a college from nothing and graduated a class of three. More than that, he continued, the College now had enough undergraduates enrolled to require "that all the classes of the Classical Course be organized at the beginning of the next collegiate year in August. "Thus," he concluded, " . . . during the five years of my lease, the school will have been built up to collegiate proportions."

CHAPTER ELEVEN

President Lucian H. Hammond

PRESIDENT VICKROY had presided over the birth of the College and saved it from infanticide. When he handed it over to his successor, it had a fair chance of life.

But Lebanon Valley College was still in swaddling clothes. It was the second president, Lucian H. Hammond, who put it into academic dress. He produced the nucleus of a real library, some scientific apparatus, a few scholarships, and an alumni association. He also launched an endowment campaign. Under his regime, college sport (at least baseball) was introduced. Best of all, in view of the College's chronic undernourishment, he obtained the support of the Pennsylvania and Virginia Conferences without throwing co-education overboard.

President Hammond had been long immersed in the academic tradition. Born, September 7, 1825, in the town of Worthington, Franklin County, Ohio, he had early shown an aptitude for learning. Fifteen miles north of Worthington is the town of Delaware, seat of Ohio Wesleyan University. He entered that institution "about 1849" (the college records of that time are scanty), and completed the excellent Classical Course offered there. It gave him a good introduction to the intellectual currents of the time, introducing him to the higher mathematics, the various sciences, philosophy, logic, ethics and theology, and the English Language. It gave him concentrated study of much of the best ancient classical literature: Homer, Virgil, Horace, Herodotus, Livy, Xenophon, Cicero, Thucydides, Tacitus, Plato, Aeschylus, Euripides, and Sophocles. He graduated in 1853 with the earned degree of Bachelor of Arts. After the customary probation period of three years, he received his M.A. *in cursu.*

In 1854 he joined the faculty of Mount Pleasant College, which the United Brethren Church had recently established in Westmoreland County. When Mount Pleasant closed its doors in 1858 and was absorbed by Otterbein, he became Professor of Greek at the latter institution. From 1866 to 1868 he was Professor of Ancient Languages at Cottage Hill Female College in York,

Lucian H. Hammond, M.A.
President, 1871-1876

Pennsylvania; and in the latter year he moved over to take the corresponding position at Lebanon Valley College.

So it was that, in 1871, when Lucian Hammond came with his wife to the College, he already had a good knowledge of its background, having been on the teaching staff for three of its five years of existence. He was familiar not only with academic practices in general but also with the peculiar problems of Lebanon Valley.

He was a sound scholar. In personal character, he was kindly and sensitive. At the same time he was a man of conviction. He was not afraid of facing facts, nor of drawing other people's attention to them—sometimes to his own hurt.

During his term as president, he made no great changes in the curriculum, save that he brought back the Ladies' Course, which for a time had been discontinued, and he dropped the Commercial Course. The Classical Course remained the center of the college program. For those who wanted excursions into newer fields, there were the restored Ladies' Course, the Scientific Course, the Course in Modern Languages, and the Ornamental Department (Music and Painting). When the Commercial Course was dropped, its building, the old Academy, was taken over as the Ladies' Hall.

President Hammond had a gift for music. At Otterbein he had led an orchestra. At Lebanon Valley College he conducted "vocal classes," being commended in the press for the "highly cultivated" voices he developed. It is not surprising that, under his regime as President, Music rose in status. In the 1871-1872 *Catalogue,* it is listed as a department of its own (under the general heading, "Ornamental Department") quite distinct from "The Fine Arts."

The Lebanon *Courier* of May 9, 1872, noted that "whenever we wish to hear good singing we go to Lebanon Valley College."

THE CLIONIAN LITERARY SOCIETY

During the year after Hammond's arrival, a new Literary Society, the Clionian, was established for the ladies. Three students took the lead in organizing it: Sarah Burns, Rebecca Kinports, and Ellen Jane Mark. The President and Faculty were consulted, student meetings were held, and on November 12, 1872, a constitution was adopted.

These were the founders:

Sarah Burns	Annie V. Collins
Rebecca Kinports	Maggie C. Hershey
Ellen Jane Mark	Fannie C. Killinger
Louisa S. Leisenring	Sallie A. Herr
Rebecca Schweitzer	Lizzie E. Mase
Lizzie A. Gensemer	Alice Stehman
Emma K. Rigler	Olive H. Stehman
Laura E. Saylor	Sallie J. Young
Clara J. Siegrist	

CO-OPERATING CONFERENCES

The East German Conference had been the first "cooperating conference," giving support to Lebanon Valley College from the time when the Conference was organized in 1869.

In 1872, a few months after Hammond became President, the Pennsylvania Conference decided to forego its demand that Lebanon Valley College give up co-education. Instead, it accepted the recommendation of its Committee on Education that it co-operate immediately "with the East Pa. and East German Conferences, in sustaining Lebanon Valley College. . . ." It decided to send its sons to that college's campus even at the risk of meeting young ladies there.*

The Pennsylvania Conference then proceeded to elect "nine Trustees to

---

* The danger, after all, was not excessive. At least that is suggested by a reminiscent remark made to Sara Greiner (Mrs. Earl J. Leffler), by Mrs. H. Clay Deaner, the former Ella J. Rigler, widow of the "Professor of the Latin Language and Literature and Astronomy": "In 1873, whenever President Hammond approached, the girls cast their eyes down to the tips of their shoes, to give the impression that they disapproved of males in their vicinity."

To keep the record straight, Ella Rigler (Mrs. Deaner), who graduated from the Ladies' Course with the degree of Mistress of Arts in 1877, confessed to Mrs. Leffler that her Mistress of Arts degree "prepared her for nothing but marriage."

meet with the Board of Trustees of said College." They were: "C. T. Stern, Z. A. Colestock, J. Erb, J. C. Smith, W. B. Raber, S. Schoop, jr., J. Knipp, jr., H. R. Musser, J. B. Hurst."

Next year the Pennsylvania Conference put its whole heart into the venture. After listening to President Hammond's report, the members adopted this resolution:

"That we as a Conference will spare no effort and shun no sacrifice to make Lebanon Valley College all that it should be as a Literary institution of our Church, and to crowd its halls with students thus making our co-operation practically effective."

The same Conference, in its annual meeting in February, 1875, went as far as to declare, "That we regard Lebanon Valley College as a gift of God to this and other eastern Conferences; its location, appointment and facilities being well adapted to our present needs."

The Virginia Conference was not far behind. In its February, 1873, meeting, members heard the report of the Visiting Committee to Lebanon Valley College. ". . . .we would hereby recommend that the Virginia An. Conf. enter into cooperation with the above named Conferences [East Pennsylvania, East German, and Pennsylvania] in controlling, patronizing, and sustaining Lebanon Valley College by electing six Trustees to represent us on the Board."

Whereupon the Conference elected the following: "Monroe Funkhouser, Daniel Kohler, J. Harp, J. L. Grimm, A. M. Evers and J. W. Hott."

The Committee on Education giving its encouragement, the Conference declared further, in words that signaled an end to the struggle over co-education, that "we as a Conference will use our influence in favor of said school by recommending it to our people as a convenient and proper place for the literary training of our sons and daughters."

So it is said that today Lebanon Valley College holds the distinction, among existing colleges and universities of eastern Pennsylvania, of having the longest tradition of co-education.

For a very short time, the Parkersburg Conference co-operated, and the Allegheny Conference came in for nine years, 1881–1891. The Pennsylvania and Virginia Conferences stayed with the College and have continued throughout the years to give it powerful support.

When in 1875 the Pennsylvania Conference pronounced Lebanon Valley College "a gift of God," it gave particular praise to it for three things that were President Hammond's contribution: (1) "a pretty large Library," (2) "some scientific apparatus," and (3) the prospect of an endowment.

The Library

The beginnings referred to above—library, scientific apparatus, and endowment—were modest enough.

As for the library, the *First Annual Catalogue,* 1866–1867 carried this gentle appeal: "The Boehm Library, consisting of well-selected books, is accessible to all the students. Donations in books or money are earnestly solicitated. . . ."

It has already been noted that the committee formed in January, 1867, to establish a library, had no better success in four months than to collect $89.39 and about a hundred volumes. It was not until 1874 that a real start was made. In that year, contributions in money and books began to flow in. President Hammond contributed 25 books; Professor Scribner, 50; Professor Bierman, 50; Jacob Hoke, 10. Best of all, the Board of Trustees appropriated $300.00 for the college library.

It was in that same year, 1874, that the Library received a name (the Library of Lebanon Valley College), a staff (a Librarian and a Treasurer to be elected annually by the Faculty), and a Constitution. The duties of the Librarian, as defined in the Constitution, were not onerous, and the student privileges were not excessive.

> Article IV. It shall be the duty of the Librarian . . . to open the Library for delivery and reception of books one hour each week in term time . . . for the young women, and one hour for the young men on such days as the Faculty may determine. . . .
> Article XV. Gentlemen who are graduates of the College may obtain books from the Librarian through one of the professors, and ladies who are graduates may obtain books from the same through one of the lady teachers, said professor or lady teacher to be held responsible for the safe return of books thus obtained.

The Library's first Accession Book, dated 1874, gives titles of 653 books. It is an interesting collection. The loyalty with which the conferences supported it is seen in the weight it carries of theological works. There were 16 volumes of *The Evangelical Family Library* and 25 volumes of *The Religious Library.* There were a good many children's books, such as *Precept upon Precept.* There was also a good sprinkling of the best general literature: Milton, Tennyson, Longfellow, Whittier, Scott, Cervantes, Byron, Victor Hugo, Hawthorne, De Quincey, Dickens, Emerson, Fenimore Cooper, etc. History was as well represented in such works as Bancroft's *History of the United States* in 9 volumes, Froude's *History of England* (12 volumes), Grote's *History of Greece* (12 volumes), Mommsen's *History of Rome* (5 volumes), Gibbon's *Decline and Fall of The Roman Empire* (6 volumes), and Carlyle's *Frederick the Great* (10 volumes). There was even a life of Mary Queen of Scots. There were a few elementary books on health, and occasional treatises on grammar and composition. There was *Robinson Crusoe, The Arabian Nights,* and *Tom Brown's School Days.* The list ended with Volume II of *Memoirs of Female Sovereigns* and Volumes I and II of Lander's *Travels in Africa.*

Hammond and his staff worked hard on that library, and they took deserved pride in the results. In February, 1875, he was able to report that one year ago the College had no library, and that now it had over six hundred volumes.

But that was only the beginning. On April 9 of the same year, the Lebanon *Daily News* reported: "Mr. George W. Hoverter of Annville, who some time ago purchased the library [800 volumes] of the Union Fire Company, of town, has sold the same to Lebanon Valley College." By 1876 Hammond was able to report that the college Library had swelled to 1132 volumes (evidently not all the Fire Company's books had been purchased—or preserved) and that there were "resources in hand which when applied should increase the number to 1200 volumes."

These figures may help us to understand the sacrifice of men like Hammond who gave their time to such small details in order that the dream of a well established Liberal Arts College in Annville might become a reality.

SCIENCE

It will be recalled that the Scientific Course had not as yet got very far off the ground. In 1874 it was still a three-years course, consisting principally, in the President's words, of the "English branches"—unencumbered, that is, with foreign languages.

In the 1873–1874 *Catalogue,* the Scientific Course offered a number of single-term courses (the college year being now divided into three terms, Fall, Winter, and Spring) in English: English Grammar and Analysis, English, Past and Present, Composition and Rhetoric, and English Literature. There were courses in General History, the History of Civilization, Philosophy (Mental, Moral, and Natural), Natural Theology, Evidences of Christianity, and Analogy of Religion. There was a little Political Economy, a lot of Mathematics, and a term each of Physical Geography, Natural History, Botany, Anatomy, Physiology, and Hygiene (these last three in one), Chemistry, Geology, Astronomy, and Mechanics.

It was felt, however, that some scientific apparatus and some curios were needed to stiffen the course. In 1875 the President was able to report that "the cabinet [museum] contributed by various friends of the institution is sufficiently extensive to have become of interest, and a valuable auxiliary to the department of Natural Science."

ALUMNI ASSOCIATION

A vital aid to the College came on the afternoon of June 11, 1874, when, following the Commencement Exercises, the Lebanon Valley College Alumni Association was organized, with these officers:

President: John W. Etter, '72.

Vice-Presidents: Miss Jane E. Kauffman, '72 and Rev. John K. Fisher, '74.

Secretary: Miss Sarah Burns, '73.
Treasurer: Zaranius S. G. Light, '74.
Orator: Rev. J. Wesley Etter.
Essayist: Miss Jane E. Kauffman.

At the time there were only twenty-three graduates, of whom eight had received their diplomas on that same day. But the College and its friends were looking to the future. The soundness of their faith has since been attested by the generous response of the alumni in the building campaign of this Centennial Year, 1966.

ENDOWMENT

That all was not well at the College, was clearly indicated by an article in the *Religious Telescope* of June 30, 1875, drawing attention to the unsatisfactory condition of the college finances, quarrels in Board of Trustees that had their repercussions outside, the virtual breakup of the Faculty, and the proferred resignation of the President.

> The duties of the Board of Trustees [wrote E. S. Chapman] were peculiarly difficult, owing to the resignation of three members of the faculty, and the positive disagreement of the members of the Board respecting their successors . . . It seemed to be the opinion of nearly all the members of the Board that the services of President Hammond, at the head of the faculty, could not at present be dispensed with; and hence, contrary to his repeatedly expressed desire, he was re-elected president, after his resignation had been tendered and accepted. . . .

The strain of carrying the multifarious administrative duties of those days* and a considerable teaching load as well, was beginning to tell on President Hammond. A glance at his part in the public examinations in December, 1874, will show something of his teaching responsibilities. According to the Lebanon *Courier* of December 30, he "examined classes in Plato's Gorgias, Cicero de Senectute, Greek lessons and English grammar."

During his last years at the College he put on a courageous fight for an endowment, but his strength was giving out and his temper was growing short. In his report to the East Pennsylvania Conference on February 27, 1874, at Schuylkill Haven, he bluntly declared:

> No College can be permanent without an endowment, it cannot do justice to its students, however competent its instructors may be, without a good Library and apparatus. . . .

---

* President Bierman in 1901 said of himself that "he was president, chairman of the executive committee, financial agent, acting financial secretary, kept the books of the college, had charge of all the papers belonging to the college, and also assisted in raising money at different times."—Brief of Argument, Supreme Court of Pennsylvania, October term, 1901: Paper Book of Appellant, p. 26.

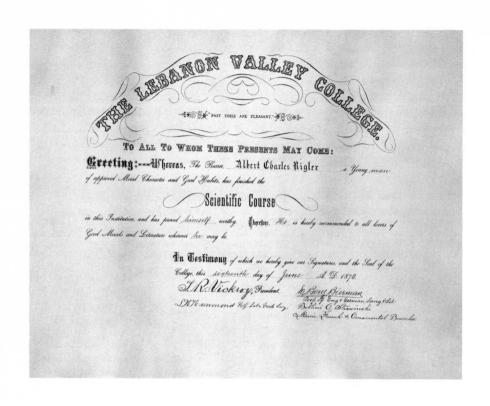

Diploma of 1870, one of the first three granted

Five dollars from each member would give the College relief, and they can spare it. Hundreds give twice this amount each year to burn segars, and will they not give this amount to enkindle immortal minds? Many families among us have hoarded treasures from which they might abstract enough for a College and yet have sufficient to bind the hands and blast the intellects of their sons. There is five times enough surplus wealth in the Conferences patronising this institution to endow it completely, and well would it be for our Church could we draw it from her coffers, even if it were cast into the depths of the seas.

The Conference, accordingly, "Resolved, That . . . we will more than redouble our efforts to place Lebanon Valley College beyond all material wants. . . ."

Two years later, President Hammond attempted to explain to the same Conferences why the endowment campaign had been a failure: "It may be in part," he said, "because the Agents, though they have worked hard, have extended their operations over too much territory, and thereby canvassed hurriedly and superficially. . . ."

Or was it that they had worked on stony ground? Boldly he went on to what he thought was the crux of the matter: "the apathy of the ministers." In contrast he cited the record of the Virginia Conference, whose ministers had "the college in their hearts," and in consequence "accomplished more for it financially than *all* the other cooperating Conferences combined."

This all-out effort to bring the constituency to face the financial facts concerning the College, when added to his other responsibilities and worries, proved too much for him. On May 17, 1876, it was reported in the press that President Hammond was "very seriously ill." On May 31, he was said to be "still in a precarious condition." On June 7, it was made known that "Prof. Hammond has resigned the presidency on account of ill health."

It was observed that most of his Faculty had resigned as well, and that a good many students had withdrawn from the institution. The immediate cause of this general exodus is not precisely known, but there is evidence that back of it lay a quarrel between the Faculty and the Board. A letter to the Lebanon *Daily News* of June 30 hinted that it was owing to "the *vindication* (!) of their 'ideal' teacher, whom they still retain," and "the manner he was vindicated. . . ."

Other complaints were aired in the press, as, for instance, by Thomas L. Stein in the *News* of June 19, deprecating "the way things have been going for some time," and in particular the "financial condition of the institution."

A reporter on the *News,* commenting on President Hammond's illness, wrote that

> the college loses an executive whose ability is fearless yet kind, and one who in his private and public life is tender and affable as the most refined nature, the cause of education [loses] a sound and thorough educator, and the church an earnest, devoted Christian. . . . His mind is perfectly at ease and composed, as he enjoys the consciousness of having been faithful to himself and to all with whom he came in contact.

He died a few months later, March 20, 1877, at the age of fifty-one, in Landisville, New Jersey. According to his former colleague, Professor E. Benjamin Bierman (the only member of the old Faculty who did not withdraw) his remains were laid "in an unmarked grave in Siloam cemetery near the city of Vineland."

Hammond's unmarked grave is a symbol of honor, the honor that belongs to all those men and women who, in the College's early years, sacrificed their careers and sometimes their lives to bring this strange, fractious, but vital and promising institution to the maturity it now enjoys.

Graduating Class of 1892

Front row: Della Roop (Daugherty), Lillie Rice (Gohn),
Anna Brightbill (Harp), Laura Reider (Muth).
Middle row: Jacob Martin Herr, Elmer Haak, Josephine
Kreider (Henry), Hervin U. Roop, Anna Forney (Kreider).
Back row: Samuel Stein, Lulu Baker, Harry Roop, Florence
Brindel (Gable), D. Albert Kreider, John Rice, Catharine P.

Mumma (Good), Seba C. Huber, Andrew R. Kreider.
This class was the largest to graduate in the history of the
College up until that time. The 25th Anniversary of the founding of the College was celebrated this year, 25 years from the
date of the charter in 1867, rather than from the true founding
date in 1866.

CHAPTER TWELVE

President DeLong Brings Harmony

UNDERNOURISHED FINANCIALLY as it had been during its most tender years, Lebanon Valley College underwent, in adolescence, a series of near-fatal illnesses. From these it made amazing recoveries, yet its friends remained anxious. In the formal ceremonies for the new president, David Denman DeLong, held on the evening of August 22, 1876, an undertone of apprehension could be detected. It was only to be expected, for the long disability of President Hammond had provided a breeding ground for noxious political weeds.

At the inauguration ceremony, DeLong essayed a cautious re-interpretation of the aims of a Liberal Arts College, in terms that were calculated not to offend anyone. "The College does not propose," he said, as reported by the *Courier,* "to teach theology, law or medicine, but it proposes to lead out in harmonious development the physical, mental and moral powers of our nature, or in other words, to qualify us to think well and act wisely in view of our relations to each other and to God."

Following the President, the Honorable Henry Houck, Deputy State Superintendent of Schools (who had come in from Lebanon on foot), spoke a not very veiled word of warning: ". . . if union and harmony prevail in the councils of the board of trustees, the executive committee and the faculty, the College will enter upon a career of usefulness and success."

To the cause of "union and harmony" the young President (born November 11, 1846, at Newville, Indiana) brought qualifications his predecessor had lacked. For one thing, he was an ordained minister of the United Brethren Church. For another, he had had training in that great school of democracy, the Grand Army of the Republic, in which he had enlisted, November 10, 1863—one day short of his seventeenth birthday. On January 11, 1864, he was mustered in as a private in Company F of the 129th Indiana Volunteers, a regiment that saw heavy service in the Atlanta Campaign and other operations of 1864 and 1865. He was mustered out, August 26, 1865.

His wife was ready to support him by taking a full share of college responsibilities, teaching and collecting funds. Years afterwards, she told Enid Daniel, '00, that when the College was facing bankruptcy, she herself went

Rev. David D. DeLong, A.M.
President, 1876-1877

out in Annville to get money, and in that way raised a thousand dollars.

They were both graduates of Otterbein University. During the Commencement Exercises of that institution in 1869, Miss E. Lete Knepper of Finley (one of two graduating in the Ladies' Department), delivered a farewell address on "The Empire of Mind." At the Commencement in 1870, Mr. D. Denman DeLong of Newville, Indiana (one of two graduating in the Classical Department), spoke his farewell on "The Magnets of the Soul." In each partner to the marriage that ensued, and in the partnership itself, mind and soul accorded well and made one music for the College. David DeLong held, besides the Presidency, the Professorship of Mental and Moral Science; his wife, Emma K. DeLong, took the Professorship of Greek Language and Literature. She is said, indeed, to have been "the first lady in America to occupy such a position."

During the six years that elapsed between his graduation from Otterbein and his coming to Lebanon Valley College as President, David DeLong had attended the Allegheny Theological Seminary and had had experience both as a teacher and as a pastor, the former at the Roanoke Classical Seminary in Indiana, the latter in Westmoreland County, Pennsylvania, at the town of Mount Pleasant (scene of the first General Conference, 1815, of the United Brethren Church) and at other stations attached to the Allegheny Conference.

This "young man, modest, wise, of good scholarship and considerable experience in the instruction and government of young men and women," as the Lebanon *Courier* called him, and "a man of grace and dignity . . . polish and culture," as the *News* put it, succeeded for eleven years in keeping the College pretty closely to the course Henry Houck had prescribed for it.

On November 15, 1876, the *News* reported that the endowment fund of the College was growing, no less than $11,000 having been secured in one week. Within a year, it was thought, $50,000 might be raised.

The year ended happily. The closing exercises of the term were well attended by townsmen and friends of the College. On Tuesday evening, December 19, an "able lecture against evolution," as the *Courier* said, was given by Philip H. Reinhard.

On Wednesday, the Preparatory Class presented their "Rhetorical," which consisted of orations and essays on these subjects: "The Girls of the Twentieth Century," "Daniel," "Aim High," "Love for One's Trade," "A Name in Life," "The American Indians," "Friday," "The Flirt," "Centennial Squibbs."

On Thursday evening the Philokosmian Literary Society presented a sparkling "Polyglot" entertainment:

H. B. Dohner, German oration, "The Beauties of a Well-Chosen Vocation";

H. C. Deaner, Latin oration, "Roman Literature";

G. F. Bierman, French oration, "Monsieur Guizot";

J. B. Crouse, Greek oration, "The Beginning is Half of the Whole";

J. C. Yocum, English oration, "The American Centennial."

The reporter for the *Courier* added a subjective note: "While we had enough to do in translating the subjects with few scattered sentences and without the aid of our dictionaries and vocabularies, we amused ourselves like the rest by eating peanuts and hoarhound candy; and took no further notes, and thought, go on, *Labor Omnia Vincit, bravo, eclat, etc.*"

The year 1877 opened hopefully. President DeLong's report to the co-operating conferences was cheerful and aggressive. He was happy at the good relations between town and gown in Annville, at "the re-fitting of the South College building, and the providing and furnishing of halls for three Literary Societies" there; at the purchase of a new piano for the Department of Instrumental Music; at the progress of the Department of Natural Science; at the unusually large number beginning the study of the classics; and at the recent religious revival among the students.

Gravely he continued: "Money is our greatest want at present, that is, an ample endowment fund." He went on to say that $15,000 had already been secured to that end, and stated his policy, which was "to raise $100,000 as endowment, as soon as it can be done"—words that were to be re-echoed hopefully and unavailingly for many years to come.

One of the problems that disturbed his first year was that of relocation. A movement had grown up in some quarters to remove the College from Annville to a larger center. While the arguments pro and con were flying about, patrons of the College questioned the wisdom of putting money into an institution that did not know where its permanent home was to be. President DeLong was pleased to say that the question of removal was (as he thought) settled.

"Lebanon Valley," he said, "is located. Annville is to be its home."

He was not a good prophet. The question of relocation remained to break the sleep of presidents and trustees for many years to come.

On March 9, 1877, the Kalozetean Literary Society came into being. Its name had been suggested by Professor Louis H. McFadden, its motto— *Palma non sine Pulvere*—by Mrs. DeLong.

These were the founders:

Horace S. Kephart	Alfred C. Dice
Simon P. Light	Clayton P. Saylor
Jacob L. Whitmoyer	William F. Garman
Allen Penn Strayer	Robert F. Strayer
Cyrus G. Richards	Nelson P. Moyer
Charles E. Rauch	Henry Marquet
John L. Garman	Harvey C. Hoverter
Bright C. Lindenmuth	Samuel T. Mower
Sealon S. Daugherty	Geo. W. Van Meter

During Commencement week, DeLong was able to close his first year in an atmosphere of harmony, both with his Board of Trustees and with his Faculty. Members of the latter were happy at the prospect of stability he gave them. "Nothing," commented the *News* (remembering the crash when Hammond went out) "is more demoralizing to students and detrimental to the best interests of a college than a constant change in the corps of instructors, and it is cheering to see that this is to have an end at Lebanon Valley College."

Undoubtedly DeLong's main task was to "hold the line"—to keep the College from flying apart, as it had nearly done before his arrival.

Under his regime, there was little change in the curriculum. Such changes as were made were rather of degree than of kind. The Classical Course remained the heart of the College program. But the Scientific Course was strengthened, being raised to four years instead of three, and given a good deal of Latin, though no Greek. The 1885-1886 *Catalogue* announced firmly that "The Classical Course is the most thorough, and should be elected by those who contemplate entering the 'Learned Professions,' and by such as aspire to the ripest scholarship or purely literary pursuits."

The Ladies' Course (which, after being dropped for a time, had come back and been elevated to a four-years course leading to a degree), was dropped again; but the degree, Mistress of Arts, was retained, to be conferred on such "lady students" as completed the four-year Scientific Course.

72

Music made a considerable advance under DeLong. In the 1880 *Catalogue,* the heading "Ornamentals" was dropped and in its place stood "Department of Music." The course of studies was treated as a unit, though one might specialize in either Piano or in Voice, and all graduates were required to have a knowledge of the Elements of Harmony.

The regular "Course of Study" in Music was introduced with this preamble: "The graduating course in Music extends over a longer or shorter period of time, as some pupils will accomplish in two years what would take others three or four years to complete." A "Post graduate" course was offered for "those who may wish to continue the study of classical music."

The 1881 *Catalogue* introduced a further advance: the granting of a diploma after a three-years' course, this in addition to a preparatory course for those who "are not already familiar with the rudiments of music."

With President DeLong came an almost complete change of teaching staff. Professor Bierman was the only hold-over from the old faculty—and he did not remain long under the new president. Among those who came in with DeLong was the Rev. Daniel Eberly, A.M., Professor of Latin Language and Belles Lettres, a distinguished figure whom the College had hoped to have as President in 1866. Another was Louis H. McFadden, A.M., Professor of Natural Science and the Greek Language. Professor McFadden was relieved of Greek next year by Mrs. DeLong, and was so left free to concentrate on his specialty.

Among other noteworthy additions to the Faculty later during DeLong's tenure were H. Clay Deaner, A.B., Professor of Mathematics and Astronomy; George W. Bowman, Professor of Natural Science (who followed McFadden in 1882); and Alice M. Evers, B.S., Professor of Instrumental Music.

Admissions standards, hitherto slack, received a tightening in an unexpected quarter, as may be seen from a statement appearing in the *Catalogue* for 1878-1879:

> Recognizing the danger and evil attendant upon the practice of carrying fire-arms, no one will be matriculated who brings with him a pistol or revolver . . . and the possession of either, while connected with the College, will be deemed sufficient cause for the removal of the offender. The attention of parents and guardians is especially called to this condition of membership in the College.

That warning was not dropped from the *Catalogue* until 1885, when all restrictions were omitted except this innocuous one: "Matriculation is regarded a pledge on the part of the student that he will obey all of the rules of the College."

Even that mild requirement was dropped from the 1885-1886 *Catalogue.* It is to be noted that in that year only two students graduated. The financial situation was such that it has been surmised the administration would have enrolled card-carrying members of the *Mafia* if they had presented themselves.

Faculty and Students, 1887

Upper: *Profs. George W. Bowman, Alice K. Gingrich, John B. Lynn* Middle: *Prof. Florence Adelaide Sheldon, Pres. David D. DeLong, Prof. Alice M. Evers* Lower: *Prof. H. Clay Deaner, Mrs. David D. DeLong, Prof. Isaiah Sneath*

As an administrator, DeLong's contribution to the College was impressive. He infused new energy into it on his arrival; and, with his confident leadership (holding aloft the banner of Union & Harmony), it pursued a fairly steady course for eleven years. He brought in a good faculty, improved the College's financial system, strengthened the Music Department, and added a new building to the campus. That was a frame structure, erected in 1883 north of the Administration Building to house the Department of Natural Science with its museum, the departments of Music and the Fine Arts, and the College Library. When Engle Hall was built, it was removed; but it may still be seen, having been turned into a residence, 336 East Sheridan Avenue.

DeLong's record was a good one; but, after ten years, tensions were building up. The President's report to the East Pennsylvania Conference (the same report in substance as that to the other conferences) in the spring of 1887 had of necessity what he called a plaintive air: "As in the past, so now, the pressing need of the institution is money. And the immediate future promises to change the need to an imperative demand. Our buildings are full of students, and more ample accommodations will have to be provided. . . ."

The note changed, as he proceeded, to one of sharp reproof (recalling to our minds the unmarked grave of President Hammond). "It is a matter perfectly inexplicable," he said, "to those who are sacrificing most for the cause of Christian education, that we allow this great home interest to suffer."

The public, however, did not notice that all was not comfortably normal. On June 15 the Lebanon *Daily News* reported that "The salubrious rays of the morning sun" ushered in the Baccalaureate sermon by the Rev. Dr. J. W. Etter. Monday, at 1:30 p.m., the grades were read. On Tuesday the Alumni exercises were held, Miss A. May Saylor being the essayist and Prof. I. W. Sneath the orator. At the Commencement Exercises, a collegiate class of no less than twelve graduated—"seven gentlemen and 5 ladies," as the *News* reported.

But behind this pleasant facade all was not well. The financial situation was threatening. It was not that the college debt was hopeless. It was only $20,000. But the methods being taken to reduce it and pay operating expenses were trivial and disheartening. According to the *Religious Telescope* of June 29, 1887:

> The Board laid an assessment of five cents per member upon the co-operating conferences, hoping in this way to reduce the debt at least one thousand dollars annually, and also assist in meeting the running expenses of the college. In order to help on this good work the male members of the faculty consented to a temporary reduction of salary, which will reduce the expenses this year $600. The lady members of the faculty also suffered a reduction of $25 each, making $675 in all. L. W. Stahl, the financial agent of the college resigned his position. . . ."

Of the professors' salaries it was reported a few months later in *The College Forum* for May, 1888, that they were "a disgrace to the church," being only a third of those in other institutions doing comparable work.

On July 26, 1887, it was reported in the *News* that "The Reverend I. W. Sneath [class of '81], professor of the German and Greek languages in Lebanon Valley College, Annville, has forwarded his resignation. . . . This announcement will occasion much regret to the students of the institution and will prove a loss to the college itself."

President David D. DeLong, who had now been at the helm for eleven years, did what he could to steer a course through these shoals. But in the end his patience snapped.

On August 4, 1887, the Lebanon *Daily News* reported: "Rev. D. D. DeLong, D.D., of Annville, today resigned the presidency of Lebanon Valley College, to take effect immediately. . . . He will return to ministerial work, several positions already awaiting his services."

The College was again at Death's door.

THE
COLLEGE FORUM
OF LEBANON VALLEY COLLEGE.

VOL. I. ANNVILLE, PA., FEBRUARY, 1888. NO. 2

EDITORIAL:

The publisher kindly requests of all who receive a sample copy of the College Forum, to remit twenty-five cents in stamps, and thus insure the monthly visits of Forum.

The kind words that have been spoken and written about the College Forum, are greatly appreciated by us. Our native modesty has, however, suffered no loss, for with the many kind words have come a few of adverse criticism upon the typographical appearance of the first number. If our friends will only be patient and support us in our effort, we hope to smarten up a bit in succeeding issues. There is even a promise of an entirely new dress.— In the meantime we comfort ourselves that beauty will shine even through tattered garments.

We call attention to the liberal terms offered to subscribers of the Forum in connection with the "Century" and "Scribner's" magazines. The monthly visit of either to a home will bring not only pleasure, but great profit. It will develop the taste of young people, in literary, and also in artistic matters and prove an educational force of great value.

We congratulate ourselves not infrequently on the high character of the great majority of our students. Many of them are conscientious almost to a fault; others have so much self respect as to shrink from anything that might, in the slightest degree, compromise them; it is the few who are restrained simply by the fear of penalty. It is a pleasure to associate with such a class of young people and to be their leaders in intellectual pursuits. Discipline is not the vexation to the spirit it often is elsewhere, but largely takes care of itself. We certainly are proud of the young gentlemen and ladies who make up the students of Lebanon Valley College.

There is nothing so impracticable as the narrowly practical. To judge of education as you would of a pair of boots, asking simply how much wear you can get out of them, or of an investment in mining shares, with an eye only to the financial returns, seeking to combine the minimum of risk with the maximum of dividend, is to degrade the greater by measuring it by the standard of the less. The utilarian view of education is not only a degraded but a degrading view to take of life and its deeper meaning. Not how much more money and how much more easily can my son or my daughter make, but how much more of a man, how much more grandly womanly may my son or daughter become, is the true basis of judgment. Not as a means of getting, but of becoming, should young people be given an education.

The authorities of Lebanon Valley College ought to have a profound sympathy for the ancient Jews, who were required to make bricks without straw, for they themselves have been asked to perform a like difficult task—to run a college without money. The management of the school in the past has been severely criticised, because a large debt has been accumulated. That no mistakes have been made in the past were a proposition as difficult to maintain as that none will be made in the future. But the great, the fatal mistake which plunged the college so deeply was not made by the management. The church made that mistake in not furnishing the money needed to run a college of the high standard required to satisfy our people and to compete favorably with the schools of other denominations. The church called for a good college, but when it was furnished, she simply neglected to pay the bills and debt was the result.

* * * * *

A college is not a business which will make money or even pay its way. It is a beneficiary enterprise, which must look to the generosity of Christian people for the greater part of its support. It cannot hope to thrive on the small income derived from its

CHAPTER THIRTEEN

President Edmund S. Lorenz

IN THE EMERGENCY that followed President DeLong's sudden resignation in August, 1887, invitations to the presidency of the College were issued by the Board to a number of eligible persons, all of whom declined. Among these were the Rev. Daniel Eberly, who until 1884 had been Professor of Latin at Lebanon Valley; the Rev. Dr. J. Wesley Etter, '72, who had preached the Baccalaureate Sermon at the June Commencement; and the Rev. Dr. H. A. Thompson, former President of Otterbein University. When classes opened on August 29, the College was without a president and without any very sanguine hope of finding one.

Clouds broke, some six weeks later, when the Rev. Edmund S. Lorenz of Dayton, Ohio, unaware of the full measure of trouble into which the College had sunk, accepted the position. He was a graduate of Otterbein, 1880, and of Yale Divinity School, and he had spent several years in postgraduate work at Leipzig, Germany. He was well known in religious circles as a fluent preacher in both English and German, also as a hymn writer and composer of religious music, and as the author of *The Gospel Workers Treasury* as well as a forthcoming book on organized evangelism.

About the middle of October, 1887, a wave of relief swept over the campus on the appearance of this "fine, quiet, scholarly man," as Albert H. Gerberich '88 (then a Senior student), has since described him. "He was very sociable and he had pleasant associations with the students."

But the shock was severe for the new president himself when he fully realized the situation into which he had stepped. It was fortunate, under the circumstances, that behind his quiet friendly manner were reserves of energy and courage capable of carrying him over rough country.

The enthusiasm and drive which he brought to his task, together with discernment and far-sightedness, gave him qualitites of leadership under which all factions for a time were able to unite. He got action.

The cataclysmic manner in which the position had been opened for him, and the arduous duties that befell him as college administrator and promoter, are best described in his own words, which have been preserved in a manu-

77

Rev. Edmund S. Lorenz, A.M.
President, 1887-1889

script history he wrote entitled, "The Lorenz Family." In Chapter XIX, an autobiographical sketch modestly entitled, "My College Fiasco," is valuable not only for the light it throws on his career but also for its first-hand information about what most of the College's early presidents had to go through.

It opens with a bang:

> But suddenly, early in October, 1887, like a bolt out of the blue, there came a call to undertake the presidency of Lebanon Valley College at Annville, Penna. It attracted me, but I was loath to give up my literary and musical plans. I also questioned my ability to endure the strains involved in such a position. Had I fully known the situation, I now think I should have refused. But my wise friend, W. J. Shuey, who, I surmise, had not fully approved of my stepping aside from active work, earnestly counselled me to accept, as did Bishop Weaver and others.
>
> So, against my own better judgment, I agreed to undertake the task and left at once to take hold of the unknown problem. On arrival I found that my predecessor, in a rage because of some opposition to some plans of his, had resigned the day before the college was to open. He sent word to the coming and prospective students that he had resigned and that the institution would likely close its doors. The school year, however, was begun, but under great uncertainties and fear of collapse. A dragnet was thrown out at once to secure a president in which I had become entangled. I had not taught since I was nineteen years old and then only in a public graded school. I knew college methods and organization only from outside. The members of the faculty, the Executive committee, the trustees, the people in the field at large were all unknown to me. Yet I had to establish the general morale in students and faculty and in the supporting territory. My chief

immediate task was to awaken courage and aggressiveness and to develop financial resources without which the school was doomed.

It was a daunting situation, but I summoned up my courage and plunged ahead, adapting two slogans I saw in the stained glass window of the Glasgow cathedral: "Gang forward" and "Poco a poco" (little by little). I had everything to learn, but learned fast.

I preached two or three times every Sunday, often in German, and was called on to lecture during the week. How I did it I hardly know, for I had no time to prepare for my public work, improvising as if I were at the organ, I suppose. I planned some small ways of increasing the college income, but deliberately avoided looking towards a regular financial campaign. My first year, as I realized, was the psychological preparation of our people to give largely when I had definite forward-looking plans that would appeal to them. I must understand the possibilities in order to plan largely and wisely.

One by one, as they came up, the problems were solved. There was a growing enthusiasm and hopefulness among students and friends. Improvements and enlargements were made in every line. Some dreams of previous years confided to me became realized because I put courage and energy and organization back of them. So the year that opened so disastrously ended with the largest attendance and the best financial report in the history of the college.

One of Lorenz's first and best accomplishments was the launching of a monthly magazine, *The College Forum.* Through its pages he presented college news not only to the faculty and students, but also to the constituency, stirring an interest in higher education and explaining the particular problems of Lebanon Valley College. The monthly *Forum,* well-written, skillfully edited, and issued at the comfortable subscription price of twenty-five cents a year, served as the first move in Lorenz's campaign for "the psychological preparation of our people."

In the first issue, January, 1888, he asked the constituency to face the facts about their college: "Our present membership is not as large as heretofore, owing to the unsettled condition of the school at the beginning of the year. . . ." By May, however, he was able to advise his readers to look back no longer, but to look forward hopefully. Things had changed so much that the College now had fifty more students in attendance than it had had the preceding year, and, as he said, another twenty would fill the chapel. There was no room for growth with the present facilities and the College had to have financial help. "A college," he continued, "cannot run on its regular income any more than a missionary society. It is a benevolent institution where students get twice as much as they pay for."

Though Lorenz wrote the main editorials, he was well supported by a staff of students and professors. The names of the founding editors should be remembered:

Editors

Rev. E. B. Lorenz, A.M., President
H. Clay Deaner, A.M., Professor of Latin

It is not surprising that President Lorenz—hymn-writer, composer, and later founder of the great Lorenz Music Publishing Company—should have planned the enlargement of the Department of Music. Whatever question there might still be in some parts of the Church constituency about Higher Education, and however reticent the Plain People might be about instrumental music in the sanctuary, the college constituency, by and large, possessed and cultivated an inborn love of music.

"Music," said Samuel Johnson, "is the only sensual pleasure without a vice."

Lorenz used music as an entering wedge in his campaign on behalf of the whole college curriculum. In the opening issue of the *Forum,* appeared an article on "Musical Culture," in which it was said that "Perhaps at no time has the importance of the study of music been so recognized and followed as now. A few years ago it was not considered essential to an education, but was an extra, to be studied if there was time; but we have arrived at that time, when no education is considered complete without it. . . ."

Lorenz found the enrollment in music ("between fifty and sixty," it was reported) in the fall of 1887 encouraging. He noticed that the public enjoyed the student recitals. In June of 1888 the Board of Trustees, on his recommendation, decided (as C. I. B. Brane reported in the *Religious Telescope* of June 27) to establish a Conservatory of Music:

> The territory between Pittsburgh and Philadelphia is unoccupied by anything of the kind, so far as I know, and the prospect for patronage north and south is equally good. The musical department of the college deservedly enjoys an excellent reputation, and by increasing its faculty and facilities as is now contemplated and proposed, its popularity and influence will be increased and extended, and thereby its patronage will be multiplied. Geographically speaking, Lebanon Valley College is well located for such an enterprise.

Plans went forward for the transformation of Music from a mere appendage to the degree-producing departments into a full-fledged Conservatory of Music offering a Bachelor's degree of its own. The *College Forum* (Lorenz's mouthpiece) for July, 1888, in reporting on the June 11 meeting of the Board of Trustees, announced that it was decided that the Music Department should be reorganized as "a conservatory of music, having five departments and a course of seven years in length leading to the degree of Bachelor of Music. This will bring the new conservatory abreast of the best institutions of the land. A good deal of enthusiasm was manifested over this project and there is no doubt that with an increase of our present' excellent facilities a large musical College can be built up."

Unfortunately Lorenz's illness interrupted these plans. No great development of the Music Department was to be seen for a number of years.

Meanwhile, however, in other ways the new president gave the College motion. Post-graduate courses were introduced. The *College Forum* for July, 1888, reported:

"Five non-resident post graduate courses leading to the degree of Doctor of Philosophy were recommended to the Faculty and adopted by the Board. This was recognized as a large step in advance."

In all, six Ph.D. degrees (not honorary) were given by Lebanon Valley College:

> Cornelius A. Burtner 1892
> Isaac H. Albright 1893
> Benjamin F. Fritz 1893
> Joji Kingora Irie 1895
> Joseph G. W. Herold 1898
> Jacob H. Reber 1898

In years to come, the College was to do itself credit by dropping the graduate work. It was found to be beyond the capabilities of her library, equipment, and small teaching staff, the College having failed to achieve the advance—the general enlargement—President Lorenz had planned for it. At the time it was introduced, however, it was a great morale raiser.

A great cause for rejoicing came in 1888. On June 11, the Board of Trustees accepted from William Bittinger the gift of a farm of 204 acres at Shiremanstown, valued between $30,000 and $50,000, for the endowment of the Josephine Bittinger Eberly Chair of Latin Language and Literature. The actual cash value of the farm did not amount to much, and the terms of the bequest proved ultimately to be embarrassing to the College. But at the time the gift was announced, it was welcomed as a gesture of confidence.

The Latin chair was named in honor of Josephine Bittinger, who was warmly remembered on the campus, according to the *Forum,* as a cultured woman of "kindly considerate ways." She was the wife of the Rev. Daniel Eberly, who for some years (1876–1884) was Professor of Latin Language and Literature at the College. He resigned in 1884 because of his wife's illness. She died the same year. It was said that on her deathbed she had asked her father,

William Bittinger of Abbottstown, to help the College. After her death, Professor Eberly used his influence with Mr. Bittinger to the same end, successfully.

The farm at Shiremanstown was subject to a life interest held by Professor Eberly, and, according to the terms of the bequest, it could never be sold. Its income was eventually to come to the College as endowment for the Chair of Latin. As it turned out, the College was to find this inalienable farm to be a liability rather than an asset. But, at the time the gift was received, it was greeted by the *College Forum* with a roar of triumph: "That Lebanon Valley College has a future no one can now venture to deny."

Yet catastrophe for the College lay immediately ahead. President Lorenz's health failed. The narrative is resumed in his own vivid words:

> Owing to the constant use of my voice in the classroom, preaching, lecturing, [it] had begun to break at inopportune moments of public address. A throat specialist prescribed a steady course of nerve tonic, strychnia, which I took three times a day. Unfortunately the effect would not be limited to the nerves of my throat, but gave a false strength to my whole system. Unknowingly I was not really adding strength, but simply drawing a check on my vital reserves every time I took a dose. I finally reached the point where nature gave me notice that I had overdrawn my account, and the inevitable collapse followed.
>
> No small factor in my nervous exhaustion was the illness and death of our baby, Paul Shuey, at the age of twenty-one months. He had reached the stage of development where he became very interesting to me and we were great pals. As I came up the walk to the house he was frequently at the window waiting to greet me with a smile that was heartening to the weary man. He had a warm spot of his own in my heart, and it was heartbreaking to lay his body away in the cemetery on the brow of the hill overlooking the village from the northwest. . . .
>
> I had gone back to Dodson, Granpa Kumler's, for what was supposed to be a month of rest. I saw no chance to complete my book on revival methods, and so decided to take the first part which only needed some strengthening in places, and adaptation to separate publication, to issue it under the title "Preparing for a Revival." So I spent my ostensible month of rest in continuous work on the MS—. I completed it and passed it over to the United Brethren Publishing House for publication and returned to my great eastern task.

The *College Forum* reported happily in its May, 1889, issue:

> After an absence of eight months spent in a school whose students all matriculate unwillingly . . . , the editor resumes his chair. During his absence the COLLEGE FORUM has been ably cared for under the general direction of Prof. Deaner, and its readers have suffered no loss. The faculty and financial agent who divided among them the work of their afflicted associate in a loyal and large hearted way which was more than admirable, are hereby tendered his sincere and most earnest thanks."

CHAPTER FOURTEEN

President Lorenz Charts a Course

DURING THE EARLY MONTHS of 1888 it became apparent that the first part of Lorenz's campaign, "the psychological preparation of our people," was beginning to bear fruit. A crescendo of voices called for a college endowment. In February, the *Daily News* of Lebanon reported that proposals were being made in United Brethren circles to try to raise a hundred thousand dollars for endowment "next year." Late in the summer, at a U. B. reunion at Mont Alto, the Rev. Dr. J. Wesley Etter of Lebanon (who had declined the presidency only the year before) made a spirited appeal for generous financial aid to the College:

> Here is a plan to endow Lebanon Valley College [he said]: pray then pay. When a man prays for a thing he becomes serious about it, and instead of continuing to pray that his hungry neighbor may be fed, he feeds him, having been put to shame in the serious moments of prayer by the revelation that he is praying God to do a thing which he himself can do and ought to do. Let us then have a day of prayer over the raising of this $100,000 endowment, and then a pay day. . . .

By the following spring, things were coming to a head. Lorenz was ready to launch an all-out financial campaign, and he charted a course for it, not by assessing five cents a head for U. B. Church members and cutting professors' salaries, but by organizing the Church from the top for an intensive financial drive.

In the *College Forum* for May, 1889, a main article entitled "The General Conference and Education" opened with President Lorenz's forthright, clear, and discerning statement of the problem. He showed, with figures, the perilous condition of all the Church's colleges. "The road to bankruptcy lies plain before our eyes, and *the end all too near.* . . .

> What is the cause? The causes are many: the early prejudice against education in our church, its genius for producing a change of character rather than for nurturing or developing it, the rural character of our people bringing less sense of the need of education, the fixedness and unremunerativeness of the financial capital of our people invested as it almost exclusively is in farms and rural property, the lack of academical training among our ministers, are among the

more important ones. The chief trouble, however, is that there has been no systematic effort made to counteract these adverse influences. We have been trying to reap without sowing. We have tried to get money from our people for an object in which they had no spontaneous interest and in which no effort had been made to get them interested before asking their assistance. . . .

The remedy then lies on the surface—create in the people an intelligent enthusiasm over the subject of education by systematic and thorough instruction and encouragement, by the pulpit, the press, by special methods and plans—by every avenue by which we can reach them.

Toward that end, he made a number of specific proposals for action:

1. Let the General Conference provide for a quadrennium of educational agitation, an aggressive campaign systematically outlined and thoroughly organized whose purpose shall be announced as the raising of at least half a million.

2. The conference should instruct the Board of Bishops in a very definite way to emphasize this phase of the church's work in every possible way. . . .

3. Elect a board of bishops whose sympathies with the educational work are so aggressive as to make the work suggested above a pleasure, not a task.

4. Elect as editor of the *Telescope* a man who shall develop even further the educational plans of the present administration, whose sympathy with such a general movement shall have a contagious power. . . .

5. Let there be a general educational secretary elected whose whole time shall be devoted to the cause and whose duty it shall be to prepare education literature of all kinds, and in a variety of forms, with which our church should be sown knee deep in a systematic way. . . .

6. Commit to the board of Education the duty of preparing a plan of campaign. . . .

7. Let us have a 'College day' for the whole church which shall be made a permanent feature of our church life. . . .

This is no new plan. Eight years ago the General Conference provided for a campaign of eighteen months, but set no mark to be reached, and provided *no one to push it*. The plan was good but it was not carried out. . . . We believe our church is now ready for such a movement.

Motivation and organization, those were his keynotes. And timing! He did not play his trump at once. He went to work vigorously but quietly on a vast plan of improvement. If it seems to us now, with our historical hindsight, to have been ill-advised and recklessly adventurous, we should remember that it was safe-guarded, as he believed, by the assured aid of powerful outside donors. The extraordinary story, with its climax in the summer of 1888, is best told in Lorenz's own words:

To begin with, he did not think Annville a suitable place for the College.

. . . I thought it ought to be moved to Harrisburg, the capital of the state. To announce my decision openly would have been suicidal, as it would have given the absolutely certain opposition a chance to anticipate me by checkmating my every move. Not more than four or five men whom I felt I could trust implicitly knew of my plans, and that was one too many.

I managed to get an appointment with U. S. Senator Don Cameron on a Saturday when he was at home on a weekend. He had several thousand acres of land lying between Harrisburg and Steelton, and I was sure he would be accessible to a proposition not only to increase its value very largely, but also greatly to hasten its being brought into a lively market, by establishing a college on part of it.

I found him willing to promise me ten acres for my purpose. I warned him that I should want him to quadruple that, but was glad to have that much for a start. He also promised me to spend a week in visiting the leading financial people of Harrisburg and to organize a movement to assure that city's providing the necessary buildings. The United Brethren Church was to raise an adequate endowment fund as its share of the enterprise.

The Harrisburg end was to be taken care of on the quiet, so that I could spring the proposition on the college trustees and supporting conference as an accomplished and official offer and so prevent reactionaries and Annville interests from defeating it.

So I left Senator Cameron full of enthusiasm and courage. The next day, a Sunday, I preached at Stoverdale Camp, a great East Pennsylvania Conference summer center, with unusual vigor, but with some strange nervous experiences whose meaning I did not understand.

He came to understand the symptoms a few days later. After a sleepless night of train travel, he reached Annville at about six in the morning, and suffered at last the collapse he had for so long been unconsciously inviting. His heart gave out and his life for a time was despaired of.

"Of course," he concludes, "with that collapse, all my great plans for the institution collapsed as well."

I soon saw, that, unless I was removed from Annville, I should never recover, for in spite of every kindly intention to spare me, the problems of the college were brought to me. I could not read, could not even endure to be read to, could not write a letter. For weeks I lay without moving my little finger, unless I was disturbed. I was merely vegetating.

As soon as I gave the slightest hope that I could be moved, I was taken to the train to start for Dodson. I was in serious doubt whether I would reach it alive, so weak and irregular was my heart action. Even when I got to Dodson, it was uncertain whether I would reach Mamma's old home alive.

Their family doctor had been wired for from Dayton, and came at once to take charge of my case. . . .

In a little while my strength was evidently increasing and presently I was able to sit up and occasionally move about in my room. Little by little my strength increased until I was able to creep back, metaphorically speaking, to Annville and slightly supervise the appointment of teachers for the heavy spring attendance and the planning for Commencement.

This venture into the active world proved too much for him. He collapsed again.

As soon as I realized how serious was my condition, I offered my resignation as president. But sympathy and appreciation of what I had accomplished, and,

Rev. Daniel Eberly, A.M., D.D.
Professor of Latin and Belles Lettres

perhaps, a realization that a nearly dead president was better than no president at all, led the Executive Committee to refuse its acceptance. At Commencement the slow improvement I was making and the suffering incident to even the little I was doing made it clear that my return to work was out of the question. Again I resigned, and this time peremptorily. But the Executive Committee came back with the request that I choose my successor.

This I consented to do; foolishly, for I was in no condition to conduct the delicate negotiations needed and had no private secretary to take care of the correspondence which I was not yet able to undertake. The result finally was that I reluctantly consented to the election of the brother of a bishop who urged his appointment. He was a good preacher and had a forceful personality, but had no discretion or administrative capacity. During his single year in the position he undid a good deal of the work of building up the morale among the supporters of the college, I had accomplished.

So I limped back to the West, a broken man, with even yet no assurance of prolonged life, much less of restoration.

He recovered, after some time, and lived a long and useful life, working in the fields of literature and music and as the founder and successful business head of the great Lorenz Music Publishing House of Dayton, Ohio.

C. I. B. Brane in the *Religious Telescope* of June 27, 1888, summed up Lorenz's career at the College in this manner:

Last Year's Success,

when you pause to consider it, is something exceedingly strange and marvelous. When the fall term opened, the institution was without a president, and the outlook was doubtful and gloomy. The remaining members of the faculty deserve praise for their prudence and devotion during that unsafe and unsettled condition of affairs. About the middle of October, Rev. E. S. Lorenz, A.M., entered upon his duties as president of the college, and in a short time he and his associates turned defeat into victory and made the past year the most successful in the history of the school. I suppose that this strange but fortunate turn was a simple expression of interest upon the part of the Lord in the welfare of Lebanon Valley College; but it also serves to illustrate the fact that He works through the instrumentality of competent agents. . . .

A beautiful postscript to his college career was provided by the Harrisburg *Telegraph* in a news item which was reprinted by the *College Forum,* September, 1889:

Ex-President Lorenz Goes West.
Lebanon Valley College's Late President Will
Reside at Dodson, Ohio.

Rev. E. S. Lorenz, ex-president of Lebanon Valley College, and his family, left the city yesterday for Dodson, Ohio, where they will reside with the father of Mrs. Lorenz, a son of ex-Bishop Henry Kumler, until Mr. Lorenz shall have recovered from his affliction. Two years ago Mr. L. was called to the presidency of Lebanon Valley College of Annville. His unassuming manner, united with great learning, his earnest efforts and untiring zeal in behalf of the college, his large heartedness and wide sympathy, enabled him at once to gain the affections of the students of the institution, the co-operation of the church under whose direction he labored and the respect of the community at large. Had his health permitted his labors to be continued the college, under his direction, would doubtless have attained a degree of enlarged prosperity hitherto unknown in its history. Already much was done in preparation for the carrying out of such measures as would infuse new life and lay the foundation upon which to raise the institution to a place of efficiency and completeness unsurpassed by any of the kind in the U. B. Church. The sympathy of all who came in contact with Mr. Lorenz goes with him, and the most earnest desire is expressed on every hand that his health be restored and his services retained to the church for many years.

Tower of the Old Administration Building

The New Bell,
Installed in 1890 and recovered from the fire in 1904.
Inscription: "Secured and Donated
by Students of 1889 & 1890."

Sketch by John Heffner, '68

CHAPTER FIFTEEN

President Cyrus Jeffries Kephart

AFTER THE LONG ILLNESS of President Lorenz, the advent of Cyrus Jeffries Kephart—"a larger man, physically and mentally," as the departing president said on Commencement Day—brought to the campus new visions of hope and glory.

"He comes, not as an experiment, as I did," said Lorenz, "but has had two years of successful experience as President of a College and a number of years as Professor of Mathematics and the languages."

A newspaper of Des Moines, Iowa, where Kephart had held a United Brethren pastorate, described him as "not only a competent man but . . . also an indefatigable worker."

A. W. Drury, in his *History of the United Brethren Church,* speaks of him as "a ready presiding officer," one who possessed both "the facility" of his brother, Isaiah Lafayette Kephart (editor of the *Religious Telescope*) and the "massive force" of his still better-known brother, Bishop Ezekiel Boring Kephart.

Miss Anna Kreider of Annville today remembers him as "a very powerful man and speaker—such force that one might almost be afraid of him."

His tenure of office was short, but it served to introduce to the College the dynamic (though controversial) "Kephart Dynasty" of which more will be heard in the next chapter.

Kephart seemed to possess all the qualities needed for success in such an elementary struggle as the College was then engaged in. Cyrus Kephart's family heritage in America, like that of the late Bishop John Russel, came from land-clearing pioneers. Cyrus's great-grandfather, Nicholas Kephart, born in Switzerland, had come to Pennsylvania about 1750. His son Henry had married Catherine Smith, an Englishwoman. Their son, Henry, Jr., (Cyrus's father) married a Pennsylvania German, Sarah Goss, daughter of a Revolutionary soldier.

Grandfather Henry Kephart had taken the family west to the Allegheny Front in 1804, settling in Decatur Township near Osceola Mills, south of present Philipsburg. There Cyrus Jeffries was born in 1834, the last of thirteen

Rev. Cyrus J. Kephart, A.M.
President, 1889-1890

children. He grew up in the neighborhood of a dense white pine forest. In that region, some still living have memories of a childhood game, leaping from giant pine stump to pine stump (the forest having been lumbered over) to see who could travel farthest without touching the ground.

His father, who swung a good axe, had a mind also for books. With his own hands he helped build the log schoolhouse which Cyrus and his brothers and sisters attended.

The early upbringing of the Kephart boys was rugged. They "received thorough training in woodcraft," writes Lewis Franklin John in his *Life of Ezekiel Boring Kephart*. "They felled the trees, hewed timber, constructed rafts and conveyed them down the river, run sawmills, made shingles, and conducted brief business enterprises of their own. . . ."

In 1859, the Kepharts moved still farther west to a farm beyond French Creek in Mercer County, halfway between Meadville and Franklin. There Cyrus went to school until he was fifteen, and at sixteen began to *teach* school. By 1869 he was enrolled at Western College in Toledo, Iowa, where his brother Ezekiel was then president. He graduated in the Classical Course in 1874, and, having received license to preach, undertook his first pastorate at Toledo.

He entered Union Biblical Seminary at Dayton, Ohio, in 1875, and graduated with the degree of B.D. in 1878. After graduation, he became principal of Avalon Academy, which in 1880 became Avalon College. Later he served as Professor of Mathematics at Western College, leaving this post in 1887 to take the pastorate of the East Side United Brethren Church in Des Moines, Iowa. It was while he was here, two years later, that he was invited to the presidency of Lebanon Valley College.

Bringing his family to Annville, he installed them in what was the President's house, which Lorenz had built on College Avenue.

In the August, 1889, issue of the *College Forum,* he made his bow to the college constituency:

> I do not deem it necessary to make any very extended statements in this connection. I am glad to say that I feel honored in being called to fill the place made vacant by the resignation of one who, by his manly conduct and untiring energy, endeared himself so much to the people. While I hope to be worthy the confidence of the readers of The Forum, and of the friends of the College, as to whether I shall be, I must leave to them to judge.

Judgment on his short term of office cannot be made fairly without an understanding of the conditions that confronted him at the time of his formal inauguration, which took place at Mount Gretna, September 3, 1889.

It was a period, as must be apparent from the events narrated in the preceding chapter, of great uncertainty. The sudden resignation of DeLong had shocked the College's sponsors into a display of energy which Lorenz had begun to steer into productive channels. Then in a few months came Lorenz's nearly fatal illness, which grieved the community and left his ambitious, half-finished plans dangling in the air. One of these plans, the proposed relocation of the College, ignited a controversy that was to blaze for years.

It should be remembered, too, that the dominant interest in the Valley at that time was agriculture. In consequence, Annville was as yet little touched with the liberal atmosphere of nineteenth century industrialism. Most of her people were comfortably conservative, in religion as well as in politics; and some of them were suspicious of scholars like Kephart who encouraged students to ask questions as well as to memorize facts.

Kephart, a big man physically with a powerful mind and a great gift of expression, set out to make the constituency realize its need of college—trained men and women, and to rouse them to action: that is, to send their sons and daughters to Lebanon Valley College and, for their benefit, to remove its present financial handicap.

He went about his task in several ways. One was by the building up of pride in the alumni. The October, 1889, issue of the *College Forum,* provided its readers with an analysis of the alumni record—to reassure doubters as to the efficacy of the College's instruction, and to reassure them also as to the direction in which it was steering the Church's young people:

While something is being written respecting the individual graduates of the College, it may be interesting to our readers to know something of them as a body. The graduates now number 149; the first class having completed their work in 1870. Of these 48 are ladies, 101 gentlemen. 135 have completed one of the collegiate courses, and 19 have completed the course in music-five having completed both. 39 of the graduates are now either in the regular ministry or preparing for it; 7 are occupying professorships in the schools of the church; two are connected with the faculty at Yale University; 19 are teaching in other relations; six are practicing medicine; eight are attorneys-at-law; nine are merchants; many of the ladies are queens royal in the home; 3 are dead; the remainder are scattered in various avocations.

There is much in this record to rejoice at. One-fourth of the entire number of graduates are in the ministry. This ought to give encouragement to those who see so clearly the necessity of an increase of qualified men in the ranks of the ministry. Lebanon Valley College has done a most important work for the Church, and it is not yet twenty years since its first class graduated. With a hearty support, who can estimate what it may do in the next twenty years?

In the November issue of the *Forum,* appeared a ringing call, written by Sarah M. Sherrick, Professor of English Language, to the young women of the Church to prepare themselves at college for the opportunities and responsibilities which the approaching twentieth century would undoubtedly open to them:

Our Girls

Every true woman considers herself blest in being permitted to live in this last quarter of the 19th century. Never before has she had such privileges and opportunities, and so nobly has she met the responsibilities which these involve, that the world no longer refuses her fair field for competition for equal labor.

But if being a woman to-day means so much, being a girl with a new century and all its manifold possibilities opening up before her and leading doubtless into new and broader fields of thought and action, means a great deal more. As the woman of to-day stands head and shoulders above her mother in influence and usefulness, so she may expect her daughter to occupy a still wider sphere of activity. That much prated "woman's sphere," which our grandfathers and great uncles guarded so jealously is ever shifting its border, and so widely has it extended to-day, that those worthies were they to return to earth would doubtless be lost in attempting to fix its circumference. That such a sphere exists, we will not question. The question is rather, who shall fix its boundary?

But do the girls of to-day realize their opportunities, and are they preparing themselves for the responsibilities which must soon be shifted on to younger and stronger shoulders? Is this work so gloriously begun in the 19th century to be carried forward with the same impetus into the 20th? Girls, what do you say? Are you getting ready for your part?

Clear-headed and unafraid, Kephart continued to voice the College's financial needs with disconcerting candor. Gone were the days when the conferences thought they could make money out of the College, as they had done when they leased it to Miles Rigor and Thomas Rhys Vickroy. They had come to realize that tuition fees could not support an institution of higher learning. The need of an endowment was understood and accepted. But Lebanon Valley College's present endowment was so pitifully small that it was quite insufficient to pay operating expenses and faculty salaries. Bankruptcy lay ahead, just over the next hill.

In the spring of 1890, Dr. Henry B. Stehman, '73, called for the wiping out of the College's floating debt of $10,000 before June 1st. He offered to pay one of the hundred proposed subscriptions of $100 each. When the offer was published in the March, 1890, issue of the *Forum*, the editor (President Kephart) added this comment:

"Dear Friends who read this, our Church needs a College in the East. Must have it. But it needs a College well supported, out of want." He called for the immediate acceptance of Dr. Stehman's offer.

In the April issue, he declared, "Money *must* be provided to meet the expenses of the College"; and he urged the opening of membership in the Board of Trustees to college graduates (who knew exactly where money was needed) and to business men (who knew how to get it).

The question of Board membership had been raised by Dr. Stehman, Superintendent of the Presbyterian Hospital of Chicago. He had suggested in the March, 1890, issue of the *Forum* that laymen should be elected to the Board of Trustees.

> I am satisfied [he wrote] that the said Board (of Trustees) should be, in due time, composed for the most part of former students of the College, who are business men . . . . If these cannot be gotten, select other successful financiers, so that the business experience of such men may be brought to bear upon the conduct of affairs at the College.

So began the movement to put business blood and academic know-how into the affairs of the College.

In the same issue of the *Forum,* there appeared a comparison of Lebanon Valley College's method of appointing trustees (by the cooperating conferences), with that of Yale, Harvard, Rutgers, Johns Hopkins, Iowa College, Lafayette College (Easton), Cornwall College (Iowa), the University of Wooster (Ohio), and Dickinson College in Carlisle. It was found that, in all but one of these, incoming trustees were appointed by the incumbent trustees, that is, by men who knew the inner circumstances of their institution. The exception was Cornwall College, and even here two or three of the trustees were appointed each year *by the alumni.*

"Is it not reasonable," said the writer, "that the men who have the immediate charge of a college, who stand close by it and know all its needs, are best qualified to choose the men who manage its affairs?"

Another controversial issue was raised when Kephart directed the attention of the College's sponsors to a certain essential condition of the intellectual discipline which all agreed it was the function of a college of Liberal Arts to undertake. It is condition more widely understood in our day than it was in his: *the scientific spirit of inquiry.* He gave warning in the August, 1889, *Forum,* through an article written by his brother, Bishop E. B. Kephart, of what would happen if this were neglected at Lebanon Valley:

> There is not one department in the whole realm of human knowledge that is not open to investigation; and the generation now preparing to enter the college will be a generation of investigators in a much wider sphere than their predecessors. As they will be required to look over a broader field, so also must their qualifications be accordingly. As a rule, man's advance in knowledge is determined by the facilities afforded him for acquiring it. The time is upon us when the equipment of a college and its facilities for imparting instruction weigh much more with the intelligent student and the wise parent than does the fact that it is under the auspices of this or that denomination. Yes, the time is upon us when equipment and facilities for learning will determine what institution will get the students.

Meantime the students at Lebanon Valley, unaware of Kephart's skirmishes with his Board, attended classes, prepared their "lessons" (as these were still called), and enjoyed a rare day off, such as, for instance, "Chestnut Day." An article in the *Forum* (October, 1889) describing this colorful corner of "student activities" merits reprinting as an authentic voice from the period.

> . . . Chestnut day at L. V. C. is a day that has clustered around it many pleasant memories. . . . At the request of the Juniors, the faculty granted the 4th inst. as that day. The morning dawned brightly. It was just as the Juniors had predicted. They always know. The students convened in the chapel as usual. Devotional exercises were conducted by President Kephart. The President gave a few good suggestions as to how to make the day a success. They called forth a hearty, good laugh. . . . Soon the familiar step, tramp, tramp, the girls and boys are marching, was heard, and peals of laughter echoed and re-echoed all along the line. We wonder if Grant's line of march was so mirthful, when he said he would "fight it out on this line if it took all summer." Grant was at the head of this line. Nothing of unusual interest occurred along the way, save the failure to get a few apples which tempted the "boys." At last Gravel Hill was reached. The view is grand, and enraptures the eye of the most slow to see the beauty in nature. The greatest difficulty we found was to get some one to climb the trees. From the conversation along the way, we concluded that the gentlemen were as skillful in climbing as the young school teacher in the "Hoosier School Master," but to our sorrow we learned that good talkers are poor doers. However, some, braver than the rest, like little Zachius, did climb the trees.
>
> In all, there were several gallons of chestnuts gathered, but few were saved for winter use. By some unforeseen circumstance, the dinner failed to come. The Juniors, with the speed of a gazelle, came after it, and by 12:30 all were partaking of it. Dinner over, games, foot races, leap frog, etc., were indulged in for several hours. We returned home in time for supper, feeling a little tired physically. The grove gave us new life and made us realize more fully that "all work and no play makes Jack a dull boy."
>
> [Signed] "A Good Time."

The winter of 1889–1890 witnessed a memorable event. According to the *College Forum* (February, 1890), it was at the suggestion of President Kephart that "a movement was set on foot at the close of the Winter Term by the students to secure a new bell to replace the old one which was indequate for the present demand of the College."

Mention of such a replacement stirred memories. The old bell bore the date, 1866. It was placed in the New College when it was built. Since that time, for twenty-two years, it had "controlled the goings and comings of the students." Twice it had tolled the death knell: first, for Miss Fannie Burtner in 1875; second, for President Garfield in 1881. On April 30, 1889, it had sounded the centennial of Washington's inauguration as President of the United States.

To the raising of the new bell on Saturday, January 18, 1890, in which students and faculty, town and gown participated, the *Forum* devoted one of its happiest purple passages:

> . . . At 12:45 the work began under the direction of Messrs. Jere Staver, Adam Gingrich and Daniel Gingrich. Faculty, students and a large number of citizens were present with willing hands and did good service. The fifth story was reached at 2:30. At 3 the old bell pealed forth farewell tones and then was lowered from the cupola by the students. Its littleness and inferiority was only noticed when seen in contrast with the new one. At 3:20 the bell was on the cupola. Ten minutes later it was on the frame. How the news was heralded that the bell was safely in its place. At 3:45 the rope was attached. Prof. Lehman then began to ring it where twenty-one years ago he rang the old bell. What joy filled the hearts of all as the sweet strains were heard. What for nearly two months was talk and anticipation, was a grand reality. The music which it wafted was sweet. It was like the music of chimes. . . . People who live far out in the country heard, for the first time, the call of Christian culture from Lebanon Valley College. . . .

Reading today the Forum's description of "The Bell Entertainment," which followed some time after the raising, carries one back into the gay, perfumed innocence of an earlier age.

"For several weeks," ran the report, "the monotony of school life was truly changed to a cadence of bells. As the time drew near, everyone was talking of bells and belles."

When the great evening arrived, those who braved the rainstorm—and they were many—saw up on the chapel platform the old bell. The program opened with an instrumental solo, *Le Printemps,* by Miss Nettie Swartz. As the old bell began to ring, Mr. E. S. Bowman spoke a farewell. While the old familiar notes were dying away, the new bell pealed forth the tones that ever since (for over three-quarters of a century) have ravished the ears of campus dwellers.

Then Miss Johns sang a solo, "My Neighbor"; Miss Joyce Kreider spoke a history of "Famous Bells"; and Messrs. Schuyler Enck and David Eshleman gave a humorous duet, "Oh Yah! Don't, Dat Was Fine!" Tableaux followed, Miss Anna Brightbill representing a lady of "Ye Olden Time" in a Martha Washington costume, and Miss Ruth Rigler "A Modern Belle"—"one of the sweet little girls of the day, with her long cloak and big hat with nodding plumes, finger in her mouth, and innocence playing in her eye."

Next came a "sextette by members of the Washington Cornet Band." Miss Elvira Stehman recited "The Bells," by Poe. Mr. Horace Crider led a troop of nine men, "The Dumb Bells" (including Messrs. Morris Bowman and Raymond Kreider) through thirty minutes of much applauded gymnastics.

The Misses Anna Kreider, Mary Kreider, and Lottie Herr were encored (and reportedly stole the show) with a costumed rendition of "Three Little Maids" from *The Mikado*.

The evening ended happily with "The College Bells," consisting as the *Forum* said, of "bells and belles with bells." The old bell rang, the new bell rang, and the six lady ushers who wore little bells on their wrists bowed to each other and rang the bells, bowed to the audience and said goodnight.

President Kephart severed his connection with the College in less than a year. There was no explosion. He explained his resignation on the grounds of his "personal financial situation." (The President's stated salary was $1050 and payment was uncertain—as his successor was to discover.) He accepted the pastorate of Trinity Church, Lebanon, some months before his resignation from the College took effect. From January to June, 1890, he held the two positions, pastorate and presidency, and then left the College to devote himself for a few years to the pastorate alone. In 1904 he accepted the presidency of Western College, his *Alma Mater*.

In his last issue as editor of the *Forum* (June-July, 1890), he ran an editorial headed "The Duty of the Hour" in which he made a final plea for a good endowment.

> There must be action now. The question is no longer whether the East needs a college. That question is settled affirmatively and has been for years. Lebanon Valley College will soon be twenty-five years old; but what an existence! During all those years practically without an endowment.

It is true that he had himself secured an addition to the endowment fund, but it was still absurdly small. The Bittinger Farm, now valued at $25,000, was "not productive." If the present endowment were productive, he noted, the total income would be about $1200. But the annual deficit (not including running expenses such as fuel and repairs) was $1793.86. The loss could be stopped in only one way, by a good endowment.

He reiterated the cry former presidents had uttered despairfully at the end of their terms: "There has already been too much delay. The college has suffered, the church has been hindered and hampered in its growth, and God's cause has been impeded."

CHAPTER SIXTEEN

President E. Benjamin Bierman

ON KEPHART'S RESIGNATION, the Board of Trustees elected as his successor the Rev. George M. Matthews, A.M., of Dayton, Ohio, but he declined on grounds of health.

That the College itself was not in health, was everywhere known. Professor John E. Lehman, as devoted a college supporter as the institution has ever known, made no pretense about it in the letter he addressed "To Former Students" and published in the August, 1890, issue of the *College Forum.* He took it for granted that his young friends already knew the worst about L. V. C., but asked them to share his own faith in the College's future.

It is a revealing letter. Remember as you read it what Lehman and his colleagues on the staff were undergoing. His daughter, Mrs. Edith Lehman Bartlett, recalls hearing her parents speak of the lean years when professors took their families for meals to the college dining room in lieu of salary.

> Perhaps some discouraging reports concerning the College have come to you since you are at your homes [wrote Professor Lehman]. Rumors are afloat, I know, that are not calculated to inspire much confidence, but I am glad they are *only rumors* and there is no foundation for their truth. The outlook for the College financially is really better to-day than it ever was, I believe every word of that. To be sure there is a little difficulty on hand to meet a few pressing claims. If a few thousand dollars can be raised, (and I am sure it can, the church will not let the school die for so paltry a sum), then the breakers can be safely passed and beyond there is clear sailing. The College fail? *Never!* with an endowment fund of nearly twenty-five thousand dollars, about one hundred and fifty alumni whose hearts beat warm for it and forty thousand United Brethren to stand by it, and who will come to its rescue when its needs are properly presented to them.

The presidency that Matthews had declined was accepted by E. Benjamin Bierman, who was inaugurated in the fall of 1890. He was well known on the campus, having been a professor at Lebanon Valley from 1867 to 1879.

His Prussian ancestors had come from the province of Westphalia in the German Empire to Pennsylvania shortly after the American Revolution. His father's people had lived in Berks County, and his mother's in Lancaster

E. Benjamin Bierman, A.M.
President, 1890-1897

County, for many years. He was born near Reading on December 1, 1839.

After some years in private schools, he entered the Lehigh County Normal School at Emmaus, Pennsylvania, and in 1857 entered the Reading Classical Academy, where he spent four years. He was married in 1862 to Miss Anna M. Isett. He taught for a time at Tremont, Pennsylvania. Afterwards he served as Principal of Hamburg High School until 1867, when he was called to join the first faculty of Lebanon Valley College. That same year Lafayette College gave him an honorary A.M.

Though he had not graduated from college, he was, as the Lebanon *Daily News* said of him in its issue of May 15, 1874, "a thoroughly educated gentleman." And, indeed, his education had to be thorough to encompass all the varied duties of his college career, which extended—with interruptions—from 1867 to 1909. He joined Vickroy in the College's first year as Professor of the Normal Branches and Principal of the Model School. When the Model School was dropped, he became Professor of English and German languages and Literature. Later, as Professor of Mathematics, he settled down into the field in which he was to make his chief reputation, although his years as President of the College (1890–1897) and as Treasurer (1906–1910) were important because he piloted the ship of learning through some stormy seas.

One of his avocations was the study of Astronomy. In the 1877–78 and 1878–79 *Catalogues* he was listed as Professor of Mathematics and Astronomy. One of the cherished memories of L. V. C. kept to the end of his life by the late Rev. Dr. Samuel J. Evers, '81, former Pastor of the Union Memorial Church of Glenbrook, Connecticut, was that, as he wrote, May 14, 1964, "Prof. Bierman invited us now & again to his Recitation Room to hear of the wonders of the 'Heavenly Bodies.'"

In 1879, Professor Bierman left the College with a snap that still lives in memory. The story was told to the writer by Mrs. Laura E. Muth, of the class of 1892:

> Quite a number of years before he became President, he was on the administrative side of the college, and in a committee meeting they had a disagreement. Now Mr. Bierman at that time was a very dignified gentleman, and he said: "Life is short. Peace is sweet. I am leaving," and he resigned.

He was already something of a public figure by the time he returned to Lebanon Valley as President. From 1878 to 1880, he had been secretary of the Higher Education Department of the National Teachers Association. In the latter year he was a delegate to the Republican State Convention and served on the State Central Committee. After leaving Lebanon Valley, he was twice elected (1900 and 1902) to the State Legislature.

It was the hope of the Board of Trustees that Bierman's Pennsylvania Dutch background and his local experience would fit him to lead the College through its present emergency.

"He understands our people," said the *Forum,* "and can work with them and for them to the very best advantage."

Those still living who were children in Annville in his day, remember his tall frame, topped with the high silk hat he often wore, and his extreme short-sightedness. Small children on the street were frightened when he stopped to speak to them, peering through thick lenses into their faces.

WEATHER FLAGS

A few days after the fall term opened in 1890, a new sight greeted those who looked out on the college campus: a set of colored flags on a pole issuing weather reports. This L. V. C. service was less precise than is expected of our observatories today, but, by reason of the wider range of its flagged alternatives (e.g., "warm" or "cool," "fair" or "rainy"), it was less liable to error.

It was part of what today would be called a national (or international, Canada co-operating) hook-up. The United States Signal Service, a few years before, had organized a continental system of weather forecasts. It was decided to establish a weather station at Lebanon Valley College. So it was that, on September 16, 1890, Professor Albert H. Gerberich, '88, was appointed "displayman" for this part of the Lebanon Valley.

It was Professor Gerberich's duty, as the *College Forum* reported in its October-November issue, "to observe the temperature, the direction and velocity of the wind, and the conditon of the barometer at certain hours every day,"

Albert H. Gerberich, '88

and to telegraph his findings to the Signal Office at Washington. He had also to display flags every morning to indicate (from information received by wire) *, what the weather was likely to be in that vicinity.

The flags displayed were four in number:
A *white* flag for *fair* weather;
A *blue* flag for *rain*;
A *black* triangular flag for the *temperature*: placed *above* white or blue to signify *warmer*, placed *below* to signify *cooler*;
A *white* flag *with square black center* for a *cold wave coming,* to be displayed forty-eight hours in advance.

THE QUARTER CENTENNIAL

The College by this time, like any other adolescent, was counting its years. In 1892, it celebrated its Silver Anniversary or Quarter Centennial.

Why it had not been celebrated in 1891, twenty-five years after its founding in 1866, is difficult to say. Perhaps Bierman was too busy. In those days the President—as he himself was to say later in court—*was* the College. He presided over the faculty, kept peace with the Board, taught four classes, shopped

---

* About 1867 Western Union had run a line through Lebanon Alley, between the old Academy and the site of the New College.

100

for the College (e.g., bought winter coal for it on his personal credit), handled the finances, kept the books, solicited students. Perhaps, on the other hand, the College in 1891 was too much disturbed by the renewed debate over relocation to be in a mood for celebration. Or perhaps the financial situation was too uncertain for an evening of congratulations.

Whatever may have been the actual cause of the delay, the celebration of the Quarter Centennial *a year late* was excused on the grounds that it was an appropriate anniversary of the granting of the College Charter in 1867.

The event, when it came, was thus described in the *Forum* for June, 1892:

> The Quarter Centennial exercises of Lebanon Valley College occurred on Wednesday evening, June 15, it being twenty-five years since the College started on its career as a chartered institution. The many friends of the College gathered in the chapel until it was filled to its utmost capacity. Conspicuous among them on this occasion, was John Huber, of B. from Chambersburg, who is rising unto the 84th year of his age.
>
> The Washington Band Orchestra, of Annville, consisting of seven of the prominent members of the celebrated Silver Cornet Band, furnished the music for the evening.
>
> With President Bierman, the following gentlemen sat on the rostrum and took part in the exercises of the evening, viz.: Judge McPherson and Rev. C. J. Kephart of Lebanon; D. W. Crider, of York, president of the Board of Trustees; Dr. D. Eberly, of Abbottstown; Rev. J. W. Kiracofe, of Mechanicsburg; and Rev. C. T. Stearn, of Chambersburg.

President Bierman spoke briefly on the College's history. Judge J. B. McPherson, of the Dauphin and Lebanon Judicial District, spoke on "The Mission of the Smaller College." Former President Kephart followed with a discussion of the Church's changing attitude toward Higher Education, and Professor Daniel Eberly spoke of the struggles for existence from which other colleges had triumphantly emerged.

> Rev. C. T. Stearn was then introduced. He said he was not there to make a speech, but to tell them that the field lying immediately west of the main building had been purchased for the college, and that $1500 were needed to pay for it, and he wanted to secure that amount then and there. He succeeded in raising $1200 in subscriptions. The balance has been assured.

In conclusion, President Bierman read a letter from former President Vickroy, whose faith had carried the College through a difficult beginning and who now viewed its future with confidence.

> . . . I saw the College when it had neither student nor name; I saw it when arms were raised to strike it to the ground; I gave my young life's energies to counteract these influences, and for all I did for it, to-day I give God profound thanks that he gave me the strength and courage to do this work. . . . Many young men and young women have gone forth from these walls into the various walks of life to benefit society.

... I now look into the dim future and the faith by which the elders obtained a good report enables me to behold unseen things. As the years roll on I see the children, grandchildren and a long line of their descendants flocking back to this spot bringing with them thankofferings to endow the College and provide the needed means for the highest and best education. . . .

RELOCATION

The two great issues which Bierman inherited from his predecessors were those of *relocation* and *endowment*.

The question of relocation had been simmering since the College was founded. It boiled over, not for the first time, in a heated debate at a meeting of the Pennsylvania Annual Conference at Mechanicsburg, on February 28, 1891. It was learned that Chambersburg and Hagerstown, Maryland, had been quietly bidding for the College.

That the revival of this old controversy was dangerous, was only too apparent. In its issue of March 16, 1891, the Harrisburg *Call,* which advocated bringing L. V. C. to the capital city, reported that

> . . . many ministers and members of the church realizing that a re-location is necessary, are refusing to aid it in any manner whatever, and the withdrawal of their support lessens the chances of success, for the necessary funds cannot be secured to furnish the college with appurtenances in keeping with the times. A very decided stand was taken by the Allegheny conference at its last session, when it passed a resolution that it would withdraw its patronage if the college was not moved to a more desirable locality. The students in the institution at the present time also recognize the need of a change, and sent a resolution to the conference which convened in Mechanicsburg recently, stating that they thought a re-location of the college was necessary and that they also desired better equipment, and unless the request for the latter was complied with they would apply for admission to other seats of learning.

The Harrisburg *Patriot* reported that former President Kephart "and others prominently identified with the college would like to see it in this city."

The *Call* resumed its coverage of the controversy on April 4 with the remark that the agitation over the removal of the College had so angered the citizens of Annville that they were roused from their lethargy and indifference at least to the extent of publishing in the Annville paper denunciation of the students for having sent requests to the co-operating conferences that the College be relocated.

The Lebanon *Daily News* wound up its coverage of the relocation issue on June 19, with a report that the Trustees of the College had dropped the matter. "The fact of it is," said the paper, "as it was well known by the attorneys of this bar, who had given the removal their attention, that whatever action the Board of Trustees would take would be of no avail, as the buildings were so surrounded that legally the removal of the college could not be made." See page 31.

The College Board put it another way: "Resolved. That we can not entertain the thought of abandoning what we now have unless an offer, thoroughly guaranteed, be made of grounds and not less than one hundred thousand ($100,000) dollars."

ENDOWMENT

Bierman, like every president before him, called for an endowment; but, being not devoid of astuteness, he did so without too great a show of urgency. He was a sensitive, peace-loving man, and his policy was to avoid stirring up animosities. At the same time, he allowed former President Kephart of Lebanon to use the pages of the *College Forum* for more vigorous assaults on the apathy and parsimony of those who should be helping the College.

Despite these stick-and-carrot tactics, the endowment campaign remained stubbornly immobile, or very nearly. To make ends meet in any fashion at all, Bierman adopted the strictest economy. Faculty salaries, his own included, fell into arrears. It has been said of him that he "almost starved to death"—and the rest of the faculty with him.

There was inevitably a quick turn-over of the teaching staff. Yet a few devoted souls stuck by the institution that seemed to have forgotten them. Bierman himself took the lead in "Operation Bootstrap." In 1891, the President with John Lehman and other professors repapered their classrooms at their own expense to spruce up the place for the returning students. Mrs. Bierman sent out an appeal for each "sister" in the Church to contribute two cents "for aid in refurnishing and making more homelike the rooms and halls of the Ladies' Building." They collected $71.34.

Somehow Bierman kept the College alive. No one but a Pennsylvania Dutchman could have done so. He understood the local people, and they him. Today Mr. Sam Saylor of D. L. Saylor's Coal and Lumber Company in Annville recalls those days:

"Bierman and my father were great cronies. When the College was in financial trouble, he [Bierman] would come and say, 'The Trustees won't give me any more coal. Give me a load of coal. I'll see that you get your money.' And my father would give it to him."

As late as President Keister's day, a decade later, a professor's pay at L. V. C. was inferior to that of a local factory worker. David K. Shroyer, '26, in a letter to the writer has described the straits to which his father—the Rev. Dr. Alvin E. Shroyer, '00 (a professor loved and honored "on this side idolatry")—was put to keep his family alive and to entertain the many visitors to the college who turned up there for food and lodging.

> . . . We had a yard full of chickens, a large garden with many fruit trees and extra rooms, so the Shroyer home became the official hostelry for visiting missionaries, conference superintendents, bishops, evangelists, performers, and what have you!

. . . I can remember one year when the College was behind approximately one year in the payment of salaries—we managed to exist by exchanging poultry and eggs at the Kinports' grocery store for food and clothing staples, imposing upon the good nature of the coalmen, repairmen, milkman, tax collector, etc. for extended credit. In the summer months my father worked in the Shoe Factory making heels to supplement our meager living. He could make approximately $5.00 a day at that job which was far more than he could make as a college professor at that time. . . . Throughout his days people were wont to take advantage of his good nature—carrying a heavy schedule they added additional duties of registrar, athletic association representative, and on occasion, janitor and house-servant. We used to help clean-up the campus and for years the uniforms of the various athletic teams were washed in our cellar in a series of wash-machines, that my Father rigged up. The football and baseball shoes were recobbled in our cellar as well. In addition, failing students, whose situation was well known to my Father, would come over any time that might be free for tutoring. I can still see them offering a quarter for a half-hour or hour of tutoring—the offer of payment was made but rarely, if ever, accepted.

As the end approached of Bierman's seven years as college president (during which time his own salary of $1,050 a year had fallen deeply into arrears) he grew more and more aware of the truth contained in a statement made in 1893 by Z. A. Weidler, Chairman of the Educational Committee of the East Pennsylvania Conference. It was that in its inception Lebanon Valley College's heritage from the Church was "a hostile environment, an apathetic constituency, and a feeble patronage."

In his last report to the East German Conference, Bierman threw aside his usual cautious, let-us-not-offend-each-other manner and spoke with the point and vigor of a free man—one who has seen the truth and is not afraid to speak out.

He called on the Church to lift Lebanon Valley College out of its crippling debt, "or," he said, "we shall . . . stand in the eyes of God as unworthy servants. . . . The Church cannot roll off this responsibility. . . . When religion bids farewell to learning it will degenerate into fanaticism."

Of President Bierman's general contribution to Lebanon Valley College, the Rev. C. I. B. Brane said that Bierman had borne "burdens enough to bury a giant," and had, indeed, saved the College's life. Looking back upon the turbulent days of the College's famine-fed adolescence, one sees that he had managed to give it a measure of quiet healing for a span of seven years.

It had, however, become a seemingly settled tradition at the College that presidential exits should be accompanied by thunder and lightning. After Bierman left in 1897, he sued the College for back salary and got it.

CHAPTER SEVENTEEN

Student Life in the Nineties

DURING BIERMAN'S PRESIDENCY (1890–1897), student activities, as we understand them today, had hardly got off the ground. In the days when a graduating class of ten or a dozen was considered large, there was little need for more than the Literary Societies and the Y. M. and Y. W. C. A. to provide a main outlet for the students. There were, of course, other temporary organizations like the Prohibition Amendment Club, which was founded in 1889, Professor John E. Lehman being then the President and W. H. Washinger the Vice-President. Its meetings were well attended, and it gave the students an outside interest. The State Inter-Collegiate Prohibition Association, organized in Harrisburg in 1893, conducted oratorical contests to which the College in that year sent O. E. Good as a contender.

Student life without theatricals, movies, radio, television, dancing, smoking, motor cars, or a grandstand and cheer leaders, is difficult for us today even to imagine. Because of the absence of such amusements, recalls Mrs. Edith Lehman Bartlett,

> the students of that day had to seek their entertainment where they could find it, and walks and excursions into the country were common and gathering arbutus in Steinmetz's Woods was one of the things that every spring was extremely popular. The students in groups, or perhaps in pairs more likely, would stroll out to Steinmetz's Woods and gather the lovely little flowers that then grew so plentifully.

In this connection, Mrs. Bartlett contributes a poem (of unknown authorship) which she received from the late Mrs. Ida Bowman Richards, daughter of George W. Bowman, A.M., who was from 1882 to 1890 Professor of Natural Science at the College.

ARBUTUS

High on a northern hill
There is a place I know
Where stony earth is still
Half blanketed with snow,
And last year's mosses hide

Under the melting drift;
Whence come, with frost defied,
Spring's first, fresh, fragrant gift.

Impatient of tomorrow,
On stems as tough as hope,
Small leaves, as dark as sorrow,
Unfurl on that far slope—
And tiny, clustered flowers,
Pink, passionate, and sweet,
Are plucked in Steinmetz' bowers,
A nosegay for my sweet.

Students at L. V. C. in the early nineties were for the most part a quiet, sober-minded lot, far removed from the rah-rah boys of a later era. There were occasional pranks of a not very subtle kind, such as bringing a horse and buggy on to the chapel platform before morning prayers. But such things were exceptional and not taken for granted as the ever-ready paddles of the Death Leaguers were to be two decades later. Members of the female sex, while not as demure as they had been in the days of President Hammond, were equally far removed from the high-stepping, baton-tossing drum majorettes of today.

Mrs. Laura Reider Muth, recalling the Victorian atmosphere of her graduating year, 1892, contrasts the restraints of those days with the freedoms of today, and does it without too much nostalgia.

> I think we were just a little snobbish. If a young man had to do manual labor or do work around the campus, he wasn't quite as popular as the young men that were sent by their parents. We girls didn't think quite as much of them. And another thing that amuses me is to see people walking with their lunch packages. We wouldn't have thought of carrying a lunch package in the open. That was far below us. . . .
>
> None of our girls would have thought of going into somebody's house to do housework or do baby sitting. We didn't think of going out to earn any money. We would have done it as a favor, but not for money. Our parents—it was their job to put us through school. Now, you put yourself through school if you can.

In the 1890's, college sports at Annville were only beginning to come into prominence. There had, of course, always been interest among the men in "physical exercise." But for a long time the college authorities were caught between two fires; the animal spirits of youth and the moral fervor of many of their elders. Students who were athletically minded were in consequence advised to satisfy themselves with country walks or perhaps go in for track.

Nevertheless, games of a sort were indulged in. Croquet "on the lawn" was popular, and baseball was organized as early as 1882. The Annville *Gazette* of April 26 in that year, under the heading "College News," made this announcement:

"We are thoroughly organized for playing base-ball. Already the fourth 'nine' has elected officers. Some challenges have been received, which will be given attention in due time."

For all that, Mrs. Muth remembers that in her day there was as yet nothing of the intercollegiate rivalry associated with college sport of more recent times. As late as 1893, a writer in the *Forum* seemed to find great athletic progress not only in the College's possession of "one of the finest ball grounds in the country," but also in its "two tennis courts" and "a beautiful croquet ground."

Yet a change was already coming. The June, 1893, *Forum,* found it necessary to defend "athletic sports" against the charge that they were "a ruination to student life." Both the charge and the defense suggest that a movement was on foot to recognize sports as an integral part of the college program. Next year, when the Athletic Association was founded, both the hopes on the one hand and the fears on the other were realized. Competitive athletics had come to be accepted by the College.

It was not, however, until 1897 that football became fully organized. Football, from the start an amazingly popular sport, soon turned student interest in intercollegiate athletics into a burning fever.

But that transformation came, not under President Benjamin Bierman, but under his successor, Ulysses Roop.

Meantime, for a small college like L. V. C., it was natural that the acquiring of a gymnasium should loom large. In 1882, the members of Kalo dug out a gymnasium underneath the south end of the old main building. It was heralded in the *College Catalogue* for 1883 with this announcement:

"There is a Gymnasium in connection with the College, under the control of the Kalozetean Literary Society, to which all students have access during certain periods of the day. A small fee is charged."

In 1894 it was stated that "The room is open from 3:15 to 4:50 p.m. All are welcome."

The *Catalogue* that year noted that in the gymnasium "A careful Director has oversight of these exercises to guard against accident and immoderation."

That was also the year Kalo announced, "The gymnasium has been thoroughly renovated, copious wardrobes have been made, and a beautiful club and dumb-bell rack has been placed near the entrance"; and by 1897, under the administration of President Roop, the Kalo column in the *Forum* could carry the proud news of "a shower bath and a tub bath" installed in the gymnasium.

All through the difficult years of the College's first half century, the religious life on the campus was one of the binding forces that held the institution together. The way in which that influence worked among the students is beautifully revealed in a letter of November 9, 1964, from Mrs. Mary R. Hough, L.H.D. (Mary Richards, '97) who, with her first husband, Ira E. Albert, '97 (after whom Albert Academy in Sierra Leone was named), was for many years a missionary in Africa.

Mrs. Hough was born and brought up in Annville, where the College's influence, as she says, though not always recognized, was nevertheless pervasive, especially among the growing children of the town. Her own experience in childhood confirms this:

I was a member of the Gleaner's Mission Band of the local church, which was periodically raising money to give children in Africa the opportunity to go to school. I sold walnut taffy which mother made to help in the project. The College dormitories gave me an unfailing consumer resource. Students not only bought hundreds of my taffy patties but a number became my longtime friends. I came to love the College and am sure it had an indefinable influence on my early years. . . .

There were inspiring occasions during my College years when returning missionaries spoke to the students at chapel. One such occasion impressed me deeply. In the fall of 1894, my Sophomore year, several new missionaries on their way to Africa, spoke one night in one of our churches in Lebanon and came to the College for a very early chapel service. In order to give interested members of the local church an opportunity to hear them, I went before breakfast, up one side of Main Street and down the other side notifying them of the early chapel service. A large part of the student body followed the Missionaries to the train and gave them an enthusiastic sendoff.

The extracurricular religious features of college life in that day were strong and vital—student prayer meetings, Bible study classes, Y. M. C. A. & Y. W. C. A. had a strong influence in strengthening my religious life and aims.

I was President of the Y. W. C. A. while W. G. Clippinger was President of the Y. M. C. A. Our financial resources were meager so we pooled them in order to send a delegate to the Student Conference at Northfield, Mass. Mr. Clippinger (later President of Otterbein College) was sent in the summer of 1895 and I was sent in the summer of 1896.

This conference with leaders like D. L. Moody, Robert E. Speer & a host of like minded men and women, made a tremendous impact on my life.

It was here on an unforgettable evening out on Round Top that I made the decision to be a missionary if God called for me. . . .

I have always felt that L. V. C. had a *very* large share in preparing me for and in determining my life work.

CHAPTER EIGHTEEN

The Story of John Lehman

WHILE BIERMAN WAS Professor of Mathematics at Lebanon Valley College, John Evans Lehman, '74, was one of his best students. When Bierman became President of the College, Lehman was one of his best professors. There was a saying in L. V. C. circles a generation ago, "From Bierman to Lehman to Wagner." No higher compliment could be paid to the College than a reference to this mathematical trio who spanned a period in college history of some seventy years.

There are many graduates who remember Dr. Paul S. Wagner, whose eager plans for the College were an inspiration to both students and faculty. But today not so many are left who remember Professor John E. Lehman, whose scholarship, wit, and friendship were in themselves one of the College's best institutions.

No better introduction to John Lehman's early life can be found than in a biographical sketch that appeared in the college *Bizarre* issued by the class of '06 in their Junior year, that is, in the spring of 1905, shortly after the Administration Building, which John Lehman as a young man had helped to build, was destroyed by fire.

To the question whether the sketch might have been written by Professor Lehman's son, Max (author of the College Song, "To Thee, Dear Alma Mater"), who in 1905 was a Sophomore, Max's sister, Mrs. Edith Lehman Bartlett, replied in a letter of July 19, 1965:

"It *may* have been Max. Certainly he was capable. However, I strongly suspect it may have been Tom Stein, a former student of the College, a close friend and admirer (I believe) of my father. Mr. Stein was at one time the professor of German and I believe he grew up with papa."

Certainly whoever wrote it pushed a pen with punch as well as grace, and did so with the roguish intimacy that bespoke a warm and completely trusting friendship.

JOHN EVANS LEHMAN

JOHN EVANS LEHMAN was born near Lititz, Lancaster County, September 11, 1850. He is of Welsh descent on his mother's side, and of German on his father's side. The nearest approach to fame we have been able to trace in either family is Robert Evans, his great grandfather, who was nothing more than government surveyor, to whom, however, we might trace his mathematical tendency.

At the age of four the family moved to Avon, Lebanon county, where John began his education, as a mischievous boy, receiving his floggings thrice daily. As an inspiration to him in his school-boy efforts, his father at one time offered him a twenty-dollar gold piece, if he could succeed in catching his teacher with a difficult problem in arithmetic. He never received the twenty-dollar gold piece. By his mother he was bidden to sleep with his school books under his pillow, in hope that he might in that way imbibe their contents.

At the age of eleven the family moved to a mill southeast of Annville, still known as Bachman's mill. Here he partly learned the trade of a miller and in the old saw mill sawed off a little finger, the absence of which is still evident. He continued his education at the "Heilig" school house, under the direction of such men as A. R. Forney, W. B. Bodenhorn, the late county superintendent of public schools, and the Hon. J. H. Imboden, all of Annville.

About the year 1865 the family moved to Annville, and John attended the town high school. Shortly after this Lebanon Valley College was founded, and the only building was the present Ladies' Hall. The growth of the school soon demanded an additional building, and John stood by as an inquisitive boy of fifteen when ground was broken for the Administration building which he saw destroyed by the fire of last December. He was employed as a helper in hauling bricks and carrying mortar while the building was under construction.

In the fall of 1868 he was employed as janitor in the College. The work then consisted in sweeping, bell-ringing, and taking care of the seventeen stoves, by which the two buildings were then heated. His contact with students and student life created in him a desire for an education, therefore at the end of the year he asked permission to enroll as a student and earn his way by doing only part of the janitor work. The request was granted and at the age of eighteen he entered the preparatory class of the college. His duties required him to rise at four o'clock in the morning to start the fires, and at five he rang the rising bell, statements which might startle a Lebanon Valley janitor of 1965.

In his junior year he laid down his broom and coal-shovel and earned his way by tutoring. He graduated in 1874 at the head of his class.

The year after graduation he taught in the public schools of Schuylkill county in the times when teachers "boarded round." If his reputation as a teacher did not begin there, he made a name for himself as an old-time singing school teacher.

For the following six years he was chief forfeiting and re-instating clerk in an insurance office in Lebanon. In the year 1877 he was married to Miss Fisher from Hamburg, Pa. This acquaintance and courtship began while both were students at the college and continued under greater difficulties than similar college affairs of the present day, for the social life of the school was very different from the present. The men were not allowed to stop and talk to the ladies in the halls, or on the walks, nor call on them in the parlor, nor take walks to Lovers' Retreat and other interesting spots. Even under those difficulties happy matches were made then as now.

The duties of a clerkship, however, proved too monotonous for him, and anxious to get into educational work he secured a position as teacher of Mathematics and Greek in Fostoria Academy, Ohio. He spent four very successful years there.

In 1885 he was elected to the chair of Mathematics in Western College, and to the Principalship of West Virginia Academy, and to the head of the Preparatory department of Otterbein University. He decided to accept the latter, and after two years of faithful service, he was called to his Alma Mater to fill the position he now holds—called to a professorship in the school which twenty years before he entered as janitor. During the early years of his professorship he took a course in higher Mathematics under Dr. Wm. Hoover, of Ohio State University and later spent a summer at Cornell University, doing advanced work under Prof. McMahon. He is so well known in this section of the country that it would seem useless to give any detailed account of his twenty years work here.

He has grown to be part of the school. The students always found in him a true friend and willing helper, always more ready to serve others than himself; obliging and kind almost to a fault. Kind and patient with an earnest student, but severe with the listless and indifferent, he is of a sunny disposition when all goes well. He has decided opinions of his own, but gives in gracefully when you agree with him.

He has a host of friends among the students and alumni of Lebanon Valley College and he is respected and held in the kindest regard by all who know him.

Further details for the John Lehman story have been contributed by Max Lehman's younger sister, Edith Lehman (Mrs. Ralph Bartlett of Baltimore), class of '13, who very kindly consented to an interview, of which what follows is the substance.

While he was yet a full-time janitor at the College, observing the students and talking with them, John Lehman enjoyed so exciting a glimpse of the world of knowledge that he resolved to join them in pursuit of the Good, the True, and the Beautiful. In college, he registered for the Classical Course and graduated in 1874 with the degree of Bachelor of Arts, adding an A.M. to it later, and subsequently receiving from his Alma Mater an honorary degree, Doctor of Science.

While in college, he met the young lady, Rebecca Fisher, who was to be his wife and to help fix his mind on a scholarly career. Her father was of German extraction, whose forebears were much interested in education. Mr. Fisher gave the land, built the schoolhouse, and himself hired the teachers in his Berks County community. He then drove around to solicit pupils among the farmers and workmen thereabouts.

John Lehman after graduation taught school for a short time in Rebecca Fisher's neighborhood. Their ensuing marriage was described by the Lebanon *Daily News* of November 14, 1877, in such terms as to show how well thought of the young couple were in Lebanon County:

> Mr. J. E. Lehman, in charge of the Assessment Department of the Home Office of the U. B. Aid Society, at this place, was united in marriage to Miss Beckie K. Fisher, of Hamburg, yesterday a.m., the ceremony being performed at the residence of the bride's parent, by Rev. Samuel Etter, of the latter place. The happy couple arrived here last evening, and immediately went to their house on East Cumberland Street, which had been fixed up neatly and furnished before the wedding. May dark clouds, aye, even shadows ne'er appear in the horizon of their matrimonial life, and may happiness ever be at its zenith.

After teaching Mathematics for a few years at Fostoria Academy, he accepted a position at Otterbein University in Westerville. It was there that his son Max was born—the Max Fisher Lehman who seemed destined to win great honor for the College that graduated him, but whose career was cut short by the First World War.

In 1887 John Lehman came to Lebanon Valley College as Professor of Mathematics. Intent on his own intellectual advancement, he spent his spare time working, with great encouragement from his professors, toward a Ph.D. from Ohio State University. All was going well, and he expected to get his doctorate in 1894; but, as the time approached, financial pressures (college salaries being in arrears and his family circle growing) forced him to drop this work. It was his greatest disappointment, but he did not allow it to dampen his interest in the college that had opened to him the world of the mind. For the rest of his life, three great interests continued to occupy him: his family, the College, and the Church. He satisfied all three by a life of uninterrupted devotion to the struggling institution at Annville.

His avocations were astronomy and music. He procured the first telescope for the College—not with his own funds, for he had none, but with the help of wealthy patrons of the sciences like the Rockefellers and the Carnegies. He developed a club for people interested in astronomy. They used to come

112

out to his house at the corner of Main and Ulrich streets, and there set up his telescope and study the heavens. He used also to gather the children of the neighborhood. He would tell them stories about the stars, and then let them look through the telescope for themselves.

He loved music. He led, and on occasion sang first tenor in, the Lebanon Valley Quartet, which provided music at college functions, at religious camp meetings, and at churches celebrating College Day. He was for a time leader of the choir in the First United Brethren Church in Annville.

The *College Forum* for January, 1888, ran this note about him: "His help in preparing the Christmas music was greatly appreciated by the Annville U. B. church. It is not generally known that the Professor is a musical composer and author, but such is none the less a fact. 'Rippling Rills from the Fountain of Song' has his name on the title page."

He had an effervescent wit. Mrs. Bartlett tells how, at a Philo-Clio joint session, when he was called upon for extemporaneous remarks, he delighted his student audience with a talk on the subject of "Tics."

"You know," he began, "there are many kinds of tics"; and he launched into verbal antics about such things as mathematics and statistics, politics, and rustics till he had them all in ecstatics.

John Lehman was a rare personality, a man who seasoned his love of teaching, music, the stars—and one should add the novels of Charles Dickens—with a deep concern for humanity. Yet, with all his kindness, he was an upholder of academic standards in a day when the temptation was almost overwhelming to regard anyone as a good student who had money to pay his bills. He made friends more readily with those who could think mathematically, but he was universally loved as well as respected.

A signal honor was conferred on him, December 28, 1905, when the Board of Trustees, on the resignation of Dr. Roop, appointed Lehman President *pro tem.* of the College.

The 1907 *Bizarre* said of his son, Max:

> Everything he does, he does enthusiastically whether it's singing a song, taking part in a class scrap or taking a girl to a concert, and everything which he does, he does equally well. He is one of the first tenors of the Glee Club and one of chief pleasures of his life is to sing. He has held various offices during his college course and the latest of these is treasurer of the Athletic Association. . . ."

When Max was killed in France during the First World War, Professor Lehman suffered a shock from which he never wholly recovered. He continued to lecture at the College, but much of the flavor had gone out of his life and the zest from his teaching.

The Lehman name will always be honored at Lebanon Valley. The chair Dr. Barnard H. Bissinger holds today is the John Evans Lehman Professorship of Mathematics.

The Men's Dormitory (Kreider Hall)

CHAPTER NINETEEN

President Hervin Ulysses Roop

THE MISHAPS AND FRUSTRATIONS of its first thirty years had left Lebanon Valley College and its friends in a highly depressive state. But suddenly, in 1897, there came a change. As though awaking out of a bad dream, the College discovered there was nothing the matter with it after all. Its future was secure.

The cause of this happy revolution was the advent of the new president, the young (aged twenty-eight), handsome, scholarly, and socially gifted Hervin Ulysses Roop. In energy, he has been called "a ball of fire." That is an impression that survives to this day in the memory of some of the alumni. He was of the modern academic type: alert, with a pleasant campus manner, an impressive platform presence, a spate of degrees after his name—A.B., A.M., Ph.D., all of them earned, and a charming, cultured wife with a ravishing singing voice.

In seven years, he brought to the College all the buildings (except South Hall) that most of our alumni remember from their student days: Engle Hall (the Conservatory), the Carnegie Library (now the Lounge), North Hall (for many years the Women's Residence), the Men's Dormitory (Kreider Hall), the present Administration Building, and the Central Heating Plant. He brought in a good faculty, added new courses, modernized the Library, more than doubled the size of the student body, and put Lebanon Valley suddenly into a respectable place in the American scholastic world.

Before coming in as President, Dr. Roop had spent his time acquiring the ingredients of success in the academic world he was to enter. To begin with, his family heritage was United Brethren. He was a great grandson of Jacob Roop (1782–1875), "one of the pioneer preachers," as Dr. William A. Wilt writes, "of our church in Dauphin, Lebanon, and Lancaster Counties."

He was born, November 16, 1868, of Pennsylvania Dutch parents, on a farm near Highspire, Pennsylvania. After attending schools at Highspire and Steelton in the Harrisburg vicinity, he entered Lebanon Valley College in 1888. Enrolled in the Classical Course, he soon distinguished himself as a brilliant student and an active leader in college affairs. In his freshman year he was elected corresponding secretary of a student political club known as

Rev. Hervin U. Roop, Ph.D.
President, 1897–1906

"The Republican Phalanx."

At graduation in 1892 with the degree of Bachelor of Arts, he delivered what the *College Forum* called "a masterly oration" on a subject his later career was to exemplify, "The Sovereignty of the Individual." He himself possessed the qualities that make an individual sovereign in whatever society he moves; and he strengthened these for the career he had planned, in either teaching or the ministry, by pursuing graduate studies at Union Biblical Seminary in Dayton, Ohio, where he graduated with the degree of Bachelor of Divinity; at Wooster University, from which he emerged with the degree of Doctor of Philosophy; and with shorter periods of study at Cornell University, Leander Clark University, and the University of Pennsylvania. In 1895 he was ordained to the ministry of the Church of the United Brethren in Christ.

His main career turned out to be in teaching. In 1892, he became Professor of English and Pedagogy at the Cumberland Valley State Normal School at Shippensburg, and in 1895, Professor of English and History in the famous Rittenhouse Academy in Philadelphia. While President of L. V. C., he taught some classes in Philosophy, Pedagogy, Bible, and Oratory.

On assuming the presidency, he at once set the College's face forward, calling for more books for the library, more equipment for the Sciences, and, in a word, more money. Wisely, however, before pressing the financial issue, he made it his business to inspire confidence by reducing the debt. He brought it down in the first year from $40,000 to about $10,000.

116

To the outside world he was the ideal college president: "a very distinguished personality," as a former student, Miss Anna Kreider of Annville, remembers him. "They were a wonderful couple [Dr. and Mrs. Roop], cultured and popular. He was a man of great energy and charm, poised, and gentlemanly. Mrs. Roop, with her wonderful voice was—oh, how shall I say it?—she was simply *supreme.*"

The students as well as the townspeople had confidence in him. They went to him for advice, and came away satisfied.

He was "a man of dignity," recalls Mr. Gideon R. Kreider, "He carried himself well. His voice from the platform was good, and he had a rather suave way of speaking that would appeal to an audience."

His energy and charm made him a leader, and a touch of genius made his leadership effective and wholesome. His first concern, as already said, was to get the finances of the College in shape. Soon an optimistic spirit came over the campus and the constituency behind it. This, together with good soliciting methods (Roop spent his summers attending to this) brought in a host of students. Within three years he had more than doubled the registration in the Classical and Scientific courses, and more than tripled the total college enrollment. The institution found itself no longer operating in the red. There was a surplus income, which was applied against the debt.

An editorial in the *College Forum* for April, 1898, struck the new note:

> The spring term opens up very auspiciously. Twenty-five new students have already registered and ten or fifteen more are expected before another week rolls by. To see the busy wheels of progress about the institution in a thousand and one ways; to see the old and new students full of zeal and determination; all portends a spirit of thrift and advancement, such as old L. V. C. has not witnessed for many a day.

By 1902, President Roop was setting a definite financial goal before the co-operating conferences: $50,000. That goal was reached in 1904.

Meantime he had enlarged and strengthened the Faculty. Himself a product of wide contacts in the university world, he wished to foster a cosmopolitan academic tone. To that end, he brought in Professor Herbert Oldham, F.R.S., a graduate of Trinity College, Dublin, who had studied also at the London College of Music and on the Continent. Professor Oldham introduced new courses, new ideas, and a cosmopolitan air such as the College had never seen before. His worldly experience, recalls Gideon Kreider, was greater than that of all the other faculty members put together.

Not being able to pay salaries sufficient to attract many such men, President Roop used his family connection to draw good men to the College: men such as the Rev. Lewis Franklin John, his brother-in-law; Rev. Benjamin Franklin Daugherty, another brother-in-law; and his father-in-law, Bishop E. B. Kephart, brother of the former President Cyrus Kephart. Bishop Kephart remained on the faculty throughout Roop's tenure of office, teaching at different times International Law, Biblical Antiquities, and Archaeology.

During this time, a new curriculum was organized, following a system which had recently been adopted by Johns Hopkins University. The twelve college departments were set up in five groups, each with a faculty adviser: Classical, Philosophical, Chemical-Biological, Historical-Political, and Modern Language.

Scientific studies, though still in their infancy, received great encouragement.

> The first course in Biology at Lebanon Valley College [wrote the late Professor S. H. Derickson] was given in 1899. There was not even a room that could be called a laboratory. Each student brought whatever equipment he pleased and paid for it and it became his property. Even the first compound Microscopes used for class work were bought by students. The following year when Prof. Enders had charge of the work he collected money from the students and bought their instruments and note books for them at wholesale rates to save their money and to procure uniformity in the work.

Many other improvements were made by President Roop. He introduced the Dewey Decimal System in the Library. He introduced the first four-year Bible course given in the College, one hour a week for all students. It was a properly integrated course of lectures, covering each year successively one of these four topics: *New Testament History, Old Testament History, Prophets and Poets of the Old Testament,* and *New Testament Doctrines.*

On Roop's recommendation, the co-operating conferences in 1903 agreed that there should be on the Board of Trustees a maximum of five college alumni and, in addition, five Trustees-at-Large.

College athletics came very much alive under Dr. Roop. In 1897, the College had its first football team. At first, games were played on the College campus. In 1898 the season opened with a home game in which Harrisburg High School was the visitor. There was no score.

The October *Forum* that year announced that athletics was receiving special attention. Games had been scheduled with Susquehanna University, Ursinus College, Gettysburg College, and the State colleges. Readers were assured that, under Coach Stees, the College would do itself credit. The writer noted the significant fact that the gymnasium was "now under the control of the College authorities."

Basketball appeared in the 1903–1904 season. The girls as well as the men had their teams. At first the college chapel, in the old Main Building, provided the "cage"—the benches and also the rostrum being removed. The coach was John Gillis, Director of Athletics.

The progress of intercollegiate athletics spelled problems for the Faculty. The minutes of that august body are illuminating:

April 4, 1905. "On motion it was agreed that all members of athletic teams

The Faculty, 1903

Front row: *B. F. Daugherty, J. T. Spangler, H. U. Roop, J. E. Lehman, H. Oldham*
Second row: *N. C. Schlichter, Edith H. Baldwin, Frances Shively, Etta Wolfe
Schlichter, Emma R. Batdorf*
Third row: *S. E. McComsey, W. M. Heilman, H. E. Enders*
Fourth row: *T. G. McFadden, L. F. John, C. H. B. Oldham, T. S. Stein,
H. H. Shenk*

be required to take not less than ten hours of regular work in any department of the college."

May 9, 1905. "The committee on standing of baseball players reported this recommendation: that one 'outside' pitcher be allowed this season in games where absolutely necessary. . . ."

President Roop's greatest achievement was in the building campaign he initiated. Within a few months of his arrival as President, it had become evident that the buildings on the campus were totally inadequate for the astonishing inrush of students. Roop made his plans for a Greater Lebanon Valley, won the co-operation of the Board of Trustees and the conferences, and electrified the town of Annville with prospects of local employment and academic prestige.

Engle Hall (the Conservatory) was the first building to go up: a four-story, brownstone edifice in Corinthian style, completed in 1899. It was the gift of

The Old Administration Building after the fire

Benjamin H. Engle, a Harrisburg contractor, and a trustee of the College from 1898 to 1911.

The new hall at once relieved some of the overcrowding. It contained a large auditorium with an organ, where the morning chapel service could be held as well as concerts, theatricals, and term examinations. There were classrooms and practice rooms for the music students, and special rooms for the literary societies.

The next structure to be erected was a north wing added to the Main Building. The contractor, Benjamin H. Engle, ran it up in good time. When, in the fall of 1900, it was ready for use, it doubled the dormitory capacity for the men.

At Commencement, in 1902, there was great rejoicing when President Roop announced the coming gift, by Mrs. S. L. Brightbill and her son, Morris E. Brightbill, of a new gymnasium. Foundations were laid where the Gossard Library stands today. But there were disappointments ahead. Mr. Brightbill hesitated and the work stopped. The foundations remained for some time a symbol of hope to some, of disappointment to many. The students nicknamed it "the Phantom Gym." It came to be used chiefly in the midnight exploits of the Death League.

Andrew Carnegie contributed money for a college library building, the cornerstone of which was laid in June, 1904. In June of the following year, this comfortable little edifice of brick with stone trimmings, in Italian Renaissance style, was dedicated.

CHAPTER TWENTY

The Fire

WITHIN THE SPACE of a few hours on Christmas Eve, 1904, the Administration Building of Lebanon Valley College was turned into a blackened skeleton. Next day, Christmas, the Philadelphia *Sunday Press* ran this report of what had happened:

> Lebanon, Pa., Dec. 24.—The main building of Lebanon Valley College, Annville, was destroyed this evening by a fire of unknown origin.
> Flames were discovered burning fiercely in the southern wing of the building at 6:45 o'clock and the town's one fire engine was useless on account of the absence of an adequate water supply. Therefore the efforts of the firemen were devoted to saving what little property could be removed.
> Fanned by a high northeast wind, the flames spread quickly through the building and within two hours only the blackened walls were left standing. . . .

"It burned like a brush pile," said one spectator, Miss Anna Kreider. But no lives were lost. The dormitories were empty.

The origin of the fire has never been determined. A man walking by on College Avenue that evening had seen a light in the basement under the President's room. Entering the building, he found flames shooting up the elevator shaft. He at once gave the alarm, but by the time the Rescue Fire Company of Annville arrived the three stories were all in flames and the roof was ablaze.

Annville residents watched in awe. For many miles around people wondered at the glow in the sky. Oliver Butterwick remembered all his life the fascination of watching the lighted sky from a window of the Butterwick house in Lebanon.

Horace Boltz was at his home at the west end of Church Street when the fire started. He came over to the campus and watched most of the night in fascinated awe.

> It was a wonderful fire [he said]. The College had a shingle roof. There was a strong wind from the east, and those burning shingles sailed right over my house, all over the west end of town. Some of them landed half way to Clear Spring (near Millard Quarries.) Nothing else caught fire from them. That was because it was snowing at the time—well, kind of half snow and half rain.

121

Two little girls watched the fire from the sidewalk on College Avenue. "Oh," said Edith Lehman to her companion, Edith Gingrich, "now my Daddy will be out of a job!"

But nobody was out of a job. Although personal effects of the students were lost to the amount of eight or ten thousand dollars, and the books and official papers of President Roop were destroyed, the College made immediate arrangements to carry on. It is the recollection of some that a meeting was held on Christmas Day in the church to consider plans for a new building.

Certainly on Tuesday, December 27, the Board of Trustees met to consider recommendations that had been already prepared by the Executive Committee. According to the rough minutes of that meeting:

> Dr. Roop stated that the object of the meeting was to take action at once to provide funds for the erection of new buildings to take the place of the main College building which was destroyed by fire on the night of Dec. 24, 1904.
>
> President Ulrich read the following resolutions of the Executive Committee which were adopted on motion of Bishop Kephart & seconded by Bishop Mills.
>
> (1) That preparations be made to re-build at once.
>
> (2) That a thorough and systematic canvass of the members of the church within the co-operating territory & friends of the College everywhere, be made immediately for funds and subscriptions to funds, for the purpose of rebuilding.

There ensued tumultous activity on the campus. President Roop was at his best, planning for immediate reorganization. Rooms had to be found for students returning after the Christmas holidays. The residents of Annville opened their homes. Classrooms had to be found for the various departments. Engle Hall and the Ladies Hall (South Hall) offered their facilities. Science took up quarters in the basement of the Library.

By January 12, 1905, the Executive Committee was ready with comprehensive plans looking not merely to the restoration of what had been lost but to the raising on the campus of an almost totally new and far more efficient Lebanon Valley College. The minutes of that meeting make interesting reading.

> . . . President Roop stated the Executive Committee minutes were destroyed in the recent fire and hence there were none to be read. All the other records contained in the safe in the administration building were also destroyed. On motion of S. P. Light, Esq. and H. B. Dohner, Dr. Roop, H. H. Kreider, and I. B. Haak were appointed a rebuilding committee. The action of this committee in employing Mr. A. A. Ritcher, Lebanon, Pa., as architect to prepare plans and to superintend the erection of the four buildings, viz., an administration building, a boys' dormitory, a science hall, and a central heating and lighting plant, for the sum of twenty-five hundred dollars complete, was approved.
>
> The action of the committee in giving the contract for the removal, cleaning, and piling of the brick of the ruined building to Matterness & Fink, of Annville, Pa., for the sum of one dollar and twenty-five cents per thousand was approved . . .

122

The prospect of money for rebuilding was no mirage. On December 30, President Roop had called on Andrew Carnegie at his residence in New York, and had received promise of some assistance. The offer when it came electrified even Dr. Roop. The Lebanon *Daily News* reported the incident in typical fashion:

> President Hervin U. Roop, of Lebanon Valley College, Annville, today made public announcement of the receipt of a letter from Andrew Carnegie in which the millionaire philanthropist promises to give $50,000 toward the erection of a Greater Lebanon Valley College, on condition that an equal sum is raised by the college, exclusive of the insurance recovered on the fire destroyed administration building. The magnanimous offer came as a New Year's greeting for the Carnegie letter was delivered to Dr. Roop on last Monday, and insures the early erection of the four proposed new buildings.

On January eleven there went out a letter, signed by President Roop, to friends of the College, reminding them of the catastrophe to the main building, which had contained "the President's offices, the recitation rooms, the dormitory rooms for 120 boys, the science department, and the central heat plant. The total loss is estimated at $85,000, the insurance is $48,000. . . .

> I have secured from Mr. Andrew Carnegie [he continued] the promise that he will subscribe the last half of $100,000. This puts upon us the responsibility of raising $50,000 at the earliest possible date in order to meet his condition. And so we earnestly appeal to you and solicit your liberal aid in this hour of our great need. You may have six or more months in which to pay your subscription, if desired.

Money flowed in. Alfred Cochran contributed $25,000 for the proposed Science Hall, the East Pennsylvania Conference, $20,000 for the general fund. Money was raised in a multitude of other, smaller ways, as when the ladies of Annville put on a bazaar and a public supper on the College's behalf. The professors paid generously out of their small salaries, many of them as much as $100. According to the college ledger, Andrew Carnegie paid the last of four instalments on his $50,000 on October 10, 1905.

So it was that, after the fiery night of catastrophe, instead of despair a fever of optimism seized the College and the community. The *Forum* for January, 1905, had this to say:

> When we look at the mass of ruins that disfigures our campus like a huge scar it is hard to see in it anything but the ghost of the building we saw for the last time before our vacation. . . . Our truer vision shows us a picture of a group of modern structures springing up from the ruins of the old Administration building.

Masons and carpenters were soon busy all over the campus. In the spring of 1905, a new Administration Building—in "Tudor Gothic and Cambridge" style—rose out of the ashes of the old. By the end of the year it was under roof.

The same year, construction started on an "Oxford-Cambridge" style dormitory for the men on the southwest corner of the campus. Some suites in it were occupied before the end of the 1905–1906 college year. A new Ladies Hall [North Hall] in an "Elizabethan" style, was started in 1905 and ready for occupation by the opening of the next college year. The new Central Heating Plant was actually in operation on October 22, 1905.

It was also in October, 1905, that ground was broken for a four-story science building. Plans for this ambitious structure called for a whole floor to be given to each of the three science departments (Biology, Chemistry, Physics). A museum was to be in the ground floor hallway, while the fourth floor was to be reserved as a Conservatory for Animals.

Undoubtedly the year 1905, which saw seven buildings under construction on the campus—the Brightbill Gymnasium, the Carnegie Library, the Administration Building, a new Ladies Hall, the Boys' Dormitory, the Heating Plant, and the Science Building, was a miracle year for the College.

But that was also the year of the Big Trouble. The Horn of Plenty was running dry. The flow of money dwindled to a trickle. The college debt showed its ugly head again and would not be downed. Mr. Brightbill lost all interest in his gymnasium (which had made several false starts), and for the last time work on it stopped. Work stopped, too, on the science building. Worse yet, work stopped on the Administration Building, and was not resumed until some time later when it was completed with funds diverted from the science building.

Dissatisfaction rose on every side. Hope deferred maketh the heart sick—and sometimes the head. Complaints were leveled at the President, insinuations, accusations. Old jealousies and sores were opened. Whispers that the fire was of incendiary origin were heard. Charges of various kinds, from nepotism to forgery, were aired in conversation and in print. Gossip broke into convulsions. The College, the Church, and the town split into two parties: those for and those against the President.

In the midst of the uproar, President Roop resigned. On the morning of January 1, 1906, Lebanon Valley College was again without a president.

CHAPTER TWENTY ONE

Aftermath

THE RESIGNATION OF President Roop did not heal the College's wounds. He remained a controversial figure until (at his request) his body was laid to rest in the Mount Annville Cemetery, September 24, 1955, the Rev. Dr. William A. Wilt, College Pastor, conducting the graveside services.

To understand the 1905 confusion and its dangerous consequences, it is not necessary to review the charges against him. These were never proved. It is sufficient to examine a few documents which will show how strongly the college constituency divided for and against him.

The first of these is his resignation:

Dec. 28, 1905.

To the President
and Members of Board of Trustees:-
I hereby tender my resignation as President of Lebanon Valley College to the Board of Trustees to take effect Jan. 1, 1906, & agree that my five year contract with the College shall be abrogated upon condition that I be paid forthwith the balance of my salary for the current year, amounting to $1500-, my Expenses amounting to 161- and the amount paid by me for reimbursement of students who suffered losses by fire Amounting to $175-

Cordially yours
Hervin U. Roop.

On the same day, a committee which had been appointed to examine the charges against Dr. Roop, drew up the following report and presented it to a special session of the Board of Trustees on January 5, 1906:

We, your committee appointed by the Board of Trustees of Lebanon Valley College, respectfully report:
That:-The charges having been withdrawn conditioned that the following arrangement be ratified by the Board of Trustees and Pres. H. U. Roop, having resigned as President of Lebanon Valley College and agreed to abrogate his five-year contract in consideration of the payment to him, forthwith, of the balance of his salary for the current year amounting to Fifteen Hundred ($1500.00) Dollars, his expenses to date amounting to One Hundred Sixty One and 41/100 ($161.41) Dollars, and the amount advanced by him for reimbursement of students suffering losses by the fire, amounting to One Hundred Seventy Five

($175.00) Dollars,—The committee appointed to investigate and report upon the charges brought against Prest. Roop and others, would respectfully recommend that the said resignation be accepted upon the terms stated.

And we would further recommend that such steps be taken as may be deemed necessary to restore Public Confidence.

<table>
<tr><td></td><td>W. H. Ulrich</td><td></td></tr>
<tr><td></td><td>John C. Herkert</td><td></td></tr>
<tr><td></td><td>W. A. Lutz</td><td>Committee</td></tr>
<tr><td>Annville, Pa.</td><td>Henry Wolf</td><td></td></tr>
<tr><td>Dec. 28, 1905</td><td>J. G. Stehman</td><td></td></tr>
</table>

According to minutes of the Board, this was also the day (December 28) when the Trustees adopted a resolution praising Dr. Roop's contribution to the College's advancement.

> Whereas, Dr. H. U. Roop has this day tendered his resignation as President of Lebanon Valley College, and,
>
> Whereas, during his administration extending over a period of eight years the standard of scholarship has been materially advanced, the student body augmented almost fourfold, the assets of the college more than quadrupled and a handsome group of modern university buildings nearly completed, and the college generally has prospered as never before in all its history, therefore,
>
> Resolved, First, That we express our profound and sincere regret at the severance of his official relations with the college.
>
> Second, That we tender our great appreciation of the high efficiency with which he served the college both as President and Treasurer.
>
> Third, That the life, growth and prosperity of the college has been chiefly due to the wise and aggresive policy, untiring energy and strong personality of Dr. Roop. . . .

The month of January, 1906, was full of embarrassment for Lebanon Valley College. Dr. Roop, whose resignation had taken effect the first of the month, was planning a trip to Europe, but he was still in town. The Board of Trustees was having difficulty in finding anyone to take his place. A strong movement gathered head to re-appoint Dr. Roop. Whereupon four members of the faculty—Hiram Herr Shenk, Norman Colestock Schlichter, Howard Edward Enders, and William Calvin Arnold—threatened to resign.

The crisis that ensued is best told in the minutes of a Special Session of the Board held on January 22, 1906:

> Mr. H. Ulrich [President of the Board], having declined to serve as President of the college, to which position he had been elected, the place therefore was vacant.
>
> On motion of D. D. Lowery, seconded by D. Eberly, Dr. H. U. Roop was reinstated as President of the college by a vote of 12 yeas and 9 nos. S. P. Light, D. D. Lowery and D. Eberly were then appointed a committee to wait on Dr. Roop and inform him of his reinstatement as President. The committee proceeded

on its mission and soon returned with Dr. Roop in person, who spoke for himself, declining to serve as President of the college unless he were elected to the position by a practically unanimous vote upon the part of the Board. . . .

The matter of selecting a President for the college was left in the hands of the Executive Committee.

During the disturbed interim that followed, the noise of discord both within and without the College, was shrill and ugly. Fortunately the steady-minded John Lehman, Dean of the College and President *pro tem.,* took hold and kept the institution alive.

In the long run, the greatest harm done by the controversy over President Roop was to the student body. Unsettled by the furor and therefore a prey to the cynically minded, the students drifted into a condition of near anarchy that made life intolerable for the next two presidents.

The Administration Building

*North Hall (until 1957 the Women's Residence, later
Keister Hall—a residence for men)*

Engle Hall (the Conservatory of Music)

128

Carnegie Library (now the Carnegie Lounge)

Football Team, 1901
J. Walter Esbenshade, manager, with hat and tie;
to his right, Donald J. Cowling, later president of Carleton College.

129

Y.W.C.A. Cabinet, 1906–1907

In a charter dated November 1, 1906, Lebanon Valley College was cited as a charter member of the Young Women's Christian Associations of the United States of America. Seated: Helen Ethel Myers, Alice K. Lutz (Kreider). Top Row: Edna D. Yeatts (Hager), Elizabeth L. Stehman (Cowling), Alice M. Zuck, Neda A. Knaub (Hambright), Effie E. Shroyer (Kinney), L. May Hoerner, Elizabeth H. Rechard (Barnhart).

CHAPTER TWENTY TWO

President Abram Paul Funkhouser

THE EXECUTIVE COMMITTEE of the Board of Trustees, at a meeting on March 9, 1906, elected the Rev. Abram Paul Funkhouser, A.M., to the College presidency.

Abram Funkhouser, eighth president in forty years, was born December 10, 1853, in the Shenandoah Valley, at Harrisonburg, near Dayton, Virginia. He was the son of Samuel Funkhouser and his wife, Elizabeth Paul. Although a native Virginian, he was not a stranger to Annville, having begun his college career at Lebanon Valley. The *Catalogue* of 1873–74 lists A. Paul Funkhouser, from Dayton, Virginia, a Freshman taking the Classical Course, Room 23, New College (the Administration Building). He transferred later to Otterbein, and, after attending one year, graduated there with a B.S. degree in 1882.

He had good church connections. In 1869, at the age of sixteen, he had been known as the "Boy Preacher," having delivered his first sermon in that year at Mt. Solon, Virginia. Later, as a member of the Virginia Conference, he served several circuits, became Presiding Elder of the South Branch District, was several times a delegate to the General Conference, was for years a Trustee of the United Brethren Publishing Board, and in 1897 became Associate Editor of *The Religious Telescope.*

Considering the desperate condition of Lebanon Valley College in the early months of 1906, what appeared to be most immediately necessary was to put at her head a man of affairs with sound business experience. Mr. Abram Funkhouser seemed to be just the man.

Before he came to L. V. C. as president, Funkhouser had had considerable experience in politics, and, as a Republican in Democratic Virginia, had had quite an extraordinary career. At Harrisonburg, he had edited *The People,* which changed its name to *The State Republican,* and through it he espoused the causes of prohibition and clean politics. As the presidential election of 1896 approached, he was mentioned strongly for the position of Postmaster General in the McKinley cabinet. Failing in this, he was appointed Postmaster at Harrisonburg, where he remained for eight successful years.

The Rev. Dr. William A. Wilt (for many years College Pastor at Annville)

Rev. Abram P. Funkhouser, A.M.
President, 1906–1907

who was acquainted with him at Harrisonburg, remembers him as a strong and fluent speaker, liberal in his theology, interested in the ecumenical movement, a worker for the union of the United Brethren with the Methodists.

The power of his dominant personality can perhaps best be seen in a curious incident that occurred in 1896. It is thus described (probably by his editor) in his posthumously published volume, a *History of the Virginia Conference* (1921):

> In 1896 Dr. Funkhouser originated the idea of a Confederate excursion to Canton, Ohio, the residence of William McKinley, then the Republican nominee for President. Though almost unaided in his plan, he chartered three trains and these carried two thousand veterans and their sons to the Republican Mecca.

He possessed great qualities, but some of them in excess. Energetic, independent, full of initiative, he was preeminently a leader—but not a graceful follower. An easy speaker, full of ideas and with an unfailing flow of words (he spoke without notes), he was a better talker than listener. Hesitant about accepting advice, and so abrupt in his manner that he left the impression—especially on young people—of arrogance, he drew the following words of not quite unstinted praise from the editor of his book, Oren F. Morton:

"He considered no discouragement, paused at no obstacle, waited for no council, and listened to no applause."

When in March, 1906, Professor Lehman introduced the new President to the students at chapel, he used, in pure good humor, words to which another fifteen months were to give ironical significance:

"Since my association with the College, I have seen five presidents come and go, but for some reason I keep on going."

The situation into which President Funkhouser had stepped was as critical as his (or the College's) worst enemy could have hoped for. For one thing, the college finances, which had never been very good, had recently suffered a nearly fatal wound. For another, student morale was approaching its nadir.

The College debt had risen to $81,000 and was climbing rapidly. By July 1, when E. Benjamin Bierman (who a few years before had won his suit against the College for back salary) became College Treasurer, the debt had risen to $86,089. The quarrel over President Roop had frightened away some of the College's best friends, and their aid was withdrawn. Work on the new Administration Building was interrupted. When, a few months later, it was resumed, this was accomplished, as already noted, only by the diversion of money from the new Science Building, for which contracts had been signed. The repercussions of this deal approached the same magnitude of disaster as that which the diversion of funds had been intended to forestall.

College salaries were on the block. In the minutes of the Board of Trustees for June 11, 1906, it was reported that the outlay for salaries alone was $17,-856.91, while the income from tuition was $11,355.38, "leaving a deficit of $6,501.33." The Board tried to meet this threat by cutting salaries, and saved three thousand dollars.

The President had a further ingenious proposal for making ends meet. However convincing its arithmetic may have appeared in bare outline as he presented it to the Trustees on June 11, 1906, it disclosed such a strange incomprehension of college affairs—time-tables, student electives, and professors' specialization—as must have amazed Dean, Registrar, Faculty, and students (if they heard of it).

> . . . we can never hope to have our people thoroughly enlisted for the college, until we do business on a business basis. . . .
>
> And I am glad there is a plain possible way by which to do it, and that without lowering our standards in any way, or lessening the amount of work now done. By an examination of the courses of study for the Fall term, I learn that the actual hours required per week in class room work are 67 in the college courses proper and 66 in the preparatory, making a total of 133 hours per week. This work is now being done by eleven persons whose work has averaged less than fourteen hours per week. If the day's work was made five hours, then six persons would more than do all the work required, if only four hours then seven would be able to do it. I note these facts that it is possible to reduce numbers without reducing the amount of work, a fact which I trust will be made use of only as actual necessities demand. . . .

It may be amusing today to read about the College's twists and turns, borrowings, refinancing, law suits, judgments and costs and pleas for suspended execution in order that the institution might keep its doors open. But the drama was not amusing at the time to professors who had families to feed. Not only were their salaries cut, but payment of any kind was uncertain. A letter of December 7, 1906, addressed by members of the Faculty to the Executive Committee, is illuminating:

Gentlemen:-

The undersigned members of the Faculty urgently request that you make some definite arrangement for the monthly payment of their salaries at a specified time so that they can conduct their business affairs upon business principles and with promptness.

Respectfully,

J. T. Spangler	H. E. Spessard	N. M. Heilman
J. E. Lehman	B. Trovillo	F. A. Roach
H. H. Shenk	John S. Shippee	J. Lehn Kreider
S. H. Derickson	H. H. Harbour	

An even greater threat to the future of the College lay in the decline of the College's standing in the eyes both of the Church and of the academic world. A main cause of this decline was a mood of cynical irresponsibility descending upon students who had breathed the rancid air of disillusionment and distrust marking the last months of the Roop controversy. It was seen in a sharp increase both in the number and in the violence of student misdemeanors. Even more serious was the alarming increase—until it became nearly universal—of cheating on examinations.

President Funkhouser, the unfortunate victim of this deteriorating situation, lasted only fifteen months, declining re-election when his first full term was up in June, 1907. The times were "out of joint," and he, with all his great qualities, was not fitted, either by temperament or training, to mend them.

Under the best of circumstances, it would have been difficult to follow Roop, a glamorous "prexy" who had brought an air of cosmopolitan distinction to the College, and who maintained (till near the end) just the right touch with the students. Funkhouser, by comparison (as recalled by a former undergraduate), was much less the cosmopolite, and he was not altogether at home among college students. He did not understand the coltish high spirits of young men emerging from the strict discipline of Pennsylvania Dutch homes into campus life with twentieth-century freedoms. He could not shrug off small student misdemeanors—in the happy manner, for instance, of Professor G. A. Richie, class of '13 (who married Belle Orris, of '15). Many graduates remember the classic scene when Dr. Richie, leading chapel, was interrupted by the machine-gun pounding of a hidden alarm clock. He stood quietly before the student body until the noise died away. Then, smiling, he said: "All right, boys. I don't mind bells. I like them. In fact, I married one." It was a marvelous denouement, healthy for student-faculty relations.

President Funkhouser, no doubt with the aim of staving off more serious misdemeanors, was inclined to make a moral issue of such pranks. One such case is disclosed in the minutes of a Special Meeting of the Faculty held at 12:30 p.m., October 1, 1906:

> The object of the meeting was to arrange for the proper discipline of some members of the Sophomore Class who had disturbed Chapel service by carrying a Freshman bound hand and foot and wrapped in green cloth, upon the rostrum while President Funkhouser was reading the Bible. . . .
>
> Dean Spangler reported [at another Special Faculty Meeting in the evening] that Messrs. Peter [Patrick] Carnes, Warren Stehman, Gideon R. Kreider assisted by A. D. Flook admitted that they had carried Robert D. Kreider into the Chapel and stated that it was not their intention to disturb but that they thought they were bringing him in just as the service was closing. The[y] further stated that they were very sorry for the offense.

The culprits were made to sign an apology (which had been prepared for them by the Faculty), and this was read later before the assembled student body.

According to one of the principals in that escapade, President Funkhouser did not have the knack of tempering discipline with "graciousness." In consequence, recalls the same informant, the students "almost had a riot or two on account of the things he made us do."

Admittedly, the undergraduate reaction was thoughtless and cruel, not to say dangerous; but it was at least understandable and, considering the low state of college morale at the time, it was all but inevitable.

Hostility to President Funkhouser came to a climax, so the story runs, at a reception in the Carnegie Library. The lights went out. In the darkness, someone emptied a bag of flour over the President's head, and a moment later someone else anointed him with a watering can. When the lights came on, he was

A sight to dream of, not to tell!

It would be unjust, however, to remember President Funkhouser only for such instances of student disaffection. He did great good for the College in ways unknown to students at the time, and it is for this his memory should be preserved in high honor.

Mr. Richard P. Zimmerman of Chambersburg contributes a tradition that brings to focus President Funkhouser's most essential contribution to Lebanon Valley College's continued existence.

> I have heard that Funkhouser saved the College in a most dramatic way. The sheriff was either at the College or on his way, when Funkhouser turned up with the money he had got from the Zimmermans of Chambersburg (no connection with my family). Funkhouser had managed to borrow the money. It was as dramatic as could be. You may quote me if you wish.

Detail is lacking, but that the legend has a basis of truth is apparent from the College's business correspondence during the spring of 1906.

It will be remembered that, when Roop resigned, the College was heavily in debt, and building operations on the campus had come to a standstill. Donors to the Rebuilding Fund withdrew their support. In consequence, work on the desperately-needed Administration Building was halted. The Brightbill Gymnasium and the Science Building remained mere holes in the ground.

Heroic measures had to be undertaken if the College was not to "die on the vine." Steps were initiated by the Trustees to place a large loan. At a Board meeting on January 22, 1906, "S. F. Engle [father of a later Acting President, Ray Engle] was appointed to act with B. H. Engle [S. F.'s brother and the donor of the Engle Conservatory], to try to secure a $50,000 loan for the college."

That was a large sum in those days, and Lebanon Valley's credit was not healthy. For months the mortgage loan eluded pursuit. Meetings of an anxious Board were held on March 16 and again on April 10.

Meanwhile creditors were becoming uneasy. Suits against the College were threatened and instituted. Mr. William Weikel, the architect and contractor for the abandoned Science Building, informed the College through his lawyers that he would "insist upon taking judgment on the whole amount of the claim on February 20th," adding that he would not insist upon immediate execution of judgment, but only wished to be in a favorable position if the worst happened to the College.

Pressed by this and other judgments, which entailed galling losses in costs, the College succeeded in arranging for a mortgage loan. But it was not a cash transaction. The College had to float a ten-year, five per cent, gold coupon bond issue (with the aid of the Keister family of Western Pennsylvania) before the Harrisburg Trust Company (of which E. Keister was Assistant Secretary) would accept the mortgage.

The weeks went by and still the College had no money it could use. The bonds were slow in finding purchasers. Creditors became increasingly aggressive. The black clouds of bankruptcy were gathering overhead. In a desperate effort to speed up the bond sale, President Funkhouser journeyed to Scottdale, headquarters of the Keister family whose money was in coal and coke.

During the President's absence, the storm broke. From the College Treasurer, W. S. Arnold, came a despairing letter, dated May 26, to S. F. Engle in Palmyra:

"President Funkhouser has gone to Western Pennsylvania, and if he does not come back with favorable report I do not know what can be done next."

Two days later, May 28 (*before the loan was placed*), President Funkhouser, back in Harrisburg, sent the college Treasurer two checks "covering the Graybill and the United Metile Company's claims," with instructions to get certified receipts and send them "as quickly as possible" to the Harrisburg Trust Company.

Was this the crisis and the transaction out of which grew the legend of Funkhouser, the Zimmermans, and the Sheriff?

On June 3, the $50,000 bond issue was placed, and Lebanon Valley College resumed the payment of bills.

President Funkhouser's report to the Board of Trustees on June 11, 1906, gives a summary of the transaction and some explanation of the delay:

> By the action of your Executive Committee, on March 9 last, I was chosen President of this institution. The matter of providing for pressing liabilities required immediate action, and a meeting of your Board was held on March 16, when the necessary steps were attempted to conclude a first mortgage loan of $50,000. Legal objections were made to the action of this meeting, and another Board meeting was held on April 10, and it was then confidently expected the loan would be placed and the whole matter closed by the first day of May. It proved to be a month later, June 3, when the bonds began to be delivered. The bonds bear interest from May 1, and on November 1 next the first installment of $1,250 in interest must be paid. Almost my whole time has been required to complete this transaction, so that the work I had planned to do has been delayed, and we face another year with very little work done specially in its behalf. . . .

When President Funkhouser's term came to an end and he declined re-appointment, the Trustees on June 10, 1907, passed this resolution:

> . . . That we the Board of Trustees of Lebanon Valley College, now assembled in annual session, do hereby express our appreciation to President A. P. Funkhouser for his willingness to accept the Presidency at such a critical period, for his earnest toil, and untiring zeal in behalf of the College; and commend him for his integrity, business sagacity, and for his excellent qualities as a Christian gentleman.

First Basketball Team, 1903–1904
Front Row: *"Cully" Warlow, Arthur J. Jones (manager), Hocker.*
Top Row: *Tom Beddoe, Edward E. Knauss, James, Alvin Binner (captain).*

The Old Alumni Gymnasium decorated for a dance

CHAPTER TWENTY THREE

President Keister Balances the Budget

WHEN THE Reverend Lawrence W. Keister, B.S., A.B., A.M., S.T.B., accepted the presidency, feelings of relief and even exultation swept the College. Keister himself was well thought of, and he was a member of the distinguished Keister family of Western Pennsylvania, owners of coal mines and coke ovens. Henry Frick (at one time key man in the coke industry and for years Andrew Carnegie's right hand man) had made his start under Solomon Keister, the new president's father, to whom Frick had been apprenticed and under whom he had learned his trade.

Suddenly Lebanon Valley College found itself in touch with the great world of finance and industry. It stirred the imagination.

Two days before President Keister assumed his duties (which, by action of the Board of Trustees, was at the hour of noon on June 12, 1907), the Finance Committee made two recommendations which the Board, looking into the future, immediately adopted:

"That any person who will pay $20,000. or more to the College shall have the privilege of naming a chair.

"That any person or family that pays $100,000. to the College shall be called the chief patron of Lebanon Valley College, and the School shall be their memorial. . . ."

Lawrence Keister was born, August 28, 1856, on the Keister farm in Upper Tyrone Township, near Scottdale, Westmoreland County. A frail child, he was the last of six children (Albert, Abraham, Frank, Fenton, Mary, and Lawrence) born to Solomon Keister by his first wife. Though Solomon owned a farm, he was not a farmer. His money was in coal mines and coke ovens. In youth he was something of a dandy. His colorful vests are still remembered. But he was converted, changed the pattern of his life, and became one of the leading laymen of the United Brethren Church.

Lawrence Keister's early education was in a log schoolhouse to which he rode several miles with two of his brothers on their "old white horse," as he used to tell his grandchildren. He was converted at the age of fourteen in the Jacob Creek Methodist Episcopal Church. Resolved to give his life to the

Rev. Lawrence W. Keister, D.D.
President, 1907–1912

Christian ministry, he went up to Otterbein University in the fall of 1877. He graduated with a B.S. degree in 1882. The same year he entered the School of Theology of Boston University, graduating in 1885 with the degree of S.T.B. (Bachelor of Sacred Theology). While in Boston he came under the influence of Phillips Brooks.

On graduation from Boston, he married Cora Cormany (A.B. Otterbein, 1885). Continuing his education, from Leander Clark College he received the degree of A.B. (1888) and A.M. (1891).

Entering the ministry of the United Brethren Church, he served pastorates at Morrellville (near Johnstown) and Greensburg. Failing health sent him to California, where he spent nearly three years in fruit farming. When he returned to the East, he served important charges in Wilkinsburg and Scottdale. At the time of his call to Lebanon Valley College, he was pastor at Mount Pleasant in Westmoreland County.

President Keister's arrival in Annville was without fanfare, and throughout his career he sought no publicity for himself. He was not what would be called a born administrator, being sensitive, somewhat uncalculating, and not much given to compromise. But he had the best qualities of what Oliver Butterwick (then a student) was to call "a brilliant, lovable Christian gentleman." He was high-minded, generous, unassuming, and utterly genuine. He would rather have died than pose for effect.

His granddaughter, Mrs. Ray E. Kiefer, of Scottdale, writes:

His contributions were many although he always said, "Now we mustn't tell anybody about this." He was always interested in helping young people to acquire an education. He would often "loan" them money, to be repaid when they were well established, not back to Grandad, but by helping some other youth with his or her education. . . .

As you can see by his poetry, he loved nature, children, small animals, good music, and above all he loved his Lord simply, humbly, completely. His ideals were very high. To some he seemed strict and uncompromising. He was. He knew the Way; he was doing his best to lead others, and he would not vary one inch. I remember his complaining that he could not tolerate ministers preaching a watered-down version of the Bible (and he never hesitated in telling them so.)

His warm hopes for the College and his high ideals were expressed in lines he wrote for the 1909 Year Book:

OUR COLLEGE

And here's my pledge to L. V. C.
My measure full, my off'ring free.
Let all these halls with life abound
Joyous and thoughtful and profound.
Let merry laughter ring again,
From lips of maidens and of men;
While serious thought finds serious speech
From lips of taught and those who teach.

Arise, thou Star of L. V. C.
Shine out with greater brilliancy,
Illuminate the mind, the soul;
Make human thoughts to us unroll;
And thoughts divine our hearts impress
While Christ our Lord each heart shall bless.

So here we pledge ourselves to thee,
Thou undimmed Star of L. V. C.

During his time at the College, many improvements were made. Walks of crushed limestone, six feet wide, were laid around the campus, a thousand feet of them. Buildings were renovated. The roofing of the Administration Building was at last made rainproof. Funds were raised to equip the science laboratories. From an anonymous "friend of higher education" (evidently Henry Frick) came a large gift to, and a name for, the Tyrone Biological Laboratory.

Student government (by the Senior-Junior Council) was strengthened. The Department of Oratory came alive under the redoubtable Miss May Belle Adams, whose reiterated "Chest out, chin in!" punctuated her classes in Public Speaking. It was she who started the custom of presenting a Shakespeare play on Commencement Day, and who, in 1912, directed the first May Day pageant at L. V. C.

Dr. Keister fought hard for higher scholastic standards at the College, and tried to bring under control some of the loose practices that were developing out of the new furor for intercollegiate sport. The faculty minutes show half-hearted attempts to eliminate the already entrenched evils of paid college players and of the so-called students who enrolled in the Academy for as long as the football season lasted and played on the college team.

A certain class of student could not forgive Dr. Keister for the steps he took to eradicate these evils. When he and the Faculty rejected the plea of the Athletic Association for "Athletic Scholarships," resentment boiled over and the Senior-Junior Council (the student government) resigned in a body—with consequences to be detailed in a later chapter.

President Keister's greatest contribution to the College lay in rescuing it from its financial Slough of Despond and setting it on its way again. His tactics were to dispel the gnawing fear of debt as a shapeless but invincible spectre by breaking up the whole financial problem into its component parts, and proposing a course of action to meet each of these separately.

As he saw it, there were three things to be done: match current expenses with current income, pay off the present debt, and build a good endowment fund. Meanwhile he nursed the College back into an almost-lost mood of hope and confidence by means of sizable financial contributions (always unheralded) made by himself and his brothers.

The proceeds from tuition and room rent had been found to be (contrary to the hopes of the founding fathers) altogether unequal to the demands of salaries and upkeep. Yet to break even with current expenses was a prerequisite to the success of the whole campaign. To help make ends meet, therefore, President Keister quietly contributed his salary to the college treasury and in addition paid many of the small bills out of his pocket. With this help, and with certain economies (such as the elimination of one professorship at a saving of $1,000), the College was enabled to plug this hole in the dike of its budget.

Paying the debt, however, was another matter. It was large and growing. On June 12, 1907, as he reported later to the Co-operating Conferences, the debt was $89,581.21. A year later it was $92,434.56, "an increase for the year of $2,903.35."

In the same report of October, 1908, he drew attention to the crippling interest payments:

> It is plain that the College cannot pay its way and also pay interest at the rate of $4,195.64 a year. Last year there would have been no deficit had there been no interest to pay. The cash solicited, $11,878.75, added to the income from the cooperative circles, $1,248.82, temporarily relieved the financial stringency of the College. Had there not been about $6,000.00 put into improvements the debt would have been diminished by about one-half of that amount.

To the Board of Trustees on June 1, 1908, he had outlined steps proposed to handle the debt:

> The Executive Committee at its regular session, April 7, authorized an immediate effort to raise $100,000.00 to cover the entire debt. The Plan adopted requires the signature of one thousand persons to a note of $100.00 each or the equivalent on condition that $50,000 be secured in this way on or before Jan. 1, 1909, and on condition that the College continue the Canvas to secure $100,000.00 on or before January 1, 1910. An agent, D. E. Long, has been placed in the field to solicit notes on this plan.

Next year the President was able to report:

> The debt effort ordered by the Board at its last session has been pressed within $2,243.00 of the mark set for January 1, 1909. Considering the financial depression and other active hindrances the result at this time is really gratifying. My time has been given to this work as fully as possible. The College agent, D. E. Long, has succeeded in this arduous work beyond the expectation of all his friends.

To the Co-operating Conferences in October of that year, 1909, he said:

> . . . The Treasurer's report dated March 31, 1909, showed the debt to be $77,280.67, a decrease of $12,300.54, as compared with my last report. . . .
>
> During the past year there was some reduction of interest and discount, and some decrease in expenses. There was also an increase of income from tuition and room rent. Hence the estimated deficit for this year is less by $2,192.00 than the estimated deficit for last year. The efforts of the Conferences and the Board of Trustees are bringing forth the right results. . . .

In October, 1910, he reported the debt to be down to $62,883.40, a reduction of $14,397.27; and by October, 1911, it was down to $48,925.95, a further reduction of $13,957.45.

To see how this was accomplished, it was necessary to look back a little. Soon after coming to the College, he sketched for his brother, Abe (Abraham L. Keister), an early plan for wiping out the debt:

> Annville, Pa., March 8 1908
>
> Dear Brother A. L.
>
> I write to you today concerning a proposition I have in mind. It may seem like an impossible one but more & more I think it can be worked. The debt of the college is something less than $90,000 & I have the idea 1000 persons can be found who will give $100 each. Of course $1000 counts for 10 when one man gives it. . . . Can not our family give at least 100 of these shares? I think the offer would lead to securing $50,000.00 as a first result & then $100,000 by the year 1910.
>
> I want to get $50,000 by Jan. 1st 1909 & I believe the first half would greatly aid to get the second by Jan. 1st 1910. These people have money but they do not give in large amounts. Never have & never will. So this plan adapts itself to their habit. I am told 100 pastors would take each one or more shares. . . .

Cast of She Stoops to Conquer, *1911*
Prof. May Belle Adams, coach, stands at extreme right

If the above proposition is approved I will give my share & try to get it going as soon as I have secured all I can for current expenses from the churches.

Your brother
Lawrence Keister

A year later, he wrote:

Annville, Pa. May 31st 1909.

Brother A. L.

Since I left Scottdale I have been thinking of a certain thing. My hopes of covering the whole debt are better now than ever before. Of course pledges are not always paid. Mr. Rettew of Harrisburg says we must have $20,000.00 above the debt before we are sure of it. May be if I get the whole well covered the family would consider endowing a chair for $20000.00 in honor of father. This idea has been before my mind for several days. I would be glad to know what you think of it.

There is no record at the College on any single contribution by the Keister family of a sum as large as the proposed $20,000 or even $10,000. No chair has been named in honor of Solomon Keister. But the College's financial records show that the Keister family (four brothers, their sister Mary, relatives Sarah B. Cochran and A. J. Cochran, and "a Friend") contributed quietly about $50,000. It was entered under various ledger categories, such as the "College Debt Fund," the "Contingent Fund," the "Science Department," and "Sundries."

Letters exchanged by Lawrence and his elder brother, Albert, will explain what was constantly going on:

May 31, 1910, Scottdale, Pa.

Brother Lawrence:-

    As the school year is near the close I am writing you to know if you have sufficient funds to pay all your teachers in full. I think this should be done in order that the school may have better standing. You let me know at once as there will be some here for that purpose if needed.

Yours Respectfully
Albert Keister

Lebanon Valley College
President's Office   Annville, Pa.   June 1st 1910
Brother Bert,

    Yours of yesterday is at hand. In answer will make the following statement.

I estimate that we need for closing up all current accounts $2697.00.

We owe the teachers $2005.00.

The bank balance today is $1096.85. This can be applied on current expenses.

We have $615.94 in bank for special use.

I am hoping each conference will pay $500.00 inside of ten days. This will bring us $1000.00.

We have some outstanding accounts that may come in. I have paid out about $100 [more] on debt than I have received from that source, or for that purpose.

So far as I can see $1000 ought to clear the College nicely, on running expenses for the year.

[No signature]

Contributions came also from the Co-operating Conferences, from individual churches, and from friends of the College; but the bulk of the debt reduction came from gifts by the Keister family.

It is doubtful if there would be a Lebanon Valley College today if Lawrence Keister had passed by on the other side.

A "snow" job, winter of 1961

April 1, 1913
Courtesy Fred S. Kreider, Jr.

CHAPTER TWENTY-FOUR

Ollie Butterwick and the Death League

HAZING HAS ALWAYS BEEN a college problem. Even in Victorian days, when the Dove of Decorum brooded over the Lebanon Valley campus, there was practical joking of an elementary kind.

As the years passed and the student body grew in numbers, hazing at L. V. C., haphazard at first, evolved itself, in the good old American way, into an organization with a local habitation and a name: its name, the Death League; its habitation, under the night sky. Sometimes its rites were celebrated in the crater of the extinct Brightbill Gymnasium, at other times amid the tombstones of the Annville Cemetery. Its motto, according to the 1913 *Bizarre,* was "Sufferance is the badge of all our tribe."

In President Keister's day, the Death League already possessed a hoary tradition, but how old the organization was is difficult to determine, for campus traditions age quickly, college generations being only about four years in length. The 1912 *Bizarre* (which appeared in the spring of 1911) memorialized March 17 of that year in these words: "Death League celebrates its 44th anniversary." If that statement is correct, the Death League originated in 1867, the year the College received its charter. But a little doubt of such antiquity is permissible. Not unlikely the calendar was drawn up by a member of that awesome body in order to cover its iniquities with the mantle of age.

Undoubtedly its members thought of themselves (in their better moments, if these may be presumed) as performing a service to society—the service being none other than that of bringing down the proud, of exposing egotism and discomposing egotists. They were, indeed, much feared by (among others) the Malvolios of the campus.

For light cases of Malvolio's malady—which, as is well known by upperclassmen, is epidemic among freshmen—a mild curriculum was prescribed: a course, as described in *Bizarre,* "in barking, rooting, moonlight sonatas and blowing out electric lights." For hardened cases a stiffer curriculum was offered, to be taken at the wrong end of a paddle.

In form, the Death League was patterned after the Ku Klux Klan. It was a secret society, and its members, when on duty, wore white sheets and hoods.

The *Bizarre* quoted above gave a list of its officers in a not too difficult cipher, which may be of interest to their descendants:

High-cock-a-lorum. . . . . . . —pp—nz—ll—r.
Big Devil. . . . . St—hm—n.
Little Devil. . . . . L—ng.
Paddler. . . . . .C. R—y B—nd—r.
Faculty members ex-officio.

The Death League was both feared and revered by members of the incoming class. That paradox was put into verses entitled "The Midnight Summons" by John Karl Lehman, '11, son of Professor Lehman. From the vantage point of his Junior year, he compressed a freshman's agonies on being confronted with the Death League, into a parody of Poe's "Raven";

Once upon a midnight dreary, while I pondered, weak and weary,
Filling up my empty cranium with facts and scientific lore—
While I nodded, almost sleeping, suddenly there came a creaking,
As of someone gently sneaking, sneaking down the corridor.
" 'Tis some Sophomore," I muttered, "sneaking down the corridor—
Only this and nothing more."

As I calmly went on cramming, in my cranium knowledge ramming,
Sharp the sound of doors a-slamming, rang throughout the corridor.
Quickly then there came a tapping, as of someone gently tapping
As of someone gently rapping, rapping at my study door—
All of this and something more.

Up I sprang with knees a-quaking, heart a-beating, hands a-shaking,
For I knew what meant that gentle tapping on my study door.
While I stood with heart a-thumping, soon there came an awful stumping,
And I knew that they were bumping, bumping in my study door—
So I thought I'd better open
Open up that study door.

There they stood all slowly beckoning, dressed in white and calmly beckoning,
Leading me off to reckoning, for my wicked deeds of yore—
'Twas no need to be refusing, or they soon would force be using,
And my dignity abusing,
If I'd answer, "Nevermore."

Soon they on the way were leading, and across the campus speeding,
While with prods I was not needing, still they urged me on before,
Never once a chance of turning, though with rage my heart was burning,
Still by prods they kept me going, urging me still on before,
Only this and nothing more.

Then the dismal silence broken, by a whispered word and token,
And I heard my name being spoken, and I shivered to the core—
And my thoughts need no expressing, you can easily be guessing
How I felt out in the midnight,
Seeing things ne'er seen before.

I soon the strangest stunts was doing, imitating cats a mewing,
Or blowing out electric lights, as did other fools before—
Last of all the "Oil of Gladness," received with many a sting of sadness,
Soaking out all of the badness, and the evil deeds of yore,
All of this and plenty more.

After it was past and over, and I lay beneath the cover,
Thinking and considering, what had just been done before—
I soon came to this conclusion, that amid all this confusion,
I would take my needed lesson,
And be better than before.

Oliver Butterwick, '12, was a younger brother of Robert R. Butterwick, Professor of Philosophy and Bible, a courageous man, liberal in theology and a vigorous exponent of academic freedom of thought. Ollie, who was already a legend at the College when the present writer came on the staff in 1925, had been the mainspring of the Death League during his college years and, after graduation, became its chief apologist. A few months before his death in 1964, he generously consented to a long, tape-recorded interview. As transcribed, it reads like a confession of faith rather than of error, for Oliver Butterwick believed—as Robin Hood did—that on the whole his exploits had been for the good of mankind.

In the interview, Mr. Butterwick explained the psychology, as he understood it, of the Lebanon Valley campus, and so accounted for the prep-school exuberance of some of its extra-curricular activities.

> We were a very homogeneous mass, not a heterogeneous. The great percentage of us were United Brethren. We came from very poor homes, with a puritanical background of rearing, and when we got there we were a little like spring heifers when they're left out in the pasture. We ran wild.

In this connection Ollie spoke with respect and affection of his father, a good, strict Pennsylvania Dutch disciplinarian, with no hanky panky about relativity where sin was concerned:

> At home I had one of the finest fathers that I guess was ever born . . . but that was before the age of the gray line. Today you have a gray line. Things, they are neither right nor wrong, you know. It's a little right and a little wrong. But back home father would point his finger at me and say:
> "Listen, sonny. As long as you put your feet under my table, there are certain things you are going to do and certain things you are not going to do. March!" That meant upstairs. We had a woodshed right in the house, and I visited that woodshed quite often with father, and he administered ethics.

Ollie was an extrovert, gregarious, possessed of an outrageous hunger for humor, and fertile in expedients to satisfy it. He was a leader among the more active-minded students, restrained from the excesses of some of them by his innate chivalry and a fundamentally conservative outlook on life. He was not, however, in his youth, an "organization man," but a strong individualist. All his life he treasured as a compliment what Professor Derickson had said to him one day when Ollie presented himself before the Board of Trustees as spokesman for an "anonymous" petition.

"You know," said Derickson, as Ollie recalled, "this college would have been better off if you had never come here. You caused more trouble than all the rest put together."

Unlike Justice, the Death League under Ollie's leadership was a great respecter of persons. Freshmen—any freshman—could be fun, especially when you tied a ministerial student to a tombstone in the Annville Cemetery at midnight and made him deliver a two-hour sermon on "The Dead." But the League's best moments by far were those in which their shots reached the professors.

Ollie and his Death Leaguers now and again stole chickens from the professors, who used their backyards to eke out their meager salaries. One night they acquired in this manner six Rhode Island Reds from Professor Lehman and six Plymouth Rocks from Professor Shroyer and invited these popular members of the Faculty to a student feast. When the meal was served, all who were "in the know" secretly enjoyed the praise these professors bestowed on their own barbecued fowl.

John Smith Shippee, A.M., Professor of Latin and French, lived in the southwest corner of the dormitory. He had a defective eye and a habit of walking about in his bare feet. One night the boys went down town, bought two gallons of molasses, poured it over the floor in the corridor adjoining Shippee's room, pounded on his door with a long stick, and enticed him out. As Dr. Watson said of Sherlock Holmes' adventure with the Giant Rat of Sumatra, the world is not yet ready for a full report on the case.

Professor C. C. Peters, A.M. (Philosophy and Education), taught a course in Logic which Ollie Butterwick attended. Since Professor Peters was Dean of the College, he inevitably drew special attention from the Death League, and many stories are still current about him. The one Ollie liked best to tell occurred in Peters' classroom, which was situated about where the President's room is now. The windows were ten or twelve feet above the ground.

> A friend of mine [said Ollie] went out and stole some chickens from the caretaker, and we put these chickens in Dr. Peters' room, and left the windows open about that far [two or three inches].
> I intentionally was late in coming to class. I opened the door and you could have heard a pin drop.
> Professor Peters says, "Mr. Butterwick," he says, "you're the one we've been waiting for. . . . The class has decided that you are the only one that can fathom this problem in logic. . . ."
> I said, "What problem?"
> "Well, he said, as you have observed, there are five chickens in this class-

room. . . . Now the problem is this: How was it physically possible for these chickens to jump from the ground twelve to fifteen feet away and hit that small aperture"—I'll never forget the word he used—"small aperture and fly in these windows without any sign of any kind on the window frame. How could that be?"

They had been debating that for the last ten minutes.

I said, "Professor Peters, there is no problem, and there is only one solution. The chickens didn't fly in. They were put here by somebody. I don't know who."

"Well, now, who could conceive of anything so dastardly?"

Ollie Butterwick's proudest exploit was one that took in (by excluding) the President, all the Faculty, and the whole student body. It was a grand slam.

Ollie told of it in his vivid, free-wheeling way:

Johnny Lehman and I one night, we didn't know what to do. They'd meet in my room and figure out devilment.

Incidentally, did you know Dr. . . . .? He was on the Board of Trustees. He was a United Brethren minister, and he'd come visit the College, and he'd always sleep in our room. And the first thing he'd say when he came in, he'd say, "Well, Ollie, what do you have lined up for tonight?" And then we'd think of something.*

Johnny got some stove cement and some wire, and we got into the Administration Building with those keys [pointing to a set—still a prized memento], and we wired every window on the first floor, every window to the radiators, with the result that nobody could get in—and we put cement in the locks, with the result that they couldn't open the doors. It was about four o'clock when we finally got back—I finally got back. My roommate I never trusted on a thing like that.

So I was up early and I looked out my window and I saw the Faculty was meeting at the west side of the Administration Building.

So I walked over and I said to Dr. Keister, "Doctor," I said "what's going on here?"

He shook his head.

I said, "What happens?"

"I don't know; but some rascal," he said, "locked this building, and we simply can't get in to have classes today."

I says, "Now, Dr. Keister," I says, "far be it from me to pose as an angel. I am not an angel. But," I says, "this is going too far. I'm a poor boy. I've got to *pay* for my education, and I can't afford to miss two days classes."

He put his arm around me, and said, "I always knew there was *some* good *somewhere* in you."

We didn't have any classes for two or three days.

There were some things from his college days that Oliver Butterwick regretted, as the next chapter will show. But the exploits of the Death League, taken as a whole, were sweet to his nostrils until the end. The pleasure of recalling them, drew forth a strange but beautiful tribute to his Alma Mater:

---

* Something like the modern "Candid Camera," but with more tang.

All of those incidents sort of accumulated and gave us a wonderful life. If you were to ask me now what did the four years at Lebanon Valley College mean to me, above all and anything else, I wouldn't hesitate. I would say, Professor Wallace, there are two phases in my life that I shall never forget if I live to be a thousand years old.

First, the happy childhood I had at home. No money, but wonderful parents and a lot of fun, because both my father and mother had understanding in the rearing of children.

No. 2, the four years I had at Lebanon Valley College. While I had wonderful professors, I learned to appreciate good literature, I had a nice foundation in chemistry—but I have forgotten all of that. I can look at calculus today and I won't know what it's all about. I have a French dictionary over here—I can't read French any more.

But the four years that I had on the campus, the social life of that campus, meant more to me in preparing me for life than all I had learned out of text-books, because they taught me how to meet people, and cope with people; because I learned then and there that we're all basically pretty nearly alike, and that's true. And if I had a boy, and he went to college, and he came home with A's, I'd beat him, because I'd know he'd be missing something.

Professor Wallace, today—of course I'm older, living probably in the past—but I don't believe these boys and girls are getting out of their college what we got. There is such a thing as being too serious as you go through life. There is more to life than just this matter of getting a lot of knowledge.

What I liked best about that little college of ours—For forty-two years I was on the road. I was connected with the largest tobacco house in New York City, and I travelled all over this part of the country, and I had the pleasure of sitting down in club cars, pullmans, in hotel lobbies, and meeting all types of men. They'd pride themselves that they were graduates of M. I. T., Yale, Harvard, Princeton, but I was amused at how little they knew. All the engineer could talk about was his own specific engineering. They didn't have a rounded life, and I raise my hat to the President of M.I.T. today:

"Go back to the Arts. You've got to have a well-rounded life, and you can't get it in Engineering."

They don't know what to talk about. They aren't interested in anything but seeking the Almighty Dollar.

Well, a dollar didn't mean so much. I never had it. As a boy I knew we were happy without it, and I'm happy today without much of it. But I get my pleasure elsewhere. And that's what I got out of Lebanon Valley College.

CHAPTER TWENTY-FIVE

The Disturbance of the Eighteenth

LIKE THE STORIES of Robin Hood and the legends of guerrilla warfare (when the guerrillas are on your side), the exploits of the rasher spirits among the students are fun in after years to hear tell of. But they had another side. Unless this darker side be turned up for a moment to the light and exposed for what it was, it will be impossible to understand what was happening in Funkhouser's day and Keister's. There was a breakdown of campus loyalties. Gangs of students roamed the campus at night, spreading terror. Vandalism was rife. Lebanon Valley College was acquiring a reputation, far and wide, as "that awful place."

A passage from David Shroyer's letter to the present writer, dated April 24, 1964, is pertinent:

> The town kids always scouted the death league performances whenever we heard their midnight hue and cry. We would secrete ourselves in the dark places of the Campus and see the unearthly goings-on that made a terrific impression on us at that time. While youngsters, from our position of safety, we got some enjoyment out of the antics and sufferings of the victims, but as I grew older I recognized these performances as being put on for the morbid enjoyment and pleasure of a select few in humiliating and inflicting pain and suffering on those of their fellow-students outside the chosen circle. From the very beginning they had a pseudo-claim to be a policing authority among the male student body but over the years they were always a matter of concern to the faculty and, needless to say, to the general student body, for some of their excesses. From the earliest time of my memory they were a hooded group looking like a Ku Klux Klansman. I always felt for the most part they were made up of the gang most needing discipline, rather than those who disciplined—not always, but in many cases the roughest elements of the athletes made up the hard core of the organization and there is no doubt about the fact that they did strike terror in the hearts of the underclassmen when they heard their eerie cries near the midnight hour. In every instance they held a drumhead court-martial on trumped-up charges and the victim had no chance—sorry was the fate of anyone who incurred the displeasure of any of the membership. There were instances in my knowledge when fellows dropped out of school rather than face the wrath of the death league and this was a continuing cause of concern to the administration and faculty. They never, however, seemingly had the strength of conviction to outlaw the group. They

did, as you undoubtedly remember, try to restrict their activities somewhat and in my day they were no longer masked or hooded but they operated in much the same manner and the only difference—the victim was masked or blindfolded. I had my experience with them. As a freshman I was called to a late afternoon session on some trumped-up charge. I was blindfolded and led into one of the larger rooms in the dorm where you were forced to bend over and grab your ankles, after which they plied with great enthusiasm the paddles they had cut out of woodstock anywhere from ½″ to ¾″ in thickness with holes and slits cut and drilled through the paddle. I received the worst beating of my life—when I got home my trousers and backside were one, having been annealed together by the dried blood. I had to soak the pants off me. Mother was so outraged by the incident that she went to her Uncle, Aaron Kreider, who was then Chairman of the Board of Trustees, who was ready to make an issue of it and toss everybody out who had anything to do with the affair, but I prevailed upon them to forget about it—I would wreak my own vengeance on the perpetrators as I was afforded an opportunity. I did have some satisfaction in calling the bluff of some of the "gang" on a man-to-man basis in succeeding years! Shortly thereafter the banning of physical violence became the rule of the School and the death league as such died. A long delayed death—it still, however, is one of the fond memories of those who were on the right side of the fence!

On the night of January 18, 1911, the campus turned an ugly side toward President Keister. The incident was long remembered in college circles as the Disturbance of the Eighteenth.

After the lapse of more than fifty years, witnesses no longer agree *in toto* on what precisely passed, moment by moment, on that incredible evening, yet all agree on the essentials. Ollie Butterwick, the principal witness, denied all personal complicity in the affair. His version has been recorded on tape. Dr. S. O. Grimm ("Sam Grimm" at that time) who was also present, corroborates Ollie's denial of guilt, but questions some of his more picturesque details. Dr. Grimm (a member of the Death League and editor of the 1912 *Bizarre,* issued in 1911) assures the present writer that it was not the Death League as such but an "accidental group that assaulted President Keister with water, etc."

The Rev. Dr. Samuel G. Ziegler ("Sam Ziegler" in the Dorm), in a letter of May 16, 1965, to Dr. Grimm, has contributed an explanation of the circumstances that had drawn Dr. Keister to cross the campus from his home on such a night:

> As I recall the President recommended some fixed limitations on our athletic program, for what particular reason I am not sure, except for the fact that he constantly emphasized scholarship as over against athletic achievements. As I see it now that was the proper thing to do. But then (1911-12) with the full vigor of physical youth this seemed like a wild program to the male portion of the student body.
>
> The Senior-Junior Council (of which you [Sam] were a member at the time) got mixed up in it and resigned which left the restless student group without any

governing body. I recall Prof. Shenk talking to me about our resignation and inquiring how to proceed. President Keister asked to confer with me and other members of the Council in my room. Why a room in the dormitory and not his office I do not know. As I recall, you and Ollie were there at my invitation, being resident in the dormitory. You are well aware of what happened. Of that I had no previous knowledge, neither had I made known the fact that the President was coming in the dormitory.

Snow lay deep on the campus that night when President Keister made his fates-tempting call at the Men's Dormitory. He first saw Ollie Butterwick, who was an important member of the Senior-Junior Council (predecessor of the Men's Senate). Grimm and Ziegler agree that Keister had come to try to reach an understanding with members of the Council about student government. It may also be that he was moved, though belatedly, to take certain advice that Professor R. R. Butterwick had once offered him.

R. R. and I [said Ollie] met with Dr. Keister one day, and Rob told Dr. Keister: "Dr. Keister, you've made the big mistake of your life. Now here my brother, Ollie, has the ability to more or less guide this campus. Now, instead of bucking him, why don't you solicit his abilities? He could lead this campus along your lines.

At this time student resentment against President Keister over grievances, real or fancied, had reached a boiling point. Some found this quiet, round-shouldered gentleman too passive, too indecisive. Some thought him too hasty, too quick in taking sides. Others complained that he was not sufficiently interested in intercollegiate sports. This was something that touched Ollie Butterwick, manager of the football team.

Now, take athletics [said Ollie]. We had no help from the College. We would open our football season with the Carlisle Indians, which was murder. I remember when we were up at Carlisle—Pop Warner was the coach—and they'd bring out eight, nine, and ten teams, all about the same brutality that you could look at. Jim Thorpe! I tackled Jim Thorpe more than once, yes, and listen, it was just like water off a duck's back.

A gang of students gathering one night (before the 18th) in Ollie Butterwick's room, some hotheads proposed, as Ollie tells the story, that they go out to the Millard quarries, steal some dynamite, and blow up Dr. Keister's house (Sheridan Hall).

I had to change this whole direction, because it was a case of vandalism. So I prevailed upon them, "Let's go out in the town and gather some of these outhouses and string them on the campus." That would sort of relieve their pressure.

The advice was taken, but somehow the grievances remained.

The spark that set off the Disturbance of the Eighteenth was the action taken by the Faculty at a meeting held, 4:00 p.m., President Keister presiding, on the day in question. Present were Professors Shenk, Lehman, Shroyer, Wanner, Spessard, Schlichter, Dodge, Parks, and Adams.

A letter was received from the Athletic Association requesting, as the faculty minutes record, "that athletic ability be considered as well as scholarship in awarding scholarships."

The faculty response is thus recorded:

> The secretary was instructed to inform the association that there are no scholarships which can be awarded according to this request, but the faculty would be glad to be informed of any persons qualified for the available scholarships who are also athletes and, that the faculty would be glad to administer any athletic scholarships that might be established.

So much for preliminary background. From this point the narrative continues in Ollie Butterwick's vivid and breathless way, exactly as he told it at his home in York on Saturday, February 1, 1964:

> It was the Eighteenth of January. The snow was at least eighteen inches to two feet on the campus. And there was a knock on the door—of our door— and here was Dr. Keister come over to see me. He had something to take up with the Senior-Junior Council.
>
> I says, "Dr. Keister, I'm sorry, but," I says, "this is no place to meet. Let's go over to Sammy Ziegler's room and Paul Koontz'."
>
> So we go to Sammy Ziegler and Paul Koontz's room; and we weren't there more than five minutes, ten minutes at the most, when, BING! Out go the lights in the dormitory. and I knew something—but I had nothing to do with it.
>
> Now, Tommy Hensel, a classmate from Lykens, he had brought a packet of squibs. I don't know if you know what they were. They used them in the mines to light off dynamite. You'd light them and PSSSSSSSSSSSS. We were in this darkened room and these squibs came squirming in through the bottom of the door. It was enough to scare anybody. Dr. Keister, he jumped on the table, and you could see he was scared blue.
>
> And this gang hammered on the door: "We want blood. We want blood. We want Prexy's blood."
>
> "Well," I says, I says, "they're going too far," to Sammy.
>
> So Dr. Keister says, he says, "Mr. Butterwick, would you mind opening that door? You can stop them if anybody can."
>
> I said, "Dr. Keister, if I put my head out of that door," I said, "my life's at stake. I wouldn't think of it."
>
> Then they kept it up for some while. . . . So I did venture out. "Now," I said, "what is this all about?"
>
> "Well," they said "we're going to give him a ride and we're going to have some fun tonight."
>
> In a sense, they didn't mean any harm.
>
> "Well," I said, "you let up for about five minutes. That will put me in good with him."
>
> "All right, we'll quit."
>
> So I went back, the lights still off, and in about five minutes the ruckus started again. And then I figured something must be done.

So I opened the door and I bellowed out. I says, "Now cut it out. That's enough of this."

And—You've been in the Men's Dormitory—sort of semicircular stairway. This was on the second floor. Well, I lugged Dr. Keister by the arm through the balcony, round the baluster; and as I was just about ready to touch the landing, I heard a voice from upstairs, from the next floor: "This way out!" and I knew something was going to happen, and I jumped back, and poor Dr. Keister was just ready to step down when two buckets of ice-cold water—January the Eighteenth—just soused him.

How he ever made that circular stairway, I don't know. . . .Well, that was known as the Disturbance of the Eighteenth and three boys were suspended, and they were just as innocent as could be.

Sam Grimm (now retired Professor of Physics) who was present in Sam Ziegler's room corroborates the body of Ollie's tale: the unexpected arrival of Dr. Keister, the hammering on the door, the cries for blood, and the final "baptism," as *Bizarre* was to call it. He questions the squibs, the climbing on the table (wondering if Ollie may not have confused two separate incidents), and the sprint across the campus, but he adds some picturesque detail of his own.

The Senior-Junior Council had resigned in a rage some weeks before, he remembers, and the situation had been deteriorating ever since. "The situation was already so tense that we wondered why Keister came to the dormitory. We felt he was going to be in trouble—and we forgot all that we had to say. Then the lights went out.There was a clatter of cans. . . ."

The incident was not closed on the night of the Eighteenth. The faculty minutes of January 24, 1911, record the suspension (with some hesitancy) for two weeks of Ollie's roommate and one other student. Ollie says a third was sent home. None of them, he assured the writer, was a participant in the affair. Dr. Grimm agrees that "the wrong men were suspended."

For Ollie Butterwick, the Eighteenth left an unhappy memory: "The one thing I regret to this day, and yet I was innocent of it, and yet accused."

For his person, he had a good alibi, with Sam Grimm, Paul Koontz, Sam Ziegler, and President Keister as witnesses; but he was torn two ways in his sympathies: understanding the boys' resentment, yet drawn to President Keister as "a good man, an honest man," whose misfortune it was, as he said, to be unprepared except financially for the emergencies of college leadership.

Following the Disturbance of the Eighteenth, *Bizarre* in its calendar of events noted January 18th as the day on which the "Boys have 'Baptismal Services.' Who did it?"

Ollie thought he knew, but he is gone. One can still, perhaps, hear his breathless voice: ". . . . Those three were the instigators of it, but those are not the three that were sent home. So that will give you an idea."

Bizarre's calendar for the spring of 1911 shows the Death League triumphant.

[March] 2 Knobby trick—door knobs disappear from "Ad" building. "100 in board offered for apprehension of the criminals."

6 Death League meets: Preps and Freshmen find out who they really are.

17 Death League celebrates its 44th anniversary.

24 Death League takes in new members.

Next year's *Bizarre* memorialized January 18 as the "First Anniversary of 'Disturbance of the Eighteenth.' No visible signs of any probable tornado, cyclone or deluge."

The Death League, invisible and invincible, seemed destined to survive any storm.

President Keister, however, though about to retire, was still to be heard from. On June 10, 1912, at the last meeting he was to chair of the College Board's Executive Committee, the following resolution was adopted:

"That the organization in Lebanon Valley College—known as the Death League, shall be abolished."

It was a princely gesture, reminiscent of King Canute's rebuke to the tide.

After withdrawing from his labors as a college president, Dr. Keister returned to Scottdale, where he built himself a white brick house and inscribed over the fireplace the words: "Dun Movin'." There he lived to the age of eighty-nine, much loved by his neighbors.

In a small tract entitled, "Life in Review," he penned a deft portrait of himself.

> I grew up on a farm, became a Christian at fourteen, a minister at thirty, and never retired. Luke 9:62.
>
> I was anxious to be useful but was not ambitious for honors and office, and my wishes were more than fulfilled. Mark 10:43, 44.
>
> I found that answers to prayers were wisely limited by the wisdom of God, and so it was safe for me to pray. Mark 7:7.

CHAPTER TWENTY-SIX

President Gossard and the New Era

DURING THE PRESIDENCY of Dr. George Daniel Gossard, Lebanon Valley College entered a new world: that of the comfortably-endowed, fully-accredited modern American college of Liberal Arts.

To say that, is not to belittle the work of preceding presidents. In its long struggle for recognition and acceptance, the College had had many partial successes. There had been Vickroy's well-rounded curriculum—without students to profit from it, Roop's handsome circle of college buildings—without funds to complete them, Keister's bid for high academic standards—without proper support from the students or the Board. Under Dr. Gossard, the College had all the students it could accommodate, sufficient funds to expand yet keep out of debt, and higher standards along with enthusiastic support from the student body and the Board of Trustees.

So great a success, achieved as it was within ten years of his coming to the College, was a surprise to some who had questioned his qualifications as an educator.

He was born near Greencastle, Franklin County, on November 26, 1868. His father was Hilary Gossard, a farmer. His mother was Anna Mary Rebecca, née Zentmeyer. His early education was in the public schools of his native county.

When the family moved across the neighboring border into Maryland, he transferred to the public schools of Washington County in that state. After preparatory studies in the West Virginia Normal and Classical Academy at Buckhannon, West Virginia, he entered Otterbein University in 1890. There he enrolled in the Classical Course, graduating with an A.B. degree in 1892. Deeply religious and feeling a call to the United Brethren ministry, he entered Union Biblical Seminary in Dayton, Ohio, where he graduated, after losing one year through illness, in 1896 with the degree of B.D.

Ordained in 1898, he served pastorates, first, on the Marion Circuit, where he had three churches to attend to; then at Shippensburg; and finally at Salem Church in Baltimore, where he remained for ten years. His success in Baltimore brought him the honorary degree of D.D. from Lebanon Valley College in

Rev. George D. Gossard, D.D.
President, ~~1908~~1912 – *1932*

1910. Two years later, after the resignation of Dr. Keister, he was elected to the presidency of the College.

What Dr. Gossard lacked in academic administrative experience, he made up for in energy, enthusiasm, and a genius for getting on with people. Energy and enthusiasm are qualities which easily get out of hand. Fortunately Dr. Gossard was blessed with a natural courtesy that rested on warm and sincere friendliness toward those around him. He was a Christian by instinct as well as by conviction.

For the president of a college which, for some years past, had been plagued with student fractiousness, Dr. Gossard's quick understanding (even if not sharing) what others felt about matters in dispute, was the greatest help to him in winning what he called the "loyalty" of the student body.

His dignity was innate. Whether or not he was in agreement with you, he met you on your level and, if possible, on your terms. Reproof from him could be as engaging as a compliment. For evidence of that truth, an unprejudiced witness, Ollie Butterwick, will take the stand:

> Dr. Gossard—we all loved him, you know—he preached in our church, First Church in York, and, after the service, while we were shaking hands, I said to Dr. Gossard, "Dr. Gossard, you had me a little worried during your service."
> He says, "Why?"
> "Well," I says, "I was afraid you would end up in Kadesh-barnea, because of

all the sermons I've ever heard you deliver, you always end up in Kadesh-barnea."
And he put his big, huge arms around me, and he says: "Ollie Butterwick, if I had you on the campus, I'd pin your ears back. But," he says, "there's one thing I want to tell you. I wish that I could have had the pleasure and the experience of being at college for six months when that gang of yours was there. Things are so quiet. There's nothing doing at all. I miss that campus life."

When Dr. Gossard became President, the Board of Trustees gave him a few instructions. The first of these was to restore harmony, if that were at all possible, between the administration and the student body. In this, with the help of his wife, Ella Augusta (Plitt) Gossard, who was a gifted hostess, his success was immediate. His approach to the students was conciliatory without being soft. He let them see that, within limits, he liked what they liked. It was not condescension that led him to allow the boys to hoist him up into a truck with them to celebrate a football victory. He enjoyed it.

Dr. Gossard's interest in athletics pleased both the undergraduates and the alumni. Within a month of his appointment as president, he was able to report to the Conferences: "The students are quite enthusiastic over the Athletic outlook, and gratefully appreciate the concessions made by the Executive Committee."

Athletic scholarships were granted on a generous scale. The football line grew harder and heavier, the backfield more aggressive. Those were the days of Carl G. Snavely, '15, and the first great team L. V. C. ever had.

To understand the effect on student morale of this change in administration policy, it is necessary to look back a little.

In 1911 the college had only fifteen men on the football squad. There was no scrub team. That year the five college teams L. V. C. played ran up a total of 152 points against Lebanon Valley's 0. In the game that year with the Carlisle Indians, who played Wounded Eye, Jim Thorpe, and Joel Wheelock, the College was beaten 53-0.

It was Ollie Butterwick who captured Snavely. Ollie wanted a "punt" for the team: i.e., an "educated toe," such as Bobby Reigle, '26, exhibited some years later when he electrified grandstands by dropping field goals from back of the fifty-yard line. Carl Snavely, it seems, had it, and Ollie traveled to Danville on the Susquehanna to get him.

Carl said afterwards he had had at the time no intention of going in for higher education, but Ollie was a great salesman. He put his arm around Carl's shoulder and said, "You are going to College." Carl came next day. The rest is history, football history. In 1965, Carl Snavely was one of eight persons elected to the National Football Hall of Fame.

By 1914, Lebanon Valley had a superb team. They ran up a score in eight games of 234 points against their opponents' 22, and *mirabile dictu,* they held the Carlisle Indians to a score of 7-0. There was to be nothing like that again until the days of "Hooks" Mylin, coach, with Charlie Gelbert and the team that beat Brown University.

RONDEAU TO FOOTBALL
by Harold T. Lutz, '23

When football reigns, the hardening ground
Is plowed by cleats; the air profound
Is oft perturbed by rousing clash
Of men whose courage, strength and dash
Make e'en the distant hill resound

As plunging madly, goalward bound,
Against the hostile line they pound;
Resistance acts just like a lash
When football reigns.

Now 'round the end swift as a flash,
Their doughty rivals they abash.
Behind the goal the man is downed,
Once more the gridiron king is crowned,
As echoing cheers together crash
And football reigns.

—The Crucible: Football Number, IX, No. 3

Almost immediately after Dr. Gossard's election, the alumni rallied round, so that in October, 1913, he was able to report that an old dream was coming true. With the consent of the Executive Committee of the Board of Trustees, the Alumni Association was "placing a Gymnasium in the south end of the Administration Building. This," he said, "will meet a long-felt need in the student body and is greatly appreciated by them all."

Not only the students and the alumni, but also the Faculty and the Board of Trustees took pride in the Alumni Gymnasium. When completed in 1914, it took the place of two floors (the upper one cut away except for a small track around the circumference) at the south end of the Administration Building. Students "on the carpet" today, either in the President's or in the Dean's office, may hear beneath their feet (if they ever let their minds wander) the ghostly cries of sophs and frosh playing off a basketball tie.

To the ambitious new Gymnasium the Administration Building contributed a large share of its floor space: seven thousand square feet, according to the announcement in the 1914 *Catalogue*. In addition to the gymnasium proper, the ground floor yielded space for locker rooms for men and for women, shower baths, an apparatus room (with parallel bars, wrestling mats, a vaulting horse, etc.), a "team room," and a handball court. For many years the "gym floor" was used also for social affairs such as the colorful Hallowe'en Party and (when restrictions were relaxed) college dances. There was even talk of adding a swimming pool at the north end of the building, if the Chemistry Lab. could be moved.

162

Relay Team, 1914
Joel Wheelock, William E. Mickey, Paul L. Strickler, David J. Evans

It is not to be supposed, however, that Dr. Gossard spent his first years snuffing the incense of student adulation. Behind the scenes, the College was in danger, as it had always been. The shadow of debt hung over it. A timid endowment campaign in 1913 did little to remove the peril. Without Lawrence Keister and his brothers pouring money into the College's General Fund, the books would not balance. The debt was getting out of hand. In the summer of 1915 a rumor spread among prospective students that the College was closing its doors.

Miss Gladys Fencil tells about it: "My sister Betty had planned to come to college in the fall of 1915, but the report had reached us that it was a question whether or not the College would open in the fall. So we had to delay our arrival in Annville until it was definitely settled that the College would open."

By 1917, Dr. Gossard, had been in office five years. He had fully sized up

Girls' Basketball Team, 1918
Front row: *Louisa Williams, Marguerite Engle;* Second row: *Ethel Rupp,*
Merab Gamble, Helen Bubb, Sadie Houser

the situation, and had made valuable connections throughout the college constituency. Sure of his ground, he undertook with all his vast optimism and energy the College's first well-planned, well-managed endowment campaign. That it was also the first one to fully realize its objectives, is not surprising when it is remembered that the Hon. A. S. Kreider was a powerful ally, paying all campaign expenses and serving as director.

Plans for the campaign had been maturing for some time. A report of the Committee on Education to the General Conference of the Church in May, 1917, recommended that, as part of a general church movement to raise $2,-000,000 in endowment for all its various colleges, Lebanon Valley be encouraged to raise $250,000 from its own constituency.

In June of the same year, the College's Board of Trustees at its annual meeting, passed a resolution: "That the effort be continued to raise $250,000 at the earliest time possible; that $80,000 be applied to debt and current expenses and the balance on endowment and buildings."

"The task seems herculean," said Dr. Gossard in his large, eager way to the

East Pennsylvania conference in October, "but it appeals to the heroic—to the best that is in us."

A few weeks later, on November 16, 1917, the campaign was formally opened at a special meeting of the Board of Trustees held in Annville "to formulate methods and plans for collecting an adequate endowment fund of at least $250,000."

A planning committee was appointed, consisting of Bishop W. H. Bell; Dr. S. C. Enck, Superintendent of the East Pennsylvania Conference; Dr. A. B. Statton, Superintendent of the Pennsylvania Conference; the Hon. A. S. Kreider, President of the Board of Trustees; and Dr. Gossard, President of the College.

The Virginia Conference, a doughty ally which, it may be remembered, had at one time given Lebanon Valley College the strongest financial backing of any of the co-operating conferences, was at the moment too much engrossed with looking after its own Shenandoah Collegiate Institute. "We are sure, however," said President Gossard, "it will help all it can." The main load was carried by the Pennsylvania and East Pennsylvania conferences.

In 1918, a year later, President Gossard, in a report to the Conferences, was able to say:

> . . . The campaign was conducted by a strong Executive Committee with Bishop Bell, Chairman. The Hon. A. S. Kreider was unanimously elected director of the campaign. The territory was divided into 27 groups and each was presided over by a group leader. These groups were further arranged into five zones, with one or more men presiding over each zone. The organization extended to the local churches and was complete in every form.
>
> . . . When everything was ready the command to go forward was given. Sixteen thousand individual notes were signed and about one thousand cash subscriptions were made.
>
> Too much credit cannot be given Congressman Kreider and his corps of trained workers for the masterly and successful way in which he conducted the campaign. The total amount pledged was $382,357. . . .
>
> We thank personally every man, woman and child who in any way with their prayers, sympathy, service or money, contributed to the success of the campaign. . . .

It was not to be expected, of course, that "sympathy, service or money" should be the *universal* response to hard-boiled letters of solicitation. One pastor, at least, objected to a preliminary request to furnish the names of some members of his congregation who were "good prospects." A copy of a letter written from campaign headquarters and now preserved in the College Memorabilia Room, gives more than a hint of the language the good pastor had used:

May 1, 1918

My dear brother, we are not trying to rob these people; we are not trying to

The Hon. A. S. Kreider

gouge them or take their money from them by force, or go to them and say that their pastor told us they are worth a certain amount, and can pay a certain amount, and insist upon them paying it. No-No-No. . . .

In the main, the co-operation was superb. In his report to the conferences, Dr. Gossard asked "That God may bless all the United Brethren in the East. . . ."

At the close of his seventh year (1919) in the College, the President looked back as a veteran might have done at the close of a long but victorious campaign.

> At the beginning of the present Administration seven years ago [he reported to the Conferences] it was asked that three definite things be accomplished. They were first, a better and more loyal spirit among the students, second, a larger student body and third, an adequate endowment fund.
>
> I am pleased to state what everybody knows, that all of these objects have been accomplished.

That this success had been achieved during the years of the First World War made it all the more remarkable. The student body had been seriously reduced by the drafting of men into the armed services. To offset a situation that threatened the solvency of colleges all across the country, the Federal Government instituted the S. A. T. C. (Student Army Training Corps) program. Suddenly the Mens' Dormitory at Lebanon Valley College found itself turned into barracks.

The Student Army Training Corps

The men who occupied it were draft registrants who had enlisted voluntarily for training as officers or technicians in the "War for Democracy." In the unit at Lebanon Valley College, there were three officers and one hundred men, with two sailors "attached for duty." The enlisted men took work with the regular college classes, and in addition received special training in battalion drill, battalion guard mount, and "the development and solution of field problems."

To have soldiers drilling on the campus of Lebanon Valley College might have shocked the Mennonite ancestors of some of the girls who watched them. The Calendar of Events in the 1920 *Quittapahilla* (published in the spring of 1919) contains many glimpses of Lebanon Valley's war-time campus:

> [Tuesday, September 24, 1918.] School opens. Everything strangely military. S. A. T. C. squads drilling all over the campus. Boys' dorm now called "barracks." The army's the main thing.
>
> [Friday, October 4.] S. A. T. C. quarantined. [The flu had struck.] Students told in chapel that they may go home if they choose. . . .
>
> [Sunday, October 6.] . . . All but 15 leave. . . .
>
> [Saturday, October 12.] Dreary days. And it rained. . . . A squad of S. A. T. C. men detailed to entertain the girls. Each one appears at North Hall in the evening with a box of chocolates.
>
> [Saturday, October 19.] Privates Bachman, Harvey, and Giles forget they aren't in college and start some old-time roughhousing. And then they get a week K. P.

[Sunday, October 20.] Sergt. [Norman] Bouder brings Lieuts. Haight and Richardson over and introduces them to the ladies. The S. A. T. C. orchestra adds to the evening's entertainment.

[Thursday, November 7.] Rumor that war's over. Teachers can't keep young patriots in classes. Excitement runs high. Bells ringing and whistles blowing. The army does a snake dance on the campus. Parade in town.

[Friday, November 8.] . . . Rumor false.

[Monday, November 11.] Awakened at 4:30 A.M. by the bells and whistles of Lebanon. Peace here at last. Great jubilation. No classes. College and town parade the streets in the early dawn. S. A. T. C. goes to Lebanon to parade in the afternoon. Big celebration in Annville in the evening. Girls dress in white and carry Japanese lanterns.

[Wednesday, December 11.] S. A. T. C. disbanded. . . . Young Clionians parade around all day with strange, gold symbols on their faces and hair combed back tightly.

[Thursday, December 12.] Unsettled conditions reign supreme.

With peace abroad and the campus demilitarized, college life came back to normal.

[Wednesday, January 29, 1919.] Door knobs of all the buildings lubricated with an over-dose of axle grease. Tombstone in front of Library covered with tar. No [hymn-] books in chapel. Faculty beats 'em to their game by singing "Onward Christian Soldiers," and "My Country 'Tis of Thee."

[Tuesday, February 4.] The ever-famed Freshman-Sophomore game is partly played, when Prof. Grimm declares it against rules and breaks it up. Long the angry billows roar.

[Wednesday, February 5.] The morning after the night before. Strange sights greet the eyes on the campus. Chapel chairs in a ring around Prof. Grimm's grave. . . .

Delphian Literary Society

On November 4, 1921, a "Reception for Prospective Members" of a new Literary Society, the Delphian, was given. Words of welcome were spoken for the Seniors by Meta Burbeck, for the Juniors by Kathryn Kratzert, and for the Sophomores by Ruth Oyer.

The following are listed in the "Secretary Book" as charter members:

Meta Burbeck	Kathryn Balsbach [Balsbaugh]
Effie Hibbs	Mary Hershey
Larry [Erdean] Lerew	Regina Edris
Gertrude Gingrich	Matilda Bowman
Verna Hess	Ruth Baker
Betty Smith	Elsie Clark
Kathryn Kratzert	Lola Desenberg
Helen Hughes	Isabelle Smith
Mae Reeves	Sue Zeigler
Martha Gingrich	Martha Zeigler

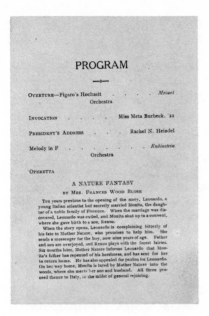

PROGRAM

OVERTURE—Figaro's Hochzeit . . . . *Mozart*
Orchestra

INVOCATION . . . . Miss Meta Burbeck, '22

PRESIDENT'S ADDRESS . . . Rachel N. Heindel

Melody in F . . . . *Rubinstein*
Orchestra

OPERETTA

A NATURE FANTASY
BY MRS. FRANCES WOOD BLOSE

Ten years previous to the opening of the story, Leonardo, a young Italian scientist had secretly married Monita, the daughter of a noble family of Florence. When the marriage was discovered, Leonardo was exiled, and Monita shut up in a convent, where she gave birth to a son, Renno.

When the story opens, Leonardo is complaining bitterly of his fate to Mother Nature, who promises to help him. She sends a messenger for the boy, now nine years of age. Father and son are overjoyed, and Renno plays with the forest fairies. Six months later, Mother Nature informs Leonardo that Monita's father has repented of his harshness, and has sent for her to return home. He has also appealed for pardon for Leonardo. On her way home, Monita is lured by Mother Nature into the woods, where she meets her son and husband. All three proceed thence to Italy, in the midst of general rejoicing.

Delphian Literary Society,
Second Anniversary,
Engle Conservatory,
Friday, February 22, 1924

Anna Long	Marion Strayer
Kathryn Long	Helen Hostetter
Frances Durbin	Dorothy Longenecker
Dorothy Fencil	Kathryn Nissley
Florence Siefried	Maude Wolfe
Helen Mealey	Betty Brenneman
Esther Singer	Alta Bingham
Mary Yinger	Stella Hughes
Rachel Heindel	Mae Reider
Ruth Oyer	Margaret Walters

On November 7, officers were elected:

President ....Meta Burbeck
Vice President ....Verna Hess
Corresponding Secretary ....Kathryn Kratzert
Recording Secretary ....Mae Reeves
Treasurer ....Dorothy Fencil
Critic ....Effie Hibbs
Chaplain ....Ruth Oyer
Warden ....Esther Singer
Board of Trustees ....Erdean Lerew
Gertrude Gingrich
Helen Hughes

At a meeting on December 2, Ruth Baker was elected Pianist.

169

Dr. Grimm and Miss Gladys Fencil in the old Registrars Office

CHAPTER TWENTY-SEVEN

"Ask Gladys"

UP AND DOWN the halls of Lebanon Valley College, the most frequently heard words for the past many years have been, "Ask Gladys."

Miss Gladys Fencil has known the College intimately since the day when her sister, Betty, entered it as a student in 1915. She herself entered in 1917, graduating in 1921 with an A.B. degree in Modern Languages. In the latter year she joined the College's secretarial staff, and, during succeeding years, moved from office to office and from position to position as Assistant Registrar, Alumni Secretary, Admissions Director, Registrar, Administrative Assistant, etc., etc., etc. With her phenomenal memory, she has become a treasure-house of information about the curriculum, college finances, students, and alumni. Her wise judgment has made her a safe counselor for faculty members in search of guidance. Competent but unassuming, she has become one of the College's most loved and revered institutions. "Ask Gladys" is, as it were, a referral to the Supreme Court.

When asked, during an interview for the present history, how she came to possess this wealth of useful knowledge, she replied:

> I think it came from working with the records. I worked in the Business Office [under Mr. Barnhart], so I got the financial background of the students; worked in the Registrar's Office [under Professor Grimm], so I got their scholastic background and the personal information, and then later on, when I became Alumni Secretary, we followed the alumni after graduation. . . .

It should be added that her memory has the assistance of an observant eye and great powers of concentration, and that, by a happy coincidence, she has always an air of easy relaxation. You are never made aware, when she answers your questions, of the miracle she is producing.

When F. B. I. investigators came around, as they did now and then (college graduates being often employed in sensitive government positions), they were astonished at her memory for detail. One of these men, wishing to interview the Librarian about a former assistant but not finding Miss Myers in the Library, asked where to look for her.

Gladys replied: "She lives at 120 College Avenue. If you go out and walk up the street to your left, you'll find a pavement that has just been scrubbed and there is where she lives."

The Federal agent was amused at two things: the Pennsylvania Dutch custom of scrubbing the sidewalks, and Gladys Fencil's knowing which pavement at that hour would be wet.

Enshrined in the memory of her student days are patriotic glimpses of the First World War as it touched the L. V. C. campus.

"The girls," she recalls, "were knitting khaki sweaters and writing letters to the boys who were already gone, and making fudge to send."

The S. A. T. C. at that time dominated the campus. Gladys and her classmates watched the men drill in squads of eight about the campus. In particular she remembers one dreadful moment when, as it seemed to very innocent bystanders, a squad leader was about to wreck his detachment:

"We saw one group headed straight for a tree, and just in time the leader called out, 'Halt!' and then the next command was 'About face!' and they headed off in the other direction, much to our relief."

Then came the Armistice and the never-to-be-forgotten mustering out. The flag was flying, with just enough breeze to keep it streaming. The bugles played, the captain spoke, and the boys were dismissed.

This deeply moving moment brought memory of the boys who died in action:

> Max Lehman, '07,
> Marcellus Von Bereghy, '19,
> Miles Thornton, '20,
> Earl Williard, '21,

and others who also died in service:

> Norman C. Potter, '18,
> Solomon Kirkley, '20.

Miss Fencil recalls the Endowment Campaign of 1918, for in the summer of that year she helped address envelopes. She had good reason to remember the fact that campaign headquarters were on the third floor of the Administration Building (in what had formerly been the Art Room)—good reason to remember, because it always seemed such a long way down with the mail. There was no elevator. Those who planned the new Administration Building no doubt remembered that the elevator shaft had been the chief conduit of the flames that destroyed the old building.

The Business Office of the College, when Gladys started to work in it in 1921, was in charge of Mr. Albert Barnhart, Agent of the Finance Committee. Clear-headed, methodical, crisp-spoken, brave as a lion, and utterly dependable, he proved himself to be a great organizer. In this capacity, he did the

College much credit when the Association of Colleges and Secondary Schools of the Middle States and Maryland sent round an examining committee to look into the College's finances.

> He set up the books [said Miss Fencil], which had been done, prior to that time, only in an amateur fashion. He organized the different funds, and he kept very accurate records. When we had to make out the monthly and annual reports, we had supporting data. We even had supporting data for the supporting data!

But even in Mr. Barnhart's premises there were problems, the chief of which came from an unexpected quarter: the printing press used in place of a duplicating machine.

> Mr. Barnhart had formerly been a printer, and he bought for the office a rotary printing press, and it was up to us to learn to set type. There were three of us working in the offices at that time [Margaret Rice, Verda Miles, and Gladys Fencil]. We were the entire secretarial staff for the entire college. We had to learn to set up type, to arrange it on the frames. We didn't mind so much the setting up of the frames, but it was the tearing down that we objected to. Every individual letter had to be put back into its particular groove.
> Mr. Barnhart was a farmer at heart. He went on the theory that it was best for the campus if the grass would seed itself. So each summer he would let the grass go to seed. And so it did until the time we had an irate parent who came in and had to cross the campus from the Administration Building to North Hall —and after that Mr. Barnhart had the grass mowed.
> I remember the first mechanized lawnmower on the campus. Bert Gingrich had rigged up a motor on one of the hand lawnmowers, and Park Brighton was assigned to mow the grass. Park evidently didn't have the correct instructions, and I looked out the window one day and saw the lawnmower going across the campus with Park Brighton running after it. That was the beginning of mechanization on the campus.

Bert Gingrich was the campus plumber. In his head he kept a minute map of all the underground pipe lines—information which Professor Grimm unavailingly tried to get him to commit to paper. He carried it proudly with him to the grave.

Bert served other functions as well. For one, he was the campus meteorologist or weather predictor.

> If anybody wanted to know whether it was going to rain, in case of May day— "Ask Bert Gingrich." He predicted some weather by the caterpillars. If the caterpillars grew their fur real thick, it was going to be a very cold winter.

Professor Grimm, the Registrar, was a magnificent organizer. The examining committee already referred to pronounced the work of Professor Grimm in the Registrar's Office and of Mr. Barnhart in the Business Office, to be altogether superior.

That commendation seems the more remarkable when one remembers the difficulties under which Professor Grimm and his loyal assistant had to work.

Miss Fencil vividly recalls those lean years:

> We had Room 4, which is the room directly across from the Business Office. We had in it one large conference table, and some comfortable chairs. I had a typewriter which was placed on the base of a sewing machine stand. And we had one set of wooden files, consisting of four medium-sized drawers with six or eight small drawers above.
>
> That was in 1921. The records had been burned in the fire of 1904, so we had nothing prior to that; and from 1904 to 1911 the College records, the Academy records, and the Conservatory of Music records were kept in separate books. In 1911 individual card records were introduced.

Miss Fencil, however much she may have disliked the printing press as a substitute for a duplicating machine, has pleasant recollections of the official college printer, Anselm Hiester, whose cluttered-up shop (modelled, apparently, on the old-fashioned country store) was situated just off the campus at the corner of White Oak and Church Streets.

> He was a very busy man. When you went in, he was always busy and always told you how busy he was; but yet would very much object if you left without paying a little visit. So, if you did pay the little visit, you really got your work done faster and you got a better job.
>
> He didn't send out bills to the College, and Mr. Barnhart was particular about asking every month for a bill. But he would get no reply, until finally the end of the fiscal year would come around and Mr. Barnhart really felt he had to have this bill to clear his accounts. So Mr. Heister would then get his bill out, which would run maybe a thousand or two thousand dollars. He would report then he had been saving—holding these bills in reserve in order to get money together to put a roof on his house, for example, or something of a similar nature. Finally Mr. Barnhart did get him to send bills monthly, but then we found that the checks were not being cashed very promptly and at the end of the year we would have checks out. But at least we did know what the bills were.

Three professors whom Gladys Fencil recalls from her student days, 1917-1921, were Professor Samuel H. Derickson (Biology), Professor Charlotte F. McLean (English), and Professor May Belle Adams (Oratory and Dramatics).

Miss Adams impressed everyone with her energy and initiative. She had a mobile, expressive face, and she gave her classes exercises in visibly registering emotion. Gladys Fencil remembers that on one occasion she instructed a group to register feelings on hearing a cry of "Fire." The class ran out of the room and did not return.

> In addition to serving as a teacher of Public Speaking [said Miss Fencil], she was Preceptress at South Hall. And nobody went up or down the hallway or up the stairs without the door opening at the bottom of the stairs and Miss Adams looking out to see who might be coming and going.

Dr. Charlotte F. McLean startled her first class in Freshman English because, out of consideration for the students' pocket books, she advised them to buy slates (which she had priced at Wanamakers in Philadelphia) instead of paper and lead pencils. One boy did, but the rest of the class declined, for auditory reasons.

Dr. McLean was well-respected as a teacher, but, as happens so often with all of us, it is little things that are remembered.

> We liked her hat. It was a fur hat, shaped something on the order of a football helmet. When she would come to class, she would put it on her chair and proceed to sit on it.
>
> She had another little peculiarity. In the dining hall in those days, some of the cups didn't have handles. She would drink her coffee and then drop her cup on the floor.

Dr. Derickson—scholar and administrator (for a few months Acting President) was at the peak of his form in Gladys' student days.

> Professor Derickson—then known as "Prof. Deri"—had a love for his work that you very seldom find in anybody—to the point of really ruining his health. When we came in as Sophomores to take his General Biology course, he had been ill, I believe as a result of overexposure while watching birds. He wasn't allowed to speak aloud. He spoke in a whisper during that year, and we whispered back.
>
> I remember well a bird study class. We would go out in the morning and look for birds. We wouldn't see a bird or hear a bird, but Prof. Deri would start to whistle bird calls, and before long we had birds all around. I remember particularly one time when we went to the woods, he made the sound of a young bird, as though it had been hurt, and he had a squirrel running up and down his arm hunting for the bird.
>
> He said, "We'll go over here and see the heron."
>
> Well, I don't know if the heron knew he was coming or not, but when we got there, there was a Great Blue Heron.
>
> And we would go to Gretna, and he knew every plant around the place. I just never knew anybody who had the knowledge of the countryside he had.

Lebanon Valley College's communication services in 1921 depended largely upon "shanks' mare."

> We had a phone in the Business Office and in the President's Office and those were the only ones in the Administration Building for quite a while. Calls came in on the Business Office phone for the faculty as well as business transactions. So, if a faculty member was called on the phone, you would ask if it was important. Yes, it was always important! So we would go up and get the faculty member to come down and answer the phone. And, of course, for long distance calls you'd travel a little faster. Then, finally, the Registrar's Office did get a phone, and so for many years we had the three phones. Now we have a central switchboard with over twenty extensions in the same Administration Building.

The main campus entrance
Gate posts by the Class of 1914, tower clock by the Class of 1913

CHAPTER TWENTY-EIGHT

Accreditation

DR. GOSSARD'S two decades as President saw the College grow into maturity.

"During his administration," wrote Professor Derickson in *La Vie Collègienne,* April 21, 1932, "the size of the student body, the number of teachers, the amount paid to teachers have been multiplied by more than three times. Considerably more than half of the alumni have graduated during this period."

These figures touch only the surface of what Dr. Gossard accomplished. His real contribution was to change the whole character of the institution and to reorient its objectives. Through the steps taken to win a place for the College on the list of accredited institutions issued by the Association of Colleges and Secondary Schools of the Middle States and Maryland, he brought it into full fellowship with the American Liberal Arts fraternity. These steps were taken with the support of the Faculty, student body, Board of Trustees, and Co-operating Conferences; and they were taken without in any degree weakening the College's foundations as a Christian institution.

There had always been at the head of the College men who understood the secret elixir of a Liberal Arts College, which is this (with apologies to John Keats): *Freedom brings Truth, Truth Freedom.* "For what earth, air, fire, and water are to animate nature, freedom is to learning," said Alfred Whitney Griswold, former President of Yale. But so conservative had been those upon whom the College had to rely for support during its first fifty years that it had been unable to break convention and deliberately cultivate intellectual curiosity.

There was, however, arising a powerful ally of those who believed in intellectual freedom. This was an organization, founded in 1887, first known as the College Association of Pennsylvania and subsequently, after a number of changes, as the Association of Colleges and Secondary Schools of the Middle States and Maryland. Lebanon Valley College (then under President DeLong) was a charter member.

When it was proposed in 1921 that this Association should publish a list, prepared by a special committee, of approved colleges in its area, Lebanon Valley hoped to be numbered among the elect. When it was learned that, in many particulars, she failed to come up to standard, the shock was severe.

It appeared that the College lacked sufficient endowment to be financially safe, that there were too few Ph.D's on the staff, the professors were overworked and underpaid, student admissions requirements were remiss, the Academy should be discontinued, the Library lacked a trained librarian and its list of periodicals was not up-to-date. In a word, the Association's Commission on Institutions of Higher Education, as explained by its chairman in a letter of November 22, 1921, "did not find it possible to place Lebanon Valley College upon the list."

With a burst of energy such as the College had seldom seen before, Dr. Gossard poured out his influence upon the Board, Alumni, and college supporters everywhere to win the means with which to improve the College's standing with the new accrediting agency. He took his disappointment without rancor or frustration. He knew the examiners who had visited the place had been nonplussed by some of the weaknesses discovered there. He knew at the same time that they had been pleased with the vitality and promise of the institution. They were only too anxious to speak well of it.

The Crucible, in its issue of December 10, 1921, had this to say:

> We must give credit where credit is due. Sometime ago, when certain authorities were passing thru our precincts looking over things in general in and about the college, two phases of college work received especial commendation. It was their confidential opinion that they had never found the business books and records of a college in better condition than those kept by Mr. Barnhart, the agent of our finance committee. Also, the system of our registrar, Prof. Grimm, was declared faultless and unexcelled, ranking high in efficiency above that of the average college and university.

Dr. Gossard sensed what the members of the examining committee felt, namely that Lebanon Valley College had the vital spark and needed only *direction* and *encouragement* to become a first-rate institution of higher learning.

On January 10, 1922, Dr. Gossard addressed a letter to Dr. Adam Leroy Jones, Chairman of the Commission on Institutions of Higher Education:

> . . . I am writing you a letter covering the points at issue that concern the Committee on Standardization. . . .
>
> (1) On Endowment we now have $308,746.43 invested and yielding an average of five percent. Besides this we have subscriptions amounting to $127,000, of which $80,000 will not be due until October 1, 1922. Besides this, we have been receiving $8,000 a year for the past seven years from the co-operating conferences. In addition to this the General Education Board is contributing $8,000 a year for this year and next toward teachers' salaries. You can see from these figures that we are beyond the limit in income required by the Commission. . . .
>
> (2) We have secured a trained Librarian [Miss Helen Ethel Myers] and are paying her $2,000 a year.

The Faculty, 1924–1925

Front row: *R. R. Butterwick, Ruth Engle, Mary C. Green, President*
G. D. Gossard, Ethel Mary Bennett, Helen Ethel Myers, C. R. Gingrich.
Second row: *J. T. Spangler, H. H. Shenk, Harold Bennett, Andrew Bender,*
E. E. Mylin.
Third row: *S. O. Grimm, S. H. Derickson, J. E. Lehman, B. H. Redditt.*
Top row: *O. E. Reynolds, T. B. Beatty, F. H. Hardman, R. P. Campbell,*
E. E. Stauffer, Harold Malsh.

(3) As to the periodicals, we think our list is the equivalent of other colleges in the State, however, if you desire to suggest additions that need to be made we shall be pleased to add such numbers.

(4) Now as to the Faculty, I beg to state that we added one professor with the Ph.D. degree last summer after we received your letter of June 30. His name is Andrew Bender. He received his Bachelor's degree at Lebanon Valley College and the Doctor of Philosophy degree from Columbia University. He is a very able man. The authorities of the college have authorized the securing of a man with the Ph.D. degree for the Chair of Education. We will add such a man without a doubt [Dr. O. E. Reynolds, who came in 1924]. About 80% of our graduates of the last six years have gone into the teaching profession. The same committee authorized the election of a man with the Ph.D. degree for the department of Latin. This too will be done without fail [Dr. Harold Bennett came later in 1922]. Other Professors with the Ph.D. degree or its equivalent will be secured as vacancies occur or the need requires.

(5) As to salaries I am pleased to report that three of our professors are being paid $2500 each for the school term and six of them are being paid $2420 each. . . .

(6) Our professors teach twelve to sixteen hours per week. There are two exceptions, one in the department of Latin where the classes are small and one

in Mathematics where a duplication of sections made it necessary to do good work.

(7) . . . (A) I am pleased to state that at a joint meeting of the Executive, Finance, and Faculty Committees it was voted to "require for admission not less than four years of academic or high school preparation or its equivalent" in accordance with the requirements of your commission. . . .

(B) The academy will be discontinued at the end of this year.

Dr. Gossard took opportunity to call on each of the fourteen commissioners individually. In his charming, open-hearted, sometimes naive, but always frank and disarming way, he drew their attention to the College's indomitable spirit, its grass-roots origin, its survival against all odds, its good buildings, its faculty growing in size and attainments, and the distinctive role it was playing in bringing higher education into the homes of its community.

The Commissioners must have pondered the question: Was Lebanon Valley College, after all, doing what they themselves had advocated—serving its particular community with a full understanding of that community's capacities and idiosyncrasies?

At a regular meeting of the Standardization Commission of the Middle States Association held in New York on May 26, 1922, Dr. Gossard appeared in person and addressed them on behalf of his institution. He made no false pretenses. He admitted the College's precarious past and its present difficulties, but he proclaimed his confidence in its future if it were accredited. He was irresistible.

"Within a minute," as he reported to the Conferences, "the commission voted unanimously to place Lebanon Valley College on the approved list."

In a letter of June 1, 1922, Dr. Gossard concluded the incident in a burst of boyish high spirits:

My dear Doctor Jones:

I want to thank you and every member of the Commission on Standardization for the very happy news which came to me first through Dr. Irvine who caught me at the sub-way station, second, by telegram and third by letter. . . .

I did not reach home until midnight Saturday, then I kept the delightful news to myself until the Chapel period on Monday morning when I told the story to students and faculty keeping them in suspense until the last sentence was spoken. I am sure it would have tickled the heart of every member of the Commission to see and hear the demonstration. One fellow came to me afterward and said, "I have not been so happy since I was in a revival three years ago. . ."

Sincerely,
G. D. Gossard

CHAPTER TWENTY-NINE

The Benders

DR. ANDREW BENDER
(From the 1948 *Quittapahilla*)

Amid the ever surrounding mass of test tubes and beakers
　Works a man who has put his heart and soul into a fight;
A fight on the upward way—the way of truth,
　A fight to better his field, himself, and his college.
To this man we dedicate this book.

Through his many years in the service of humanity,
　Through his triumph over partial blindness and great loneliness,
He served his country in time of need, and humanity always.
　It is to this man we dedicate this book.

True leader, friend, and ever-guiding counselor,
　Human dynamo, working that others may better live;
Patient teacher, even with the least of us, a genius in his own right.
　It is to him we dedicate this book.

It is because he explaineth when everything is so dark,
　It is because he upholds "John 8:32",
It is because he lives with molecules—always hoping to meet
　　a new one
　(Or a new way to meet an old one),
That we, who profited by his influence, his sincerity,
　And his wealth of knowledge,
　Do dedicate to him this book.

Dr. Andrew Bender in his laboratory

MRS. RUTH ENGLE BENDER
(From the 1948 *Quittapahilla*)

At the side of the man with the test tubes
 Stands a woman whose life is music.
The seldom found blend of artist and homemaker
 Unusually thoughtful, kindly and sympathetic.
To this woman also we dedicate this book.

As a teacher—patient and understanding,
 As a civic leader—aggressive and energetic,
As a friend—kind, loving and generous,
 As an artist—supreme.

In her church a constant worker, a doer of good and right deeds,
 In her home a fine hostess and homemaker,
As a woman—cultured, sweet, and gentle,
 Devoted to her family, church, college and community.

It is because she brings sunshine to darkened lives,
 And is tireless in her devotion to others;
It is because her life is composed of music and love,
 And all that is fine and honest,
That we, who have been taught not only how to play or
  write music—
 But how to make hearts sing,
Do dedicate this book.

CHAPTER THIRTY

Momentum

IT WAS TEAM WORK among the Conferences, the Board of Trustees, the Business Office, the Faculty, and the student body that, under Dr. Gossard's personal leadership, had won for Lebanon Valley College the great advances of his first decade. It was team work again in the second decade that, despite his failing health, enabled the College to continue its momentum.

The success of the endowment campaign in 1918 had given the College a new sense of power—an assurance, as Dr. Gossard said, of its "ability to meet emergencies, and put across big propositions." The further success of the campaign for accreditation left, however, a danger: that the supporting Conferences might think that all was now accomplished and in consequence turn their attention aside to other concerns.

To meet this danger, the President reminded them that Lebanon Valley College, in entering adulthood, had acquired the responsibilities that go with it. In particular he asked the Conferences to observe that neighboring colleges of other denominations, in order to hold their positions in a world which put increasing demands upon scholarship, found it necessary to keep on enlarging their endowments. Lebanon Valley College was no exception. It must have more money. He outlined plans for a supreme effort to raise the College's present endowment to the neighborhood of a million dollars—after first wiping out a debt of $88,247.

With the dazzling sight of a near million dollars in their eyes, the 1924 Campaign Committee elected as director J. Raymond Engle of Palmyra, engaged a professional money-getting firm to handle the rough work, and put forth a burst of energy that surprised even itself. With the aid of ministers, laymen, and every soul within reach of Dr. Gossard's infectious enthusiasm, the campaign was conducted with such pride and determination as enabled Dr. Gossard to make this report to the Co-operating Conferences in 1925:

> The past year in many ways has been the greatest in the history of Lebanon Valley College. First, it witnessed the completion of a great financial campaign in which $700,000 was subscribed for the college for endowment, debt and faculty salaries. Second, the paying of the debt of $88,247.08 by the two annual con-

ferences, East Pennsylvania and Pennsylvania, is considered one of the greatest achievements in the history of the institution. This debt hung as a millstone about the neck of the College for many years. These great conferences after subscribing hundreds of thousands of dollars for endowment, said: "We will not let our college fail, but will help it in this time of its greatest need and opportunity." Therefore, on March 31, 1925, East Pennsylvania Conference brought a check for $54,123.54 and Pennsylvania Conference a check for $34,123.54. Truly this was a godsend, for it not only paid the debt but made possible funds from the General Education Board (Rockefeller), New York, to the extent of $175,000 and greatly inspired our people with a determination to put their College on its feet and send it on its way in the great work of Christian education. Third, the graduating of the largest class (seventy) that ever went out from its halls.

In 1923, the curriculum was overhauled and some important changes were made. A total of 124 semester hours (exclusive of Physical Education), with a grade of C or better in half that number, was required for graduation.

The system of Majors and Minors was introduced in place of the old Group system. As the *Catalogue* was to announce with but little change (except for an increase in the number of semester hours required and for some additional courses) for the next thirty years and more:

> . . . As part of this total requirement [124 hours], every candidate must present at least 24 semester hours in one department (to be known as his Major), and at least 16 semester hours in another department (to be known as his Minor). Both Major and Minor must be selected not later than the beginning of the Junior year, the Minor to be suitably related to the Major, and chosen with the advice and approval of the Head of the Major department.
>
> The A.B. degree will be awarded to those fulfilling the requirements for a Major in the following departments: Bible and New Testament Greek, English, French, German, Greek, History, Latin, Mathematics (Arts option), Political and Social Science, Philosophy and Religion.
>
> The B.S. degree will be awarded to those fulfilling the requirements for a Major in the following departments: Biology, Chemistry, Mathematics (Science option), Physics.
>
> The B.S. in Ed. degree will be awarded to those fulfilling the requirements for a Major in Education, but in this case two Minors of not less than 16 semester hours each must be presented.

Throughout his presidency, Dr. Gossard maintained the improved relationships between students and Administration he had secured on his arrival. He accomplished this in subtle ways, through his own sympathetic insight into young minds. He could be strict (as, for instance, in the close faculty censorship he established of *La Vie Collègienne,* the student newspaper which succeeded the defunct *College News.*) In most things, however, he preferred a more liberal policy, relieving explosive pressures by reducing inhibitions. He would not allow the Administration Building to be locked at night lest locks should only tempt the Death League to break in.

He believed that healthy relations between the sexes would be encouraged by greater freedom of association than their demure grandmothers had known. His attitude toward the formerly inflammable subject of dancing will serve to illustrate his liberal tendency.

Dr. S. O. Grimm has an interesting reminiscence about Dr. Gossard in this connection:

> The dancing problem was a very vital concern in the 1920's, and I quite well remember that President Gossard was very much concerned about the whole problem. On one occasion, I now recall, he was in his office at the same time that there was an affair going on in the college gymnasium. And up to that point dancing at such functions had been strictly forbidden. I was in the Registrar's Office for some purpose, and, seeing that President Gossard was in his office, I dropped in to see him.
>
> Noticing that he was somewhat disturbed, I said to him, "What are your principal problems at the moment, President?"
>
> And he said, "Well, I've just been reflecting on the situation which now presents itself in the gymnasium, and I have just made up my mind that I'm going to go down there and say to them that they may conduct a dance with my blessing."
>
> He went down, and thus for the first time in the history of the College a dance was permitted by the official blessing of the President of the College.

The triumphs, financial and scholarly, of 1918, 1922, and 1924, were only the beginning. The visible effects of her financial victories—doubly precious to a college emerging from more than forty years wandering in the wilderness of debt—were seen in repaired buildings, a more beautiful campus, and improved equipment for the science laboratories. They were also evidenced in more adequate salaries (gone were the days when professors took their families for meals to the college dining hall in lieu of salary), and in a more highly specialized staff.

Year after year, Dr. Gossard (with an eye over his shoulder on the Middle States Association's accrediting committee) reported the growing number of Ph.D's on the Faculty: Dr. Andrew Bender in 1921, Dr. Harold Bennett in 1922, Dr. O. E. Reynolds in 1924, Dr. Paul A. W. Wallace in 1925, Dr. Paul Wagner in 1926, Dr. E. H. Stevenson (a Rhodes Scholar) and Dr. Mary Stella Johnson in 1928 (these two producing shortly thereafter a conjunction of names to correspond with their conjunction of dates). Dr. V. Earl Light entered in 1929.

In that year, 1929, the President reported that thirteen members of he Faculty had "the Doctor's degree, its equivalent or more." Among those with the "equivalent or more" were Milton L. Stokes, M.A., LL.B. (his Ph.D. came later), and Miriam R. Polk, A.B., M.D., who had come in 1926 and 1928 respectively, as well as a number whose long professional training and experience had received recognition in the form of honorary degrees. "Madame" Green (Mrs. Mary Capp Green), though without a college degree, brought from her many years abroad in Florence, Berlin, Johannesburg, and especially Paris, a wealth of experience and cosmopolitan elegance that made her so much loved and respected during her long career as Social Dean of Women. For six years (1922–1928) Ethel Mary Bennett (wife of Dr. Harold Bennett) was Professor of French Literature and German.

In 1930, Dr. Raymond T. Ohl, fresh from experience in Rome, Italy, joined the staff. The year 1931 brought four more Ph.D.'s: Dr. George G. Struble in English, who was to be for over thirty years Secretary of the Faculty and after 1949 Chairman of the Department of English. Dr. Alvin H. M. Stonecipher in Latin, who was soon to be Dean of the College; Dr. Lena Louise Lietzau from Vienna, for many years Professor of German; and Dr. Chester Baldwin Pond, assisting Professor Stokes in Business Administration.

In the great adventure of building a strong L. V. C., the new flock of teachers (from all over the world) joined enthusiastically with the local corps of already well-established professors: John Evans Lehman, James T. Spangler, Hiram H. Shenk, Samuel Hoffman Derickson, Alvin E. Shroyer, T. Bayard Beatty, Robert R. Butterwick, Christian R. Gingrich, Madame Green, Samuel O. Grimm, and G. A. Richie.

Professor Grimm's career will illustrate the wide-ranging duties performed by the early corps of teachers at the College. There were giants in those days! His active service at L. V. C. has in this Centennial year set a record of fifty-five years. It began in 1911, his Senior year, when he was an Assistant in Biology. On graduation with the class of 1912, he was appointed Principal of the Academy. Next year he added to that position an instructorship in Physics, which in 1914 became a full professorship. In 1916–1917, still Principal of the Academy, he was also Professor of Physics and Professor of Education. In 1920, having shed the Academy, he added to his two professorships, Physics and Education, the duties of the Registrar. In 1923 he dropped Education but took on Mathematics, and remained from 1923 to 1949 Professor of Physics, Professor of Mathematics, and Registrar. Today he continues to hold the rank of Professor of Physics.

In a fine spirit of team play, these veterans and the new recruits together (men and women from different backgrounds and of healthily divergent views) worked closely together building foundations for what they believed in their hearts to be a glorious future for L. V. C. This happy academic family was Dr. Gossard's final miracle.

His twentieth year in office was his last. He died, April 17, 1932, "in harness" as he had wished.

In his death, the College lost a powerful advocate and each member of the Faculty and the student body, a considerate friend: one who, as Dr. Derickson said, loved simplicity, was unpretentious, and was always accessible.

From the pen of Dr. Hiram H. Shenk, long-time Professor of History (and for some years also State Archivist in Harrisburg), whose eloquent lectures for years enraptured audiences not only at the College but all over Pennsylvania and neighboring States, and whose weight in church and academic councils had won for him the nickname of "the President Maker," came this tribute:

> From the days of Dr. Gossard's election to the Presidency of the college to the time of his death, his whole life was dedicated to the interests of the institution. He had no outside interests. . . . His generosity and his sympathetic spirit enabled him to appreciate the problems of the students, and to no appeal from them did he turn a deaf ear. . . .
>
> His gentlemanly bearing, his unfailing courtesy, his forgiving spirit have left lasting impression on all who had the privilege of being associated with him.

Best of all tributes is a discriminating and understanding appraisal of the man and his works by Dr. Harold Bennett. Dr. Bennett (the founding-President of Laurentian University in northern Ontario) had his initiation in administrative work at Lebanon Valley College under Dr. Gossard.

A Tribute to George D. Gossard

By a former member of his staff at Lebanon Valley College, Annville

I remember Dr. Gossard as a big, vigorous, jovial gentleman with a Baltimore accent and a heart that embraced all mankind but kept a special compartment for the sons and daughters of United Brethren, for whom he coveted a better education than was common in that time and place. He was always the champion of underdogs—especially of athletic underdogs who could play football. It nearly broke his heart when exam results showed a string of D's and F's, and at such times the Faculty had to be firm with him. On the whole, however, he wanted higher standards at L. V. C. and succeeded in his endeavor to have it accredited as a recognized degree-granting college. He assembled a faculty which was unusually good for such a small institution, and in spite of the Pennsylvania thrift that characterized his constituency, managed to pay them respectable salaries. He matched an offer which I had received from a much bigger college [Carleton, of whom the President was then Donald J. Cowling, L. V. C. '02] and sold me the idea that a Pennsylvania valley was a much pleasanter place to live than the western prairie. I have never regretted my six years of service under his administration.

Many of the abler students I knew at L. V. C. responded so well to instruction that they went on to graduate studies in the great universities and achieved distinguished careers. Under Dr. Gossard's leadership the college became a source of pride to a church and a community which, before his time, had regarded a college education as an extravagant interruption of the formative period in which a young man or woman of the industrious, thrifty Pennsylvania stock prepared for the serious business of life.

Cyrano de Bergerac, 1928

Nancy Ulrich, Paul Barnhart, Byron Sheetz, Russell Oyer, Edward Orbock,
Millard Miller, Henry Kohler, Bruce Behney, Uhl Kuhn, John Beattie, Elmer
Keiser, G. Edgar Hertzler, Calvin Keene, Frances Hammand, Alice Kindt

Dr. Gossard was neither a scholarly pedant nor a financial wizard, but he won the loyalty of men of learning and the support of men of means. He was the right man at the right time for Lebanon Valley College.

A Roman emperor once said that where he found a city of brick he left a city of marble. Dr. Gossard might truly have claimed that where he found a weak college, uncertain even of its right to exist, he left an institution firmly established in public esteem and with its foundations truly laid for permanence and excellence.

Harold Bennett, Professor of Classics
in Lebanon Valley College, 1922–28.

CHAPTER THIRTY-ONE

Tribute to Paul Wagner

"FROM BIERMAN TO LEHMAN TO WAGNER": so runs an old saying at the College in honor of a great mathematical continuum which ran from teacher to student for sixty-seven years.

No history of the College would be complete without a tribute to the incomparable Paul Wagner, class of 1917. It is fitting that it should be written for this centennial occasion by his distinguished colleague and fellow-campaigner in scholarly well-doing: Dr. Harold Bennett. Dr. Bennett was at one time Josephine Bittinger Eberly Professor of Latin Language and Literature at Lebanon Valley College, later Principal of Victoria College in the University of Toronto, and more recently President *pro tem.* of the newly established Laurentian University of Sudbury in northern Ontario.

Recollections of Paul S. Wagner

By a former colleague on the staff of Lebanon Valley College

A tall handsome young man with curly dark hair and a merry twinkle in his eye—this was the Paul Wagner whom I knew as a friend and colleague at L. V. C. in the nineteen-twenties. His official title was Professor Paul S. Wagner, Ph.D., head of the department of Mathematics, but everyone called him Paul—even, I suspect, the undergraduates, whose most intimate greeting to me was "Hi, Prof!"

He was a boy from the town of Hershey who demonstrated that the Pennsylvania stock could produce great scholars. With a doctorate *cum laude* from Johns Hopkins, he could have had an appointment in any of several big eastern universities, but he chose to return to his Alma Mater—perhaps because he had been raised in the United Brethren Church, or perhaps because he welcomed the challenge and potential of the struggling little college at Annville.

Being a bachelor when he joined the staff, he lived in the men's residence. I can't recall that he was ever appointed Dean or Don, or had any other title of authority, but I can bear witness to his easy, benevolent control over the

Paul S. Wagner, Ph.D.

young hoodlums of the "Men's Dorm," who were no better (and no worse) than the average dormitory types who enliven every university and college campus.

He was a loyal supporter of President Gossard and fought many battles for him in Faculty councils, where he was recognized as a fair-minded arbiter of standards and never lost the respect of any colleague, whether in the younger group who (like most young university instructors) felt they must assert their disciplinary toughness, or among the elders who had grown a bit weary of the fight and had subsided into a *laissez-faire* complacency.

After he married the niece of the President's wife, I felt sure that he would in due course become Dr. Gossard's successor. In this expectation, however, I was mistaken and disappointed. Perhaps the trustees were not yet ready to entrust the college to a layman, however devout in his Christian faith, or perhaps they already had an inkling of his uncertain life expectancy. His premature death, which followed closely upon that of President Gossard, was a tragic blow to his young wife, to all his friends, and to the college which he had so magnificently served. In any history of L. V. C., he must be recorded as one who saw "the shape of things to come," and whose hopes and aspirations for the college are now being realized under the leadership of his one-time pupil and protégé, Fritz Miller.

Harold Bennett, Professor of Latin Language
and Literature,
Lebanon Valley College, 1922–28

190

CHAPTER THIRTY-TWO

Interim

ON THE DEATH of President Gossard, the Board of Trustees unanimously elected its chairman, J. Raymond Engle, LL.D., as Acting President of the College.

It was a wise choice. Ray Engle, as he was familiarly known, was a son of Samuel F. Engle of Palmyra (donor of the Engle Conservatory) and Agnes Balsbaugh Engle. He was not a graduate of Lebanon Valley College, having received his B.A. from Yale and an LL.B. from the University of Virginia. But he was steeped in the L. V. C. tradition. For most of his life, Palmyra was his home. His sister was Professor Ruth Engle Bender of the Conservatory Faculty, and he himself had for many years been connected with the college administration. Since 1916 he had been a member of the Board of Trustees and since 1930 its chairman.

A judicious executive and at home in the faculty circle, he was able to hold things steady during the six months interval between President Gossard's death and the selection of his successor.

In September, 1932, an encouraging report to the Board was jointly signed by Dr. Engle, Acting President, and Dr. Paul Wagner, Assistant to the President. It provides a fitting close to Dr. Gossard's administration:

> The senior class in the College Department this year numbered 94. In addition to this, there were four seniors in the Conservatory of Music, making a total of 98 to receive degrees. This is the largest number to be awarded the Baccalaureate degree in the history of the institution. The total college enrollment for the year was 384, for the Conservatory 76, Extension Department 165, Summer School 138, making a total of 763 students with a net total of 653.
>
> Perhaps an outstanding achievement of this year was our securing recognition for the Conservatory of Music with the Department of Education of the Commonwealth of Pennsylvania, for the course in Public School Music and the Supervision of Public School Music.

This last success was a tribute to Miss Mary E. Gillespie, Director of the Conservatory, who had planned and worked specifically to this end. It was also a tribute to Dr. Gossard and to Mrs. Bender (former Director of the

J. Raymond Engle, LL.D.
Courtesy Mrs. Ruth Engle Bender

Conservatory), whose forward-looking policies had prepared the ground.

Miss Ruth Engle had joined the Conservatory staff as an instructor in piano in 1919. From 1922 to 1924 she was on leave of absence pursuing her musical studies in New York. On her return to the College in 1924, she was appointed Director of the Conservatory.

At this time the Conservatory was conducting a course in Public School Music for teachers. When the State Department of Education raised the standards for Music Education, Lebanon Valley College was found to be financially unable to meet the requirements of a four-year course for State accreditation. Under the circumstances, the College could no longer attract music students preparing for Public School teaching.

As Mrs. Bender told the story:

> . . . We came to the place when we had to decide: will Lebanon Valley have a Conservatory or will it merely be a number of private studios?
>
> The Conservatory faculty was about to give up in despair when, at the close of the Endowment Campaign . . . [in 1924], Dr. Gossard came to me and said, "I think Lebanon Valley is now ready to give some consideration to the Con-

servatory." Of course that was good news. After collecting the necessary information and requirements the four-year plan was presented to the executive committee and finally passed by the Board of Trustees. Much credit must be given to Dr. Gossard, Mr. J. Raymond Engle, who presented the plan to the Executive Committee, Dr. Derickson and Dr. [John H.] Ness. Naturally this new project would mean additional expense, not only in an enlarged faculty but also in added equipment and general repair of the third floor of the Conservatory. I remember Dr. Ness making a very significant statement at the committee meeting—said he, "I've observed that whenever singers, organists, and choir directors are trained musicians, you have a better choir, and hence a better church service." This statement seemed to turn the tide, and the plans were adopted.

In 1928, Mrs. Bender began active negotiations for State accreditation. It was a rule with the Department of Education that accreditation for Public School Music could be given only after inspection and approval of a four-year course *in operation.*

. . . Too much credit cannot be given the members of the class of 1932 [wrote Mrs. Bender]. They all knew that should the plan fail and the Conservatory not receive recognition, they would be obliged to take examinations to enter another college to receive their degree. In spite of this knowledge, they had enough faith in the Conservatory to stay on. Without those seniors, inspection and recognition would have been impossible for we had to have a four-year program in operation.

In 1930, Miss Mary E. Gillespie, who had organized Music Education in the University of Delaware, was brought in and made Director of the Conservatory to prepare for State inspection in 1932.

We were glad [continued Mrs. Bender] when the ordeal of inspection was over. Notwithstanding many complimentary remarks by the state officials we were still in doubt as to what the decision might be. A few weeks later we were informed of our complete recognition for offering courses leading to the Bachelor of Science degree in Music Education. There are two types of accredited colleges: one, for teaching music, the other for supervising music. We applied for the teaching rights, and of their own free will, the state granted us supervising privileges— the highest possible honor that can be bestowed on any college.

In 1931, Edward P. Rutledge and Ella R. Moyer were brought in to strengthen the staff, and in 1933 came D. Clark Carmean and Nella Miller. With these added to the former members of the staff (Mary E. Gillespie, Ruth Engle Bender, R. Porter Campbell, Harold Malsh, and Alexander Crawford) the Conservatory set its sights higher: accreditation by the highest national agency.

That honor came in November, 1941, when the Lebanon Valley College Conservatory of Music was elected to Associate Membership in the National Association of Schools of Music; and, after the required period of probation, was granted full membership in 1944.

E. N. Funkhouser, LL.D.,
turning the sod for the Lynch Memorial Building, with Trustees William H. Wor-
rilow, Sr., LL.D., Rev. S. C. Enck, D.D., and Rev. William A. Wilt, D.D., looking
on. Dr. Funkhouser was a member of the Board of Trustees, 1917–1962, and
President of the Board 1942–1962.

Courtesy D. Clark Carmean

194

CHAPTER THIRTY-THREE

President Clyde A. Lynch

AT A SPECIAL MEETING of the Board of Trustees on September 30, 1932, Dr. Clyde A. Lynch was elected to the presidency. He was a man of great promise. Born in Harrisburg, August 24, 1891, the son of John Henry Lynch and Carmina Blanche (Keys) Lynch, he received his early education in the Harrisburg public schools. He finished his preparatory work in the Lebanon Valley Academy in Annville, and entered Lebanon Valley College in 1914. He graduated in 1918 with the degree of Bachelor of Arts. On June 30, 1914, he married Edith Basehore of Harrisburg.

While still in his teens, Clyde Lynch had dedicated himself to the United Brethren ministry, and for the remainder of his life pursued a double career as preacher and educator. His interests were wide, his energy stupendous. In 1909 he received Quarterly Conference License to preach, and Annual Conference License in 1910. In 1916, while a student at Lebanon Valley College, he was ordained.

Before coming to college, he had served for a year, 1911–1912, as regular pastor on the Centerville Circuit in Lancaster County. In 1912, while still a preparatory student, he received appointment to churches in Linglestown and Rockville in Dauphin County. Throughout his undergraduate career, he continued to serve these two churches.

Of a deeply emotional nature and torn by conflicting impulses, Clyde Lynch at first found difficulty in adapting himself to the equable, dispassionate atmosphere of academic life. It was the Rev. Alvin E. Shroyer, Professor of Bible and Greek, who saved him for his subsequent high honors in the educational field.

Professor Shroyer's son David writes:

> I remember Clyde very well, when he was in College. When he first came to school from Harrisburg he had a very difficult time getting adjusted. . . . Clyde came to my Father and said he thought he could make the grade if he could come under my Father's daily influence. He wanted to move into our home; unfortunately, at the time all of our rooms were filled for we always had two to four college boys living with us, in addition to Prof. Wanner. But it was deter-

Rev. Clyde A. Lynch, D.D., Ph.D.
President, 1932–1950

mined that he could come to school on the early morning train from Harrisburg and return on the later afternoon train. My Father would provide a desk in his study and Clyde could live with us during the day when not in classes. This arrangement worked out very successfully and we both know of the mark Dr. Lynch made in the field of Religious Education.

To Clyde A. Lynch, as to many another college boy, Professor Shroyer brought the turning point in a life.

After graduation from Lebanon Valley College, he entered Bonebrake (now United) Theological Seminary at Dayton, Ohio. During his student days there, 1918–1921, he served as pastor of churches at Antioch and Pyrmont in Montgomery County, Ohio. With a B.D. from Bonebrake, he returned to Pennsylvania, serving as Pastor at Ephrata from 1921 to 1925. In the latter year, he received the A.M. degree from Lebanon Valley College.

From 1925 to 1930, he was pastor of the U. B. Second Church in Philadelphia. In recognition of his services to the church, his Alma Mater in 1928 conferred on him the honorary degree of Doctor of Divinity. Still pursuing his scholastic career, he enrolled in the Department of Psychology at the University of Pennsylvania, where, for two years, 1928–1930, he was Assistant Instructor in Psychology. From Penn, he received an A.M. degree in 1929.

Having finished the required courses leading to the Ph.D. degree, with

196

only his thesis to write, he was able to accept a call to the faculty of Bone-brake in 1930, where he served as Professor of Homiletics and Practical Theology. In 1931 he received the degree of Ph.D. from the University of Pennsylvania.

So it was that in 1932, on the death of President Gossard, the Board of Lebanon Valley, who had wanted a good speaker to make the College better known and who for years past had been seeking to fill the faculty with holders of the doctorate, seized the opportunity of getting a good speaker and a Ph.D. at the same time for the top position. They appointed the Rev. Clyde A. Lynch, A.B., A.M., D.D., Ph.D., President of the College. It was understood that Dr. Paul S. Wagner, steady, tactful, and experienced in local college affairs, should be Assistant to the President. Paul's illness, however, soon ended this happy partnership.

The energies that had been so conspicuous in Dr. Lynch's student days were now turned to the account of the College, and, as the wheels of world-wide history turned, all his powers were needed. To bring the College safely through the lean years of the Great Depression and immediately thereafter to untangle the agonizing problems of the Second World War as they affected the small Liberal Arts colleges—that was the task to which he gave without stint the remainder of his days.

Like all college presidents, he found himself "a slave to the public." Unlike most of them, he would not have changed this condition if he could.

"Well, after all," he wrote to Professor Edwin H. Sponseller, author of *Crusade for Education*, "I think that I should rather live a busy life and drop off suddenly some day than to spare myself too much and live to a ripe but uneventful old age."

He arrived on the Lebanon Valley campus on November 23, 1932, and proceeded to acquaint himself, as he reported to the East Pennsylvania Conference, with the duties of his office. The first of these was to keep the College before the public. That became his prime mission. Through rain and shine, snow and sleet, sickness and health, he attended to it faithfully and triumphantly.

> Since last commencement [he informed the Board, June 1, 1934] I have delivered 133 addresses. 92 of these were religious, 28 educational, 9 civic, and 4 fraternal. The policy of the Finance Committee to enable your president to render his services to the churches of our cooperating conferences without expense to them has created new interest and a growing spirit of cooperation with reference to the college. . . .
>
> I have attended the more important state, regional, and national meetings of the various educational associations and have represented the college at a number of academic convocations. . . .

Next year he reported 127 addresses delivered,

The Lebanon Valley College Band, 1933
Prof. Edward P. Rutledge on extreme left

including commencement addresses at Reinerton, Leola, Wernersville, New Holland, Womelsdorf, John Harris at Harrisburg, Shenandoah College, and the Nurses' Training School of the Good Samaritan Hospital, Lebanon.

One of the best things Dr. Lynch accomplished in his first years at the College was the cleaning up of the Men's Dormitory (Kreider Hall). In the mid-thirties, it was a living museum of hoodlumism. The proctors could do nothing. It may be recalled what had happened to Professor Shippee in Ollie Butterwick's day.

The Faculty was much disturbed by the problem. Dr. Grimm, who had been asked to investigate, said he would be unable to make a full report unless it could be recorded on asbestos! In desperation, the Faculty considered placing a young couple in the Dormitory to see if a woman's presence might not help. Professor and Mrs. Carmean volunteered.

When they went in, they were shocked at what they found: "Not one door in the building left intact," as they recall. "They had all been kicked in. Plaster on the ceilings was water-soaked, coming off in chunks with the lath showing.

Window panes were cracked and broken. Walls were pocked with bullet holes and brown-streaked with tobacco juice. Floors were covered with litter. The stench was nauseating."

The new proctors issued no commands. They did not spy. They did not preach. They let the boys know they were there to help. The boys asked to have the dormitory redecorated, and offered to pay increased room rent to help finance it. The College complied. The building was re-wired (providing convenient outlets), and the dark interior walls were redone in light paint. The floors were covered with an attractive linoleum. A proper shower room was installed in the basement. Hitherto, two showers in a dark little stall had had to suffice for 125 men.

It worked. Within five years, when the Carmeans moved out, tradition in the Dormitory was completely changed. No more doors were torn off their hinges and thrown downstairs. Forgotten was the night when Earl E. Wolf, '31 (today a retired U. S. Chaplain with the rank of Lieutenant Colonel) was driven out of a second-story window and nearly killed. Almost forgotten, too was the malodorous evening when John R. Gongloff, '38, fired a shotgun from his window and killed a skunk.

The Girls' Band, 1935

Life Work Recruits, 1936

Human nature had not changed, but the unobtrusive presence of a lady and a gentleman had drawn out a latent chivalry which then "took over."

In the college world, an unhappy consequence of the great Depression was a reign of unbridled competition between colleges in student solicitation. Scouring the countryside for prospective freshmen became a faculty activity in which it was considered shameful not to engage. A few professors, during the student-hunting season, devoted a large part of their time to it.

One of the more wholesome effects of intercollegiate competition was the introduction of Competitive Scholarship Examinations. The custom was inaugurated at Lebanon Valley College on May Day (May 5), 1934, when ninety-one students, representing forty-six different high schools, gathered on the campus to compete for "Three full-time tuition scholarships, three half-tuition scholarships, and three day-student scholarships of $50.00 each." These were to be divided between the College and the Conservatory on a 2:1 ratio.

It was hoped that these visitors (even those among them who failed to win an award), once they had been treated as guests of the College and admitted without charge to the day's student events, would carry abroad word of the congenial atmosphere in which L. V. C. students pursued wisdom.

A more direct form of competitive advertising came from the newly established college Press Service. It had been organized with the assistance of members of the staff of the Lebanon *Daily News.*

Beginning in May of the same year, the College conducted a weekly program over a Harrisburg radio station. Other forms of "public relations" were resorted to. College buildings, personnel, and activities were photographed fore and aft, and pictures were prepared for distribution throughout the constituency. A regular *Alumni Bulletin* was published, and an Alumni Secretary was appointed. For the benefit of prospective visitors, "Lebanon Valley College" road signs were set up on the highways.

Trying to infuse something of his own activism into the faculty, Dr. Lynch encouraged his professors to bowl, play basketball, write, speak, join clubs, and attend more educational meetings.

With the aid of these and other public relations measures, the College weathered the Depression. Between 1933 and 1938, the enrollment of full-time students remained substantially the same. But the Depression had taken heavy toll of the endowment. Despite an increase in student fees and a decrease in faculty salaries, the College was again facing a financial crisis—the ghost of which was supposed to have been laid by Dr. Gossard. There was talk of a new endowment campaign.

Then came the war. For two years its purely European phase cast an ominous shadow. After Pearl Harbor, the national emergency threatened every small college in the country. At L. V. C. the male student body shrank pitiably. Dr. Wallace had to cast his annual Shakespeare play from the class roster of young ladies. It was not until the G.I.'s began to replenish male ranks that English 66 could produce *Henry IV,* Part I, with C. Alvin Berger and Thomas J. Schaak as Prince Hal and Falstaff.

Dr. Lynch's report to the Board in 1943 echoed an old appeal that had been all too familiar during the College's emaciated childhood:

> . . . our cooperating conferences and the denomination should stand in readiness, as certain other denominations are doing, to provide emergency financial aid to the College, if the enrollment and reductions cannot save us from financial distress. It is absolutely impossible for the College to be self-sustaining in this dark period of the world's history. Unless such aid should come, Lebanon Valley College will likely become a deplorable casualty of the war. . . . The government is not out to save the colleges but primarily to serve the armed forces. . . . If our college is to be saved, we must do it ourselves, and there should be no delusions to the contrary.

He announced the organization of a General Campaign Committee to raise

$550,000 "for the purpose of creating a Physical Education Building, of increasing our endowment, and of liquidating our indebtedness."

Dr. Lynch was a psychologist. He understood the constituency, and the people (to whom he had contributed so ungrudgingly his time and talents as a speaker) understood him. The financial campaign, headed by Dr. E. N. Funkhouser, who contributed all the campaign expenses, was a great success, even though it had been undertaken in these difficult war years. On May 19, 1944, the President was able to make a cheerful report to the Board of Trustees:

> Of the twelve years of my administration this college year has been the worst of times and the best of times: the worst of times because there are sixty-nine fewer students here than at the corresponding period last year and a minus difference in the total registrations of the two years of 139, resulting in a deficit of over $18,000, the best of times because of our having exceeded a half-million dollars in our campaign to raise $550,000 for the erection of a physical-education building, the augmenting of the endowment fund, and the liquidation of an indebtedness in the amount of $50,000, representing the balance of more than $279,000 spent during the last twenty years for plant additions, improvements and repairs, $58,000 of which was expended for capital outlays during the last

The Green Blotter Club at the home of Dr. and Mrs. Struble, 1939
Courtesy D. Clark Carmean

President Lynch lays the cornerstone of the Physical Education Building
Courtesy D. Clark Carmean

nine years. But we are thankful that conditions are not worse—a major depression and a global war are not altogether conducive to the prosperity of liberal arts colleges. . . .

The student shrinkage continued. Under pressure of the national emergency, manpower regulations were repeatedly changed. More and more men were drawn into the services. Anxiety on the campus mounted. To the distress at casualty lists involving graduates and undergraduates, there was added uncertainty with regard to the College's survival.

For a time, the loss of students had been slowed by deferments granted certain classes of men: ministerial students and those preparing for careers in some of the sciences. But even these were now uncertain. In February, 1944, colleges had been given a quota of possible deferments, for which claims were to be filed with the National Roster of Scientific and Specialized Personnel of the War Manpower Commission. But, reported Dean A. H. M. Stonecipher to the Board on May 19, 1944, "Soon after this was arranged, the whole plan

Dennis Sherk Presenting the Colors, 1942
Courtesy D. Clark Carmean

was abolished. . . ." For a time local boards were able to postpone, at least to the end of a semester, the calling up of the deferred men. But announcement came that there were to be no more deferments after July 1st.

As it turned out, government aid to the colleges came in a flood at the end of the war. On May 11, 1945, Dean Stonecipher was able to announce to the Board the main features of the projected G.I. Bill of Rights:

> The veteran may receive from one to four years of education, depending upon the length of his service. He is entitled to a maximum of $500 a year for institutional charges for tuition, food, books, etc. In addition he will receive $50 a month for subsistence, if without dependent, or $75 a month if with dependent. These provisions are generous and will be of great service to the ex-soldier and of advantage to the colleges.

With the return of peace, President Lynch presented to conference, in September, 1945, a brief summary of the College's active contribution to the nation's war effort:

> Now that victory has been achieved it should be remembered that approximately 150 alumni and 250 undergraduates are reported in the College Office as having been in the armed and auxiliary services. Twelve were killed in action or died of wounds; two suffered accidental death, nine were wounded and four were prisoners of war. Five faculty members are still in the service.

The year 1946 saw many students and four faculty members returning to the campus. The faculty members were Frederic K. Miller (President-to-be), W. Merl Freeland and Joseph Battista of the Conservatory, and Coach "Jerry" Frock.

In September, President Lynch was able to make a cheerful report to the East Pennsylvania Conference: "We have emerged without indebtedness, have acquired considerable property, have completed a successful financial campaign, have raised our endowment to a million dollars and have the largest student body in our history."

By 1948 he could report a still larger enrollment: 817 full-time students, of which number 445, or 53%, were veterans. It was not without reason that he had observed a few months before that "there has not been a normal college year during my incumbency." The sudden influx of students had its own embarrassing effects. Classes were too large and teaching schedules were overloaded.

But the veterans were a blessing to the College in more ways than one. Not only did they provide financial security to the College but scholastic maturity as well. The comment of the English Department may be pertinent at this point. These men, who had seen life at its intensest, understood the thrust of great literature; and for the most part they responded more readily than others to the Good, the True, and the Beautiful. "Out of the strong cometh forth sweetness."

By 1950, full-time enrollment was beginning to recede. In that year it dropped to 760. Few veterans were now entering. But Dr. Lynch's task had been accomplished. He had seen the College surmount two dangerous crises, the Depression and the War. More than that, he had begun to build anew. On May 6, 1950, he laid the cornerstone of the Physical Education Building which he had come to look upon as his very special project, and which, when completed, was to bear his name.

All through these difficult years, 1932 to 1950, neither Dr. Lynch nor Mrs. Lynch had ever spared themselves. He made himself always available for outside speaking engagements, as the Board at the outset had asked him to do. She made herself the friendly hostess at home, entertaining students untiringly and with a warmth rendered the more pointed by her remarkable gift for remembering names. Her "at home" days—one for each of the four classes, Freshman, Sophomores, Juniors, and Seniors—will not soon be forgotten.

For some time past, President Lynch's health had been uncertain. In the summer of 1950, the doctors ordered him to cancel all speaking engagements, and he "scratched" seventy-two from his calendar for the remaining four months of the year.

A few days later he died, August 6, 1950—like Dr. Gossard still "in harness" as he had hoped to be.

Solomon Caulker, '41
Vice-Principal of Fourabah Bay College, Sierra Leone,
one of a group of African leaders who were educated
at Lebanon Valley College. He died in a plane crash
near Dakar, August 29, 1960, on his return from the
International Conference on Science in the Advance-
ment of New States, held at Rehovoth, Israel.

Among the others, Alfred Tennyson Sumner, '02,
was the author of grammars of the Mende, Sherbo,
and Temne languages. His son, the Hon. Doyle
Sumner, Minister of Natural Resources, Sierra Leone,
attended Lebanon Valley College, 1936–1938.

Courtesy D. Clark Carmean

College Glee Club, 1947–1948

Athletic Council, 1937
Front row: *C. R. Gingrich, E. H. Stevenson, R. R. Butterwick, C. G. Dotter*
Top row: *Emerson Metoxen (coach), President C. A. Lynch, M. L. Stokes,*
J. W. Frock (coach)

May Queen, 1949
Janet Weaver, Queen; Martha Miller, Maid of Honor
Courtesy D. Clark Carmean

CHAPTER THIRTY-FOUR

The Annual Murder

LEBANON VALLEY COLLEGE has always filled its quota of student pranks. Though the mode may change, the spirit that prompts them will be with us as long as the generations continue to replenish themselves with young; and oldsters, though they may inveigh against the ill discipline of modern youth, will always recall with satisfaction their own peccadilloes of the day before yesterday.

All humor is said to be based on the unexpected, the incongruous. This will explain the special attention the Death League gave to ministerial students. It used to take these gentlemen at night to the cemetery, tie them to tombstones, and have them preach for hours to the dead.

The awe in which the Death League (or its heirs and assigns) was held did not derive entirely from physical violence. Its members knew how to appeal to the imagination.

> I had the strangest feeling the other night [wrote a freshman, Norman M. Bouder, October 10, 1940]. I was ready for bed when two upper-classmen knocked on the door. When I opened the door, they stepped in, the one holding a foot and a half long paddle, and the other a five foot paddle. I still don't know what they wanted, but at any rate they asked who my roommate was, looked casually about and left. It was very impressive.

The scattering of iodine crystals—but it would be unwise to develop this theme in a book that might fall into the wrong hands. For the same reason we shall not elaborate the story of some college chicken stealers, who, summoned to report at the town magistrate's office, gathered in a body about that diminutive structure, locked the door, picked up the building with all its contents, and carried it away. Adults may apply to Mrs. Laura (Reider) Muth, '92, of Hershey, for fuller detail. Better left untold, also, is the adventure of Edith Lehman, '13 (Mrs. Ralph Bartlett) who, with her classmates Lottie Spessard and Florence Christeson entered the chapel at midnight intending to remove the hymnbooks and put tacks on the professors chairs on the platform—only to be interrupted by her brother, John Lehman, and his friends, who after all, as she remembers "did a better job." They silenced the organ and removed all the chapel seats.

Old Freshman Rules and their infraction make picturesque telling. It was remarked in 1941 by Norman Bouder, then a sophomore, that, "The persons who are making this years punishments sure have a sense of humor."

It seems the Men's Senate had just punished a Junior, who had been turned in by a Senior for failure to observe class standing. They required him to sit on the front six inches of his chair in the dining hall and eat a "square meal" for two meals.

"A cocky football player, a freshman, must hobble himself with a foot of ¼ in. rope and wear a gag and boxing gloves.

"The prize one has been put on a freshman who has been turned in for two weeks. He must wear a green ribbon under his chin and tied into a bow on top of his head, must roll up his trousers above his knees, suck a lollipop, and pull a toy after him wherever he goes."

All freshmen that year were obliged to carry matches, to say "hello" to everyone, to "tip their dinks" to all women, and never to walk on the grass.

In the history of malefaction at L. V. C., no case in memory can surpass the Theft of the African Leopard and its astonishing aftermath, the Purloined Buffalo Horns.

The stuffed leopard from Sierra Leone, West Africa, prized gift of the missionary William M. Martin, '18, who shot it, reposed for years in the Tyrone Biological Museum on the third floor of the Administration Building. One night it disappeared, and its whereabouts for some time thereafter remained a campus mystery.

It turned up at length in Lebanon, its abductors having deposited it at night on the steps of the old Post Office at the corner of Eighth and Chestnut Streets. The police of Lebanon are entitled to credit for its discovery and capture. A patrolman driving up Eighth Street in a cruiser car saw indistinctly— day was just breaking—a strange object on the steps. In the half light, the leopard looked larger than life. The officer stopped the car, sprang out, and pulled a revolver. For one split second he had the animal at bay—and for the rest of his life enjoyed the joke on himself.

It had been Dr. Gossard's policy to leave the Administration Building unlocked at night lest locks prove a temptation to student pranksters. But, after the recovery of the leopard, it was thought unwise to leave its precious pelt exposed to such as might wish to emulate the exploit of its first abductors. Arndt Brighton, appointed its bodyguard, was stationed in the hall opposite the only door to the Biological Laboratory.

One night, while he was sitting in front of that doorway, a pair of buffalo horns disappeared from the museum behind it. They were soon recovered, having been left by the student burglars conspicuously on the roof of the heating plant. But the mystery how the horns could have been abstracted

210

went long unsolved. The only door to the museum had been under strict observation. The windows had not been tampered with. Nothing had been broken, nothing disturbed. There were no footprints.

The writer is not sure that the case has ever been completely cleared up, but this is what he has heard. College boys climbed to the roof of the building and opened a trapdoor above the museum. One boy was lowered head first, and, suspended by his heels, lifted the horns from the top of a case. Rumor has it that it was Bill Clark, '39, who made the descent and Charlie Brown, '39, who held him and pulled him back.

There was one student hoax (aimed at the freshmen) which, repeated year after year and always successfully, achieved such perfection of form and distinction of style as to bring it into the realm of the highest folk art. That was the Annual Murder. It was more than a campus affair. All Annville was proud of it. It was talked about throughout the college constituency. Graduates told their younger brothers and sisters. Many of the freshmen had heard of it before they came up. But so well was the dénouement prepared for, the action gathering momentum over a number of days, that when a shot was heard and an upper-classman was seen stretched out on the grass with tomato ketchup trickling from his mouth, no freshman suspected the possibility of deception. The reality of what they had seen was so overwhelming that even a categorical statement from authority that the thing was merely make-believe (as Miss Myers assured hysterical girls under her care in West Hall) had no effect whatever on minds carried away by the notion that they had witnessed the passing of a Christian soul.

Superb action and timing were the keys to success. The theme was as old as the Blue Mountains—but to freshmen it was as new and soul-satisfying as the epic of Troy had been to the ancient Greeks. The gist of it was simple: Boy Steals Girl from His Roommate. (It had to be his roommate for the sake of convenience in preparing next day's script.)

One circumstance, peculiar to L. V. C., contributed to the success of the deception. It was an old tradition on this campus—only very slowly being liberalized—that once a boy had dated a co-ed, they were "hooked" for duration—the duration, that is to say, of their college careers. To break that compact, short of graduation, was a scandal.

So it came about, in late September or early October every year, that when student A was observed going to the post office with student B's girl, a hushed awe and apprehension fell over the campus. Upper-classmen understood, but played their supporting roles without a miscue. The girl at issue was tearful, pleading, courageous. Between the male principals, protests were exchanged, taunts, recriminations, and at last blows, producing all over the campus a crescendo of mass tension. On the last night of all, Student A again took student B's girl to the post office and returned to quarters with the air of a conqueror.

It was at this point that there arose the greatest danger of a give-away, for members of the faculty and the citizenry of Annville (appraised of the impending tragedy by a reliable grapevine) had taken up advantageous positions among the trees within sight of the Men's Dorm. That danger, however, had been anticipated. Instructions had been issued to all freshmen in residence to remain in the dormitory for a House Meeting.

Professor and Mrs. D. Clark Carmean, who for years were proctors living in the Dorm, have left record of the night's doings. An established routine was usually followed.

> Just a few minutes before ten o'clock, the aggrieved party would reek of alcohol, take a gun, knock on the doors, and look for his rival, so all the freshmen would know he was on the loose. On the stroke of ten, he would catch his man in the archway and shoot him.
>
> The man shot, had a capsule of ketchup in his mouth, and bit it. Blood appeared to dribble down his chin.

At about the same time, another revolver was fired through an open window and thrown out on to the grass to provide incriminating evidence for such Perry Masons as should be drawn into the case.

> The freshmen [continues Mrs. Carmean] on hearing the shot, would pour out of their rooms but stand at a distance. The murderer would run; there was a car waiting for him. The murdered man [after the college nurse had administered first aid] would be put in a car, and then the freshmen were put in cars to give blood. Many of them were in their pajamas. They [the drivers] would drop them at the door of the hospital and tell them to run inside and tell what they had come for. They asked at the desk, but were told, "There is nobody of that name here." When they got out, the car was gone.
>
> In 1939 the murder took place on a cold night in October. We knew that a number of freshmen had gone to Lebanon, but not all of them had come back. One party in particular was missing. At eleven o'clock we got a car and drove to Lebanon. We found a little group standing on the street waiting for a lift. They didn't know that it was all a fake. When they found the murdered man was not at the one hospital, they walked across the city to another hospital. Bob Tschop ['39] was one of those freshmen, and Raymond Smith ['39] (now an attorney) was another. There were about three more.
>
> When Wilbur Leech ['37] was at L. V. C., the person killed was a Catholic, and they sent Leech to get a priest. The priest, who knew about it, was playing cards. He said, "I'll come when I finish this hand." Leech got so excited he tipped the table over. . . .
>
> Robert Tilford, a freshman, leaped on the running board of the car supposedly taking the dying man to the hospital (they planned just to drive the victim a few blocks and then turn back), and they had to keep on driving. He was a conjuror, and he thought he was helping by making a noise like a motor siren. So they took him to Lebanon. They sent him in to the hospital to alert the staff, and when he came out they had disappeared.

Mike Smith, who sold soft drinks on Railroad Street, was known to have taken a correspondence course in the Science of Detection. He was, accordingly, called in as an expert on crime. The police were sent for. The town constabulary came obligingly and kept a straight face, being in the know. Once an over-enthusiastic freshman managed to bring in a state policeman, who came quite innocently, expecting to find a case of homicide—much to the subsequent embarrassment of the College, which received an official admonition.

While all this ferment was going on, the murderer was usually holed up behind drawn blinds in some professor's or townsman's house, waiting for the hue and cry to die down and for the hour of truth to strike.

Just one more thing had to come, the finishing touch. We leave it to an eye-witness to introduce it in appropriate context at the conclusion of his deposition. Norman Bouder is writing to his parents from the vantage point of his sophomore year:

October 5, 1941

. . . The annual murder is under way to its climax this coming Wednesday night. It's a lot of fun building up the story of how the one fellow is taking the other's girl away from him.

October 8, 1941

Well, the murder is in full swing. Last night during supper, Dick Beckner and Walt Ebersole had another fight. Walt went so far as to throw a chair at Dick. It is very well planned this year. Walt is the murderer; it is his girl that is going out with Dick. The murder takes place tonight, and Walt and Dick had another fight just outside of chapel this morning.

October 12, 1941

Well, Wednesday night as you know was the night of the "murder." It went off really very well. This year at a few minutes after ten four shots were heard, and the "killer" escaped. Dick Beckner, the corpse, was lying on the ground, with "blood" running from his wounds in the chest.* He was shot on the campus, about fifty feet from the archway. For several minutes the crowd of students was held back, and since there was very little light, the shooting looked real. A few of the girls were crying, and finally Janet Schopf came screaming across the campus only to faint when she saw Dick. Dick was then placed in a car, but before the car pulled away, the ambulance arrived and Dick was transferred from the car to the lighted ambulance. About five minutes after the ambulance was gone, a call came for blood transfusions and all the freshmen volunteered willingly. One freshman was sent to get Dr. Brubaker, and when he returned he reported that Dr. B. came to the window and said that this had occurred for the last 23 years. The freshman said that he thought the Dr. was crazy and should have his license revoked. I got in a car with two other upperclassmen and three freshmen and we went to the Lebanon Sanatorium. When we returned, Walt had been captured and a trial was held in Philo Hall; Walt was convicted of murder and then Dick's ghost turned up unwounded, to wish the class of '45 good luck. The rooms were very thoroughly wrecked and some fellows didn't get back until 3 a.m. One football player didn't get back until 7:30 the next

---

* For chest wounds, mercurochrome was preferred to ketchup.

morning. He had spent the night at Mount Gretna on a porch swing and covered with a rug.

The Annual Murder became a casualty of the Second World War. It survived the war itself, but, after peace was declared and veterans came to the campus, they watched the evolving Triangle with indignation, and not all of them were content to play a neutral role.

"A group who had been in the War and knew commando tactics," report the Carmeans, "planned to take care of the man who was cutting in on the other man's girl. One of that group told us they were going to do that. There were other reasons, but there was a real fear that harm was going to come to someone during the make-believe."

By Faculty action, the murder was banned. Since it was not, and by its very nature never could be, a clandestine affair like the Death League, the injunction held firm.

The precise routine which has been described on the preceding pages was not at all times adhered to. Professor Shroyer one year gave protection to an unwilling victim whose life had, at one point, been actually in danger. As David Shroyer narrates, the murderer that year was not the jealous lover but a man who had become demented without warning. A student he chased, being totally unsophisticated in these affairs, thought his time was at hand.

At the time he was a resident in rooms that were made available to about 20 boys in the unused portion of the Conservatory. [He] "ducked out of a window onto the 18″ ledge that runs around the perimeter of the roof and outdistanced his pursuer for, in his deathly fear of the fate that was to befall him, he had no fear of the narrow ledge. The murderer in turn was quite concerned about the ledge, and [the victim] had his chance to escape. He came running over to our house, his breath coming in choked spasms and his eyes distended in fright. . . . he dashed in the back door and without a word ran to the second floor and crawled under a bed! Needless to say the murderer had to search for another victim, but those who saw the staged scene never forgot it! I saw many enactments in passing years but few were as successful as that one!

214

Freshman-Sophomore Tug of War, 1964

Gossard Memorial Library, January, 1965

Courtesy Bruce C. Souders

216

CHAPTER THIRTY-FIVE

President Miller Fulfills a Prophesy

I now look into the dim future and the faith by which the elders obtained a good report enables me to behold unseen things. As the years roll on, I see the children, grandchildren and a long line of their descendants flocking back to this spot bringing with them thankofferings to endow the College and provide the needed means for the highest and best education.

Thomas Rhys Vickroy, 1892

THE YEAR 1950 was a difficult one for the College. The Depression, followed by the Second World War, the G. I. "explosion" (when the student population rocketed from about 200 to 800), and the Korean War which reduced it sharply again—all these had inevitably left rough edges at the College. In 1950, the Commission on Institutions of Higher Education (the accrediting agency of the Middle States Association) advised the College to undertake certain adjustments and to complete them no later than 1952.

That was the uncomfortable situation with which Dr. Frederic Keiper Miller was confronted when, in August, 1950, after the death of President Lynch, he was elected Acting President by the Board of Trustees.

Questioned about those difficult days, Dr. Miller said: "The Korean War had posed many problems: Student enrollment, loss of faculty, the concern of the nation in the warfare then going on; and so all of our energies were directed to keeping the College open and alive."

In this Centennial Year, 1966, the College stands high in reputation among its academic associates. Dr. Miller is not only President of Lebanon Valley College but also former President of the Pennsylvania Association of Colleges and Universities as well as former President of the Evangelical United Brethren Administrators. The College is accredited by the Middle States Association, and President Miller is a member of that body's accrediting Commission, the very agency that had stimulated the College in 1950 to raise its sights.

How that transformation has taken place is the subject of this chapter.

By birth, training, and aptitude, Dr. Frederic K. Miller was exactly fitted for the presidency of Lebanon Valley College, and the time was ripe for him.

He was born in Lebanon, Pennsylvania, the son of the Rev. Dr. Harry E.

Frederic K. Miller, Ph.D., Litt.D.
Acting President, 1950–1951
President, 1951–

Miller, who for forty-one years (1904–1945) served as pastor of the ever-expanding Lebanon Salem, "mother of churches." Active and courageous, a vigorous partisan but open-minded, Harry Miller was feared, respected, and loved (all at once) by men of every section of the United Brethren Church, whether they were conservative or liberal.

"Fritz" Miller, on graduating from Lebanon High School, came up to the College in 1925. He soon distinguished himself on the campus as an "all-round" student: scholar, athlete, and leader of men. Graduating with the class of '29, he went on to continue the study of History at the University of Pennsylvania, winning an M.A. degree in 1931 and a Ph.D. in 1948. During the intervening span of seventeen years, he acquired experience as an Assistant in History at the University of Pennsylvania (1931–1933), and as a teacher of Social Studies and coach of basketball at the Lebanon Senior High School (1933–1939). Invited to teach at his Alma Mater, he served as Chairman of the Department of History at Lebanon Valley College from 1939 to 1950.

No less important to him in his preparation for the administrative position to which he was soon to be called, was his term of service (for which he was granted two years leave of absence from the College, 1943–1945) with the U. S. Army in Europe. From 1948 to 1950, he was Assistant to the President of the College.

Appointed Acting President immediately on Dr. Lynch's death, he so ably demonstrated his fitness for the emergency that on June 1, 1951, the Board of Trustees elected him President. On November 13 following, he was formally inaugurated.

The first college issue with which he was faced was, to use his own word for it, SURVIVAL. The report on the College by the Commission on Institutions of Higher Education had been less than wholly favorable. Dr. Miller and his Board knew very well that to lose accreditation by that body would place the College at an almost hopeless disadvantage.

At the outset, President and Board came to an understanding.

"Fritz" Miller, son of his father, put the issue quite simply and firmly: "Do you want a *good* college?"

On receiving an affirmative answer, he stated boldly the financial implications of such a declaration: money for faculty salaries, for a good library, for properly-equipped scientific laboratories, for more dormitories, for a dining hall, for a chapel.

The Board liked his mettle and agreed to his terms. They gave him full support. Under the leadership of the Board Chairman, Dr. Elmer N. Funkhouser, and the two Conference Superintendents, the Rev. Dr. David E. Young and the Rev. Dr. (later Bishop) Paul E. V. Shannon, the Board joined him in a massive campaign to restore the confidence of the Middle States Association and, having accomplished that, to continue in the same direction until at last the faith of the College's founders should be fulfilled.

To an alumnus coming back to the College after a long absence, the change seen in the campus today is startling: new buildings everywhere and a vast extension of college property—west of White Oak Street, east of College Avenue, North of Sheridan Avenue, and even across the railroad tracks. Still more remarkable is the change in the scholastic atmosphere. The College has lost its parochialism and its resentful feeling of inferiority.

How has this change come about?

As Dr. Miller recalls those early days, the Board at the outset agreed to make the improvement of faculty salaries the No. 1 item on the *agenda*. It appeared to be a prime necessity if the College was to attract and hold the kind of faculty it needed: men and women highly specialized in academic training, yet broadly cultured; lovers of the Good, the True, and the Beautiful; in sympathy with the aims of a Christian liberal arts college; and persons of a kind to take root in such a place and give it their lives.

If money is the root of all evil, it is also the key to much good. Dr. Gossard used to say to prospective donors, "There is nothing the matter with this college that money won't correct." In recent years this thought has penetrated to the right places.

Heartening evidence of the increased acceptance of responsibility by the College's three major constituencies—the alumni, the Church, and the business

Gossard Memorial Library
A corner of the main reading room

community—was seen in the success of the Development Program of 1955–1956 under the leadership of Dr. Elmer N. Funkhouser, Chairman of the Board of Trustees. The original Pattern for Progress had a goal of $900,000, but the campaign was so successful that ultimately $1,090,000, was raised, of which the Church contributed approximately $500,000 in its United Crusade, while our alumni, business community, and friends raised the rest. At about the same time the College was greatly encouraged by a grant of $159,200 from the Ford Foundation, and in subsequent years by a greatly enlarged Annual Giving Program. Such support made possible the immediate erection of needed buildings, and gave the strongest assurances for the future.

On May 18, 1957, three buildings were dedicated: the Gossard Memorial Library, the Science Building (in memory of Dr. Andrew Bender and Dr. Samuel Derickson), and the Mary Capp Green Residence Hall for Women. Mrs. Green herself attended, together with members of the Gossard, Bender, and Derickson families.

The Gossard Memorial Library

The opening in June, 1957, of the Gossard Memorial Library, saw the happy conclusion of a ninety-year-old Battle of the Books.

The movement for a proper college library had begun modestly enough with this announcement in the 1866–1867 *Catalogue:* "The *Boehm Library,* consisting of well-selected books, is accessible to all students. Donations in books or money are earnestly solicited for this Library."

A library committee of three persons—Mr. Cyrus A. Loose, Mr. David Crider, and Miss Sallie M. Rigler—was appointed in January, 1867, to found the College Library. That the community was not too sympathetic is seen in the fact that, when the committee made its report four months later (on May 12), they had collected only a hundred books and $89.39 in cash toward expansion. To say that their *hopes* were fulfilled is to take a very long view, for library expansion, though steady, was exceedingly slow for the first fifty-four years—that is, until 1921, when the Middle States Association gave the College a wholesome brush with death.

Some of the more significant stages in the evolution of the college library are listed below:

1874. The Library's first accession book listed 653 volumes. The Board of Trustees appropriated $300 "to replenish the college library."

1876. President Hammond reported that the Library had 1132 books.

1878. The Philokosmian Literary Society opened a Reading room in the basement of the Administration Building. There 9 dailies, 26 weeklies, and 24 monthlies were accessible on payment of a small fee. Soon the other literary societies followed suit. The four libraries (College, Philo's, Kalo's, Clio's) together were the real nucleus of the coming College Library.

1883. The Library was given quarters in the new frame building facing College Avenue that housed also the departments of Natural Science, Music, and Art. "The Library," announced the *Catalogue* of 1882–1883, "is our great ally and aid in instruction."

The Prayer Corner in the Library

Dr. Donald E. Fields, Librarian, and his staff, 1962–1963

1888. The College Library was reported to contain 2,600 volumes.

1900. The Library-Science-Music-Art building was sold and removed to another site (where it still stands) on Sheridan Avenue near Ulrich Street. The College Library was given quarters in a room on the first floor of the Conservatory of Music.

1902. The three literary societies contributed their books to the College Library: Philo, 895 volumes; Kalo, 1,000; Clio, several hundred.

1903. The College Library adopted the Dewey System of classification.

1904. Andrew Carnegie gave $20,000 for a new library building, the cornerstone of which was laid the same year.

1905. The Carnegie Library was opened, with Reba Lehman Librarian.

1921. The greatest single advance in the early development of the College Library was made with the appointment of Miss Helen Ethel Myers, the first fully professional librarian. This appointment was one of the principal moves made by President Gossard to win accreditation by the Middle States Association.

Miss Myers' first problem as Librarian is best explained in her own words:

> When I first came to the Library, it was nothing but a playground for the students, and the Faculty had no respect for it. I had to break down that prejudice. Professor Derickson stood by me. He saw the chairs had been taken out of the Library and used for other purposes. They were all brought back, so we had chairs in our reference room for people to sit on. Then I secured the first really

Lynch Memorial Building
Courtesy Bruce C. Souders

good appropriation for books the Library had ever had. The first valuable book we bought was the Oxford English Dictionary. In the end, we had the Faculty back of us.

By selling textbooks, the Library managed to build up a little cash reserve, and so was able to bind its periodicals and make such purchases as the complete Index of the New York *Times*. Gradually the Library filled up its stack space, upstairs as well as down. Special collections came in: the Hiram Herr Shenk Collection of *Pennsylvaniana,* the Henry S. Heilman Library (purchased and donated by Dr. E. N. Funkhouser), the C. B. Montgomery Memorial Collection (donated by his sister, Mrs. H. H. Norton of Philadelphia), and the College Archives, which Miss Myers herself, President Lynch, Miss Gladys Fencil, and more recently Mrs. D. Clark Carmean have done most to gather. Inevitably the movement for a larger library gathered momentum.

When the Gossard Memorial Library was opened, it almost immediately became the focus of the College's intellectual life. "The true university in these days," wrote Carlyle, "is a collection of books." Faculty and students at L. V. C. would seem to agree. Student use of library facilities doubled at once.

"If ever an addition proved itself in the first year of operation, surely this one did," said Dr. Miller.

The year 1957 saw also the occupancy of the new Mary C. Green Residence Hall, and the partial use of Science Hall.

In December, 1955, the College had purchased the A. R. Kreider Manufacturing Company properties west of the campus, which included a three-story brick building on White Oak Street opposite the Men's Dormitory. This was transformed into Science Hall and dedicated in memory of Dr. Andrew Bender, '06, and Dr. Samuel H. Derickson, '02. In January, 1957, the Chemistry Department under Dr. Howard A. Neidig, '43, moved into the first floor. Later the Biology Department under Dr. Francis H. Wilson and Dr. V. Earl Light, '16, took position on the second and third floors, the removals being completed by September, 1959.

If 1957 was the College's *annus mirabilis,* 1958 ran it a close second. It was on July 16, 1957, that ground was broken for the new College Dining Hall, but it was not until September, 1958, that it came into use. Appetites increased in the large, comfortable, main dining room, with cafeteria service for breakfast and lunch, and waiter service for evening dinner. It proved immediately a morale builder, proving what women of discriminating mind have always known: that one way to the understanding heart is through the digestive tract. If further evidence be needed of that humble truth, it may be found in the enthusiastic student (and faculty) reception of the snack bar opened, 1958, in what had once been the Carnegie Library.

Foreign Language Laboratory

In the Psychology Laboratory

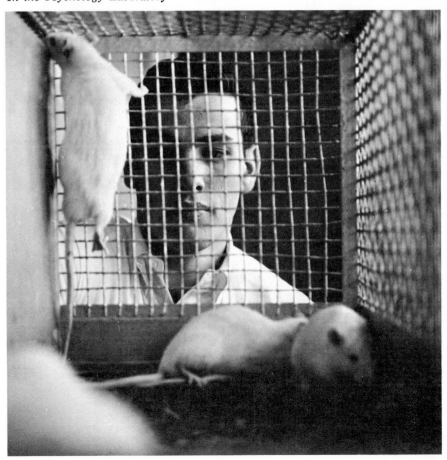

Learning the principles of neutron radiation
Bruce Bean, '68, with long-handled tongs, places the plutonium in position.
Courtesy Bruce C. Souders

The Laser Light is demonstrated by Harold A. Lutz, '65.
Courtesy Bruce C. Souders

Miss Mary E. Gillespie,
Director of the Conservatory of Music, 1930–1957
Courtesy D. Clark Carmean

The Concert Choir at the Washington Cathedral, March 28, 1965
Courtesy Bruce C. Souders

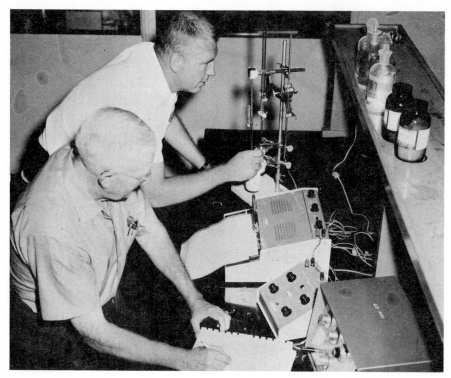

The College's Chemistry Laboratories have been the center for the Laboratory Development Program of the Chemical Bond Approach Project. This program is devoted to designing an improved curriculum for teaching chemistry in secondary schools. It is financed by the American Chemical Society and the National Science Foundation.

Honors Students
in an informal discussion with faculty members
and guests from other campuses.

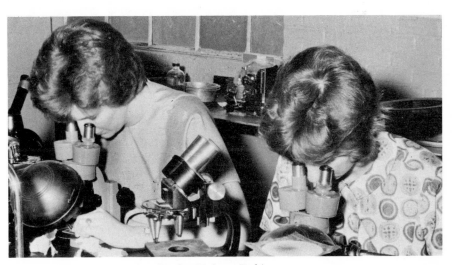

In the Biology Laboratory
Students examine biological materials through
compound and dissecting microscopes.

Hammond Hall,
dedicated with Keister Hall, another men's residence, October 29, 1965.

The Basketball Team of 1952–1953
entered NCAA tournament as Middle Atlantic Conference Champions, beating
Fordham 80–67 before losing to Louisiana State and Wake Forest.
George R. (Rinso) Marquette, Coach and Dean of Men since 1956; Richie Furda,
Co-Captain; Marty Gluntz; Howie Landa; Lou Sorrentino; Herb Finkelstein (Fields);
Don Grider; Bob Blakeney; Leon Miller, Co-Captain; Bill Vought; Jim Handley;
Howie Kosier.

It was in the same year, 1958, that the student society, Delta Tau Chi, aided by the East Pennsylvania Conference and the Pennsylvania Conference, presented to the College an altar for the "prayer corner" in the Gossard Memorial Library. Dedicated by Bishop George E. Epp in memory of the late Bishop Paul E. V. Shannon, '18, who had been a devoted friend of the College, the corner is now in daily use for prayer and meditation.

Meanwhile the old Administration Building underwent corresponding change. Laboratories were set up on the third floor for Dr. Jean O. Love's Psychology Department and for Dr. Sara Elizabeth Piel's Foreign Language Department. The Physics Department, under Dr. Jacob L. Rhodes, '43, and Dr. Samuel O. Grimm, was moved from the second floor to the first floor and basement, its former place being taken by Dr. Barnard H. Bissinger's statistical laboratory and library-seminar room for the Mathematics Department.

Other physical improvements, too numerous to mention, transformed college accommodations. Private residences were purchased, renovated, and renamed, providing further dormitory space, new offices, and an air of spaciousness and efficiency the College had never seen before.

Among the many influences contributing to L. V. C.'s new intellectual outlook and the decline of parochialism, one of the foremost has been the widened geographical base from which students are recruited. Another has been the increase in faculty travel. Sabbatical leave (introduced in the college year of 1956–1957), of which Assistant Professor Theodore D. Keller, '48, was the first to avail himself, has done much to widen horizons. So also has the bringing to the campus of increasing numbers of scholars from other colleges and universities for lectures and student conferences. The invitations now being extended to learned societies to hold their annual conferences on this campus is another sign of academic maturity.

Best of all, perhaps, in contributing to widened vision is the Faculty's growing initiative in studying its own programs and adapting the curriculum to meet the challenge of today's "explosion of knowledge." New courses and new programs are being introduced. Conspicuous among the latter is the Department of Elementary Education, established under the leadership of Dr. Clyde H. Ebersole. The interrelations of various academic disciplines are being explored. Certain major changes in the curriculum are aimed at enlarging the student's vision of Man's development.

Admissions standards have been tightened. The Honors Program (which provides special sections for superior students in certain courses, and also, through the Independent Study program, provides opportunities leading to departmental honors) while it is still in the experimental stage, is stimulating some students and through them tending to leaven the whole student body. Faculty members also, with fewer administrative duties on their shoulders, have more time for scholarly activity and growth.

The Faculty, 1964

Increasingly, Lebanon Valley students are developing intellectual initiative. Evidence for this is found in the far greater number of those who now go on to graduate study, and who do this, not merely because their chosen profession may require it, but because they love learning for its own sake.

The importance of this attitude has been fittingly expressed in a commencement address by the late Dr. Alfred Whitney Griswold, President of Yale University:

> My moral, then, is plain and my charge to you is simple: To do good you must first know good; to serve beauty you must first know beauty; to speak the truth you must first know the truth. You must know these things yourselves, be able to recognize them by yourselves, be able to describe, explain, and communicate them by yourselves, and wish to do so, when no one else is present to prompt you or bargain with you. This knowledge has been the purpose of your education. Hold true to that purpose. No price, no mess of potage, can equal its value to your country and yourselves.

In this age of space exploration and social revolution, there is great strain upon young minds seeking to orient themselves in a changing environment. Their inevitable questionings and occasional stirrings of revolt have drawn big headlines and disturbed their elders. Lebanon Valley College has not been immune, for the perplexities that bother our young people lie at the root of things and are universal. Young men and young women, no matter how good the advice they receive, must in the end come to their own terms with life's riddles—unless they are to become mental robots and follow a dictator. That students are grappling, however clumsily, with major problems is one of the healthy signs of our time.

> You have been reading, I am sure, that the era of student complacency and conformism is drawing to a close [reported President Miller to the Conferences in 1962]. Student activity in politics and in some of the controversial areas of today's world is increasing. On balance it is our impression that this is a good sign. For too long those who will be leaders in the next generation have been entirely too engrossed in their own affairs. These signs of disquiet will bring accompanying heartaches to be sure, but as our nation faces the problems of the next decade it is well that our students are showing increased interest in participation in campus, community, and national affairs.

"These young people," reported Dr. Miller a year later, "need sympathetic understanding and guidance both at the College and at home."

It is a situation that calls for "the discriminating mind and the understanding heart," a situation in which Dr. Miller sees great opportunity for college influence. With this in view, he created the new office of Chaplain of the Col-

Architect's Sketch of the College Chapel
Containing a sanctuary to seat a thousand people, together with facilities for student religious organizations and classrooms and offices for the Departments of Philosophy and Religion, it will be the center of the College's religious life.

235

lege, a position first held by the Rev. (now Bishop) W. Maynard Sparks, '27, and now by the Rev. Dr. James O. Bemesderfer, '36.

Dr. Carl Y. Ehrhart, Dean of the College, attributes the College's comparative freedom from the extremer forms of student agitation to the frankness and openness of the relations existing here between students and Faculty. Communication between the two is quick and constant. Student government (which has a long tradition at the College) is well administered. The relations between the student governing bodies, men's and women's, with the Faculty are excellent. Each has a high respect for the other. When disciplinary action is called for (except in small cases involving such things as the freshman "dink and tie" rules), the student governments present recommendations to the Faculty. The Faculty seldom disagrees—except, occasionally, in the direction of mercy, for the student governing bodies lean over backwards to play no favorites and to administer justice.

To George R. Marquette, Dean of Men, and Miss Martha C. Faust, Dean of Women—both of whom are sympathetic but firm in their convictions—and to Dr. Carl Ehrhart, Dean of the College, much is owed for the excellence of student-faculty relations.

"People," explains Dr. Ehrhart, "tend to live up to the level of behavior expected of them."

While the College has given to students a freedom that would have appalled their grandparents in President Hammond's day, it has also made quite clear what its convictions are in the matter of right behavior. The result is a harmony not surpassed on other college campuses.

As we approach the end of this brief narrative of a Pennsylvania college—its birth, adolescence, and coming of age—there is a question that calls for a frank answer. Has Lebanon Valley College fulfilled the hopes of its founders?

Certainly it can be said in this Centennial Year that the College, after long probation, has become what the citizens of Annville had in mind when they donated the old Annville Academy to the East Pennsylvania Conference for the establishment of *an institution of learning of high grade.*

It is an institution of which the alumni are rightly proud: first, because of its present status in the society of American colleges and universities; and second, because of the fight it has put up (starting without students, money, or academic know-how) to achieve the honored position it now holds.

But the College's success is in more than mere status. It is in the high function it is performing. It will be recalled that Cardinal Newman declared the object of a Liberal Education was to produce a habit of mind "of which the attributes are, freedom, equitableness, calmness, moderation, and wisdom. . . ." Granted that L. V. C.'s students have not at all times shown such

*The 1965 Outstanding Alumnus Award
is presented to Dr. Carroll Roop Daugherty, '21, by Dean Carl Ehrhart.
Other winners of the award since its inception in 1959: Dr. Robert L. Roudabush,
'31; Dr. E. D. Williams, '19; Dr. Bruce M. Metzger, '35; Miss Lottie M. Spessard,
'13; Dr. Samuel O. Grimm, '12; Miss Gladys Fencil, '21; and Charles H. Horn, '19.*

calmness and wisdom as might have been desired, nevertheless the moderation and good sense of the student body today is evidence that Lebanon Valley College is moving in the right direction.

Calmness and moderation are good, but they are not all. Our graduates are producers, active men and women, exerting public influence—Christian influence, helping their fellow men to meet the problems of a narrowing world in a patently expanding universe.

Their record is heartening to behold: whether in our own country in the field of business, the Church, and the professions, or abroad as missionaries, diplomats, and members of the Peace Corps. To name but a sampling of the more recent graduates, it is heartening to follow the careers of such men as these:

Dr. Carroll Roop Daugherty, '21, Professor of Labor Economics at North-western University, author of *Labor Problems in American Industry* and many other books;

Dr. H. Darkes Albright, '28, Chairman of the Department of Speech and Drama at Cornell University, author of *Working Up a Part,* co-author of *Principles of Theatre Art,* translator of Appia's *The Work of Living Art,* currently General Editor of the *Books of the Theatre* series;

Dr. J. Calvin Keene, '30, Professor of Religion in the St. Lawrence University, co-author of *The Western Heritage of Faith and Reason;*

Dr. James H. Leathem, '32, Professor of Zoology and Director of the Bureau of Biological Research at Rutgers University;

Dr. Bruce Metzger, '35, Professor of New Testament Language and Literature at the Princeton Theological Seminary, Member of the Institute for Advanced Studies, editor of the *Oxford Concise Concordance to the Revised Version of the Holy Bible* and of the *Oxford Annotated Bible, Revised Standard Version,* and author of *The Text of the New Testament: It's Transmission, Corruption, and Restoration* and many other works of Biblical Criticism;

Dr. Russell Getz, as Conrad Beissell, conducts the Ephrata Cloister Chorus.
Courtesy Bruce C. Souders

Dr. John P. Marbarger, '38, Research Director in the Aeromedical and Physical Environment Laboratory, University of Illinois, and editor of the *Aeromedical Journal of the United States;*

Dr. John H. Moyer, '39, Chairman of the Department of Medicine, Hahnemann Medical College and Hospital, who has discovered new treatment for Hypertension;

Robert B. Wingate, '48, Fellow of the Royal Society of Artists, one of the world's foremost medical illustrators and supreme in the depiction of eye surgery;

Dr. Russell Getz, '49, Coordinator of Arts, Department of Public Instruction, Pennsylvania, who has restored the music of the Ephrata Cloister for present-day musicians and now directs the Cloister Chorus in its annual concert.

As returning graduates move about the campus in 1966 and see on every hand the signs of growth: a new chapel, library, dining hall, science building, and residences; as they examine the latest *Catalog* or visit the lecture rooms and see how the Faculty has grown in numbers and attainments; and as they sense the *esprit de corps* among Faculty and students alike and see the pride now taken in the College by the church constituency and the community at large, a pride confirmed mathematically by the figures of recent endowment campaigns—they will see what Christian statesmanship can accomplish. For it is under the leadership of "Fritz" Miller, man of affairs and son of the revered Harry E. Miller, former pastor of Salem E. U. B. Church in Lebanon, that this has been brought about. He took the helm during a time of trouble. With the loyal help of the co-operating conferences, the Board of Trustees, Faculty, Administration, Alumni, and friends, he brought the ship into safe waters. More than that, he has refitted the craft for line duty with an armada of other colleges of the Liberal Arts in the supreme task of preparing our young people for leadership in a world alternately chilled by the shadow of the mushroom cloud and warmed with hope of better things to come if humanity can be brought into fuller understanding of Man's responsibility to Man.

Assuredly the College has fulfilled, and more than fulfilled, the hopes of its founders. If Miles Rigor and Thomas Rhys Vickroy were to return today, they would be happy to find that our graduates, lay as well as clerical, had discovered new ways—unsuspected a hundred years ago—of serving their Master by helping their neighbors.

It would be safe now to call back John Russel. Bringing to earth with him the wisdom of Eternity, he would rejoice at the rich meaning of this Centennial Year. His voice would roll out over the campus, dilating, not on his old text, "Knowledge puffeth up" (he himself in the meantime having learned humility) but on a passage from Isaiah, 33:6, that touches our present condition: "And wisdom and knowledge shall be the stability of thy times."

Valedictory

We salute the men of foresight and faith who founded Lebanon Valley College as a co-educational institution of the Liberal Arts; the men of courage and conviction who tended and defended it during its infancy; succeeding presidents, faculties, alumni, boards of trustees, co-operating Conferences, together with the people of its local community, friends throughout the United States and beyond its borders in Canada, England, Germany, France, Switzerland, Sweden, China, Japan, India, Sierra Leone—all who have in any way helped to uphold the College through good years and bad. They are truly the graduates to be honored in this Centennial Year.

But 1966 is not only a graduation, a time of remembrance. It is also a Commencement, a time to look forward.

So it is that Lebanon Valley College extends to all its well-wishers greetings appropriate to this academic occasion:

SALVETE, COLLEGII AMICI.

Appendices
and
Bibliographical Notes

Appendix A

A manuscript from the pen of Valentine Kline Fisher describing his life at Lebanon Valley College from 1875 to 1880 arrived too late for use in the body of this book. Through the kindness of the author's son, Lawrence M. Fisher of Garrett Park, Maryland, the College is permitted to print it as an appendix.

MEMOIRS OF A BERKS COUNTY COUNTRY-MAN

By Valentine Kline Fisher

Edited by Lawrence M. Fisher

Introduction by L. M. F.

Lebanon Valley College has had a strong influence on four generations of the Fisher family, beginning with Jacob Fisher of Berne, Pa., about 1867.

His eldest son, John K. Fisher, graduated with the class of 1872, his youngest son, Valentine K. Fisher, with the class of 1880. Two other children, Samuel K. and Rebecca Fisher Lehman (wife of Professor John E. Lehman), attended for various periods of time. Lawrence M. Fisher, son of V. K. Fisher, entered Lebanon Valley with the class of 1909 but graduated from Pennsylvania State University in 1910 after spending a year at L. V. C. Ethel Fisher Steiner, daughter of Lawrence Fisher, spent 3 years at L. V. C. but graduated from Pennsylvania State University in 1942.

John K. Fisher and the Rev. J. Wesley Etter were the first ministerial students to be graduated from Lebanon Valley. They were the first members of the conference to take a full theological course. They were ordained in 1876 after having been graduated from Drew Theological Seminary. The Rev. John Fisher served the College Church at Annville, Pa., 1878 to 1883. He served various other charges in Pennsylvania and died in Lebanon, Pa., June 18, 1890, at the age of 40.

Valentine K. Fisher served as Superintendent of the Salem U. B. Sunday School, Berne, Pa., for 27 years, receiving a medal from the Pennsylvania Sabbath School Association for "fifty years of Sabbath School service" awarded June 29, 1933. He was a brother-in-law to John E. Lehman and was a trustee of Lebanon Valley College 1896-1906. He died Oct. 8, 1936, at the age of 79. Dr. Clyde Lynch, President of L. V. C., preached his funeral sermon. — *L. M. F.*

College Experiences

It was in the summer of 1875 when my father came to me, out in the spring-house field, where I was plowing, over by the railroad, and told me that brother Samuel had given up the idea of going to Lafayette College, would in fact, not go to any college, and that I should get ready to go to Lebanon Valley College at Annville, the following morning.

In the spring of 1875, at the close of the college year, a controversy arose in connection with the hiring of the teaching staff at Lebanon Valley College. Some of the students, brother Samuel and I. A. Loose among them, did not like what was done. So Sam spent nearly the entire vacation studying at home trying to prepare himself to enter the sophomore class at Lafayette College at Easton. But he got discouraged, and for several reasons gave up any future thought of a college career. . . .

The term had begun when I arrived. I had to enter the Preparatory Department and had rough sledding to make the Freshman class the following term. I was put up with a young man in room number 27, next door to the room my brother John had occupied for five years. This young man also was a Fisher by name, George Fisher. He came from Dauphin county and proved to be a distant relative. He was a short stout fellow with lots of self-confidence, and proud as he could be.

He was even more poorly prepared for school than I was. At least that was my opinion. He lasted that year but did not turn up at college the following year. He was a cousin to the Reno boys at Hamburg, Frank and Charles.* I came across him only once afterwards, at some camp meeting, the location of which I do not now recall.

The first year at L. V. C. passed without any out-standing occurrences. The hardest ordeals for me to face were the Friday afternoon "oratoricals" as they were called. In them we had to express our thinking upon a given subject in writing, in the form of an essay which we were required to read in our respective divisions. Every month we were obliged to write an "oration" which we were expected to deliver on a Saturday night from the rostrum in the chapel. These were the greatest bug-bears of my whole college life. How I dreaded to get up before that chapel, crowded to the doors, and recite a lot of stuff, in which there was nothing worth while, and nobody knew it better than I did myself! But I did as well as I could, and many compliments were paid me.

---

* Their parents were William Reno (1825-1895) and Maria Fisher (1828-1875).

The school year ended and I came home for my vacation. Before my vacation had ended my father had died. My prospects for returning to college were slim. I had entirely given up the idea. Father's affairs were in terrible condition; even worse than we had realized at the time of his death. It was decided we would try to keep the estate intact and Samuel would take over the mill business the following spring. The farm was rented for three years. What I was to do was not very clear, but I remained on the farm with the intention of staying home until the following spring when the farm stock was to be sold. Sam, being the oldest of us at home, assumed the role of dictator, but I would not compel myself to be submissive. So I stepped out of the scene by going back to college. This was in October, 1876. When I got back to college I was again out of regular order because I was about a month late. But I had worked ahead in my preparatory year, somewhat, so that before the year was out, I had caught up with my class and was in regular order and good standing again. The year went by without any outstanding happenings beyond the routine of college life.

As soon as I entered college I joined the Philokosmian Literary Society, the only literary society at the college at that time. The Clionian Literary Society was organized in my junior year. I took my place in its proceedings in full, and enjoyed its activities as much as any feature of my college life. I belonged to its various cliques and parties such as usually spring up in similar organizations.

I wish to say here that I was not one of the brilliant scholars. I always moved in the upper class of students, however, and had a leading hand in moulding the student movements and activities. When students were taken into consultation by the faculty, in regard to the advisability of making any move on behalf of the student body, I was advised with as much as any one else in the social life of the college.*

I always held my own. And never, as I remember now, was any slight shown me, from the time of my freshman year on. Although I came late in the opening term, I was made head of my division at the table, a position cherished by those to whom the place was given. I kept it until the end of my junior year, when I boarded outside the dormitory.

An experience which has always remained a pleasantly remembered event of my college life was a public reception given to A. L. Groff upon his return from Europe, where he had gone to attend the Paris Exposition. I was the host, and a Miss Clara Craumer the hostess. It was a gala event, carried out in the best style we knew. After the rehearsal the event came off gloriously. It was quite an eye-opener to us unsophisticated country jays. The latter years of college were very much given to similar occasions. There were several sociables

---

* Later V. K. F. served for a number of years on the Board of Trustees of Lebanon Valley College.—L. M. F.

given during the winter seasons. All the students were invited, even urged to attend. They were, as a consequence, well patronized. In the fall there were chestnut parties. I remember two of them when the whole student body went out to Gravel Hill, to the woods, ostensibly for chestnuts. The time was spent in outdoor games of various kinds.

One of the outstanding events of the college social program was the annual anniversary of the Philokosmian Literary Society. There was considerable rivalry in this event as to who were to be the select few to have the principal parts in it, such as who were to be the orators, and who would be the presiding officers. At one time the competition was so close and the excitement so high that the senior student who aspired to the presiding officer's post collapsed before the election took place and never recovered sufficiently to preside. The secretary of the society had to fill his place. I had the honor to preside at this event in my junior year, and also had an oration in my sophomore year.

Another event to which we all looked forward was the joint session of the Philokosmian and Clionian Societies. Everybody put forth his or her best efforts, both in literary performance and in gallantry. This was also an annual event.

Of course the most important events of the year took place during the commencement weeks. Each graduating class tried to outdo the preceeding class, and tried to study out a new feature, a new idea. Class day was the most fruitful in new exploits. The class history and class jokes brought out jolly surprises of all kinds. The class of '79 was the most outstanding class in my recollection. It was made up of strong men and women; in every way a class superior. With a few exceptions all completed the classical course. All were financially able. They made the best showing.

Athletics were of the most meager sort. There was some attempt at baseball but it was not organized. True there was always ball-playing. A few clubs were brought together occasionally, being organized whenever a game was to be played. This had to be gone through with whenever any playing was to take place; mostly after 4 o'clock and before 5:30 when the supper bell rang and everyone dropped the ball and bat for supper. After supper only the most enthusiastic reported on the ballfield. The rest strolled uptown or somewhere else as the mood moved them.

On Saturday afternoons there was quite a crowd on the field, and once in a while the boys from town came to the field with a club made up of town boys to play a scrub team of students. I was never a good player. For some reason I was a poor hitter. I could catch most any ball with my bare hands. We had no padded gloves then, and a real hot ball stung sharply. Those who stood in the catcher's box invariably had "knuckled" finger joints.

I had some umpiring experience. I was taken along with our team for that purpose whenever they went to a nearby town to play. This did not happen often, but I remember a very exciting game we played at Myerstown with the Palatinate College there. I was umpire and was highly commended by their captain for fair decisions. I also went along with the town club to play a team at Lebanon. They had been given the old fair grounds, and an immense crowd came out to see the game. There was even a policeman on hand. But we could not play because we could not keep the diamond clear. Finally I handed the ball to the Annville team and called it off. There was quite an uproar thereat, but the policeman advised me to do so in order to avoid real violence....

There were the usual student pranks common to the small colleges, but no hazing in my time at all. We did not even know of such things, and there was very little class spirit. In our class, 1880, it was confined to the wearing of a seal-skin fur turban cap and a two-colored ribbon. I don't remember the colors.* In the line of pranks, quite a few could be mentioned: some harmless in themselves, others that were directed upon some of the professors were characteristic of meanly disposed minds. They seemed extremely funny at the time, but at this distance most thoughtless and foolish and even dangerous.

In letting my mind recur to these days, in many ways, delightful and happy days, many things come back in all their vividness which I would like to blot out from my memory were it possible. And I have only a few things to deplore in which I was concerned that were in themselves vicious or unkind in their results or effects. There were a good many opportunities from which I failed to profit, or their importance failed to impress me sufficiently at the time.†

---

* Isaiah Sneath, Chris Geiger, and V. K. F. constituted themselves the *Tres Boni Amici,* Three Good Friends. Sneath, class of 1881, preached for the Congregational church in New England, went to Yale and became Dean of the School of Philosophy there. He was the Beau Brummel of L. V. C. Geiger lived in Schuylkill county at the time of the author's death, 1936.—L. M. F.

† Valentine Fisher (1857-1936), after his graduation from Lebanon Valley College in 1880, entered a lawyer's office in Lebanon, intending to "read" law. His services were needed at home helping to keep the estate together. He returned to Berne and soon afterwards married Elizabeth Epting Machemer.—L. M. F.

Appendix B

A Century of Teachers, Lebanon Valley College, 1866–1966

Ablett, Charles B., B.S., M.S., Math. and Phys. 1950–51.

Adams, May Belle, B.L.I., Oratory and Pub. Sp. 1910–22.

Aikman, Rev. Joseph G., A.M., Nat. Sci. 1873–74.

Albert, Carol, B.S., Art. 1963–65.

Albertson, Gertrude, Fine Arts. 1893–94.

Aldrich, John A., A.B., M.S., Ph.D., Math., Phys. 1948–50.

Allis, Fannie A., A.B., Engl., Mod. Lang. 1895–97.

Amen, Alexander R., B.S., Ph.D., Chem. 1952–55.

Arndt, Charles H., A.M., Bio. 1916–17.

Arnold, William C., A.M., Stenog., Tpng., Bkg., Soc. 1899–06.

Avery, Euretta A., Inst. Mus. and Voice. 1879–81.

Bachman, Ora B., Mus.B., Mus. Thry. and Piano. 1912–17.

Bailey, L. Gary, A.B., M.A., Ph.D., Psych. 1931–47.

Baldwin, Edith H., Painting and Drawing. 1899–06.

Balsbaugh, Edward M., B.S., Math. St. Teach. 1938–48.

Baltzell, W. J., A.B., Violin and Harm. 1889–90.

Batchelor, William A., B.S., M.A. Art. 1953–.

Batdorf, Emma R., B.S., Elocut. and Orat., Phys. Cult. 1901–05.

Batdorf, Joses B., B.S., Normal Dept. 1888–89.

Battista, Joseph, Piano. 1940–43; 1945–46.

Baxtresser, Margaret B., B.A., Piano. 1946–50.

Beatty, T. Bayard, A.B., A.M., Engl. 1919–25.

Bechtell, Homer F., B.S., M.A., Ph.D., Math. 1961–63.

Behney, J. Bruce, A.B., Bible and Grk. 1930–31.

Bemesderfer, James O., A.B., B.D., S.T.M., S.T.D., Relig. 1959–.

Bender, Andrew, A.B., Ph.D., Chem. 1921–51.

Bender, Ruth Engle, A.B., Mus. Thry and Piano, 1918–22; 1924–.

Bennett, Ethel M., B.A., Fr., Germ. 1922–29.

Bennett, Harold, Ph.D., Latin. 1922–29.

Bernat, Louise, Piano. 1944–45.

Bierman, E. Benjamin, (President) A.M., Ph.D., Normal, Engl., Germ., Math., Astron., Nat. Philos., Mental & Mor. Sci. 1866–79; President 1890–97.

Biesterfeldt, Herman J., B.S., Math. 1962–63.

Bilbo, Queenie M., A.B., A.M., Engl. 1925–26.

Binner, Alvin, M.E., Teach. Prep. 1903–06.

Bissinger, Barnard H., A.B., M.A., Ph.D., Math. 1953–.

Black, Amos H., A.B., A.M., Ph.D., Math., Phys. 1936–48.

Black, Ella N., B.S., Music 1896–98.

Blose, Johann M., Mus.D., Mus. Theory, Piano, Organ. 1922–24.

Boehm, Florence, Art. 1907–16.

Bollinger, O. Pass, B.S., M.S., Biol. 1950–.

Bond, William, M., A.B., A.M., Math. 1948–49.

Bowker, Lee H., A.B., M.A., Soc. 1965–.

Bowman, Betty Jane, B.S., M.A., Phys. Ed. 1952–64.

Bowman, E. S., Bkg., Pnmnshp. 1885–90.

Bowman, George W., A.M., Nat. Sci. 1882–90.

Bowman, Lewis, B.S., Chem. 1950.

Bowman, Mary Virginia, A.B., M.A., Ph.D., Engl. 1954–60.

Bowman, Urban N. Jr., B.S., Phys. Ed. 1963–64.

Bowman, Wesley H., Bkg., Pnmnshp. 1890–91.

Bowman, Zacharias A., Normal Dept. 1900–03.

Bradley, Samuel M., A.B., M.A., Engl. 1955–59.

Brown, Ethel I., Music, Voice. 1910–11.

Brumbaugh, Alice M., B.S., M.A., Soc. 1952–65.

Bugda, Peter F., B.S., M.Ed., Art. 1962–63.

Burns, Sarah, M.A., Elocution. 1868–69; 1871–72; 1873–74.

Burras, Fay B., A.B., M.A., Math. 1964–.

Butler, Ruth E., A.B., M.A., For. Lang. 1955–61.

Butterwick, Robert R., A.B., B.D., D.D., Bible & Philos. 1920–38.

Campbell, R. Porter, Mus.B., Piano, Organ, Thry. 1915–62.

Carmean, D. Clark, A.B., M.A., Mus. Ed. 1933–.

Carroll, Rhoda Z., A.B., A.M., Math. 1952–53.

Castetter, William B., B.S., M.A., Ed. 1946–48.

Cerveris, Michael E., B.S., M.A., Piano. 1963–64.

Chamberlain, Charles A., A.B., B.D., S.T.M., S.T.C., Rel. 1962–64.

Chapman, E. Winifred, A.B., Phys. Ed. 1928–29.

Chestnut, David T., A.B., M.S., Fr. 1961–62.

Christeson, Laura, Piano. 1909–10.

Colgan, Carroll M., B.S., M.A., Ph.D., Psych. 1957–60.

Colgan, Mildred M., A.B., M.S., Psych., 1957–60.

Cooper, Charles T., B.S., M.A., Sp. 1965–.

Cooper, Clara C., A.B., M.A., Ph.D., Psych. 1948–51.

Cooper, Homer I., A.B., Ph.D., Bus Ad. and Ed. 1948–50.

Cramer, Martha A., Fr. & Fine Arts. 1878–80.

Crawford, Alexander, Voice. 1927–64.

Cretzinger, John I., A.B., M.A., Ph.D., Biol. 1946–50.

Culp, Mary S., Music. 1880–81.

Cummings, Hubertis M., B.A., M.A., Ph.D., Engl. 1947–48.

Curfman, George D., B.S., M.M., Mus. Ed. 1961–.

Damus, Hilda M., M.A., Ph.D., Germ. 1963–.

Daniel, Rev. Charles S., B.S., Soc. Sci. 1898–99.

Daniel, Enid, B.S., Phys. Cult. 1899–00.

Darlington, George L., B.S., M.S., Phys. Ed., 1964–.

Darnell, Virginia, B.S., M.A., Mus. Ed. 1939–43.

Daugherty, Benjamin F., A.B., A.M., B.D., Latin. 1897–1906.

Daugherty, Samuel F., B.D., D.D., Bible. 1915–19.

Deak, Stephen, Cello. 1934–36.

Deaner, H. Clay, A.B., Math., Astron., Lat. 1879–97.

DeLong, David D. (President) B.A., A.M., Ment. & Mor. Sci. 1876–87.

DeLong, Emma Knepper, B.A., M.A., Grk. 1877–85.

Dent, Constance P., B.A., M.A., Psych. 1951–57.

Derickson, S. Hoffman, B.S., M.S., Sc.D., Bio. 1903–50.

DeWitt, Orville P., Jr., A.B., Engl. and Hist. 1899–00.

Dittmar, Emma, E., Fine Arts. 1889–93.

Dodge, Louise P., Ph.D., Lat. and Fr. 1909–11.

Dotter, Charles G., A.B., Ed. 1902–03.

Drummond, Sarah E., Inst. Mus. and Fine Arts. 1872–74.

Duffey, Buela, Piano. 1935–36.

Dunahugh, Nettie R., M.E., Math. 1901–02.

Eberly, Daniel, M.A., D.D., Lat., Philos., Hist. 1875–84; 1899–05.

Ebersole, Cloyd H., A.B., M.Ed., D.Ed., El. Ed. 1953–.

Ebersole, W. S., A.M., Grk. 1887–90.

Eby, Carrie G., Music. 1888–92.

Eby, Lillian C., Ph.M., B.O., Oratory, Phys. Cult. 1909–10.

Egli, William H., B.A., LL.B., Bus. Law. 1947–63.

Ehrhart, Carl Y., A.B., B.D., Ph.D., Philos. 1947–.

Eichinger, Harry L., B.O., Elocut. 1899–00.

Enders, Howard E., B.S., M.S., Bio. 1904–06.

Engle, M. Edna, A.M., Engl. 1907–08.

Engle, J. Raymond, A.B., LL.B., LL.D., Acting President. 1932.

Erickson, Robert L., B.S., M.S., Math. 1948–51.

Esbenshade, Edith Spangler, A.M. Engl. 1909–10.

Espenshade, Marlin, B.S., M.S., Bio. 1949–50.

Etter, J. Wesley, A.B., Pnmnshp., Bkg., Rhet., Engl. 1866–73.

Evans, William R., B.A., M.A., Engl. 1962–63.

Evers, Alice M., B.S., Music & Fr. 1883–90.

Faber, Anna Dunkle, A.B., Ph.D., Engl. 1954–.

Fairlamb, William H., Jr., B.M., Piano & Thry. 1947–.

Fagan, Robert C., B.S., M.A., Psych. 1948–51.

Fagan, Violet B., A.B., A.M., Sp. and Fr. 1948–51.

Faust, Martha C., A.B., M.A., Ed. 1957–.

Fehr, Alex J., A.B., M.A., Pol. Sci. 1951–.

Feig, Chester A., B.A., M.A., Ed.D., Ed. 1946–49.

Fencil, Louise G., B.S., Phys. Ed. 1929–31.

Fields, Donald E., A.B., M.A., Ph.D., A.B. in Lib. Sci., Latin. 1928–30; 1947–.

Fields, Frances T., A.B., M.A., A.B. in Lib. Sci., Span. 1947–.

Fink, Althea C., B.S., Art. 1884–85.

Fisher, Paul H., B.S., M.S., Math. and Phys. 1947–48.

Flint, Carrie M., Music, Instr. and Voice. 1892–96.

Flory, Leila A., Mus. Thry. 1929–30.

Ford, Arthur L., A.B., M.A., Ph.D., Engl. 1965–.

Forney, Adam R., Engl. 1872–73.

Forney, Anna R., A.B., Mus., Harm. 1894–95.

Foss, Martin, LL.D., Philos. 1960–62.

Fox, Richard E., B.S., M.S., Econ. and Bus. Ad., Coach. 1947–54.

Frank, Luella U., A.B., M.A., Germ., Sp., Fr. 1946–55.

Freeland, Merl W., A.B., Piano. 1938–50.

Fritz, John H., A.B., M.A., Hist. 1959–61.

Frock, Jerome W., B.S., Dir. Phys. Ed., Coach. 1934–46.

Frounick, Ross G., A.B., Lat. 1920–22.

Funkhouser, Abram Paul (President) B.S., A.M., 1906–07.

Funkhouser, George A., M.A., Ment. & Mor. Sci. 1870–71.

Funkhouser, Jessie P., Art. 1906–08.

Garman, Betty H., B.S., Phys. Ed., 1958–59; 1964–.

Gates, G. Thomas, A.B., LL.B., Bus. Law. 1963–.

Geffen, Elizabeth M., B.S., M.A., Ph.D., Hist. 1958–.

Gerberich, Albert H., B.S., Nat. Sci. 1890–91.

Gerberich, Grant B., B.S., Norm. Dept. 1900–03.

Getz, Pierce A., B.S., M.S.M., Organ. 1959–.

Gillespie, Mary E., B.S., M.A., Music & Dir. of Conserv. 1930–57.

Gillis, John, Dir. Ath. 1903–05.

Gilmore, Robert O., A.B., M.A., Math. 1953–56.

Gingrich, Alice K., M.A., Inst. Mus., Voice. 1885–88; 1892–93.

Gingrich, Christian R., A.B., LL.B., Pol. Sci. & Econ. 1916–42.

Gingrich, Mary Funk, Piano. 1951–52.

Gockley, Warren, B.S., Phys. Ed., 1950–51.

Good, Oscar E., A.B., A.M., Math. & Sci. 1894–98.

Gossard, George D., (President) B.A., B.D., D.D. 1912–32.

Gotwald, W. H., D.D., LL.D., Apologetics. 1903–05.

Grace, D. John, B.S., C.P.C.U., C.P.A., Econ. & Bus. Ad. 1958–59; 1961–.

Gray, Thomas W., M.E., Phys. Cult. 1899–02.

Green, Mary C., French. 1916–43.

Green, Yvonne D., A.B., French. 1926–27.

Grider, Donald M., A.B., M.A., Phys. Ed. 1960–62.

Grimm, Samuel O., A.B., A.M., D.Sci. Phys., Math., Ed. 1912–.

Griswold, Robert E., B.S., M.S., Ph.D., Chem. 1960–.

Groff, A. LeFevre, Bkg. 1877–78.

Grumbine, Irvine F., Bkg. & Pnmnshp. 1884–85.

Guitner, Eugenia E., A.M., Nat. Sci. & Mod. Lang. 1870–72.

Guyer, Roy J., A.B., B.P.Ed., Lat., Phys. Ed., Coach. 1906–09; 1913–17.

Haag, Jessie H., B.S., M.Ed., Phys. Ed. 1946–47.

Hain, W. M., Penmnshp. 1885–86.

Hammond, Lucian H. (President) A.B., A.M., Grk. 1867–76; President, 1871–76.

Hammond, Stocks, Mus.Doc., Voice. 1895–96.

Hanson, Geilan, Russian. 1963–.

Harbour, Homer H., A.B., Engl. 1906–07.

Hardman, Frank F., Mus. Thry, Voice. 1922–25.

Haring, Malcolm M., A.M., Chem. 1918–21.
Harriman, B. Lynn, B.A., M.Ed., M.A., Psych. 1950–53.
Hartz, Leah C., Stenog., Typing. 1895–99.
Haugh, John F., A.B., Ph.D., Chem. 1961–.
Heilman, Wesley M., A.B., Norm. Dept. 1889–07.
Hempt, Marian E., Art. 1916–17.
Henderson, Esther, B.S., M.A., Phys. Ed. 1935–46.
Henning, Paul F., Jr., A.B., M.A., Math. 1959–.
Herr, June Eby, B.S., M.Ed., El.Ed, 1959–.
Hershey, Urban H., Mus.D., Violin. 1894–95; 1920–22.
Hess, Paul W., B.S., M.S., Ph.S., Bio. 1962–.
Holbrook, Mary R., Inst. Mus. 1868–69.
Holliday, Jane M., B.M., B.A., Mus.Ed. 1949–52.
Hollinger, Henry B., B.S., Ph.D., Chem. 1959–61.
Hollinger, Joseph K., A.B., Phys. Ed., Coach. 1921–23.
Holtzhauser, Clara A., A.M., Latin. 1917–19.
Honker, Henry A., Norm. Dept. 1900–01.
Hott, Ella R., Ph.B., Engl. 1888–89.
Houck, Henry, Prac. Teach. 1866–67.
House, Judson, Voice. 1937–39.
Houser, Barbara J., B.A., M.A., Germ. 1962–63.
Houtz, Florence, A.B., M.A., Engl. 1948–50.
Hurlburt, Charles E., Bible. 1897–01.
Huth, Mari L., B.S., Ph.D., Germ. 1947–49.

Intrieri, Marino, B.S., Phys. Ed., Coach. 1939–44.

Jackson, Alice M., Voice. 1909–10.
Jackson, Harry Dyer, A.B., Dir. of Mus. Dept. 1908–10.
Jackson, John K., A.M., Pub. Sp., Voice. 1904–06.
John, Lewis F., A.M., B.D., D.D., Bible, Philos. 1901–08.
Johns, Mary E., Voice 1889–90.
Johnson, Elizabeth, Violin, Orches. 1918–21.
Johnston, Falba L., A.M., Engl. 1911–14.
Jolly, James A., A.B., M.A., Hist. 1964–.
Jones, Ben., Piano. 1950–51.

Kaho, Elizabeth, B.Mus., M.A., Ph.D., Mus. Thry., Piano. 1946–52.

Keister, Lawrence W. (President), B.A., S.T.B., D.D. 1907–12.
Keller, Theodore D., A.B., M.A., Engl. 1949–65.
Kenyon, Mildred, B.S., M.A., Phys. Ed. 1931–35.
Kerr, George T., B.S., M.S., Ph.D., Chem. 1950–52.
Kephart, Cyrus J. (President), A.M., B.D., Ment. & Mor. Sci. 1889–90.
Kephart, E. B., M.A., D.D., LL.D., Int. Law, Bible Antiq., Arch. 1897–05.
Keys, William S. H., A.M., Ment. & Mor. Sci. 1872–73.
Killinger, Fannie C., Mus. 1881–82.
King, Byron W., A.B., A.M., Ph.D., Dir. Sch. of Expr. 1901–03.
Kirkland, Robert McD., A.M., Lat. & Fr. 1912–17.
Kline, James L., B.S., M.S., Chem. 1955–61.
Knisley, Nevelyn J., Mus.B., M.F.A., Piano. 1954–58.
Kostruba, Helene, M.D., Russ. 1947–51.
Koth, Otto R., B.S., M.Ed., Engin. Drwng. 1956–58.
Kreider, Alice Lutz, Art. 1919–20.
Kreider, Joseph Lehn, B.S., M.A., Chem. & Phys. 1907–08.
Kreitzer, Howard M., B.S., M.A., D.Ed. Dean of the Coll. 1952–60.
Krumbine, John S., Math., Mechan., Philos. 1866–68.
Kurtz, Geraldine H., B.A., M.A., Mus.Ed. 1959–61.

Landis, Emma L., Fr. & Fine Arts. 1880–85; 1898–99.
Lanese, Thomas A., A.B.,Mus., M.Mus. Mus.Ed. 1954–.
Laughlin, Maud P., B.S., M.A., Hist., Soc., Pol.Sci. 1946–57.
Leamon, James S., A.B., Ph.D., Hist. 1961–64.
LeCarpentier, Suzanne, B.S., M.A., Mus. Thry. & Strngs. 1952–54.
Lehman, Edith M., A.B., German, 1915–16.
Lehman, John E., A.B., A.M., Sc.D., Math. & Astron. 1887–1928.
Lehman, Reba F., A.B., Fr., 1901–07; 1917–18.
Lehn, Homer M. B. Pedagogy. 1901–02; 1906–08.
Lewin, Mary B., B.S., M.S., Math. 1963–.
Lietzau, Lena L., Ph.D., Germ. 1930–52.
Light, Alma M., M.S., Teacher Prep. 1903–06.

254

Light, Fred W., B.S., Violin. 1909–12.
Light, G. Hobart, D.D.S., Phys.Ed., Coach. 1920–21.
Light, Sadie A., Elocut. 1895–96.
Light, V. Earl, A.B., M.S., Ph.S., Bio. 1929–64.
Linebaugh, Percy M., Mus.B., Piano, Thry. 1917–18.
Linscott, Hubert, B.S., Voice. 1935–37.
Linta, Ned A., B.A., M.A., Phys. Ed. 1956–59.
Lochner, Hilbert V., A.B., A.M., Econ. & Bus. Ad. 1947–51.
Lockwood, Karl L., B.S., Ph.D., Chem. 1959–.
Long, Doris, A.M., Engl. 1914–15.
Long, Lenore N., Mus.B., Voice, Thry. 1920–21.
Lorenz, E. S. (President) B.A., A.M., B.D., Ment. & Mor. Sci. 1887–89.
Lotz, John F., B.S., M.A., Ed.D., Econ. & Bus. Ad. 1946–49.
Love, Jean O., A.B., M.A., Ph.D., Psych. 1954–.
Love, John B., B.A., Math. 1956–57.
Lowery, D. D., Ethics. 1889–90.
Lynch, Clyde A. (President) A.B., A.M., B.D., D.D., Ph.D. 1932–50.
Lynn, John E., A.B., Lat., Math., Fr. 1884–87.

Mackert, C. LeRoy, M.A., Phys. Ed. 1930–31.
Magee, Richard D., B.A., M.A., Ph.D., Psych. 1961–.
Malm, Sylvia R., A.B., M.A., Ph.D., Bio. 1962–.
Malsh, Harold E., Violin. 1924–63.
Mallory, Mary E., Fr. & Fine Arts. 1877–78.
Manbeck, Mabel E., Piano. 1899–01.
Marble, Harriet L., Mus. Thry. & Voice. 1911–12.
Marsh, Ozan, Piano. 1945.
Marquette, George R., A.B., M.A., Phys. Ed., Dean of Men. 1952–.
Martin, William N., A.B., Bio. 1927–28.
Martorana, Jerome J., B.A., M.A., Pol. Sci. 1963–64.
Massinger, Charles, B.A., M.A., Voice. 1946–48.
Matlack, Jesse M., Jr., B.A., M.A., Engl. 1959–62.
McComsey, S. E., Violin, Strngs. 1901–05.
McCracken, Ellis R., A.B., M.Ed., Dir. Ath., Coach. 1954–61.
McDermad, Jno. A., A.M., Grk., Nat. Sci. 1891–97.

McFadden, Louis H., A.B., A.M., Grk., Nat. Sci. 1875–82.
McFadden, Thomas G., A.M., Chem. & Phys. 1900–06.
McGill, David W., Teacher Prep. 1903–08.
McGrath, Ralph, Ph.B., M.S., Bus. Ad. 1943.
McHenry, J. Robert, A.B., M.A., Phys. Ed. 1964–.
McHenry, William D., B.S., M.Ed., Dir. Ath. & Coach. 1961.
McKlveen, Gilbert D., A.B., M.Ed., D.Ed., Education. 1949–.
McLean, Charlotte F., A.B., Ph.D., Engl. 1917–20.
Mease, Dorothy Light, A.B., Engl. 1953–54.
Mease, Harry M., Ed. 1902–04.
Mease, Ralph R., B.S., M.A., Phys. Ed. & Coach. 1946–52.
Meily, C. Seltzer, Engl. Tutor, 1869–70.
Metoxen, Emerson, B.S., Dir. Phys. Ed. 1934–39.
Meyer, H. Lenich, B.S., M.S., Nat. Sci., Pedag., Pol. Eco. 1896–00.
Meyer, John, Cello. 1930–31.
Miller, Frederic K. (President 1950–) A.B., M.A., Ph.D., Litt.D., Hist. 1939–50.
Miller, Marion S., B.S., M.A., Hist. 1948–51.
Miller, Harvey D., Violin. 1892–94.
Miller, J. Henry, Germ., Bkg. 1881–83.
Miller, J. P., Soc. Ethics. 1897–98.
Miller, Mabel A., Voice, Mus. Thry. 1918–20.
Miller, Nella, B.S., Piano. 1933–40.
Mills, Edith Frantz, Voice. 1911–12; 1922–29.
Mills, J. S., Ph.D., D.D., Soc. 1901–05.
Morris, Edith M., A.A., B.M., M.A., Mus. Thry. 1951–52.
Morris, John R. II, B.S., Phys. 1963–.
Moyer, Ella R., B.S., M.A., Mus. Thry. 1931–42.
Moyer, M. Ella, Mus. Thry. & Instr. 1889–92.
Moyer, M. Violette, Voice. 1908–09.
Muehling, Sylvia M., B.S., M.M., Piano. 1952–54.
Müller, John H., Germ., Bkg. 1883–84.
Mumper, Lucille Shenk, A.B., A.M., Engl. 1946–47.
Mylin, Edward E., A.B., A.M., Phys. Dir. & Coach. 1923–34.

Neidig, Howard A., B.S., M.S., Ph.D., Chem. 1948–.

Neithamer, Richard W., B.S., Ph.D., Chem. 1955–59.
Neithamer, E. Jeanette, B.M.E., M.M.E., Mus. Ed. 1957–59.
Ness, Robert K., A.B., M.S., Ph.D., Chem. 1947–48.
Ness, Ruth Haverstock, B.S., M.S., Math., Chem. 1947–48.
Newall, Robert H., B.A., M.A., Engl. 1960–62.
Neilson, A. Evald, B.A., M.A., Ph.D., Eco. & Bus.Ad. 1964–65.

O'Donnell, Agnes B., A.B., M.S., Engl. 1961–.
O'Donnell, J. Robert, B.S., M.S., Phys. 1959–.
Ohl, Raymond, T., A.B., M.A., Ph.D., Lat. 1930–32.
Oldham, Charles B., Piano, 1898–05.
Oldham, Herbert, F.S.Sc., Piano, Dir. of Conserv. 1898–08.
Olin, Harvey M., B.M., M.M., Mus. 1962–63.
Orth, Andrew, B.S., A.M., Eco. & Bus.Ad. 1949–51.
Owen, Benjamin, Piano. 1936–38.
Oyer, Miriam R., Pub. Sch. Mus. 1921–22.

Parks, Sarah R., A.M., Engl. 1910–11.
Pavlidis, Theodore, B.A., B.D., M.A., Soc. 1964–.
Pease, S. Eva (Muller) Inst. Mus., Voice. 1881–85.
Perry, Sir Edward Baxter, Piano. 1922–24.
Peters, Charles C., A.B., A.M., Philos. & Ed. 1910–13.
Petrofes, Gerald J., B.S., M.Ed., Phys.Ed. 1963–.
Pickwell, Marcia M., B.A., M.S., Piano. 1958–63.
Piel, S. Elizabeth, A.B., M.A., Ph.D., For. Lang. 1960–.
Poad, Charles R., B.S., Phys. Ed. 1959–62.
Polk, Miriam R., A.B., M.D., Hygiene. 1928–32.
Pond, Chester B., A.B., A.M., Ph.D., Math., Bus. Ad. 1931–32.
Porter, Jermain D., A.B., Ph.D., Chem. 1941–44.
Pottieger, Elizabeth H., A.B., A.M., Psych. 1960–65.
Pritchard, George H., A.B., Phys. Ed. & Phys. 1912–13.

Redditt, Bruce H., A.M., Math. 1923–26.
Reeve, E. Joan, Mus.B., M.A., Piano, Thry. 1957–.

Reid, Marian, A.B., Engl., Germ. 1914–16.
Reisinger, Mary Goshert, B.S., Music. 1935–36.
Resler, Laura E., Instr. Mus. 1876–79.
Resler, Lillie A., M.A., Hist., Engl. 1874–75.
Reynolds, O. Edgar, A.B., M.A., Ph.D., Ed. & Psych. 1924–39.
Rhodes, Jacob L., B.S., Ph.D., Phys. 1957–.
Richards, Benjamin A., A.B., A.M., Ph.D., Philos. 1960–.
Richardson, Lulu M., A.B., A.M., Ph.D., Fr. 1935–36.
Richie, Gustavus A., A.B., B.D., A.M., D.D., Grk., Relig. 1925–59.
Ricker, Ralph R., A.B., A.M., Hist., Coach. 1950–52.
Rigler, Lizzie M., Music, Painting, Ornament. Branches. 1966–69.
Rigler, Ruth E., B.I., Oratory. 1907–08.
Riley, Robert C., B.S., M.S., Ph.D., Eco. & Bus. Ad. 1951–.
Roach, Florence A., Voice. 1906–08.
Robinson, Roger I., B.S., M.A., Phys. Ed. 1948–50.
Roeder, Edward M., A.M., Germ. 1907–08.
Rogers, George, Voice. 1925–27.
Rogers, Milton, B.M., M.A., Mus. Thry. & Piano. 1951.
Roop, Hervin U. (President) A.B., A.M., B.D., Ph.D., Philos., Pedag., Orat. 1897–06.
Roop, Mrs. Hervin U., A.M., Voice, Art. 1897–99.
Roulette, Kathleen K., A.B., M.S., Psych. 1948–50.
Rovers, Reynaldo, Voice. 1945–.
Rupp, S. Edwin, A.M., Soc. 1907–09.
Rutledge, Edward P., B.S., M.A., Mus. Ed. 1931–54.

Sanders, William J., A.B., Lat., Engl. 1903–04.
Saunders, Margaret, Piano. 1942–43.
Saylor, Malin Pf., F.I. (Upsala and Stockholm), Fr. 1961–.
Schlichter, M. Etta Wolfe, B.A., A.M., Germ., Engl. 1897–06; 1908–10.
Schlichter, Norman C., A.B., A.M., Fr., Engl. 1899–09.
Schmauk, Emma R., A.B., Fr. 1914–22.
Schmidt, Gertrude K., Mus. Thry., Voice. 1912–18.
Schneider, Hans, B.S., M.S., Chem. 1951–55; 1961–63.
Scholz, John P., Ph.D., Math. 1950–52.
Schwanauer, Ferenc, Ph.D., Germ. 1960–62.

Schwanauer, Johanna, A.B., Germ. 1961–62.

Schweigert, G. E., B.S., Ph.D., Math. 1934–36.

Schweppe, Frederick, A.B., M.A., Voice. 1942–43.

Scribner, J. Woodbury, A.M., Ment. & Mor. Sci. 1873–75.

Seaman, Edna., B.S., Engl. 1914–17.

Seltzer, Lucy S., A.B., A.M., Germ., Engl. 1911–18; 1922–23.

Shay, Ralph S., A.B., M.S., Ph.D., Hist. 1948–.

Sheldon, E. Edwin, Mus.B., Dir. of Conserv., Piano, Organ, Thry. 1910–20.

Sheldon, Florence A., Fine Arts. 1885–91.

Sheldon, Ida Maneval, Mus.B., Mus. Thry, Piano. 1910–20.

Shenk, Hiram H., A.B., A.M., LL.D., Hist. 1899–16; 1920–50.

Sherrick, Sarah M., Ph.B., Mod. Lang., Engl. 1889–92.

Shettel, Paul O., A.B., B.D., S.T.D., Philos., Bible. 1938–43.

Shippee, John S., A.M., Lat., Fr. 1906–09.

Shively, Frances, Harm. & Anal. 1902–04.

Shopp, J. H., A.B., Nat. Sci. 1872–73.

Shott, John A., Ph.B., Ped.B., Ph.M., Nat. Sci. & Pedag. 1892–95.

Shrom, W. P., A.M., Ment. & Moral Sci. 1871–72.

Shroyer, Alvin E., B.D., D.D., Grk., Bible. 1909–20.

Sincavage, Emma, B.S., Phys.Ed., 1963–64.

Sleichter, Mary E., A.B., A.M., Germ., Engl. 1892–94; 1909–11.

Sloca, Charles, B.S., M.A., Ph.D., Engl. 1950–53.

Smith, Anna E., B.S., M.A., Ed., Psych. 1952–53.

Smith, Carrie E., Mus. Thry. 1895–98.

Smith, Ella M., Voice. 1888–89.

Smith Ernestine J., A.B., Phys. Ed. 1948–52.

Smith, Robert W., B.S., M.A., Mus.Ed., Dir. of Conserv. 1951–.

Smith, Sarah S., B.E., Music, Fine Arts. 1874–76.

Sneath, Isaiah W., A.B., A.M., B.D., Grk., Germ. 1885–87.

Snoke, G. Mason, Pedag. 1901–02.

Snyder, Roy S. W., B.S., M.S., Bio. 1952–53.

Souders, Bruce C., A.B., B.D., M.A., Engl. 1947–49.

Sowers, Joan S., B.A., M.A., Fr. 1962–63.

Spangler, James T., A.B., A.M., Grk., Bible, Philos., Hist. 1890–91; 1897–09; 1916–25.

Spangler, Paul M., Bkg., Phonog. 1903–06.

Sparks, W. Maynard, A.B., B.D., Ed.M., Rel. 1950–59.

Spessard, Arthur E., B.I., Elocution. 1908–09.

Spessard, Harry E., A.B., Acad. Engl. & Lat. 1898–99; 1903–12.

Sponaugle, Doris I., B.S., Phys. Ed. 1947–48.

Sponseller, Edwin H., B.D., M.A., Rel. Ed. 1943–44.

Stachow, Frank Ed., B.S., M.A., Mus. Ed. 1946–.

Stagg, Shirley E., B.S., M.A., Piano. 1950–54.

Statton, Philo, Violin. 1911–13.

Stauffer, Douglas A., B.S., M.S., Engl. 1963–65.

Stauffer, Henry F., M.E., Norm. Dept. 1887–90.

Stein, Thomas S., A.M., Lat., Germ. 1901–06.

Stetson, Miss E. A., B.E., Elocut., Vocal, Normal. 1866–67.

Stevens, Justina Lorenz, B.S., Bot., Lat., Alg., Physiol. 1888–89.

Stevens, Lucile H., A.B., M.A., Fr. 1947–48.

Stevenson, Eugene H., A.B., Ph.D., Hist. 1928–38.

Stevenson, Stella Johnson, B.S., Ph.D., Fr. 1928–52.

Stine, Clyde S., A.B., A.M., Ph.D., Ed., Spch. 1938–46.

Stine, Frank L., A.B., Engl., Math. 1916–17.

Stokes, Milton L., M.A., LL.B., Ph.D., Bus. Ad., 1926–46; 1965–.

Stonecipher, Alvin H. M., B.A., M.A., Ph.D., Lat., Germ. 1932–59.

Storck, George H., B.S., M.A., Phys. Ed. 1962–63.

Strawinski, Belle O., M.A., Music, Fr., Ornam. Branches. 1869–70.

Strickler, Paul L., A.B., Phys.Ed., Coach. 1919–20.

Struble, George G., B.S., M.S., Ph.D., Engl. 1931–.

Swope, Pierce E., Norm. Dept. 1906–08.

Taylor, Elizabeth, A.B., M.A., Psych. 1954–55.

Taylor, Myron, Voice. 1939–42.

Thompson, Anna M., Ph.M., Mod. Lang., Engl. 1894–95.

Thurmond, James M., A.B., M.A., Mus.D., Mus. Ed. 1954–.

Titcomb, Eleanor, A.B., M.A., Ph.D., Fr. 1964–.

Todd, James U., B.S., Bus. Ad. & Eco. 1948–49.

Tohill, Laurence S., A.B., Nat. Sci., Latin. 1874–75.

Tom, C. F. Joseph, A.A., B.A., Ph.D., Eco. 1954–.

Toole, Robert C., B.S., M.A., Ph.D., Hist. 1956–58.

Trautman, D. L., B.S. in M.E., Math. 1949–50.

Troutman, Perry J., B.A., B.D., Ph.D., Rel. 1960–.

Trovillo, Bessie, A.B., Germ. 1905–07.

Tucker, Rosalind A., B.S., A.B., M.A., Engl. 1962–.

Turner, Gertrude, A.B., A.M., Remed. Engl. 1953–56.

Van de Sande, Elizabeth D., Art. 1896–98.

Van Steenwyk, Linda, B.A., M.A., Piano. Mus. Thry. 1961–.

Vickroy, Thos. Rhys (President) A.B., M.A., Ph.D., Lang., Math., Philos., Belles-Lettres. 1866–71.

Von Bereghy, Zeline, Violin, 1899–01; 1914–18.

Wagner, Paul S., A.B., M.A., Ph.D., Math. 1917–18; 1920–23; 1926–36.

Wagner, Robert J., B.S., M.S., Math. 1957–61.

Walker, Ella L., M.A., Mus. & Drawing. 1866–69.

Wallace, Mary K., A.B., A.M., Engl. 1926–31.

Wallace, Paul A. W., B.A., M.A., Ph.D., Engl. 1925–49; 1965–.

Walter, Anna C., A.B., Oratory, Phys. Cult. 1900–01.

Wanner, Henry E., B.S., Chem., Phys. 1909–18.

Washinger, W. H., Norm. Dept. 1889–90.

Weiksel, J. Arndt, B.S., M.S., Ph.D., Chem. 1949–50.

Wethington, L. Elbert, B.A., B.D., Ph.D., Rel. 1963–.

Weydling, George H., A.B., Ph.D., For. Lang. 1959–60.

Whitney, Henry N., B.A., M.A., Hist. 1938–39.

Wieder, Homer W., A.B., M.A., Ed. 1964–.

Wilde, Willoughby S., L.L.C.M., Mus. Thry., Voice. 1896–98.

Wilson, Francis H., B.S., M.S., Ph.D., Bio. 1953–.

Winters, Ada, Instr. Mus., Fine Arts. 1870–72.

Wisewell, George E., A.M., Lat., Fr. 1911–12.

Wissler, Willis, A.B., M.A., B.Pd., M.Pd., Econ. 1947–48.

Withrow, Letitia, Voice. 1921–22.

Wolfgang, Marvin E., A.B., Soc., Pol. Sci. 1947–52.

Wood, Margaret A., B.S., M.A., Pol.Sci. 1932–42.

Woodland, John T., A.B., Ph.D., Bio. 1950–52.

Woods, Glenn H., A.B., M.Ed., Engl. 1965–

Yingling, Richard R., B.S., Chem. 1964–.

Zimmerman, Leah M., Voice 1964–

Zuck, W. J., A.M., Engl. 1882–84; 1903–08.

Appendix C

Trustees, Lebanon Valley College, 1866–1966

Adams, Rev. John Q., 1870-71; 1873-76
Albright, Rev. Isaac H., 1888-1906
Appenzellar, Joseph L., 1942-47
Appenzellar, William O., 1903-06; 1907-21

Bachman, M. H., 1929-42
Baish, Henry H., 1903-46
Baker, B. Frank, 1897-99
Baker, Edward M., 1889-94
Baker, W. O., 1886-89; 1890-92
Barnhart, Jefferson C., 1963-
Batdorf, Bishop G. D., 1919-21; 1932-44; 1945-47
Bearinger, Josiah E., 1961-62
Beattie, Rev. W. M., 1917-32
Beckley, Rev. A. S., 1914
Berry, Rev. W. R., 1886-89
Bitzer, Charles L., 1944-59
Boltz, Stephen W., 1884-85
Bowers, S. H., 1911-14
Brandt, Carl S., 1959-
Brane, Rev. C. I. B., 1886-95
Breinig, George F., 1904-20
Breinig, J. L., 1871-74
Brewbaker, Rev. C. W., 1910-11
Brightbill, Maurice E., 1903-06
Brown, Dr. J. W., 1867-70
Brunk, Rev. J. H., 1917-39
Bryson, William D., 1962-
Buffington, Isaiah, 1914-17
Burkholder, Rev. D. R., 1883-90
Burtner, Rev. Cornelius A., 1896-99
Burtner, Rev. Edward O., 1904-10; 1913-25
Burtner, Solomon, 1874-78
Butterwick, Rev. R. R., 1904-08; 1913-19

Chamberlin, Rev. John B., 1890-94; 1896-1903
Chandler, C. A., 1933-36
Clippinger, Samuel W., 1890-1904
Coble, E. W., 1938-59
Cochran, A. J., 1910-22
Colestock, Rev. Z. A., 1871-81

Coover, Charles M., 1918-24
Coughenour, B. F., 1882-86
Craumer, Rev. Lewis W., 1866-89
Crider, David W., 1879-95
Cupp, Rev. N. F. A., 1891-94

Daugherty, Rev. Benjamin F., 1926-32
Daugherty, Rev. S. B., 1951-63
Daugherty, Rev. Samuel F., 1915-21
Deaner, Jonas S., 1875-90
DeLong, Rev. A. L., 1882-83
Dohner, Rev. Hiram B., 1893-1903
Dougherty, Rev. J. B., 1866-71
Dyche, Rev. C. P., 1886-91; 1904-06

Early, Rev. Daniel S., 1866-71
Eberly, Rev. Daniel, 1890-1910
Eby, S. N., 1884-90
Edwards, Rev. David, 1873-76
Ehrhart, Rev. Oliver T., 1931-55
Ehrhart, Paul C., 1957-
Enck, Rev. Schuyler C., 1919-52
Engle, Benjamin H., 1898-1911
Engle, J. Raymond, 1915-42
Engle, Samuel F., 1890-1915
Epp, Bishop G. E., 1951-58
Erb, Rev. Jacob, 1871-72
Ernst, Rev. Ira Sankey, 1927-55; 1957-59
Esbenshade, Park F., 1947-48
Eshenaur, Walter C., 1961-
Essick, DeWitt, 1960-
Etter, Rev. John Wesley, 1888-89
Evers, Rev. Abraham M., 1872-96
Evers, Rev. Samuel J., 1893-96

Fake, Dr. Warren H., 1947-56
Faust, Rev. Samuel D., 1889-1907
Fegley, Rev. D. LeRoy, 1955-
Fegley, Park H., 1945-46
Fetterhoff, Dr. Hiram R., 1873-78
Fisher, Rev. F., 1882-84
Fisher, Valentine K., 1896-1906
Fisher, William J., 1953-62
Fleming, Rev. Mervin R., 1918-46

259

Flook, Rev. Cyrus F., 1891-97; 1904-12; 1915-18
Forney, Adam R., 1891-1904
Fout, Rev. Julius E., 1893-98
Fridinger, Rev. Donald N., 1955-
Fries, J. N., 1886-09; 1912-29
Fultz, Rev. C. E., 1926-32
Funkhouser, Rev. A. P., 1878-80; 1889-92; 1894-96; 1899-09; 1914-17
Funkhouser, Elmer N., 1917-62
Funkhouser, Monroe, 1872-74

Gabel, Rev. Henry S., 1904-07
Garber, J. N., 1906-09
Garber, Roy K., 1942-51; 1952-64
Geesey, John E., 1962-
Gelbach, Rev. Henry H., 1876-86
Gerberich, Mrs. Ruth Evans, 1961-
Gibble, Rev. Phares B., 1921-58
Gingrich, Peter, 1868-71
Gipple, John E., 1918-48
Glen, Rev. J. Stewart, 1948-61
Glen, J. Stewart, Jr., 1959-
Glen, William R., 1927-33
Glossbrenner, Rev. J. J., 1866-68
Good, Oscar E., 1895-96; 1942-45
Gossard, Rev. George D., 1908-12; (Pres. 1912-32)
Graybill, C. L., 1928-36
Graybill, S. R., 1906-07
Gregory, Bishop D. T., 1952-56
Grimm, Rev. Jacob L., 1872-82
Grimm, Samuel O., 1952-62
Grimm, Rev. W. O., 1881-83
Groh, Samuel, 1866-67
Gross, Ezra, 1904-10
Grove, Dr. D. Dwight, 1959-
Gruber, John, 1871-72
Gruver, Rev. J. Paul, 1939-
Gruver, Rev. W. F., 1909-37

Haak, Isaac B., 1885-1904; 1907-13; 1918-21
Hain, William M., 1903-04
Hallman, Rev. G. W., 1926-35
Hammack, Rev. A. S., 1906-22
Harmon, Rev. George, 1881-90
Harp, Rev. J., 1872-73
Harp, Reno S., 1892-1904
Harper, T. C., 1908-09
Hartman, Rev. G. K., 1907-10
Haverstock, Rev. Calvin B., 1962-
Heckert, John C., 1900-11
Hendricks, M. S., 1906-09, 1911-12; 1913-15
Herr, Rudolph, 1866-89
Hershey, Rev. I. Moyer, 1916-26
Hertzler, Rev. G. Edgar, 1945-

Hill, Joseph, 1866-71
Hiser, Rev. Carl W., 1941-
Hodges, Elmer, 1909-24
Hoffman, Rev. David, 1866-71; 1880-85
Hoke, Rev. Jacob, 1872-74
Holzinger, Rev. Charles H., 1925-28
Hoover, Levi, 1866-71
Horn, Rev. A. N., 1917-26
Horn, Charles H., 1954-
Horn, Rev. Paul F., 1952-
Horst, Miles, 1945-64
Hostetter, Rev. Mark J., 1954-
Hostetter, Paris, 1951-54
Hott, Rev. G. P., 1886-91
Hott, Rev. J. W., 1872-73
Hoverter, George W., 1870-81
Howe, Rev. John W., 1873-76; 1880-81
Hoy, H. H., 1915-20
Hummel, Rev. Solomon M., 1873-82
Hummelbaugh, Rev. E. H., 1917-20
Hunsicker, John, 1908-13; 1936-44
Hursh, John, 1873-89
Hursh, Joseph B., 1871-91

Imboden, Harry M., 1932-51
Immel, H. S., 1910-21

Jones, Rev. John Owen, 1926-38
Jones, Rev. L. R., 1886-88

Kaebnick, Bishop Hermann W., 1959-
Kauffman, Rev. D. M., 1866-67
Kauffman, Rev. Gerald D., 1961-
Kauffman, Rev. Lester M., 1954-
Keedy, Rev. David D., 1874-93
Keiper, Rev. John A., 1895-99
Keister, B. Frank, 1903-10
Kephart, Rev. Cyrus J., 1893-97
Kephart, Bishop Ezekiel B., 1895-1906
Kephart, Rev. I. L., 1866-67
Kephart, J. R., 1883-86
Kern, Edward, 1898-1901
Keys, Rev. W. S. H., 1866-72
Kinports, John H., 1866-71
Kiracofe, Rev. J. W., 1876-86
Kleffman, Rev. John E., 1898-1924
Knipp, J., 1871-72
Knipp, John C., 1892-95; 1899-1904
Kohler, Daniel, 1872-74
Kohler, Rev. Fillmore T., 1949-52
Koontz, Rev. Paul R., 1919-22; 1924-27
Kreider, Aaron S., 1909-29
Kreider, David, 1867-71; 1874-86
Kreider, Henry H., 1866-1908
Kremer, Rev. Benneville, 1866-67

Lane, Rev. M. O., 1884-91
Leathem, James H., 1965-
Lehman, Rev. A. S., 1935-36

Lehman, William H., 1889-92
Light, Alma M., 1949-52
Light, Boaz W., 1889-92
Light, Rev. Ezekiel, 1866-76
Light, Gideon, 1867-89
Light, Nathaniel B., 1892-98
Light, Dr. Seth A., 1913-14
Light, Simon P., 1899-1906
Long, Rev. Aaron A., 1913-19
Long, Rev. David E., 1912-15
Lowery, Rev. Daniel D., 1904-16
Ludwig, George C., 1931-55
Ludwig, Samuel, 1896-97; 1898-99
Ludwig, Rev. Sanford A., 1896-97
Ludwig, S. R., 1906-09
Lutz, Harold T., 1939-59
Lutz, Rev. L. Walter, 1910-31
Lutz, Robert W., 1962-
Lutz, William A., 1895-99; 1900-06
Lynch, Rev. Clyde A., 1928-31;
 (President L.V.C., 1932-50)
Lyter, Rev. Joseph A., 1907-13; 1915-26

Mark, Rev. George A., 1866-86
Mark, Rev. Jacob H., 1868-72
Mathias, T. W., 1908-09
Matsko, John F., 1952-
May, Rev. Thomas S., 1952-55; 1960-
Maysilles, John H., 1895-06
McFaul, William N., 1914-23; 1924-48;
 1956-61
McKelvey, J. B., 1948-57
Medsger, Rev. J., 1882-84; 1886-91
Mentzer, Rev. Warren F., 1962-
Metzger, Maurice R., 1939-52
Meyer, Rev. John, 1867-73
Millard, Edward F., 1904-05
Miller, Rev. E. E., 1935-65
Miller, Rev. Harry E., 1903-04; 1913-15;
 1916-19; 1920-26; 1930-45
Miller, Henry B., 1897-1904
Miller, Rev. Millard J., 1939-42
Mills, Alfred K., 1921-31; 1933-42
Mills, Bishop J. S., 1901-06
Mowers, Rev. Samuel A., 1872-78
Mowrey, Raymond G., 1925-29; 1930-62
Moyer, Rev. S. N., 1907-08
Mumma, Rev. J. G., 1881-83
Mund, Allan W., 1958-
Mund, Rev. Frederick W., 1959-
Musser, H. R., 1871-72
Mutch, Rev. Charles A., 1891-1904
Mutch, Rev. C. E., 1915-18
Myer, Rev. John C. S., 1890-99

Neff, Rev. E. E., 1909-14
Neilly, J. W., 1924-25
Ness, Rev. John H., 1925-48

Newman, George A., 1898-99

Oliver, Rev. John E., 1937-58
Olmstead, Marlin E., 1903-10
Owen, Rev. John W., 1906-14
Oyer, Rev. David M., 1911-16
Oyer, Rev. Russell C., 1963-
Oyler, Andrew P., 1872-73

Peiffer, Rev. Harold S., 1958-61
Pershing, Rev. J. H., 1888-91
Peters, D. Augustus, 1906-10
Peters, Rev. Lewis, 1866-73
Plummer, Rev. F. Berry, 1910-13; 1916-27;
 1928-31; 1932-57
Plummer, Wilbur C., 1946-49

Raber, Rev. William B., 1871-74
Ranck, Rev. Ezra H., 1959-
Rauch, Charles E., 1902-06
Reachard, O. W., 1932-41
Reed, W. S., 1884-90
Renn, Rev. U. S. G., 1912-13
Resler, Rev. J. I., 1889-91
Rettew, Charles B., 1888-91
Rhinehart, Rev. Paul E., 1957-62
Rhoad, Rev. Hiram F., 1926-30
Rice, A. H., 1890-96
Rice, J. E. B., 1894-96
Ridenour, Rev. Jacob R., 1886-1906
Rider, Rev. Gordon I., 1922-49
Riegel, Benjamin, 1866-67
Rife, Melvin S., 1962-
Rife, Reuben M., 1931-34
Rigor, Rev. G. W. Miles, 1866-67; 1869-74
Riland, Albanus S., 1871-96
Riland, Rev. Paul J., 1866-68
Roop, Rev. Hervin U., 1896-97;
 (President L.V.C., 1897-05)
Roop, Dr. Jacob W., 1874-84
Roudabush, Charles E., 1926-41
Runk, Rev. Irvin E., 1911-15; 1920-26
Runk, Rev. Jacob, 1871-84; 1886-89
Rupp, C. F., 1921-25
Rupp, J. Paul, 1943-57
Rupp, Rev. Samuel E., 1915-18; 1920-26

Sampsell, Rev. William H., 1892-95; 1896-
 98
Sand, Rev. J. A., 1878-79
Sattazahn, Lloyd A., 1944-54
Sauder, Charles W., 1963-64
Schaeffer, Rev. Harry E., 1925-28; 1932-59
Schaeffer, John, 1874-77
Schlichter, Rev. H. A., 1881-84
Schultz, John, 1866-67
Schum, H., 1882-83
Sechrist, Rev. A. J., 1917-32
Sechrist, W. S., 1909-17

261

Shannon, Rev. Paul E. V., 1932-57
Shearer, Rev. Daniel L., 1959-
Shelley, John W., 1895-96
Shenk, H. W., 1948-
Shenk, Hiram H., 1919-21
Sherk, Abraham, 1866-71
Sherk, H. A., 1910-12
Shettel, Rev. Paul O., 1933-39
Shopp, Samuel Jr., 1871-72
Showalter, W. L., 1908-09
Showers, Rev. J. Balmer, 1945-51
Shroyer, Rev. Alvin E., 1908-11
Shroyer, Lawton W., 1952-
Siegrist, Michael B., 1866-70
Skelton, Rev. Sanford D., 1896-06
Slonaker, Rev. Paul J., 1945-
Smith, Benton P., 1956-65
Smith, J. C., 1871-73
Smith, Rev. W. H., 1929-41
Sneath, Jacob, 1886-90
Snoke, S. C., 1913-15
Snyder, George C., 1886-97; 1899-14
Snyder, Rev. J. F., 1912-18
Snyder, J. R., 1921-23
Spangler, A. C., 1947-60
Spangler, Rev. James T., 1895-99
Spayd, Rev. H. B., 1888-91
Stahl, Rev. L. W., 1882-91
Stahle, Col. J. A., 1878-88
Stambach, Rev. C. Guy, 1936-51
Stansbury, John H., 1914-17
Statton, Rev. Arthur B., 1898-06; 1907-25
Statton, Rev. George W., 1873-76
Stearn, Rev. Charles T., 1871-72; 1877-83; 1889-92
Stehman, John B., 1866-1896
Stehman, Jonas G., 1901-13; 1917-20
Steigerwalt, Rev. A., 1866-71
Stine, Rev. Frank L., 1918-21
Stinespring, Rev. C. W., 1897-1904
Stover, Rev. G. W., 1906-09; 1924-39
Straub, Jack L., 1914-24
Strickler, Paul L., 1954-61
Strine, Huber D., 1941-56

Swartz, Rev. Solomon L., 1886-1902

Thomas, Harry, 1920-25
Thomas, John, 1884-86; 1888-91
Thomas, Noah G., 1874-88
Thomas, Warren A., 1903-20
Tinsman, Rev. Clyde W., 1942-45
Tutwiler, Eugene, 1909-12

Uhler, Rev. William H., 1892-95
Ulrich, William H., 1883-84; 1890-93; 1897-1906; 1907-12

Wagner, Rev. W. H., 1884-93
Wagoner, Rev. George, 1883-89
Walmer, Samuel, 1866-71
Waltermyer, Woodrow W., 1961-
Washinger, Rev. William H., 1894-1917
Watson, Albert, 1931-
Weaver, Rev. J., 1868-73
Weber, Rev. Charles B., 1958-
Weidman, Rev. B. B., 1886-88
Weiss, John H., 1890-93
Welty, Rev. Mervie H., 1946-
Wengert, Samuel K., 1956-
Wier, Rev. Adam K., 1913-17
Williams, Earnest D., 1942-60
Williams, Earnest D., Jr., 1960-
Wilt, Rev. William A., 1932-35; 1937-59
Wine, E. C., 1922-31
Wine, Sylvester K., 1897-04
Wolf, George A., 1893-95
Wolf, Henry, 1901-06; 1918-29
Worriлow, John L., 1962-
Worrilow, W. H., 1944-62

Yardley, Mrs. Louisa Williams, 1931-46; 1952-61
Yeatts, C. O., 1921-24
Young, Rev. David E., 1925-62
Young, John, 1866-68
Young, Rev. Joseph, 1866-71; 1876-88

Ziegler, Rev. Samuel G., 1915-21
Zimmerman, Richard P., 1959-
Zuse, Rev. DeWitt P., 1952-63

Appendix D

TREND OF STUDENT EXPENSES OVER THE PAST CENTURY

(Minimum Cost per Year)

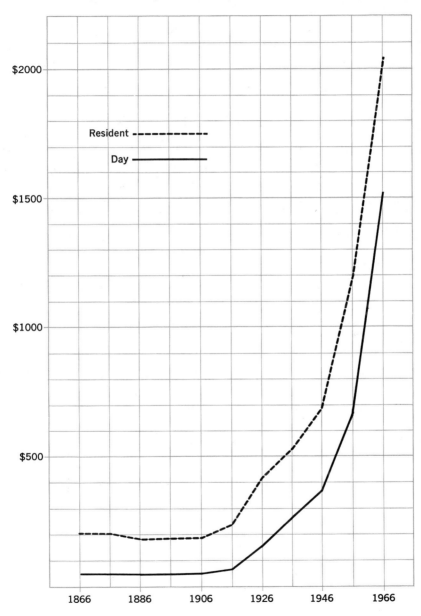

Bibliographical Note

The Memorabilia Room in the Gossard Memorial Library contains the College Archives. The fire of December 24, 1904, destroyed the earliest records; but among the administrative records and other source materials that have been preserved since that time are the following:

Minutes of the Faculty and reports of various committees;
Minutes of the Board of Trustees and its Executive Committee;
Minutes of the Finance Committee;
Correspondence and reports of the presidents;
Departmental reports;
The *College Catalog,* from 1866 to the present;
The Lebanon Valley Bulletin and the *Alumni Review;*
Biographical notes concerning alumni;
Miscellaneous records pertaining to the founding of the College;
Student research papers dealing with the history of the College;
Minutes of student societies;
College periodicals, such as *The College Forum, Bizarre, The Quittapahilla, College News, The Crucible, La Vie Collegienne;*
Various papers published by the Lebanon County Historical Society, in particular President E. Benjamin Bierman's "The First Twenty-Five Years of Lebanon Valley College" and Dr. H. H. Shenk's "The Annville Academy";
Local newspapers, especially files of the Lebanon *Courier* and *Daily News* (Microfilms of which are in the Gossard Memorial Library) and copies (where they may be found) of the Annville *Gazette* and Annville *Journal.*

The College Library contains a collection of church periodicals such as *The Religious Telescope*. Early numbers of this latter, however, are missing here. They are to be found in the Historical Society of the Evangelical United Brethren Church in Dayton, Ohio. The miscellaneous collections of this society are invaluable for any study of Lebanon Valley College.

Among the printed books of value to such a study as this are the following:

A. W. Drury, *History of the Church of the United Brethren In Christ* (Dayton, Ohio, 1924, 1931);

Henry Garst, *Otterbein University, 1847–1907* (Dayton, Ohio, 1907);

Individual histories of the several cooperating Conferences of the Evangelical United Brethren Church;

Mennonite Encyclopedia (Hillsboro, Kansas, 1955–1959);

Minutes of the East Pennsylvania, Pennsylvania, and Virginia Conferences of the U. B. Church.

Of quite particular importance are these two works:

Edwin H. Sponseller, *Crusade for Education* (Frederick, Md., 1950);

Saul Sack, *History of Higher Education in Pennsylvania* (Harrisburg, 1963).

Index

278

Wilt, Dr. William A., 115, 125, 131–132, 194
Wingate, Robert B., 239
Wining, Mrs. DeVere (Maude M. Wolfe), 169
Wolf, Lt. Colonel Earl E., 199
Wolfe, Henry, 126
Wolfe, Etta (Mrs Norman C. Schlichter), 119
Wolfe, Maude M. (Mrs. DeVere Wining), 169
Women's rights, 92
Wood, Charles, 56
Working up a Part, Dr. H. Darkes Albright, 238
Worrilow, Dr. William H., Sr., 194
Wounded Eye, 161
Wright, John R., 56

Yale Divinity School, 77
Yale University, 93, 177, 191, 249

Yardley, Mrs. Charles H. (Louisa Williams), 164
Yeatts, Edna D. (Mrs. Willard S. Hagar), 130
Yinger, Mary, 169
Yocum, J. C., 71
York, Pa., 8, 18, 156
Young, Dr. David E., 219
Young, John, 32
Young, Joseph, 32
Young, Sallie J., 61
Y. M. C. A., 105, 108
Y. W. C. A., 105, 108, 130

Zeigler, Martha L., 168
Zeigler, "Sue," 168
Zentmeyer, Anna Mary Rebecca (Mrs. Hilary Gossard), 159
Ziegler, Dr. Samuel, 154–157
Zimmerman, Richard P., 135
Zuck, Alice M., 130

The
Universe
Makers

The
Universe
Makers

SCIENCE FICTION TODAY

by DONALD A. WOLLHEIM

HARPER & ROW, PUBLISHERS

NEW YORK, EVANSTON, AND LONDON

1817

FOR ELSIE
who shares my personal universe

Contents

vi] *Contents*

The Day It Began to Come True

EVER SINCE the day that I first heard that an atomic bomb had been exploded over Japan I have had the disturbing conviction that we are all living in a science-fiction story. Atomic power and atomic bombs were old stuff to me at the time, for as an ardent science-fiction fan I had known all about them and their potential for at least a decade. But when the bomb was actually invented and used before the founding of the world state (which was the way it was supposed to have been) I knew we were in for it.

I had at that time already acquired a reputation as a science-fiction authority. I had edited and published the first anthology ever published to use the title "science fiction"—the *Pocket Book of Science Fiction* done in 1943. This was the occasion for a phone call on A-Bomb day from a New York radio station asking me to take part in a hastily organized panel discussion of the atomic bomb's significance.

Although this was the first time I had ever been invited to appear on the air, I simply could not bring myself to do so. I was too uneasy about this misuse of atomic power, too unresolved in my feelings that the world had taken one step too many over the edge of the old realism and into the world of the fantastic future. The possibilities loomed menacingly and chaotically before me, and I was not prepared to talk about it. Instead, I recommended that the station call John W. Campbell, Jr., the editor of what was then—and still is—the leading s-f magazine and the kind of man who could talk a blue streak about scientific and pseudo-scientific possibilities.

I felt then, and I have no cause to change my mind, that the world was entering into a science-fiction phase.

Certainly my thoughts that morning were a mixture of elation at the oncoming of a long-heralded science-fiction event and a sort of sickly foreboding over the fact that it had come when it did and in the form it took. That time, you will recall, was at the end of a grim war—the war was still on, though not for much longer—and we had all been promised, through the media of the press and propaganda, the wonders of the victorious world after the foes were vanquished. Much of the propaganda had, as usual, been taken from the stock in trade of science fiction. This helped in the persuasion that time and history had taken a turn into the unreal, into the misty tracks of the "Days to Come" whose heralds had been the lurid-covered magazines we had fought for so crusadingly.

I was of that pioneering group, the fanatical science-fiction fandom of the thirties, who had believed when others scoffed, who had bought these three or four wild-titled and wildly illustrated magazines and kept them alive during the time when they were among the lowest and least of the pulps that crowded the newsstands of those prewar days. We were a small group compared to the legions of science-fiction readers today—and in consequence very much a beleaguered group. Our lives tended to be bent toward each other, our world was a microcosm of our own lives, and we lived in an atmosphere of infinite horizons that could not be communicated to most of the grim and haunted world of the Depression around us.

Science fiction shaped my life and I can truthfully say I am marked by it in every way. Through it and my associations with its readers and writers I have found my profession, my life, my philosophy, my hobby, and, yes, my wife and friends. Fandom—that organized nucleus of readers—has long been split in its approach by two opposing slogans regarding addiction to science fiction. One is "Fandom is Just a God-Damned Hobby." The other is "Fandom is a Way of Life." For me the latter is the fact.

So I recall sitting at my desk after putting down the phone and thinking to myself, what should I do about the bomb? Atomic power—how many times had stories shown what a world of wonders and prosperity would be humanity's if we could tap the infinite power of the atom. Electricity would be virtually free and endless. We could rebuild the world and with such power end poverty, make the world Utopia, and finally climb to the stars. All that was implied by atomic power which, story after story assured us, would be the tap into Nature's own basic resource. Transmutation of the elements would be open to us.

Such had been the promises of atomic power as foreseen in science fiction.

But then there was the use of this same power in the form of a weapon. There would be rays of such devastating potency that disintegration would result. There would be atomic explosions rivaling the sun in terrible intensity.

If I had taken the radio offer, how should I speak? Should I say that it was the most wonderful news of the century—and that all would be utopian from now on? Or should I admit that in the hands of the old politicians and the old unimaginative generals, with the terrifying division of the world into diametrically opposed political philosophies, this power—in its first form as a superbomb dropped upon an enemy city—was something to dread, not to welcome. That henceforth, because the world was not unified and was not idealistically governed, this power was to be a Sword of Damocles hanging over all mankind and darkening the future.

Both sets of visions churned through my mind. I could not resolve it then. I felt, to be blunt about it, sick. I declined to try to resolve my conflict in a few hours.

That was one aspect of science fiction as a world philosophy. I was a believer in futures. To find that what had been a whole railroad yard of possible futures in the thirties had suddenly been narrowed down to a mere two or three sets of rails heading out—and that it was no longer a matter of daydreaming over the pages of fanciful stories but to be the facts of daily living as humanity roared on along one of those nearly parallel tracks carrying me and my own life with it—that was coming to reality too sharply.

A Life for Science Fiction

SCIENCE FICTION does not, of course, deal strictly with the future, but the major part of it does. By constant reading one acquires a group of conceptions of how the future is going to shape up, and also how it should shape up to be pleasant and how it could shape up to be terrifying.

This world we live in is definitely a world that science fiction conjectured in most of its aspects. The facts of our everyday life today were the fantasies of my youth and the years that preceded my youth. Television was prophesied in many science-fiction tales, going back to the dawn of the century, and taken for granted in the writings of the twenties and thirties. Radio had been a wonder thing in the first years of this century and the source of some wonderful tales right up to the thirties.

Airplanes? Many a great story and fascinating novel had been written about the airplanes of the future, about commercial aviation, about private fliers, aerial bombers, sky pirates, war in the air, and planes city-big as well as planes that one could strap to one's shoulders and take flight. The years following 1945 were to see the blossoming of these things.

I recall the World's Fair of 1939 with a display of future road-ways showing such marvels as cloverleafs, banked express highways, and so on. When you viewed this science-fictional exhibit, they gave you a button to wear that read "I have seen the future." True, quite true. We are living in that express highway-cloverleaf future, and we all drive it every day. In fact, it's polluting the countryside along with some of the other wonders we all envisioned: supercities, perfected insecticides, jet engines, and giant factories.

We believed in robots. They used to charge around in such daily comic strips as the original Buck Rogers, and it was not uncommon to see robotic things playing the role of Bug Eyed Monster on the covers of such dignified magazines as *Astounding Stories of Super-Science* and similar conservative titles. Robots could be built to have superbrains, and they are among us today in the form of the increasing plague known as computers. The depersonalization of business and industry is going on apace today, and that's a science-fiction concept.

We believed above all else in space flight and rockets and the multiplicity of worlds. Today, to be sure, we have the first two. With radio astronomy and constant search we may yet turn up the last. Rockets were also to lead to great events and space flight was to lead to wonderful adventures. The great events are still mainly veiled in military secrecy and the flights through space are militarily controlled and the fliers little more than hard-boiled and endlessly rehearsed test pilot-actors. Not quite the way we saw it, even though science fiction and its followers can truly claim the right to say we started it and we pushed it through.

At least two of the original seven U.S. astronauts admitted to having been science-fiction readers in their formative days. I have learned that one of the three who made that first flight to the moon itself had spent the day before the takeoff reading one of the Ace editions of Edgar Rice Burroughs. (Could it have been *The Moon Maid?*)

Is this the world that science fiction made? I think it is. One bit of research among men of science showed that a high percentage of them had been turned toward their profession through the reading of science fiction in their youth—and some still read it. The ideas we planted, the seeds we sowed (some of them dragon's teeth, yes) are in bloom about us and we are harvesting the results.

The thing that went wrong is that we may be in the wrong story. It looks to me as if we are in that basic science-fiction tale, envisioned in the thirties, where two great world empires contend with each other, leading up to a war which would leave one the victor and thereby establish the one-state world of Earth. Only after that should space flight and meeting with other intelligent beings of other worlds take place. Otherwise, a divided world confronted by a stronger, more advanced single-nation planet might face the same disasters that divided India faced with a united Britain or the tribes of America with a Spanish empire.

It looks as if that is the story we are in. We are in that tale wherein the great inventions were made before the installation of Utopia. That story never had a happy ending.

But hold it . . . let's not get too gloomy all at once. Science fiction makes no hard and fast rules. It may precede history but history never has been known to follow it exactly either. Nor, for that matter, has science.

What should be evident by now is that science fiction is not just a form of literature to be discussed as literature should be discussed—the lives of authors, the lists of their works, the evaluation of their styles. Science fiction is above all a system of ideas. It deals with ideas more than it deals with literary styles. It speculates in futurities and in probabilities. These are what are more to be remembered than the depth of character of its heroes.

Science fiction, then, is judged by the immense variety of its visions and concepts—which are as varied as the potential of humanity is varied and as multifold as the stars in the sky. It is this harvest of wonders, this garden of marvels, this vision of what could be and what could have been that makes science fiction so different and makes its readers marked for life in out-of-the-rut trains of thought.

The phases of being a science-fiction reader can be traced and charted. So many read it for one year, so many for two, so many for life. For instance, reading it exclusively can be as compulsive as a narcotic for a period of an intelligent teen-ager's life. The length of time as I see it—and I have seen and talked with and corresponded with hundreds and hundreds of such readers in my lifetime—is about four or five years of the most intense reading— usually exclusive, all other literature being shoved aside. After that a falling off, rather rapid (often due to college entry or military life or the hard stuff of getting a job for the first time). There is, I suspect, something like an 80 percent turnover in the mass readers of science fiction every five years.

Which isn't bad. It means that a higher and higher percentage of people have been exposed to its mind-tingling and vision-enlarging writings at the most impressionable times of their lives. The effect lingers on in the world around us.

There are the other 20 percent who cling to it. They are the nucleus who keep the magazines alive in bad times, from whose ranks arise the writers of science fiction and the editors too; people like myself.

I was such a young man. I started reading science fiction sporadically from the time I was eleven. I graduated from grammar school to becoming a total reader. It happened during that last day before graduation—that slack day when one still reports to school, but lessons are over and pupils sit around a classroom killing a couple of hours until allowed to go home. On that day I came to school without anything to read. While I was sitting around wondering how to occupy my mind, another student came over—one I scarcely knew, incidentally—and handed me a copy of *Amazing Stories* saying, "I think you'll like this."

That was the issue containing the first installment of A. Merritt's *The Moon Pool*. How right he was! I was hooked on the s-f magazines at that point. Nevertheless, it was a few months before I could raise the funds to keep on buying that magazine—and had depleted the obvious science-fiction books in the local library. In the interim I missed the concluding installments of Merritt's masterpiece and it was not till many years later that I was able to pick up the back numbers I had missed and find out what happened at the Nan Matal on mysterious Ponape Island.

But I do not think I read any other type of fiction from that day on for at least five or six years. (I exclude those books assigned for homework or college necessity, to be sure. I am talking about reading for pleasure.) I had found my niche.

The usual science-fiction devotee tends to be solitary and introverted in his youth. This is not an exact thing, of course, but in a general form it holds true for most of those I have met. They do not run with the pack—they are at home with their noses buried in the pages of speculation. Even if they are of a sociable nature, what they want to talk about is the wealth of wonders they have absorbed through their reading. They find that the average youth is not concerned. A little such talk goes a long way. Whereas the ardent s-f addict will talk about science and Mars and the moon and space flight and time travel all day and all night too, he soon finds that among the friends of his own age there is usually no one he can talk with about this. So he becomes a solitary until he discovers that he can correspond with others like himself. Then he obtains a typewriter and does so for hour after hour.

Such is my own history, for I was definitely that kind of solitary reader, devouring everything the magazines published, every book I could buy or borrow, and eventually writing to other fans and trying to write stories myself. The problems of daily life, getting through school, worrying about college, thinking about making a living, were never as real as the problem of how the moon flight was to be organized, what we would find on Mars, and whether atomic power would be released in our time. That was what counted.

That, to be sure, is what eventually did count. In that sense the stubborn introverted convictions of the s-f fan were ultimately to be proved right. It is that conviction, pursued with the fanaticism of a religious convert, that impressed itself upon so many who were to leave the world of fantastic literature to work in the world of scientific realities—and thereby ultimately produce those things that only some wild pulp writers had spoken of.

So it came about that the friends of my youth were found eventually among dreamers like myself. I corresponded around the country and overseas, and I met and formed clubs with similar types at home.

The history of the world of science-fiction fandom has been written elsewhere and is in any case not relevant to this book. Suffice it to say that I became prominent in that microcosm, that through it I was to determine my life trade—that of a writer and editor, and to find work in those fields. Through it also I was to meet the girl that I married and to establish my place in society.

Like many of my fellow introverts I wanted to write out my own angles of these fantastic conjectures. I had the remarkable fortune to sell the first story I ever wrote, a short piece, to Hugo

Gernsback's *Wonder Stories*. That was in 1933 and from that time on I knew that science fiction was not to be just a reading hobby but also a life interest.

I became a full-time professional editor in 1941, putting out two magazines for a shoestring publisher. My budget was nothing, literally nothing. Stories were solicited from my friends, art work was cajoled from fan artists with professional ambitions. The magazines lasted a year or so, long enough to gain me a "foot in the door" as a pro editor (at no salary), and get me hired on as a pulp magazine editor for A. A. Wyn, who had a chain of such magazines under the "Ace" imprint.

But don't think those two magazines I edited so cheaply were full of unknowns. It was in their pages that such writers as C. M. Kornbluth, Robert Lowndes, and others first made their mark, and our chief artist was Hannes Bok, who has a whole movement devoted to his name today.

It was shortly after joining Wyn (where I edited detectives, westerns, and sports magazines, but not fantasy) that I conceived and sold the first two anthologies directly dealing with science fiction, the aforementioned *Pocket Book of Science Fiction* and the *Viking Portable Novels of Science*. On the basis of those I was later to sell Avon Books the idea of a series of similar anthologies—the *Avon Fantasy Readers*—which led me to joining their staff and finding myself almost immediately their editor (by virtue of the fact that the man who hired me quit two months later). For two years thereafter there was no person in the entire editorial staff save myself. I was it—first reader and editor in chief and official and only blurb and caption writer. I will drop that line of discussion right here too—what happened to me at Avon and after is another book, which discretion indicates I ought to write only after retiring.

A Matter of Plausibility

LET US get back to science fiction. Before we go any further I had better define what I mean by it. How do I know when such and such a work is science fiction and when it isn't? When I first thought about writing this present book the *New York Times* list of the ten hard-cover best sellers had three titles that I considered to be science fiction. Of these the authors of two would probably have winced at the label, while the third could not have squirmed out of it.

The books were *The Andromeda Strain* by Michael Crichton, *Slaughterhouse Five* by Kurt Vonnegut, Jr., and *Ada* by Vladimir Nabokov. The last two authors are the ones that would have winced. The first title is unmistakably standard s-f.

What, then, is my definition of science fiction? There have been many attempts to define science fiction . . . you can find them in the introductions to anthologies and they all differ a little from each other. I do not agree with all of them—I think most anthologists are too restrictive, too tight, in their definitions. Back in 1935 I did a short article for a fan magazine in which I set forth my own definitions of the three classifications of adult fantasy:

> Science fiction is that branch of fantasy, which, while not true of present-day knowledge, is rendered plausible by the reader's recognition of the scientific possibilities of it being possible at some future date or at some uncertain period in the past.
>
> Weird fiction is that branch of fantasy dealing with supernatural or occult subjects, which is rendered plausible by the reader's recognition of the fact that there are people somewhere who at present, or in the past, did believe, or do believe in the truth of the ideas therein and is therefore willing to concede the truth of these things for the period in which he is reading the story.

Pure fantasy is that branch of fantasy which, dealing with subjects recognizable as nonexistent and entirely imaginary, is rendered plausible by the reader's desire to accept it during the period of reading.

As you see, these definitions are based upon the reader's voluntary will to believe. Plausibility is the necessary factor in all reading, mainstream as well as fantasy. To make a fantastic premise plausible one must utilize one of these three approaches. Depending upon which one you use, the classification must follow inevitably.

In the case of *The Andromeda Strain*, the premise is that a space probe satellite returns to earth contaminated by a strain of germs originating outside this planet. Although the novel is virtually newspaper stuff, its success is certainly based upon remarkable timing—for it hit the stores coincidentally with the return of the Apollo 11 astronauts to quarantine precisely to isolate and offset any lunar germs they might have picked up on the moon. The story is science-fictional in that it deals with a space probe that did pick up such a germ and what happened when it returned to contaminate a small Nevada village. The author packed it with seemingly authentic details about what are supposed to be present-day procedures in handling space probes—and since many of these procedures are still cloaked by the secrecy that blacks out much of today's scientific enterprise connected with the military, the author's depiction of what he thought those procedures were seemed both very real and very probable.

I note here that this work—which I personally found absolutely engrossing, for Crichton knows how to spin a suspense story—has been torn apart by s-f magazine reviewers for absurdities in plot and premise. I cannot criticize their objections for they make sense, but the novel was still a spellbinder and its best-seller status easily understood.

Vonnegut's *Slaughterhouse Five*, though directed at the mainstream reader, is, like most of Vonnegut's writing, a sharp-edged satire. With a grim sardonic touch, the acid edge of contrast between horror and farce, the novel tells of the bombing of Dresden in World War II through the medium of a modern middle-class American who is afflicted with a distortion of his time sense. He shifts back and forth between present, past, and future, and is also the pawn and puppet of alien intelligences from a planet somewhere else in the galaxy.

The utilization of this extraterrestrial manipulation makes the work science fiction. The public has been sold already on the probable existence of alien intelligences around other stars and also on the possibility of switching back and forth in time. Vonnegut does not neglect his science-fictional argumentation for these premises either. Hence, the work is science fiction.

Lest someone now raise the objection that Vonnegut throws his star people at us cold, I will say that one s-f premise builds and grows upon the body of s-f lore and argument that has gone before. This I will discuss at length later.

As for *Ada*, a work manifestly not intended for the science-fiction audience, and, for that matter, not very readable to the average person since Nabokov is one of the elite literary multi-level observationists, the background of the long novel is laid on what is known in s-f as a parallel world. This is one where the Russians found and colonized North America first, and *Ada*'s world is a United States not too terribly different from our own save that what would be of Anglo-Saxon root in our real land is of Russian root in Nabokov's. At one point in the novel a character indulges in a long pseudo-scientific speculation on the possibility of a parallel world wherein the English colonized America and what that world would be like—in short a description of our world.

This puts the book squarely into the realm of s-f, not of pure fantasy. For here Nabokov has built upon a whole stratum of s-f novels arguing the premise that there is a multitude of parallel worlds, all Earths, spaced apart by some alteration of molecular count or dimensional layerage, and in these other Earths history would have worked out according to other alternates of history. These "Worlds of If," to give them a popular generic name, are an increasing favorite in modern s-f writing. They afford grand fun for sociological speculation, not to mention fine arenas for heroic adventures.

One of the earliest such works, incidentally, was a collection of essay-stories, including one by Winston Churchill, entitled appropriately *If*. I would not define this ancestral work as science fiction, however, for Churchill made no effort to justify his alternate history—it was a take it or leave it presentation, in short, "pure fantasy" classification.

Let's play this string out a little more. It should be apparent that it is possible to produce the same novel as any one of the three classifications and requires often only a paragraph or two to do it. What may be unacceptable to one reader on a pure fantasy approach may be made acceptable by inventing a reasonable "scientific" premise or an occult one.

Take J. R. R. Tolkien's magnificent trilogy *The Lord of the Rings*. These adventures all take place in a world, plainly not the one we know, which the author calls Middle Earth. Tolkien makes no effort to place this Middle Earth in relation to our own Earth (Upper Earth?). He writes of it, maps it, gives its history, but he does not say anything that could pin it down in any scientific cosmology.

Middle Earth might be taking place in some forgotten past epoch, but Tolkien does not say so and contradictions of speech, time, and anthropology would immediately set in should he make such a claim. It could be a parallel Earth, but he disdains to play that game. It is too much like our own Earth to be acceptable as a planet somewhere else in the universe. Now, it would not have taken Tolkien more than a few paragraphs to have made it science fiction by choosing to utilize such a pseudo-scientific ploy and perhaps alter a few elements in his background to establish it, but he was not so interested. Middle Earth is a place one takes on faith. You believe in Frodo and his quest because a fine work of imaginative writing makes you quite willing to suspend disbelief just to enjoy it. It is pure fantasy, and that is the only classification we can give to *The Lord of the Rings*.

Or, Tolkien could have put it into the weird fantasy classification by some claim that magic does so exist, and that elves and dwarfs and the like are real beings of the supernatural world, and that Middle Earth is the world of "another plane" wherein they dwell. This would have taken even more rewriting than making it science-fictional and might very well have alienated many readers and spoiled a lot of the enjoyment. *The Hobbit,* which was published as a children's book, is probably read by children in exactly that manner—here is a part of fairyland and fairyland is real to the child's mind that does not require more erudite hocus-pocus to establish acceptance.

Andre Norton's six novels of the *Witch World* are an instance wherein a science-fiction springboard was utilized to present a planet as magical and variegated in its own way as Middle Earth. For in the first novel of the series, Simon Tregarth is on Earth escaping from enemies and finds his escape by means of a "Gate" between worlds, operated by its discoverer. We are told quite definitely that it utilizes scientific principles of an ancient and lost galactic race to transfer by means of some sort of instantaneous space warp a thing or a person from one planet of the galaxy to another. The exact location of the Witch World is not known—but it is definitely somewhere in our own space-time continuum, though so remote an area that the laws of science that work there are not quite the same as the ones that work here.

Now this Gate Between Worlds is not an Andre Norton invention either. It is one of those premises upon which science fiction today rests—ideas worked out in the past and now taken for granted when utilized today.

Science fiction is built upon such premises. Somewhere in the early days of the literature someone invented a premise, argued it out with scientific (or more likely pseudoscientific) logic and convinced the readers. Once the argument is made, the premise is at once accepted on its own word, enters the tool shed of the science-fiction writer, and may be utilized thereafter by any craftsman without further repetition of the operational manual.

As a boy I was fascinated by L. Frank Baum's Oz books. One of the things that has always struck me about those books, which may be part of the underlying reason for their popularity among American children of the twentieth century, is that they come exceedingly close to being science fiction. Baum set out to write a distinctly American version of a fairy tale, and unconsciously he hit upon plausibility premises close to the s-f mark. Oz is sometimes described as being on a parallel world, almost in those words. People from America get there through various means, often natural catastrophes, which could be easily science-fictionized into Gates Between Worlds. Dorothy gets there at one time by means of a tornado, at another through falling into the inside of the Earth via an earthquake, once thrown overboard at sea in a fierce storm and washed ashore near Oz. Similar means have been utilized by s-f writers to present Gates Between Worlds.

Even the magic and witchcraft of Oz smacks of science fiction, for it has to be learned, it follows the books of lore, it can be taught (the Wizard is taught by Glinda), and one needs scientific instruments to practice it.

I am not claiming the Oz books as science fiction, however, because they are still too much fairy tale. What I am demonstrating is that a little ingenuity and borrowing from the established propositions of past s-f writing could make them so.

Take this gimmick of the Gates Between Worlds. I have already said that one explanation for this device is the supposition of a space warp. Space warps themselves are another gimmick too, worked out in detail in someone's past fiction, at least forty years ago. The idea is that space is not continuous but may be wrinkled—"warped" sounds more scientific. Hence the argument runs: two segments of space may be separated by thousands of light years traveling along the visible three-dimensional continuum of space, yet may be touching each other because space or the universe or something is wrinkled and the two sections are touching each other like two pages of a book. The Gate then is merely an extradimensional means of cutting across this touching point and thereby avoiding the problem of having to travel those thousands of light years inch by inch.

That's one argument. There are many more, worked out by inventive writers. Another and equally prominent argument is that the Gate Between Worlds is an automatic matter-transmitter which operates like a radio or television, that is, instead of transmitting the electronic pattern of sound or sight it breaks down matter into its own electronic patterns, broadcasts them to a station elsewhere, and reassembles the pattern there into a total facsmile of the original—life and all. The *transmatter* isn't all that simple and the possibilities of confusion are endless and so are the stories that have been built upon it.

The point that I am stressing is that modern science fiction no longer requires an author to go into all this argument. He has only to say he has a Gate or a transmatter and the reader is able to supply from memory of past stories all the plausibility quotient he needs to accept this as a future probable invention.

Science fiction builds upon science fiction. As a result of this, modern stories are freer to deal with sociological possibilities and the movement of humanity under future conditions and do not have to repeat pseudoscientific propositions endlessly.

4

Verne or Wells?

SCIENCE FICTION breaks into four major classifications and any story may fit one or several of these groupings:

> Imaginary Voyages
> Future Predictions
> Remarkable Inventions
> Social Satire

Under Imaginary Voyages come trips to the moon and planets and stars, trips to the prehistoric past or the center of the earth, voyages to unexplored parts of this world such as *Gulliver's Travels* and *She,* visits to the infinitely small and the infinitely large, trips to the future, and so on.

Future Predictions covers the stories that tell you what could be happening to mankind tomorrow or in the next century or a million years from now, here or wherever in the universe, with or without man, come to think of it. Mainly it tends to involve genuine accounts of what could happen if such and such a trend or potential continues or comes to pass. Utopias are a variety of this (though they may also be found as Imaginary Voyages), as well as wars to come, or plagues, or famines. Trips to the planets obviously are both Future Predictions and Imaginary Voyages, and probably ought to include the next category of Remarkable Inventions.

In this classification would come many stories taking place in the present where we assume something has been discovered. *The Invisible Man* is an example. Again Remarkable Inventions usually are found in the previous two classifications as well.

Social Satire generally partakes of one or all of the previous classifications, but is a class by itself because of the motivation of the writer. The intent is to hold a mirror to the present, by means of the future or of an imaginary land, and thereby either make fun, a dire prediction, a somber warning, or a healthy look at where we are all going and What Does It All Mean. *Gulliver's Travels* is a good specimen of that, and *1984* also. In Social Satire science fiction becomes a means to an end but is not the end itself, as it may be in the previous classifications.

Social Satire of the past was often rather obvious and crude. The best of modern s-f usually contains a touch of it, but neither crudely nor always obviously either. Where science fiction has meaning beyond its momentary entertainment value may depend exactly on the combination of logical future prediction and compassionate social satire that the writer is able to bring to bear upon it, without being soapboxy about it.

In fact it may be said that much of the talk that goes on between full-time science-fiction writers about their ever-recurrent dream of someday being accepted fully into the mainstream of literature must derive from their awareness of the implicit social criticism of their projections. The best of modern science fiction carries social satire elements which, it must be pointed out at once in fairness to definitions, do not appear to be satirical in the old sense. Any effort to imagine what people will think and do in unrealized situations of unattained conditions can only be described as a form of satire. The reality never quite jibes.

A great deal of what seems to be maturity in modern s-f derives from its combination of these four elements in the same story, plus, to be sure, writing above the level of a penny-a-word hack.

But good writing is not a monopoly of recent authors. The quality of writing depended upon the men who were attracted to this sort of work. It is just that today, in an environment reeking of science fiction on every side and in every headline, the number of good talents being attracted is vastly greater than back in the wood-paneled airless parlors of the nineteenth century.

Verne was a first-rate writer for his day, though his work was intended primarily for juvenile readers. It is impossible to read him today without realizing that he had a talent for detail of background equal to any, that his eye for the nuances of his time was up to the level of any—it is in his dialogue and his characterizations that the juvenile level shows up strongly.

I am not here writing a history of science fiction—this has been done by others—and I recommend such studies as those of I. F. Clarke, W. H. G. Armytage, H. Bruce Franklin, and most of all Sam Moskowitz for detailed exposition of that sort. I am concerned with the flow of ideas that grew as a result of all this. So here I shall start with the two who are always listed in quick surveys as the fathers of the field—Jules Verne and H. G. Wells.

A basic divergence that can be detected through science fiction can be traced to the thinking of these two. Others wrote concurrently with them, but these two are the ones that stood out, these are the ones we remember and whose works remain available to be read as part of the beginning heritage of those who came later to the field. We know that original conceptions credited to both Verne and Wells could be traced in earlier writers—Sam Moskowitz has done a good deal of that—but it is not the misty records of medieval mariners who may or may not have sailed across the Atlantic that we remember, it is the voyage of Columbus that "fixed" the event and from which the New World derives. Similarly, submarine voyages may have been invented and described by earlier writers, but it is *Twenty Thousand Leagues Under the Sea* which we recall as the one that set the scene in the s-f pantheon.

Verne turned out a flock of remarkable premises for science fiction (or at least he produced the successful popularizations for them). In his writings can be traced not merely the submarine but the airship and the airplane, rocket weapons, voyages around the moon, telecommunication, power locomotion, city planning, and so forth. But whatever his projection, his scenes and his characterizations never changed—they were always reflected against the unvarying political scenery of the latter half of the nineteenth century. There is no evidence of social change in his works—his inventions do not change their inventors nor their users. Sometimes one like Captain Nemo or Robur may dedicate himself to righting wrongs, but the motivation even then is usually revenge or personal vindication rather than any soaring desire to move the human condition forward.

Jules Verne was and remained to the end a typical small-minded French bourgeois nationalist. His works reflect no other thinking. He saw other nationalities in the typical caricature traits common to the most vulgar political thinking of his time. He was quite capable of the crudest anti-Germanism (a product of the defeat of 1871) and the kind of cheap anti-Semitism which ultimately culminated in the French national disgrace of the Dreyfus Affair.

Verne's works stayed tightly within the restrictions of Imaginary Voyages and Remarkable Inventions, and strayed into Future Predictions with great reluctance, and into Social Satire never.

On the other hand, H. G. Wells started off in the realm of Future Prediction and Social Satire with his magnificent gem *The Time Machine,* still one of the most perfect little novels in the genre. I read this one in the public library at the age of ten, gaining the perspective of humanity carried on, changing, evolving, and perhaps disappearing as millions of years passed, and its internal differences brought about the emergence of two humanities—neither desirable, neither destined for immortality. This was social satire and unforgettable future prediction. This was Wells's introduction to the world, for it was his first great novel, the one he had written and rewritten since his school days, whose polish and concept reflected vividly the potential of the social struggle upon which the turn of the twentieth century pivoted.

Wells was a Utopian and though his writings were to encompass as many Remarkable Inventions as Verne—indeed to help fill out the armory of modern science fiction—it was his Social Satire that was dearest to his heart and was the lever with which he sought to move the world.

Even such apparent Imaginary Voyages as his *War of the Worlds* and *The Island of Dr. Moreau* are enhanced by his use of these themes—invasion from space and the biological restructuring of beasts into humanoids—not merely for shock and thrill-a-minute purposes as would have been done by Verne and the others of his ilk. They are asparkle with implications of social thinking, with mirrors held up to our mind and the suggestion to think not merely of the horror but of what should be done to change our philosophy of the universe.

One can go through the works of Wells and pick out the original concepts that seem to be "firsts" in the foundations of modern science fiction. Not merely the two listed above, and the time machine as well, but also a myriad others such as can be found by a perusal of his short stories.

My copy of *The Short Stories of H. G. Wells* is one of my personal treasures for it was a presentation to me from my mother on my fifteenth birthday. It has been read and reread innumerable times. From it I have derived many of the elements that have influenced my thinking and my life, and not the least of these was the style of writing. My short stories are not many, but they have been cast in the premise set forth by Wells, that a good story of science fiction should have but one theme that departs from the accepted and credible. Against a background of the known, one unknown factor gains impact and is best set off.

Going over the short stories of H. G. Wells strictly for Remarkable Inventions we encounter first after first in the realm of s-f basics: rivalry of insect "civilization" with humanity, war tanks, man-eating plants, diamond making, collision with another star, superacceleration of life, the shop of marvels, the man with psi talents, worship of science, germ development, travel beyond this dimension, and on and on. And if one adds the novels, we find aerial warfare, the bedlam of the over-crowded future city, size-changing foods, and atomic power.

For Remarkable Inventions, Wells had it all over Verne. For Imaginary Voyages, he was moderately deficient, but in the other two categories he soared. Therein lay the talent that put H. G. Wells into his permanent position in the world of great literature.

Wells started as something of a social alarmist, but he rapidly developed into a Utopian, a Fabian Socialist at first, a World Stater toward the end. Wellsian Socialism is a vague term—it seems to mean a combination of scientific achievement for the betterment of mankind and utilized on a social basis. It was always rather misty, expressed in general ideas, aspirations, but rarely clear enough to enable any reader to tie in with any specific social movement. Wells, to be sure, wrote innumerable political tracts, but the world of the science-fiction reader has never paid attention to them. They were destined to be outdated with great speed and are today antiquities dealing with things that seem to have no relation to today's world. But his science fiction remains the means by which he continues to influence the world. The very method he abandoned for political lecturing turned out ultimately to be his sole lasting memorial, an inextricable part of the science-fiction world that is today.

It is possible to theorize that, as in *The Time Machine,* Verne and Wells produced two diverging evolutions in science-fiction writing and thinking and that this can be detected in the dichotomy between *Analog* magazine and its competitors in the form of *Galaxy, If,* and *Magazine of Fantasy & Science Fiction* . . . and, yes, *New Worlds* too.

Consider the two: Verne, the small-minded nationalist without social content and with a fixation only on inventions and gadgets. Wells, the Utopian, concerned with social aspirations and world organization and always utilizing science fiction in context with its influence on the changing of humanity. Does it not seem that Verne would inevitably lead to a magazine like *Analog,* whose editorials, which dominate the magazine and color its contents, reflect a similarly small-minded nationalist thinking, whose stress is on gadgets and inventions, and which consciously rejects Utopianism and the changing of "human nature" to adjust to changing technologies and infinite worlds? *Analog*, which is a magazine I discuss later at greater depth, is prepared to accept alterations in all the scientific laws whether physics, chemistry, biology, or astronomy, but never in what the editor believes to be the laws of economics—which are forever fixed, perfect, immutable, and not to be questioned.

Whereas in the contents of *Analog*'s various rival magazines, put out by many editors and many publishers, no such fixation appears. The range and scope of stories in *Galaxy* and the *Magazine of Fantasy & Science Fiction* is wide open, and therein the laws of economics are as subject to change as any other. It is accepted that the better the writing the more likely will be reflected the social and psychological changes in man and mankind caused by projected futures or inventive situations. Here in these magazines and their writers seems to be reflected the other current, the Wellsian current, which says there is no scientific advancement without its impact on humanity.

It is not an accident that the one magazine espouses racism in its ugliest form, puts forth arguments in favor of slavery (Yes, I said slavery!), and insists on the deliberate revision of stories to include statements of the right of financial greed to triumph over idealistic ideas.

It is not an accident that the other magazines reject racism, cannot even conceive of anyone in this day and age seriously supporting slavery, and ask nothing of their writers save their honest opinions.

It might be argued by Verne readers that Jules Verne did write about Utopianism in his novel *The Begum's Fortune*, wherein two opposing scientific cities were set up in an unpopulated area of Oregon territory, one French, peaceful, intellectual, the other German, mechanized, war oriented. But Verne was just exercising his bent for nationalism and also playing around with the science of architecture and city planning. Of social content—nothing different from the political caricatures of the day.

It might also be argued that Wells did not invent Utopianism

. . . the 1890's were a very fertile area for Utopian writings and Bellamy's *Looking Backward* made a bigger splash in its day than ever Wells did. It was Wells who had the firmest grasp of the century to come—that science would alter it more than someone's armchair social theorizing. *Looking Backward* is pitifully antiquated in style and ideas today. Wells is still an influence.

But there are others who influenced the current of science fiction. One of these influences is the writer Ray Cummings.

As I see it, Ray Cummings bridged the gap between the era of H. G. Wells and the dawn of the science-fiction magazines which crystallized the name and the genre and to which everything modern can be traced.

5

Master of the Microcosm

VERNE wrote in the latter half of the nineteenth century. Wells wrote from 1895 to about 1920 (speaking of him as a science-fiction novelist and short-story writer only). Ray Cummings started in 1920 and his most fruitful period ran through to the late 1930's. He wrote for the pulp magazines, mostly for *Argosy All-Story* weekly and its successor, *Argosy* weekly. That fabulous variety pulp had a style all its own. It ran four serials an issue, one starting, one ending, and two in-between installments. It ran from four to six short stories or novelettes as well. In its pages appeared many of the popular writers of the twenties and thirties, including Edgar Rice Burroughs, Otis Adelbert Kline, Murray Leinster, A. Merritt, and Ray Cummings.

Cummings would have to be described as a Vernian. I know of no Utopias from him. I can think of nothing that could be called a serious sociological prediction. His novels were adventure novels, on a rather simplistic level at that. As likely as not his plot would be that of the heroic scientific young man going to the rescue of a maiden in distress. He had a style all his own, often flowery, given to gasps of wonder and incomplete sentences. He had picked up from Wells's *Time Machine* the trick of often not naming his characters as anything but The Very Young Man, The Businessman, and so on.

But Cummings was grounded in the science of the day, which was that of the early decades of this century. His novels and short stories were expressions of adventure arising from his concept of the universe. This concept is worth analyzing, for therein lies the change in s-f from those days to the present.

During the nineteenth century, and especially in its closing days, there flourished the vision of a purely mechanistic universe. The laws of nature were fixed and permanent and merely awaited their discovery. The planets revolved about the sun in fixed orbits which could be measured and predicted without fear of deviation. The sun moved through the universe in a certain direction at a certain speed and that was that. All suns and comets and galaxies moved on their ways, which could be measured and thereby the universe could be understood. Complex and wonderful it was, but essentially it was like a vast clockwork mechanism which could be mapped and mastered.

In chemistry an observed reaction could be put down on paper and would never thereafter be seen to differ. In physics mathematics proved how one force acted upon another, and that too would always be the case. In biology and geology, evolution had been traced and its course plotted to the present day and simple following of the line could tell us what to expect of future eons.

While many people had expressed doubts about the exactness of all this, by and large mechanistic thinking dominated science. It supplied answers that one could count on in that period of scientific invention—any information to the contrary merely served to obscure thinking. One did not doubt; the glory of the universe was the glory of the watchmaker magnified to infinity, wonderful to think about, and an oyster to be opened by any writer with imagination to open it.

Out of this mechanistic universe came almost all the science fiction of those days, and even after the thirties much of what came along was mechanistic in its application to science.

The mechanistic universe was dealt its death blow by the discoveries of Einstein and by the formula E equals MC squared just as much as our modern political world has been shaken apart by this same formula. Once one realizes that energy and matter are interchangeable, that the transfer of one form to the other is constantly going on, an element of chaos enters the scene. Today's cogwheel could be tomorrow's electrical storm. You can't build a wonder watch on that principle! The formula and the subsequent changing worlds of astronomy, physics, chemistry, biology, and technology have made an awful lot of the old pre-1940 science fiction obsolete. Nevertheless, concepts build upon concepts, and what we have today may be modernized efforts to restructure much of what had been wonders before.

Ray Cummings pioneered in ideas derived from the mechanistic universe that Wells and Verne had neglected. The latter because he probably never thought of it. The former because he was already in 1910 alerted to the coming shift in science, wise to the errors of Victorian science, and not interested in being a writing hack for the popular fiction magazines.

From Ray Cummings we got the fourth dimensional world— that this world could be but one of many divided in space by a fourth dimension incomprehensible to us but verifiable by mathematics. Cummings probed the intriguing possibilities of an age of aviation—his Flyer of Eternal Midnight could be achieved: it was an airliner which flew about the world at the same rate as the world's rotation, arriving at all its ports of call always at midnight. He played around with the concept of robots, the machine men of the future, and they often figured in his tales. Karel Capek had invented the word "robot" for his created humanoids of *R.U.R.*, but they were made of synthetic flesh and blood. Today we use the term "android" for such as these. Robot now means mechanical man, not meat man. Cummings played around with suggestions of space travel to come. I don't think he invented space pirates but he had novels about them.

He certainly played around with past, present, and future, binding them together in a series of novels such as *The Shadow Girl* and *The Man Who Mastered Time*. Wells had invented the time machine, but Cummings put it to full use. In his short stories he brought forth concepts of gravity and size relativity ahead of his time. But what he did best was a type of story which cannot be duplicated today simply because it was based totally on the old mechanistic concepts of space. He traveled to the infinitesimal and to the infinite (and found them both finite).

In his day science knew that matter was composed of electrons and protons, and in the popularizations of the day these were more often compared with miniature solar systems. Electrons of planetary size (comparative) revolved in fixed orbits about protons of solar size. That was it. In the minds of many the further explanation was simple: matter consisted of an infinite number of infinitesimally small solar systems, these systems composed of particles with movements similar to those of the worlds of astronomy.

So it was possible for Ray Cummings to write a novel called *The Girl in the Golden Atom* (Harper & Brothers, 1923) in which his hero, The Very Young Man, goes down in size by means of a pill invented by The Chemist until he is small enough to set foot upon an atomic electron world which then becomes in relation to him just another planet like Earth.

The size-changing pills are one of Cummings' specialties. He used them in many stories thereafter. They are composed of the same material that Alice found in the Drink-Me bottles of Wonderland, albeit Cummings advances pseudoscientific explanations having to do with chemical contraction of tissue and so on.

By means of this gimmick Cummings dares to explore the microcosmic universe. For if these electrons are truly particles of matter revolving about energy-charged sun particles, why, then, they are truly planets and must harbor life and all that accompanies planetary existence.

Ray Cummings' descriptions of his heroes' journeys into smallness are masterpieces of wonder travel. The world grows vast, the viewpoint becomes that of the microscope, then further and gradually, as our hero slips and stumbles over vast rolling molecules like so many marbles in a sack, shrinking even further until at last he falls into astronomical space and finds himself shrinking down to the surface of a world, a world with trees and plains like our own—only infinitely small!

What do they find in that microcosmic world? The same things Cummings' heroes will find in voyages to other planets, to the bottom of the sea, or to infinite largeness—a maiden to be rescued, a villain to be foiled, a good action-adventure derring-do novel. Kingdoms and republics, Napoleons and scientists, some weird animals, some fantastic cities, but always perfectly comprehensible people.

He utilized the size-changing chemicals in exploring the vaster universe, the macrocosm. Here his hero, in a space ship that grows in size rather than moves in space, grows vaster and vaster until the sun and its planets are reduced to microscopic size and the galaxies and the billions of stars too are but molecules in a universe whose relation to us is that of ourselves to the microcosmic. And what happens then? I recall two variations. One is that the Greater Universe is like ours—a planet with people and heroes and villains and a maiden to be rescued. The other is more intriguingly mechanistic—our hero finds himself on the inside of a huge shell, the shell which encircles our universe as an eggshell holds its contents. And what lives on that inner shell of the universe? You guessed it. A maiden to be rescued!

They don't write that story any more either. The concept of the microcosmic world has been dashed to pieces by the discovery of more things than electrons and protons. We now believe we have discovered how many other energy particles of the microcosm? Twenty, is it? Or more? Bodies charged with every variety of energy or not charged at all. The molecule becomes not a simple matter but a vastly complex interweaving of many energies and many particles in many many motions. Nobody today would describe the microcosmic universe as another solar system or dare to invent a voyage into it!

As for the question of the macrocosmic—is this universe indeed a particle or a molecule in some vaster universe? Who can say? Some stories hint at it or touch upon it, suggest, but do not define, for the realization of the complexity, of the ever-changing nature of existence and the impermanence of any state of being has erased the adventuresome ignorance of the days of Ray Cummings.

Certainly we do not expect to find a maiden in distress or a villain to be foiled. I see in Ray Cummings the culmination of the science-fiction story of the mechanistic nineteenth century and the beginning of the adventure story which formed the body of present-day fiction.

He completed Verne's work. He did not venture into sociology. He did not upset one's equilibrium with social prediction. His was the old Sense of Wonder played out in full.

Curiously enough, Cummings still has reader attraction. There is a trend—and has always been—to enjoy stories of derring-do in fantastic settings. This is the stuff of Edgar Rice Burroughs. I have reprinted many Cummings novels in new editions in paperbacks for Ace Books, and they have sold well and have been rewarded by the letters of young readers and nostalgic old-timers with cries of appreciation.

Never mind that their science is antiquated—there are no lost cities in well-explored Africa and no such creatures as Tarzan's anthropoid apes, but Tarzan is a permanent fixture of the world of imagination. The world of science-fiction reading has wide margins and readers are tolerant of the lack of credibility. Enough that they were credible once, that once these things seemed logical; if the storytelling is still exciting, let's read them anyway, accrediting them perhaps as fantasy—we accept them as credible because we wish to do so, not because we are any longer convinced.

What, then, of Edgar Rice Burroughs? He, too, came out of the same period that produced Ray Cummings. His stories of wonder adventure have made their mark in the world. Tarzan is a word to be found in dictionaries and is known to all languages and all lands. Tarzan himself—well, we can believe or disbelieve—but the bulk of his adventures were instances of an almost extinct branch of science fiction—the Imaginary Voyage to a lost race. There is a formula detectable in many Tarzan adventures: he finds a valley or an isolated land in which are lost people: Romans, ant-sized men, tailed men, lost Atlanteans, and so on, all forgotten by our civilization. Usually they have split into two warring factions and Tarzan inevitably gets mixed up with one side or the other. The lost-race story belongs to the roots of science fiction, it is one with Gulliver, and Burroughs makes it live to this very day.

But whereas Cummings eschewed social satire, Burroughs often indulged in it, and many of his novels are enhanced by his deliberate satirical presentation of one or another philosophy. He pokes fun at staid religion in his attack on the blond-wigged priests of Mars ("Help Stamp Out Therns" is a slogan I have seen carried about by fans at more than one convention!); he satirizes Nazism and Communism in his stories of Venus; he builds a parallel with the Earth of World War II in one of his last novels, that of *Beyond the Farthest Star;* he weaves a picture of the miseries of the conquered in *The Moon Men.* Yet his social satire was irrelevant to his popularity. It was his talent in producing wonderful adventure, of building good against evil that prevails.

Burroughs was not a very grand philosopher. His views were pretty much those of the more open-minded American middle class of this century, which were generally speaking good views indeed. He was no Utopian. He did not venture into deep science or propose grandiose schemes for social development. He sought to entertain and in so doing created marvels that caught the mind of the world and still do.

I said something about good against evil just then. I will get back to this by and by. It counts. It's old-fashioned these days but it counts. It cannot be subtracted from the reasons why Burroughs sells today as well as he ever did. Tarzan is good, always good. His foes may be mixed, but his main foes are evil, plain downright evil.

We don't get much of that in mainstream fiction these days. Too bad.

When I hear that millions of young people are reading Burroughs and enjoying him, I rejoice. It may not be brilliant science fiction, but there is a light of hope here that outshines all the sour statistics of youth gone wrong.

Burroughs had his imitators in the twenties and thirties of the *Argosy* and *Blue Book* days of science fiction. Chief among them were Otis Adelbert Kline and Ralph Milne Farley. Farley produced a series of adventure novels laid on Venus which embodied the currently exciting premises of radio—and his novels were *The Radio Planet* series. Good in themselves, they have faded away as imitations always do. Otis Adelbert Kline entered the lists with another Venus-based series of adventure novels done in a very Burroughs style. But what Burroughs had, Kline did not have in more than a mirrorlike fashion. Grand adventure, which has had its followers when reprinted (as I have done in the sixties), but, again, imitation without innovation must always remain shadowed by the work of the imitated.

6

Headquarters: Canopus

AND THEN CAME Edmond Hamilton. In the pages of a ghost-story magazine called *Weird Tales* appeared a group of novelettes of the world in danger. Science fiction from a weird story source, but science fiction back when there was but one such magazine, *Amazing Stories*, and that mainly reprint. Out of the twenties into the early thirties came Hamilton—and a sudden spark that was momentarily to light up the greatest concept of the world of science-fiction ideas: the galactic civilization.

That spark was the Interstellar Patrol. Corn, pure corn. A style marked by endless exclamation points, a gosh-wow-golly type of writing, our side against theirs plotting, a last-minute rush to the lever that alone would save or destroy the day, and a bang ending leaving everyone breathless. No characterization at all—everything strictly cardboard, and the universe very mechanistic too. And yet—the Interstellar Patrol was the crude tiny spark that hinted at what this is all about.

Modern science fiction is delineated by the farthest boundaries of time and space. And the galactic civilization is the turning point of this universe building. A civilization of intelligent beings, in contact with each other, trading with each other, banded together in some sort of Federation of the Stars to assist, to enlighten, to defend. It implies a lot—oh, how much it implies!

There it was in those crude wild formula stories of Edmond Hamilton in the lurid pages of *Weird Tales* in 1929 and 1930. The Interstellar Patrol.

Ten thousand years from now? Apparently, a patrol ship of the stars traveling many hundreds of times the speed of light. And crewed by one being each of a dozen or two dozen intelligent cooperating civilized worlds, members of the Interstellar Federation whose headquarters were on a planet of the mighty sun Canopus. One man from Earth—and the rest of the crew equals, described as fishmen, snakemen, bearmen, and beings of weirder stripe, one each from many stars. All working together as a trained crew to rescue stars from danger, to fight off invaders from other galaxies, to beat down natural disasters that would threaten the civilized worlds. Galactic civilization!

Hamilton told us little of this civilization. He never explained how ships could travel at such speeds, relying on the passage of ten thousand years of scientific progress to make that reasonable. He stated for granted an exchange of cultures but never depicted it. Cardboard does not allow any great depth of character or vision of background. But the idea, the idea!

Galactic civilization. It imples going to the moon, going to Mars and the other planets. It implies colonizing where colonizing is possible. It implies the multiplicity of worlds and the intellectual kinship of intelligent beings whatever their form. If we think, therefore we are brothers. It implies mankind covering the space between the stars. It implies making that travel sufficiently practical so that commerce between stars becomes practical, commonplace. It implies civilizations taking from each other what is desirable, presumably what is best for each. It implies an end to boundaries and the acceptance of infinite future and infinite progress outward in the universe.

It implies so much. There it was, hot on the heels of Verne and Wells and Cummings. A new young writer then, Edmond Hamilton, with the spark that lit the infinite. Hamilton is still writing, he is far more sophisticated, far more able and skilled a storyteller than the youth who pounded out those tales of the Patrol, but he surely cannot hope to surpass that concept which for one moment pushed the borders of science fiction ahead.

7

The Supreme Moment of the Cosmos

THAT WAS 1929. In 1930 there appeared in England (in the U.S.A. in 1931) another writer whose work was to further advance science fiction into the modern era and who was to present a vision of futurity so vast that none have ever sucessfully tried to duplicate it. This was W. Olaf Stapledon, and the book was called *Last and First Men.*

Last and First Men came out of the blue. Nobody had ever heard of Stapledon before, he had written no short stories for the magazines and he had apparently read little or nothing of the material that had influenced the small world of science-fiction readers. But what he came up with was a seemingly endless treasure chest of concepts and ideas which he had worked out by himself and which came forth like an explosion of wonders that threatened to transmute all thinking thereafter. What *Last and First Men* was, was nothing less than the entire history of humanity from the twentieth century to the end of the Last Men on the planet Neptune two billion years from now!

It is a magnificent book, an inspiring one. Beginning in detail, Stapledon traces the coming centuries—and this is his major weak point. For already this is out of date; trying to foretell the exact political moves of a mere twenty years must always defeat the prophet. It is easier to predict on the basis of thousands of years. So it is with Stapledon, but none have predicted as he has done.

To skip the earliest centuries, what we have is the history of eighteen species of humanity, of which ours is but the First. Each species spans tens of thousands and in some cases millions of years of history and each species has its philosophical and social problems, which inevitably bring about its downfall until the next evolutionary level of humanity evolves, takes charge of the world, and starts off again. Stapledon sees humanity as a soaring spirit, always trying, never quite succeeding in conquering the limitations of flesh and body. Advance after advance leads but to setback after setback as the universe proves to be beyond the total grasp of man's efforts. But the efforts are ever more magnificent, ever more challenging, and mankind gives the universe a great fight before it ends its struggle.

Stapledon did not believe that star flight would ever come about nor that space flight would ever prove very practical or produce any special favor for mankind. The only other intelligence man was to encounter was on Mars and the result of the war against this virus-like, utterly alien intelligence was to ruin both worlds for hundreds of thousands of years. Mankind eventually was to find and contact intelligences on other star systems, but never visit them in person. Humanity changes worlds twice. When planetary disaster overtakes the Fifth Men a few hundred million years from now, the race emigrates to Venus, by then a habitable world. The transition brings about another downfall and further evolutions; a billion years from now humanity moves to Neptune, where it finally dies out with the Eighteenth and greatest species.

The task of outlining each species, of showing advance on a scale of millions of years, should prove beyond any mortal writer's capability, but Stapledon managed to achieve it. His approach is philosophical, his philosophy is Wellsian and mystical, his patience endless, and his faith in mankind clearly unbreakable. His Neptunian men are very nearly godlike, but they are not gods. Stapledon sees advanced mankind as achieving a state of universal harmony so integrated as to create an overmind common to all. The racial mind becomes the thinking single spirit of all men and it is this mass mind, the combined brain power of millions of individuals free of the mud and muck that so bog down the First Men of our own day, that enables the Last Men to contact similar racial minds throughout the universe. The Last Men begin to envision the whole of existence and to possess, for at least a brief moment, the kind of omniscience that we would ascribe only to God.

When science-fiction readers had begun to absorb the shock of this vast opening up of futurity, Stapledon was ready with his next and greatest concept, the book entitled *Star Maker*. This is the history of the cosmos itself. It spans all of time from beginning to end. It encompasses the universes of primitive natural laws before our own and it suggests those universes that are to come after our universe disappears. In the main *Star Maker* deals with our own cosmos, with the rise of intelligence in the universe, with the development of that union of racial minds which becomes the galactic mind, and continues to that union of galactic minds which becomes for one infinite moment the universal mind, the instant which Stapledon calls the Supreme Moment of the Cosmos.

But with compassion and skill Stapledon does not throw all of this at us in one long lecture. He starts with a single human being, disillusioned, bitter, seeking the meaning of everything. This becomes the disembodied mind which soars forth first to probe the past and learn of an Earth which existed millions of years before us and faced similar problems and of its demise. Then to explore other worlds of intelligent beings (and what a variety and what wonders!). Then to witness in one chapter all that was detailed in the nearly four hundred pages of *Last and First Men*. Then on to the development of successful racial minds that did bridge the cosmos, that did manage to solve what humanity was never to solve. So on, until solar minds became galactic minds and that supreme moment. Then the slow path downward to the extinction and burning out of this galaxy and its companion galaxies. The detailed section of the rise and fall of this, our own, universe covers about a hundred billion years.

Reading the book is an experience. Is it possible to read it without being moved? Without being in some way philosophically affected? I think not. It transmuted my thinking certainly. From Wells to Cummings, add Burroughs, add others, it is Stapledon who probably instilled in me a faith in humanity I cannot wholly lose, depressed as I may become at various times with the vicissitudes of the world.

But what was its effect on science fiction? Unfortunately not as great as it should have been, for one prime reason, I suspect. While *Last and First Men* was published in America early enough to be known, it did not deal with atomic power, it did not believe in interplanetary flight, and its immediate political predictions were not convincing. *Star Maker*, which would have had a far greater impact, was not published in the United States until long after World War II. A few fans and a few writers secured the British edition, published in 1937 by Methuen, but not enough to influence what had become the main source of science-fiction conjecture, the American pulp magazines of the thirties and forties.

For me *Star Maker* acted to establish in my mind what must be termed the cosmic vision. Hamilton had spoken of ten thousand years and interstellar confederation. Stapledon spoke of the galactic unity of all intelligent minds when confronted by the enigma of the origin and destiny of existence itself—for any discussion of the whys and wherefores of the universe must ultimately be a discussion of the meaning of being and understanding. Stapledon was a mystic who based his mysticism not on mumbo jumbo, primitive omens, or the accidental configuration of the zodiac, but on the most wide-lensed view of the astronomical and biological sciences themselves.

He was not an atheist. It is not possible to read Stapledon and to see what he sees in humanity and the meaning of intelligent striving and yet view cold atheism as having much point. He is not an advocate of religion either, for that, too, seems too simple, too primitive a solution. But he is a profound believer in what one would call cosmic unity. Existence *is*, therefore existence must have meaning beyond any single mortal life.

Or, as the last of the Last Men says, two billion years from now as his race dies on Neptune: "Great are the stars, and man is of no account to them. But man is a fair spirit, whom a star conceived and a star kills. He is greater than those bright blind companies. For though in them there is incalculable potentiality, in him there is achievement, small but actual. . . . Man was winged hopefully. He had in him to go further than this short flight, now ending. He proposed even that he should become the

Flower of All Things, and that he should learn to be the All-Knowing, the All-Admiring. . . ."

But the rise of modern science fiction was not to benefit from the farther vision of *Star Maker* since that was a vision withheld from the makers of science fiction at a time when it would have done the most good. *Star Maker* was not a successful book, as far as I can see. I do not think it saw a second edition in England. Stapledon wrote other works in the thirties, two of which are masterpieces. One is *Last Men in London,* the account of two people of our own time as seen through the perceptive cosmic vision of a Neptunian Last Man. The other is in my opinion the best effort to predict the oncoming of that species of men who will be to Homo sapiens what we are to Homo Neanderthalensis. This is *Odd John,* a novel of a boy who was born out of humanity and who found a few others like himself. It ends disastrously, for Stapledon continued in the line of his first book —man must strive many times before he succeeds once. But *Odd John* is head and shoulders above other efforts to depict the same thing—the novel of the next higher species of man. (Other instances include *Slan* by A. E. Van Vogt, *The New Adam* by Stanley G. Weinbaum, *The Wonder* by J. D. Beresford, *Childhood's End* by Arthur C. Clarke, and *More than Human* by Theodore Sturgeon.)

Instead of taking off from *Star Maker's* many galactic conceptions, it was not until Isaac Asimov wrote the group of stories that were to be published as the *Foundation* trilogy that the shape of galactic Things to Come was brought into the idea-structure of s-f writing.

8

The Decline and Fall
of the Galactic Empire

IT WAS IN 1942 that the magazine then known as *Astounding Science Fiction* began the first of Isaac Asimov's series of stories which, when completed in 1949, were to become the *Foundation* novels, that series which was voted a Hugo as the "most outstanding science fiction series" of them all. The novels are *Foundation, Foundation and Empire,* and *Second Foundation.* I am inclined to think, in the context of this book, that they are the pivot of modern science fiction.

The stories published before *Foundation* belong to the old line, the stories published after belong to "modern" science fiction.

What did *Foundation* have that was so pivotal?

Nothing less than the analysis and problems to be involved with the Decline and Fall of the Galactic Empire—and its reconstruction. In so doing Asimov clarified much that was implicit in previous science-fictional projections into the wherefore of space travel and what will follow after the stars are first reached. He developed the theme of the rise of a united effort to combine all the colonized worlds under one rule, emanating from Terra Triumphant, as from Rome, and showed the faults and flaws of that unified effort. People had written of planet flight and of star flight, they had written of colonies planted on worlds that circle alien stars, they had described the hazards and perils of travels between the worlds, they had depicted the struggles for exploration, the Magellans and the Cortezes of those interstellar days.

It was left to Asimov to gather the whole together and say, they will make an empire and that empire will have its day, much as Rome, and for much the same reasons will fall as Rome fell. Between barbarians and the rise of local nationalisms there will be a period of chaos, an interstellar Dark Ages, and during that time, that Interregnum, there will arise the many star nations that are to be—the equivalents of France and England and Spain, based upon Rome but not of Rome, holding the reconstruction of Rome as an ideal but never achieving it, for time and science and the growth of mental horizons will make such a second Roman Empire forever an impossibility.

In short, Asimov applied to future history the lessons of past history. He brought to the attention of the science-fiction cosmos the fact that humanity follows patterns and that those patterns, though similar, differ in scope, differ in intensity and internal nature, that the rise of civilization follows a spiral that makes certain events seem to recur predictably but always on a new and vaster level.

The theme of his three great novels is that during the building of an empire of human-colonized worlds there grew up a body of knowledge of human potentials, human activities and historical analysis which became a science by which humanity itself could be directed, predicted, patterned much as chemists know how to organize compounds and create new materials by their knowledge of the actions of the laws of chemistry and physics.

Asimov named this science psychohistory, and in the first book he defines it as "that branch of mathematics which deals with the reactions of human conglomerates to fixed social and economic stimuli. . . . Implicit in all these definitions is the assumption that the human conglomerate being dealt with is sufficiently large for valid statistical treatment. . . . A further necessary assumption is that the human conglomerate be itself unaware of psychohistoric analysis in order that its reactions be truly random."

Students of psychohistory learned to analyze the events of a given social situation and correctly and mathematically to work out the probable results. In short, to predict with a high degree of accuracy, based upon the knowledge of all the variables, just what would happen and how and when it would happen.

This is done today with computers in many fields. To do it with all humanity, to predict accurately the historical events of next year or next century, however, is beyond our capacity at this time simply because in the relatively primitive state of our information there are too many variables, too much that is obscure or unclear about past events, and our science of psychology is still in a formative, conflicting, and anything but exact stage. Economics has not yet been fully accepted as a science —the world still follows several major economic systems—and we do not yet know what balance and proportion of strength to assign to economic motivation, psychological motivation, and environmental motivation—not to mention simple opportunism and "mutant" unpredictables.

In Asimov's novels it is assumed that during the course of the tens of thousands of years of the rise of the Galactic Empire enough data were compiled, enough information was tested, enough science was advanced to make possible a true science of social prediction. This is psychohistory.

The story of the *Foundation* novels, then, is the prediction of the imminent fall of the Empire, of a million worlds cast adrift, as commerce and the exchange of information ceases, as interplanetary wars and piracy and the onslaught of worlds turned barbarian begins the process of smashing up the Empire and reducing it to ruins. To offset this, the leaders of that science establish the Foundation, an institute of monastic devotion dedicated to tracing the course of the fall and to seeking out and assisting those factors which will rapidly bring this Dark Age to an end and restore civilization through the galaxy.

In the course of the three novels Asimov deals with the rise of planets once obscure, with the manipulations of the Foundation's secret operatives thereon, of the maneuvers of politics and psychology needed to shore up the key worlds of the galaxy to come. The second novel deals with the unexpected—the oncoming of a mutant unpredictable, a Charlemagne of galactic history whose brief personal power seemed almost for one shining moment to restore the Empire that had been, only to fall again with the death of the single leader. And the inner problem of the Foundation and its men, which were not immune to psychohistory themselves and against which corruption a secret Second Foundation had been set up—a touch Isaac Asimov alone might have been capable of.

The parallel between all this and the actual past history of Earth should be clear to anyone with any knowledge of history beginning with Rome. We see in the fall of the Empire the fall of Rome and the failure of Roman civilization. We see the efforts of innumerable little pockets throughout Europe to retain what they had learned from Rome, to set up little Romes to offset the barbarian sea around them. We see the dream and vision of restoring the Rome that was, the vision that occupied nations for a thousand years after, the same vision that caused the Kaiser of Germany and the Czar of Russia alike to bear the title of Caesar even down to our own twentieth century.

We have also in the Foundation a parallel of the Church and its monks, keeping the records, binding together the legend of Rome with religious bonds and ties of the mind even though the secular ties had been torn asunder. But we detect also a more modern parallel, that of the latter-day Church, the Communist party which seeks through a set of theories based on the premises of a pseudo psychohistory known as Marxism to predict the movements of human masses and historical change.

For psychohistory is the science that Marxism never became. Marxism, if you are not aware of it, is not just a plan for socialism or a scheme for uprisings—it was put together in the middle of the nineteenth century as allegedly a science of the movement of history. It is taught to this day as a required science in Communist party run countries.

The validity of this Marx-Engels "science" can be shown by the simple fact that after a half century as the official basis of the U.S.S.R., its innumerable students have never successfully predicted anything. Their history proceeds from one ghastly bungle to another, from one costly oversight to another, and their course among nations has been marked with incredible clumsiness, crudity, and a constant jarring departure from the "democracy" and "freedom from want and fear" that their whole crusade was supposed to achieve.

Which should not be surprising. For, while Marxism has a glib logic in its ringing analyses of the nature of society and the operations of economics, these are all nineteenth-century *mechanistic* conceptions. No "Marxist" yet dares to challenge the original premises and state the need for further data, for the inclusion of psychological information, and for further study of the not-so-simple problems of economics. Marxism predates psychology itself—and it has never yet taken even that body of information into account!

What we have is the equivalent of a man who reads the first two or three chapters of an elementary first textbook of chemistry —and immediately sets himself up as a working chemist!

I conjecture that Asimov took this basic premise of Marx and Engels, said to himself that there was a point there—that the movements of the human mass must be subject to the laws of motion and interraction, and that a science could be developed based upon mathematics and utilizing all the known data— millions and millions of variables certainly!—that would be what Marxism thought it was and never could be.

This was psychohistory. By the twelve thousandth year of the Galactic Era it was almost an exact science.

In the Foundation novels, the work of the psychohistorians succeeds. The predicted thirty thousand years of barbarism is averted and the loss of knowledge and lapse of planets into savagery is averted.

But because science fiction builds upon science fiction and one man's originations become the next man's accepted premises, the rise, reign, and fall of a galactic empire is now taken for granted in many millennia-spanning novels to come after. Not always is the galaxy restored—that particular plot belongs to Asimov. More often we have novels of adventure during the tens of thousands of years after the fall, on worlds which have forgotten their common ancestry and common heritage with Earth and other stars. Humanity is found on a million worlds on a million levels of culture from cave man to high technology— and the Galactic Empire and Earth itself are either legends, re-ligious allegories, or altogether forgotten.

Then we have novels and stories which take place during the restoration—on a higher scale—of contact between the myriad human worlds of the universe. We begin to approach the Staple-don theme of a harmony of intelligences that covers the universe.

9

The Cosmogony of the Future

WHAT THE FOUNDATION SERIES did was to create the point of departure for the full cosmogony of science-fiction future history. It is possible to analyze present-day stories and place them into that framework of millions of years to come. We can establish a pattern of premises accepted without acknowledgment. We can tell what is implied by the simple facts of a story's background.

Are the science-fiction writers wrong in utilizing a framework which is subject to such close definition? Not really. There is only a limited number of general possibilities open to human conjecture. When all the many highly inventive minds of science-fiction writers find themselves falling again and again into similar patterns, we must perforce say that this does seem to be what all our mental computers state as the shape of the future.

What, then, is this history?

First, we have the initial voyages to the moon and to the planets of our Solar System. In this sequence we also include stories of the contact of man with intelligent species elsewhere in this system—Martians, Jovians, Venusians, if any. Stories of the first efforts to set up terrestrial bases on such planets. Stories of the first colonies of such worlds, their problems internal and external, their conflicts with the parent world, their breakaway or interplanetary commerce, spaceship trade lanes, space pirates, asteroid mining, the weird wonders of the Outer Planets, and so forth.

Second, the first flights to the stars. The problem of whether science can ever exceed the speed of light—a very important one where the problem of colonization is concerned. Starships, ships that must travel centuries and contain generations descended from the original crews. Other planets of other stars. Intelligences on such planets and our problems with them or against them. Human colonies on other starry systems. Contact with Mother Earth, independence or dependence. Commerce—exploitation or otherwise.

Third, the Rise of the Galactic Empire. The rise of contact and commerce between many human-colonized worlds or many worlds of alien intelligences that have come to trust and do business with one another. The problem of mutual relations and the solution, usually in the form of treaties or defensive alliances. Implacable aliens in the cosmos who must be fought. The need for defense. The rise of industrial or financial or political powers, the eventual triumph of one and the establishment of a federation, a union, an alliance, or an autocratic empire of worlds, dominated usually from Old Earth.

Fourth, the Galactic Empire in full bloom, regardless of what form it takes. Commerce between worlds an established fact, and adventures while dealing with worlds in and out of the Empire. The farthest planets, those of the Galactic Rim, considered as mavericks. The problem of aliens again outside the Empire, and outside our own galaxy. Politics within the government setup, intrigues, and dynasties, robotic mentalities versus human mentalities. "Terra-forming" worlds for colonization. The exploration of the rest of the galaxy by official exploration ships, or adventurers, or commercial pioneers.

Fifth, the Decline and Fall of the Galactic Empire. Intrigue and palace revolt. Breakaway planets. The alliance of worlds strained beyond its limits by rebellion, alien wars, corruption, scientific inability to keep up with internal or external problems. The rise of restless subject worlds. Decline, then loss of contact with farthest worlds, crumbling of commerce, failure of space lanes, distrust, finally worlds withdrawing into themselves as the empire/alliance/federation/union becomes an empty shell or is destroyed at its heart.

Sixth, the Interregnum. Worlds reverting to prespace-flight conditions, savagery, barbarism, primitive forms of life, superstition. Worlds taking to barbarian raids on defenseless isolated planets, hastening the downfall of knowledge. Fragments of space flight, fragments of empire, some starships, some efforts to revive. Thousands of years of loss of contact. Humanity in this period becomes indigenous to most of the habitable planets of the galaxy, forgetting origins. Evolutionary changes may take place. Alterations of form to fit differing world conditions—giant men, tiny men, water-dwelling men, flying men, mutations.

Seventh, the Rise of a Permanent Galactic Civilization. The restoration of commerce between worlds. The reexploration of lost and uncontacted worlds and the bringing them back to high-technology, democratic levels. The efforts to establish trade between human worlds that no longer seem kin. Beating down new efforts to form empires, efforts which sometimes succeed and revert to approximations of the previous period, with similar results. Eventual rise of galactic harmony among intelligences. The exploration of other galaxies and of the entire universe.

Eighth, the Challenge to God. Galactic harmony and an un-dreamed-of high level of knowledge leads to experiments in creation, to harmony between galactic clusters, and possible exploration of the other dimensions of existence. The effort to match Creation and to solve the last secrets of the universe. Sometimes seeking out and confronting the Creative Force or Being or God itself, sometimes merging with that Creative First Premise. The end of the universe, the end of time, the beginning of a new universe or a new time-space continuum.

All the above and every variation on it—that's the scope of modern science fiction today.

And when some well-intentioned reporter or radio commentator calls up a science-fiction writer at the time of Apollo and asks, "Now that men have landed on the moon what will you write about?" is it so strange that he is answered with a shrug and a smile of forgiveness?

10

Of Men Like Gods

WHEN I THINK of stories that have to do with challenging God or becoming God or having a hero of godlike powers I have to think of A. E. Van Vogt. For one of Van Vogt's abiding characteristics is to make his heroes so invulnerable, so omniscient, so gifted with superhuman powers as to encourage the suspicion that his heroes are all really God in disguise.

Van Vogt is a universe maker by instinct. From the first his stories have concerned themselves with extraordinary powers, with new concepts in science or in mental gymnastics, and he constantly seems to strive to create new systems of thought and mental order which will permit the creation of supermen. It is not an accident that his first fame-making novel was *The World of Null-A*, which presumed to be an exposition of the General Semantics of Alfred Korzybski, a philosophy of semantics which was thought to be the key to truly scientific and accurate communication between men. It was a Depression gimmick idea, one of the many that sprouted in those unhappy, desperate times. Its premise was that if we could only understand each other *perfectly* we could end wars, miseries, and so on. Everything that was bad about society was due to lack of perfect comprehension of each other's words and writings. The theory of General Semantics postulated a new form of mind training designed to eliminate emotional coloration from all communications and thinking.

Actually it was never clear just what *The World of Null-A* had to do with the real General Semantics, save for the use of interesting quotations before each chapter. Van Vogt's hero turned out to be rather similar to God. Gifted by powers of clear thinking and identical mental conceptions with others trained in the mental techniques, he was virtually uncatchable. In fact he could not truly be killed. Trapped, cornered, slain, he turned up instantly elsewhere safe and whole again! General Semantics, according to Van Vogt, supplied this godlike re-creating.

That book, whose action took place in a future of the period between the interplanetary and interstellar phases, was followed by Van Vogt's effort to create a godlike being, this time by evolutionary means. It was *Slan*, with the same premise as *Odd John*, but this time presenting not an abortive immature superman, but a whole race of supermen, fighting for their place against prejudice and having a tough time of it. The book's protagonist, Jommy Cross, is a boy of *slan* roots, running from his oppressors in a fear-ridden city of the future. But *slans* are supermen, though not gods, and in some ways *Slan* is one of Van Vogt's most successful books.

Van Vogt himself is a perpetual seeker after mental godhood. Van Vogt is a talented writer who utilizes his novels to propel many novel schools of thought, making them move with dramatic skill, a talent that calls for a toboggan technique of plotting which, as he once described it, required inserting a new idea every seven hundred words!

A devastating criticism was made of his work by Damon Knight in his book *In Search of Wonder*, the sort of breakdown of Van Vogt's plots to show their inconsistencies, their flaws of characterization and plot. It was the sort of jugular dissection that Mark Twain made of the work of James Fenimore Cooper—and with much the same result: nothing. Van Vogt is still among the two or three best-selling authors of science fiction in America. Whatever may be said of his plotting, he is always read compellingly, he is fascinating, and one gains a sensation of having had one's brain exercised.

I find Van Vogt always unusual. No two works of his are ever quite alike and no one can possibly tell in advance each new twist of the toboggan slide. He embodies all the phases of the cosmic future. His stories span all time and all space.

The Galactic Empire in full bloom is, for instance, the scene of two of his best novels, *The Weapon Makers* and *The Weapon Shops of Isher*. Here in the year 4784, the Empire is at its height, the Empress Innelda of the Isher dynasty is the titular ruler of the universe. But nothing is ever taken for granted in a Van

Vogt novel. Here we have a counterforce to Isher in the form of the mysterious—and "Godlike"!—guild of the Weapon Shops. Possessed of certain scientific achievements denied to the Imperial forces, the weapon shops are not openly in rebellion, possibly may not even want rebellions. What they are is a guarantee of personal liberty even amidst the dictatorship of an empire that spans the stars. Their trick—the sale of weapons to individuals—their slogan, "The right to buy weapons is the right to be free." The National Rifle Association and the gun lobby should jump for joy with such a slogan—and Van Vogt had it more than twenty-five years ago!

Just how applicable this revolutionary slogan is is a matter of the time and the place. It was written into the United States Constitution. It is under attack right now. It, the privilege of owning personal weapons, is denied in all totalitarian and dictatorial countries. But it is not a simple proposition. It has ramifications and Van Vogt is aware of them. Once again his hero is to all intents and purposes God, himself impregnable and aided by a person who swings forever between five million years in the past and five million years in the future!

In *The Voyage of the Space Beagle,* we have a Van Vogt novel of phase two, the first explorations of the stars—and also an explosion of another science of the mind, Nexialism. The *Space Beagle* set out simply to explore the many planets of the nearby stars, it ends heading out toward a galaxy 900 million light years away in order to exhaust and shake off an almost godlike antagonist which nevertheless had met its masters in the human beings who were masters of Nexial thinking.

The Mixed Men is another interstellar epic, this time belonging to the Galactic Empire phase, wherein an Imperial ship encounters a hideout group of planet colonies. And *The War Against the Rull* is an intergalactic combat epic which must be taking place during the seventh phase of the future, for the galaxy is united and only an intelligence from outside this star cloud can break up its unity.

Van Vogt swings back and forth, like his victim of Isher, making all time and space his field, and showing in innumerable ways that man is equal to the greatest potential and is godlike

in himself. Man may vary—he may advance himself by conquest
of his own mind or by evolutionary development of the next
race, or he may deliberately remake himself into a scientifically
constructed superior form, as in the recent Van Vogt novel *The
Silkie*, whose hero is a being of that classification, able to change
shape at will, able to be a space ship and a submarine, able to
think with computerlike capacity and speed, able to play God
as far as the old-style humans were concerned.

To the uninitiated layman all this may smell of megalomania
and perhaps paranoia, but Van Vogt remains atop the lists of
the most favored and best-selling science-fiction writers. There
must be a reason and that reason is as I have outlined before:
he has an instinctual belief in humanity, he believes in the in-
vincibility of humanity, he refuses to accept boundaries of time
and space.

The fact is that science-fiction readers agree with him. They,
too, cannot believe that humanity has limitations.

Call it megalomania, if you will. There is indeed a megalo-
maniac element to most s-f novels. Whereas mystery novels deal
with the saving of a single being, or the avenging of a single
injustice, and western novels likewise, whereas war novels and
spy novels may deal with the fate of cities or armies or nations,
an incredible percentage of science-fiction thrillers will settle
for nothing less than the fate of the entire world, or some
other planet, or the Galactic Empire, or the whole of mankind,
or even occasionally the entire universe. Read through the
blurbs of a hundred paperback s-f books and count how many
have at stake not just the hero's life but a cause of planetary
vastness. Science-fiction writers are not just universe makers,
they are also universe savers.

Perhaps their vision, wide-lensed and far-ranging, is right.
Perhaps in this century and at *this time* of this century it *is*
actually the world that is at stake or all humanity—and only
science and the defenders of science can save it.

A darned near unanswerable case can be made for their being
right. If so, megalomania is not accidental.

It may also explain why this type of cosmos-spanning novel
came into full bloom only after the end of World War II.

Science fiction does not merely build upon previous science fiction—it also projects answers to the crises of the day, it builds upon the immediate present, no matter how far-flung the field of the novel.

But before we get into the matter of the very pivotal problems of the last third of the twentieth century, let us have a look at a universe maker who has been doing exactly that. I refer to Philip José Farmer and his novels of the Lord Creator Jadawin.

11

Of Gods Like Men

FARMER IS BEST KNOWN and most often referred to in critical works about science fiction as the first to introduce speculation about sex intelligently as a legitimate subject of science-fiction extrapolation. I would discuss that here too save that it has been done too often and it is not my intent to depart from what I consider to be the main drive shafts of science fiction.

Farmer's brilliant novel *The Lovers,* and such books of his as *Flesh* and *Strange Relations,* have all been analyzed and exclaimed over before. They can be fitted into the framework I have outlined but what interests me is the premise behind his most recent series, all paperback originals: *The Maker of Universes, The Gates of Creation, A Private Cosmos,* and *Behind the Walls of Terra.* For, although writers like Stapledon have speculated on humanity's rising to the point where it could compete with God, we have in these stories the premise that a physical species, akin to man in every way (emotionally and physically), had advanced its civilization and control of the secrets of nature so far that it was able to create entire universes, closed cosmoses, establish whatever arbitrary laws of "science" it wished to govern these man-made continuums, and then use them for its own private playgrounds!

The idea is the implied one behind any religious dogma of

creation. God the Creator who made the skies and the earth as outlined in the Book of Genesis never defines His motives. God established the world as He saw fit to establish it, made animals and beasts, created water and land, set the rules for night and day, and presumably laid down all the laws of nature at that time. What was His motive? We can only assume it was self-satisfaction of some sort. Surely the restrictions laid down on man, as He created him according to the Bible, imply that. The need for praising the Lord, for doing His work, and so forth, all in the various divine ordinances, would indicate that God made this universe for His own pleasure or for His own experimentation for some purpose we cannot suspect.

Take this basic premise of religion, then establish the belief that science, if carried on at its rate of progress as of this century, must inevitably uncover all the secrets of the universe, and does it not imply that mankind, so armed and so learned, can then also create self-sustained, closed-circle private cosmoses, out of our own space and time, but accessible to the builder and obeying under stress whatever whimsical laws an artificial physics and arbitrary biology or chemistry will set up? Stapledon, ultimately mystical, did not feel that mankind or even the galactic mass intelligence would be able to do more than glimpse the Face of the Creator. Less mystical, modern s-f writers are coming around to the idea that, given enough time (centuries, millennia, millions of years) and sufficient data (all that there is to know), our descendants can duplicate to their own design anything at all.

Such are the capacities of the race Phil Farmer calls the Lords. They reached a point where each made his own universe to crown his own glory. Into one of these plunged the man Wolff, from our own day, and found himself in a world of tiers, not spherical, not moving through the skies like our planets, but a flat world, with level laid upon level, like a Babylonian ziggurat, until at the top level is the house of the Lord (who turns out to be Wolff himself, whose real name is Jadawin). On each level there is a different type of civilization—all more or less related to our own world's past histories and legendry—for it would appear that Jadawin has some relationship with the universe in which this our earth exists (which we begin to suspect is also the creation of one of the band of Lords).

The Maker of Universes and its sequels are not grand cosmological epics—they are action-adventure novels, with danger and challenge à la Edgar Rice Burroughs and Sir Walter Scott. The idea is there and the mind-challenging concepts are implicit. We read, as the series goes on, of other universes and other Lords (Farmer makes it a postulate that all Lords distrust each other and are forever trying to trap and destroy each other), and the variety is awe-inspiring and constantly surprising. The novels are a veritable fireworks of new concepts in biology and fantasy lands—the creations fall over each other and the possibilities continue to burst from Farmer's mind in ever-growing array.

Farmer's pocket universes just would not have been possible to the science-fiction writers of the pre-Foundation days. They would not have been possible ten years ago. They are possible today because of the advanced state of the art, because science-fiction readers have become aware of the cosmological implications of man's progress, and because also the past few years have shucked off the fear of religious bigotry that would have inhibited writers and publishers (more the publishers than the writers, I must admit) only a short time ago.

Any religious person—God-fearing would be the right word—would presumably object to such sacrilegious ideas as that man could ever compete directly with God. The implication that God Himself might be just another mortal playing at scientific games would cause a true believer to write furious letters to publishers. But this no longer happens. Apparently science fiction no longer needs to fear the anger of the believers.

I am reminded of one of the classics of the preatomic days, C. S. Lewis' brilliant novel *Out of the Silent Planet*. This was the first of a trilogy intended as an allegorical depiction of the conflict between materialistic science and moralistic theology. The second and third novels, *Perelandra* and *That Hideous Strength*, cannot be classified as science fiction, the second being almost straight fantasy and the third primarily a thriller-suspense novel. But *Out of the Silent Planet*, with its trip to Mars, its unforgettable depiction of the three intelligent yet dissimilar races of Martians, is indeed science fiction. But science fiction with a moral—which is that a high civilization must be God-fearing and adhere to the conviction that there is a Higher Morality above that of mortal lawmaking.

Out of the Silent Planet survives as a classic on the sheer literary talent of its author, a colleague of J. R. R. Tolkien. But its message has gained no adherents in the modern writings of the field and indeed its philosophy strikes today's readers as painfully dated.

I can only ascribe this to the growing social, moral, and political crisis of our times—the crisis that started with the first test firing of the first atomic bomb and has been growing ever since. The national controversy of a few years ago as to whether or not "God is dead" is evidence of this. Such a shocking concept would not have got to first base before World War II. But in our time it became a subject that could be discussed—and sometimes accepted—in the pulpits of churches themselves.

Science-fiction writers were a little slow to recognize the implications of this debate, but the Farmer novels are an indication that as a result of it all barriers are down when the discussion of the creation of the universe and of mankind is concerned. God as a physical real being is now a valid subject for science-fictional speculation. The universe *did* start—that would seem to be a fact. How and why and when and whodunit are therefore valid speculative themes for the s-f writer.

Astronomically, the time of the apparent origin of the universe has been established and current theory seems to settle mainly on a Big Bang several billion years ago—wherein a single giant atom burst and the result is what we see about us—the parts of which are still speeding away from the scene of the explosion. All very well. It still begs the question of where did the single Primal Atom come from and what was there before it and why did it go off?

Science merely moves God a bit farther into the distance, but the human mind is not capable of the concept of personal non-existence. It is beyond our computer capacity, that's all. Hence we refuse to discuss that very primitive question of the very, very young, "Who created God?"

S-f writers can't answer that either—they must beg the question even as Farmer does. But they can and do bring a physical God right into their stories if they see a plot angle to it.

What's more they get no kickback from doing so. I have published novels such as Dean Koontz's *Fear That Man,* wherein God is depicted as an evil force and is at one point turned into a small worm and *stepped on!* I got no protests from readers. My publisher received no letters of indignation from the religious. A dozen years ago such a reference would have raised a storm. Not so any more. We live in troubled times and the old standards are dissolving.

12

Three Barriers to Futurity

HOWEVER, a vengeful God may have the last laugh yet. We are faced with three crises of the last section of the twentieth century which may yet send us all to hell. These are hurdles that the writers of science fiction must face and overcome if they are convincingly to depict any future for humanity, either here or in the stars, in the twenty-first century and those to follow.

They are the hurdles of pollution, overpopulation, and the Bomb.

I do not think that any science-fiction novel purporting to deal with the next two or three centuries can be acceptable without in some way mentioning how the author sees the solution of these problems. For stories laid a thousand or more years in the future we can assume that whatever scars will result from this century will have been alleviated by time—mutations excepted, of course. But the modern s-f writer must clear these three hurdles to make any post-twentieth-century scene credible.

The fact is that not all of them do. It is easier to ignore them, to write a story taking place in London or New York or Luna

City or Marsopolis a hundred or so years from now and treat the background as if the population of the world were just the same, as if merely the addition of a few fancy gadgets, trick language, and so on would make it acceptable as a future setting. That is bad thinking. It is hack writing. If we are dealing with something written twenty years ago, or in Ray Cummings' day, sure. We understand. But now?

Of the three problems, the Bomb has been with us since 1945. Overpopulation and pollution are recent—we have really become aware of their menace only in the past two or three years, though scientists and conservationists have been warning us for much longer than that. But they are coming to the fore now, more and more acutely every day.

Pollution is the least of the three. You scarcely find it mentioned in s-f stories, except in combination with overpopulation. I cannot at this moment think of a single novel in which pollution specifically and alone is the primary basis of the story. Oh, there are short stories and novelettes and probably novels wherein the characters, as a matter of ordinary everyday usage, carry around respirators and put them on before venturing into the streets or open air. Such stories are laid in the next hundred years. I recall tales wherein everyone wears outdoor coveralls and gloves—but these may also be radiation foils and perhaps not quite related to pollution per se.

Pollution is on the public conscience these days and, of the three problems, it seems to be the one that may very likely be taken care of properly in the next dozen years. In this respect, maybe s-f writers are correct in not assigning it cardinal importance. We have indeed polluted rivers, and the air above our cities is heavy with smog, and the countryside a grayed-out mess.

And nobody has to say anything about the increasingly bad taste of water, nor the dirt that clings to windshields and other objects.

But things are being done. The fact is that government has awakened to the matter and more and more cities are taking steps to limit pollution and contamination. In the way that governments and profit-making corporations do things, it isn't being rushed, but it is being done. Work is going on about the introduction of automobile engines of a nonpolluting type. Electric batteries will be coming back for running cars. Not overnight, but probably in time to permit some recovery. We may save a redwood or two by the time Congress gets around to it. Nobody has a good word to say for pollution, so politicians can safely support the fight against it. As for private interests, eventually they will see the light too.

I do not think pollution is a problem in itself. In connection with overpopulation, it is. It may be that, with the geometric progression of the world's population, the fight against pollution may prove to be one against an enemy growing even as we combat it. Overpopulation is going to be the hellish problem of the next ten to twenty years. If we do nothing now, by that time it will be too late. With twenty years more of the present rate of increase, the problem of overpopulation will begin to merge with the problem of the Bomb.

Science fiction has not done too well with overpopulation by itself either. It has come up but lately. Still it was foreshadowed. There were classics of the pre-forties that spoke of worlds so populated that they were but one vast city—of Earth so populated. The authors did not know when they wrote such stories that the problem of feeding such a worldwide city would be insoluble. That humanity could not stand it, and would not want to stand it. They did not know of the experiments with psychology wherein rats and other laboratory animals were tested for their ability to get along in crowded quarters. There was a limit, after which the beasts turned on each other, became neurotic, touchy, short-tempered.

Just like people cramped together in ghettos.

Just like people everywhere will be when the world's present population doubles.

In about twenty years' time.

I think of two books that have dealt with conditions of the overpopulated Earth. Harry Harrison's novel *Make Room! Make Room!* published in 1966 was the first of these. The time is 1999. The scene is Manhattan Island, in New York City. Harrison says that the population of the city then will be 35 million. It's not at all improbable.

I live in New York and work on Manhattan. It's getting pretty intolerable now, and I doubt that the population is over 10 million (in the middle of the workday). The streets are visibly more crowded, the subways and buses definitely so, more than in years past, and to drive a car through Manhattan at midday is a feat of patience and snaillike progress. Ask anyone about apartment hunting there now. Then consider the city in 1999.

In Harrison's novel his hero is lucky—he shares his one-room apartment with only one other person. ·

Only a certain number can live comfortably on even the most fertile and fortunate land. The limit is being reached, and that can be demonstrated scientifically.

Isaac Asimov has dealt with this a couple of times in his science articles in the science-fiction magazines. In the May, 1969, issue of *Fantasy and Science Fiction* magazine Asimov, without getting too panicky, reads the doom of humanity in quite simple but unmistakable words. I will quote him, he does it so well:

> I live, immersed in my work and in my content, in the richest nation on Earth, in the period of that nation's maximum power. What a pity, then, that it is all illusion and that I cannot blind myself to the truth. My island of comfort is but a quiet bubble in a torrent that is heaving its way downhill to utter catastrophe. I see nothing to stand in its way and can only watch in helpless horror. The matter can be expressed in a single word: Population.

He then proceeds to demonstrate just how many people the world can support, just how much is needed in air and food and sunlight to feed the maximum number of inhabitants, and just how the rate of population rise grows and has grown. The outlook is pretty grim; pretty nearly unanswerable.

John Brunner tackled the problem head on in his 1968 blockbuster of a novel *Stand on Zanzibar*. The title is ominous in itself. It is based on a belief that about the time of World War I you could stand the entire human race on the 147-square-mile Isle of Wight, elbow to elbow and face to face. In the 1960's the figuring went that it would take the 221 square miles of the Isle of Man to pack us all in like sardines. By 2100, says John Brunner, you'd need the 640 square miles of Zanzibar to do it.

He didn't say where we'd have to be sardined by 2300—probably on the entire continental surface of Earth. But he didn't have to. Zanzibar will be enough—by then we will be in a snarling rage at each other, already at the breaking point.

By then, says Brunner, the year 2010, the streets of any city will be such jungles that you will take your life in your hands to walk in them. The nations will exist on the barest of terms with each other and various states of undeclared war will be perpetual. Sabotage, riot, treachery, and assassination will be the standard accepted activities of a steadily growing mass of the ordinary people.

Do not let me give you the idea that *Stand on Zanzibar* is a simple book. It is a highly complex book, a vast compendium of conjecture and thought, of possibilities and potentials, with several plots and subplots. Brunner is, as you may surmise by his reference to islands like Wight and Man, English. Nevertheless, he did an amazing job of projecting a future America. He has used his eyes and his ears wisely and discerningly.

The book is not entertaining reading—what book could be with such a theme? Harrison's book is scarcely escape reading either. In some ways Brunner overdid it, crowded in too many innovations, too many themes, even as his world was overcrowded. To make matters worse—or perhaps to assist in bringing up a wealth of new ideas—he adopted the style of John Dos Passos' classic novel *U.S.A.* It makes for disconnected reading.

The book carried off the Hugo award that science-fiction readers give every year to the best of the genre. It will be some time before another work as massive and as packed comes along. Yet it was not Brunner's only such massive job dealing with an overpacked future. In 1969 Ace Books published his *The Jagged Orbit*, another blockbuster of a novel, this time taking place in 2014, and with very much the same style. This one concentrates on racial antagonisms in the rat-trap conditions of an overpopulated America. You get a pretty vivid idea of what it will take for an agile man to get along by then—sidearms, protective clothing, respirator, helmet, first-aid kit, and assorted subsidiary weapons. That's for going down to the corner store. If you have to. Better not try.

All very sour. All very grim. All quite unanswerable. If the population continues to grow, that is how it is going to be. Science-fiction writers take note. That is a hurdle that must be overcome by mankind if we are to get on with exploring the rest of this solar system and go on to the system of star colonies and all that is promised thereafter. Mankind may have immortality in the stars, as a species, but only if we can get past the rest of this century.

I do not object to publishing stories of the far future. They represent flags of hope. We do have a future worth living and fighting and working for. But we have immediate objectives that must be overcome in this, our own lifetime, our own century already in its final third. Pollution, overpopulation, the Bomb.

Overpopulation is at least a little coming to the public consciousness. Nothing very much is being done about it so far. Some talk of the Pill, of easier abortion laws, nothing much really. It had better be acted on soon, or else . . . make room! make room! Elbow to elbow, and face to face.

13

Growing Up Grim

THERE IS ONE rather obvious solution to the overpopulation problem. That is to kill off a large section of the world's population by war. A really large section—no piddling stuff like a few tens of thousands in Korea, or a few hundreds of thousands in Vietnam, or a few dozen millions in World War II. Unrestricted germ warfare might do it. Excuse me, that word "unrestricted" is redundant. There is no restriction possible on germ warfare. Germs have no nationality, no patriotism. They are all absolute egalitarians. They are color blind. Sent to kill men in green or black or gray, they will turn around and go to work on khaki and blue with complete lack of bias. And their wives. And their children. And maybe their cattle and sheep and chickens.

Under conditions of elbow-to-elbow living, the tempers of military men and government leaders may prove a lot less approachable to reason than those of today's leaders. Germ warfare is supposed to be outlawed, and the stockpiles of germs and gases eliminated. But politicians' promises tend to be submerged by future events and generals' ambitions.

We have had stories of the world devastated by plague. We have had them for a long time. They go right back to the oldest days. Verne had a story, *The Eternal Adam,* in which cataclysms destroy the human race, save for a handful. This was his very last novella; he is said to have dictated it from his deathbed. His disaster is never explained—possibly he meant to but there was scarce time to rewrite under such circumstances! (It is included in his book *Yesterday and Tomorrow.*)

The best of such novels may be George R. Stewart's *Earth Abides.* A 1949 novel of great power and skill, it was one of the first to be awarded a prize by science-fiction fandom officially. It is not a novel of warfare—a lethal disease, possibly mutated by an act of nature, wipes out all but a few fortunately immune survivors. *Earth Abides* deals then with their efforts to come to terms with an empty world, to settle their problems on a near-deserted land where cities and factories and homes still stand—with none to utilize them.

But it was not an act of war. It could have been caused by radiation. Concern about the effects of radiation on germs and plants and living beings was strong back in 1948 and 1949. Soon several other bombs had gone off. The radiation level of the entire world rose at that time. The world has never been the same since. We are all, everything living and nonliving, more radioactive now than we all were in 1944 and for all the millions of years before that.

There is something different in the postwar world. Atomic power misused to make a bomb. Atomic power misused for war weapons. The threat of atomic fusion used to destroy the enemy in time of war. The enemy—meaning all of us. It takes two sides to make a war. When both sides have the Bomb, both sides contain enemies.

Which we all know perfectly well, and have known since

1945. An entire generation has grown up in this knowledge. It does make a difference. When my generation was growing up we knew that we might have wars to fight and depressions to live through. The world might fall again into the hands of tyrannies, as it had in centuries past. But mankind would survive. Hitler might be frightening to contemplate, but mankind could survive even under a Hitler world. Five hundred years would blunt any tyranny. It always had.

We have a generation now that has grown up to believe that it cannot and will not survive a war fought with atomic weapons. The fallout alone, the half-life of radioactivated land and air . . . Bad scene.

This is also a generation that has grown up in the science-fiction world of today. It was weaned on the atomic war scene. There have been lots of stories and lots of novels about the world after the atomic war. There have been lots of stories too about the atomic war itself—the moment of truth, as it were, when the human bull sees the sword poised and flashing toward him.

I was thinking the other day of Ace Books' most unsuspected best seller, a novel I reprinted in 1954, and whose title I changed to *Daybreak, 2250 A.D.* It was written by Andre Norton as a juvenile novel, and it was her first science-fiction book-length work. She called it *Star Man's Son*, and it was published in 1952 by Harcourt, Brace and Company. I believe their edition is still in print and still sold as a children's book.

The Ace edition's cover shows a white-haired boy in fur loincloth and primitive gear poling a raft across a river which is spanned by a shattered but clearly twentieth-century bridge. It has sold continuously and rapidly for fifteen years, in printing after printing, with steady price rises to meet the rising costs of production, has broken the record for any book ever published by what has become a major paperback publisher, and continues to sell with unabated interest. Well over a million copies would be my conservative estimate of its total sale to date.

There is nothing in our Ace edition to indicate that it is supposed to be a juvenile novel. You can assume it from the fact that its hero, Fors of the Puma Clan, is a teen-ager who has not yet been accepted into full manhood in his primitive tribe living high up in the mountains. The story tells of how Fors gains his "Star" rating—the tribal equivalent of warriorhood—by going on a daring expedition into the taboo mystery lands of the level plains.

Andre Norton wrote the book for children—twelve and up, says the flyleaf on the original edition. And I am quite sure that it has been youth, twelve and up, that has made up the bulk of its readers over these many years. And what is it that these children have been, as it were, weaned on?

Fors of the Puma Clan, we are told from the start, has been in trouble with his tribe because he has white hair, which marks him as that dreaded of all things, a mutant.

> Mutant! For more than two hundred years—ever since the black days of chaos following the Great Blow-up, the atomic-war—that cry had been enough to condemn without trial. . . . Ugly tales were told of what had happened to the mutants, those unfortunates born in the first year after the Blow-up. Some tribes had taken drastic steps in those days to see that the strain of human—or almost human—lineage be kept pure. Here in the Eyrie, far apart from the infection of the bombed sectors, mutation had been almost unknown. But he, Fors, had Plains' blood—tainted, unclean— and, since he could remember at all, he had never been allowed to put that fact from him.

What these children have been weaned on is the matter-of-fact presumption that an atomic war will destroy the United States and every other known nation, will reduce the world to primitive conditions again, render most of its surface uninhabitable, deadly, dangerous, and alter the shape and form of what life may survive.

They read, without blinking an eyelash, an adventure of a character similar to a primitive Indian, full of superstition and backwoods ignorance, who pursues his dangerous expedition across a world filled with the ruins of a once-mighty but now incomprehensible civilization. They see that world now the habitat of beasts such as never existed in our time, of monsters gifted with intelligence beyond that of animals, and of men cursed with radiation changes that have made them literally a nonhuman race.

The children take this information in their stride—it is, after all, not new to them. They have heard of the Bomb before reaching the reading stage of such novels. They have heard of what might happen. They know about mutations and what they could mean. They take it all for granted. And in *Daybreak, 2250 A.D.* they enjoy an adventure story laid in what is obviously a believable, and, God help us, even predictably probable future.

The point I am making is that the people who read this book must number millions—one can assume that every hard-cover book sold is probably read by a dozen or so young people, and every paperback edition possibly gains a handful of readers too, especially if the purchaser is young. Five million, ten million, can that be the number who have read Andre Norton's post-atomic war novel? And that was over fifteen years. A lot of them —most of them—have grown up now. People who read this—and novels of a similar premise, for there were many around with the same sort of postatomic war backgrounds—must now be in their twenties and even thirties. They must be engineers, doctors, businessmen, technicians, soldiers, even fathers and mothers, housewives and schoolteachers. And to be sure a large segment must still be in college or doing their stint in the armed forces.

They all take it for granted that an atomic war will spell the end of mankind and civilization as we know it. They have taken if for granted since their childhood. They do not question that fact.

It must have influenced their thinking. It must influence what they do and say now.

It is a science-fiction concept that has been absorbed into the modern scene.

14

To Be or Not to Be

I WAS BORN in 1914, the year that might be said to have really been the close of the nineteenth century in a cultural and political sense. I grew up in a changed world, but not a world where the knowledge of doom was an accepted fact. It is hard for my generation to realize what it must be to have grown up in the generation that took and takes *Daybreak, 2250 A.D.*, for granted, as just a good science-fiction adventure of the future, no questions asked.

When I see and read about modern youth, about their rebellion against accepted standards, about their espousal of such escape mechanisms as pot and dope and weird philosophies, their efforts at establishing instant Utopian colonies, and their rejection of the standards of the generations that preceded them, I am not surprised. What else did anyone expect of the generation that grew up knowing the Atom Bomb was waiting in the wings?

We who dreamed of atomic power back in the thirties thought it would lead to Utopia. We saw atomic energy lighting the cities and powering the factories for free, powering our flights to the planets, pushing luxurious vast airplanes through the skies, leading to plenty for all.

The youth of today knew better. They were raised to know that they faced the caves again—if they survived, that is. They knew that atomic power plants are built first to power giant submarines laden with atomic rockets to help destroy the world. Atomic power plants for peaceful use—they are a superfluous expense, a rarity.

They also have had ideals instilled by science fiction, not by other sources. This generation believes in science fiction, it runs like a thread through its "underground" newspapers and through its works. The young people have read novels about atomic aftermath. They have also read such stories as *Thunder and Roses* by Theodore Sturgeon. It helped give them something of a political ideal all their own, something for their generation only.

Thunder and Roses is a short story, first published in 1955, reprinted in *A Way Home*, which is a collection of Sturgeon's stories. It is a simple story, told with the skill of a master. Emotional, deep, sensitive, written at the peak of Sturgeon's powers and the greatest intensity of his feeling. It is the story of a couple of young men in control of a secret atomic rocket launching post. It is the story of their thoughts, their hearts, their emotions when they learn that an enemy attack has destroyed America, that their loved ones are probably dead, that they alone have the means of retribution in their hands. Their defense post has survived, unknown to the foe.

Shall they launch their atomic rockets and do to the enemy what he has already done to their homeland? That is the problem. Retribution . . . is it right, or would their firing also signify the end of all humanity? The air was already polluted, perhaps no one in America survived. But over there, on the other side, obviously the enemy was alive. It was in their power to destroy that remaining half of humanity.

In the end, the man who favors retribution at all costs is knocked out by the other. While he is unconscious, the remaining American rips the launching mechanisms to pieces. He then goes outside into the polluted atmosphere, sits down. The story ends this way:

> "You'll have your chance," he said into the far future. "And by heaven, you'd better make good."

After that he just waited.

That is another way science fiction answered the problem of the atomic bomb. It is presumably a lesson that must have sunk deep into the mind, possibly the unconscious mind, of hundreds of thousands who have read that story—the same ones who read Andre Norton and the others.

In many readers it instilled one belief—that humanity may survive the atomic war after all. And if we survive, no matter how few, we can reconstruct civilization and fulfill the destiny that awaits us in the stars.

You can find this theme tucked into the background of some Galactic Empire novels—that Terra is a half-devastated world whose sons had to take to the stars to find better worlds. The progression to Galactic Empire and beyond is not halted by a brief hiatus in Terrestrial civilization. What is a few thousand years' delay in the historical canvas of infinity?

But are there no stories in which the atomic war never occurs? To be sure, but they are not too convincing. Not with over-population and the attendant madness advancing so rapidly.

Nature has a way of paring down animal populations when

they get beyond their normal food-death cycles. Wolves starve when they wipe out too many rabbits. Deer starve when they overextend their numbers without having been hunted. Lemmings dash madly into the sea when they have become too numerous for sustenance. Maladies have been charted which periodically cut back the numbers of certain species.

In the past, plagues and famines and droughts have consistently cut back the human ranks. But we have outsmarted all that. We know too much now, and our numbers are growing beyond nature's capacity. But nature may have a trick or two left. Madness of numbers, fury at close quarters, the dropping away of natural vitamins and natural sun-originated food elements may affect our capacities to resist mutant diseases and our capacity to reason logically. We do have the atomic bomb in storage in many nations. Despite the best resolve never to use it—miraculously it has not yet been used in twenty-five years of revolutions and wars—pressures build up as populations build up. It may prove to be nature's way after all.

In his article about population, which I have quoted once, Asimov does not predict the use of the atomic bomb. He makes no specific predictions. He does say:

> If we do nothing but what comes naturally, the population increase will be brought to a halt by an inevitable rise in the death rate through the wars and civil rioting that worsening human friction and desperation will bring. . . . There is a race in man's future between a death-rate rise and a birth-rate decline, and by 2000, if the latter doesn't win, the former will.

Mankind may get some sense in time. As a science-fictionist I have faith. I must admit that I have not seen any s-f novels that pointed to a believable way out. S-f novels and writers persist in pointing toward the obvious, that Sunset, 2000 A.D. which will not see the sun rise again until 2250 or later.

Andre Norton was not the only one, as I said. Others predicted it back when it counted. Leigh Brackett's *The Long Tomorrow* —she thought that the Dark Ages to come might be sustained by isolated farm communities like the Amish. Poul Anderson has written several novels of the post-atomic bomb world, including

Twilight World and *After Doomsday*. Many others, many theories, many viewpoints, many scenes. *On the Beach* by Nevil Shute is the supreme pessimistic view—not surprising since the author is not among the ranks of deep-dyed s-f writers. We s-f writers rarely let the world die. We have the farther vision. It sustains us.

15

Misreading the Maps

AFTER THAT, if you are still hanging on, it seems reasonable to turn to a book published ten years ago with the ominous title of *New Maps of Hell*. The writer was an English literary scholar named Kingsley Amis and the book purported to be a study of science fiction as he found it at that time. Considering what we have been talking about, one would suppose that the mapping of hells would have dealt with something of the same deadly serious subjects we have just discussed.

But you would be wrong. Mr. Amis' maps of hell are what he considers science fiction to be—a sort of suet pudding of literary trash with here and there a nice plum of vicious social satire sticking out and worth examining. He seems to have a special fondness for Utopias that are not Utopias, for instance.

I should not do Mr. Amis wrong: he declares himself a science-fiction addict at the very start, though he then is careful not to identify himself more closely with it than that. As a matter of fact Mr. Amis is a mainstream writer who occasionally likes to read some science fiction, and had the good fortune to talk someone into allowing him to do a witty little book about it.

I get the distinct impression that, while investigating his subject, he was being given a guided and selected tour through one particular publisher's s-f mill, for he seems to be most familiar with the works of its authors and most especially with the writings of Frederik Pohl, whom he calls the "most consistently able

writer science fiction, in the modern sense, has yet produced."
He devotes a good deal of space to a rather admiring analysis
of several of Frederik Pohl's satirical works—quite clearly he
digs the scene of Pohl's satire on advertising, *The Space Merchants,* for he quotes with evident familiarity scenes and dialogues,
none of which could by any standard be calculated to spark that
sense of wonder which is the mainspring of the devotee.

Now, I cannot deny that Frederik Pohl is indeed one of the
cleverest minds in the field. His short stories and novelettes are
gems of cunning, unusual ideas, delectable twists of the satirical
dagger here and there, and decidedly entertaining. I have
known Fred myself since our fandom days—we were both active
Futurians when that was one of the noisier fan clubs of the
thirties—a germinal club whose members have since become
prime movers of the science-fiction world that colors society today. He showed early a capacity for plot construction, for clever
turns of a phrase, for strikingly novel ideas. He was more than
usually egotistical as well—but since when is that a crime for a
creative mind?

It is clear that the talents he displayed then he matured later.
Kingsley Amis and Frederik Pohl obviously struck a responsive
chord in each other—Amis too has a deft hand at social satire
and it is not therefore so remarkable that for him Pohl was tops.

Pohl is, like most of us who came out of the Depression, something of a disillusioned idealist, a latter-day cynic. I think, however, that, while I have continued to retain my faith in humanity
and in the future, Pohl long ago scrapped his. His satires are
sincere.

I must admit that, while I usually find Pohl's short stories and
novelettes fascinating, there is something about his novels which
gives me the fidgets. They are indeed the new maps of hell
which Mr. Amis admired enough to give his entire study of
science fiction that title.

The trouble with this arch kind of study of our field is that
the critic simply has not been steeped in it long enough. He does
not reach the dyed-in-the-wool reader. He cannot reach the
man who once read s-f exhaustively for four or five formative
years before going on to create some version of the future in a

laboratory—those engineers, technicians, experimenters of today who have passed their grounding in s-f ideation and are now trying to build the future.

I started out by saying this is a science-fiction world and that the writings of the field have clearly shaped this world of today —for better or for worse. But Mr. Amis does not know it. For him I. Asimov is a man who wrote a story about robots. Olaf Stapledon is not mentioned. He cannot distinguish between Wellsian and Vernian. And I don't think he ever heard of the Galactic Empire and its Decline and Fall.

He has a good time with some of the trivia around—a few of the short stories of the day—some of the lesser works that make up the bulk of any particular year's output. He dismisses Van Vogt as a creator of supermen. And of course he goes into the usual song and dance about how too few s-f writers pay attention to character development and how too many stress only ideas and gimmicks. If they would pay more attention to turning out really fine character novels, why, then, the mainstream would stop labeling them as a low category not to be reviewed and might start accepting them as mainstream writers.

It is ten years later. I have already indicated that the lists of best sellers do contain works that must be defined as science fiction. They had to come to our field to do it. Alas, we have still no one to post against such great mainstream novels as *Portnoy's Complaint, The Love Machine, The Arrangement,* and the rest of that constant stream of psychiatrists' couch and bedroom agonies that mark the triumphs of the mainstream.

No, Mr. Amis, science fiction does not consist of new maps of hell. It does consist of endless charts of the paths open to triumphant mankind. Social satire, the bitter skewering of some of the odious aspects of the present, are but a part of our category. They are parts, not the whole. They are but one of the many facets of our infinite explorations into the unknown side of existence.

There is a persistent pattern of wailing to be found among certain critics and some writers demanding that science fiction be accepted as part of the mainstream of literature. They dislike having their novels labeled as part of a category, like mysteries and westerns. Their work, they declare, is as good as many novels by nonfantasy writers and ought to be treated by book reviewers and bookstores in similar fashion. This business of labeling gives them the horrors; they feel that it diminishes them.

I have never agreed with this. Our audience is not that of the mainstream. Our influence is specialized and what we do has a different effect than the general run of mainstream fiction, from best sellers to the remaindered losers. We are, in fact, as specialized a form as the mystery novel, so why the fuss?

But the fuss will continue. Only recently at the annual awards banquet of the Science Fiction Writers of America, a newly ordained editor for a book firm made a speech reiterating the old cry. He said, in part: "Labeling a book as s-f puts a stigma on it. Many reviewers won't even bother to look at a book if its jacket screams that it's fantasy. . . . S-f writers should assert themselves and let their books compete with the mainstream of the publishing output not as 'science fiction novels' but simply as 'novels.' "

So he published a whole series of s-f books in very nearly uniform format which did not say s-f on their covers and whose cover drawings were fairly ambiguous. Did he succeed in fooling the reviewers? Not so you could tell. Anyone intelligent enough to pay out money for hard-cover books knew what he was buying. If he didn't like s-f, he didn't buy.

As a matter of fact, labeling books "s-f" is the established technique these days of publishers who really do know their business. It is done all the time in Great Britain by such successful publishers as Gollancz, Sidgwick and Jackson, Dennis Dobson, Macdonald—their books are clearly identified with the words or their abbreviations. So, too, Doubleday and others in the United States—and consistently by almost all the paperback houses here.

Science-fiction readers do not want mainstream fiction. It is mainstream readers who occasionally must come to us for a best seller. That is when the label is missing.

But by and large mainstream fiction is literature that deals with the here and now, with people and events as they are, and which does not require the addition of the kinds of fantasy I enumerated. It is to mainstream writers we look if we want to find talented depiction of modern man in his travails. It is to science fiction we turn only if we want to get away from the travails of today to gain the broader vision of what might be, what might have been, what is yet to come.

Why should so many s-f writers therefore continue to hunger for the glory of being submerged in the world of general un-categorized fiction? There are several probable answers. They value the reviews and praise of critics whose comments grace the daily newspapers—people like Kingsley Amis. They want the bookstores to display their books in the windows for the sake of glory. They would like the Literary Guild and the Book-of-the-Month Club to tap their books and make them famous and rich and all that.

All very normal desires. All very admirable. Overlooking the various economic and publishing politics that determine what gets reviewed and what does not, and what gets book-clubbed and what does not, the best way to attain these objectives would be to give up writing what you want to write—science fiction—and write what you think the little group of "name" reviewers will praise. The fact that these writers do not take this course is evidence either that they are incapable of it or else that they really are as hooked on s-f as all of us and wouldn't be at home outside the field. I think the latter is the reality.

Since contradiction and what dialecticians call the interpene-tration of opposites are the essence of controversial thinking, I shall now do an about-face and discuss a writer who has always considered himself of the mainstream, rejects the claim to being a science-fiction writer, whose works are reviewed with respect and enthusiasm by the literary pundits of America, and who, by God, deserves every word of it and is, in my opinion, one of the most originally brilliant science-fiction writers going. I refer to Kurt Vonnegut, Jr.

16

Delivering a Cosmic Telegram

I'VE ALREADY TALKED about Vonnegut when I was discussing his *Slaughterhouse Five* at the start of this book. Of Vonnegut's seven hard-cover books, four are distinctly in the science-fiction genre and the other three are spectacular in their own way. What makes him, then, a mainstream writer rather than a science-fiction writer?

The answer is because he says so, because he never wrote for the pulps or the category magazines and because he gets the highest rates for his writings—much higher than the sums paid by the standard s-f publishers. What strange luck is it that enabled him to avoid what some of the would-be mainstream s-f writers regard as their pitfalls? Who can say? I only know that Vonnegut is unique, that he apparently caters to nobody in his storytelling, that he has a positively scintillating cynicism the like of which cannot be found elsewhere, that he packs his books with razor-edged social comments, that he apparently does not seem to take his science-fiction elements with that often deadly seriousness that so many of our regulars do.

It isn't easy. That is probably the secret. His novels have a subtle complexity that do not follow routine and his ideas are often so startlingly different as at first to seem purely whacky— except that they are not. There's no real arguing with them. Whacky as they might seem, they have a logic inherent to themselves which is often not of this world.

If this confuses you, you'll have to read Vonnegut yourself. A universe maker he most certainly is and he builds on a tangent that no one else either sees or had the infernal brass to tackle.

Let's take *The Sirens of Titan*. This one, whose title sounds like a Burroughs epic, was first published in a paperback edition. It made an historic breakthrough in the relationship between

paperbacks and hard-covers. For I recall it as the first paperback original to go from the cheap to the expensive edition,
rather than vice versa. It was reprinted in hard covers—presumably by public demand. Lately this course has been followed by
other paperbacks, but it took Vonnegut to reverse the field.
Which is characteristic.

Consider *The Sirens of Titan* then. I'll not summarize, because
I can't in this space. One theme, one of many, is very galactic.
A starship is en route from one end of the cosmos to the other.
Its mission is simply to bear greetings from one superintelligent
species to another. No interchange of art or commerce or such—
just greetings. The starship needs repairs. It pauses at an obscure
sun and planets system in an obscure and unimportant section of
an unimportant galaxy. It requires a few manufactured parts to
replace some broken bits of the engine. The planetary system
contains no intelligent life. One planet of the group, however,
is fertile and swarming with lower orders.

The space travelers therefore have the means of obtaining
their replacement parts. They intervene in this world very
briefly in order to start one of the species on that planet to
evolving upward. Then they sit back on the Saturnian moon
known as Titan, and simply wait for the inevitable. They have
plenty of time; they are quite prepared to wait a hundred
million years. They do.

The species evolves, it works its way up to primitive tool-
using levels, works its way up to making fire, learns how to
utilize metals, develops civilization, finally reaches its technological period where it has factories and engineers and tool de-
signers, and so on. When it has reached this point, our starship's
engineer goes back to the planet, places an order for the missing
parts, gets them, returns to his starship, makes the repairs, and
takes off to resume his cosmic telegram delivery!

The planet is Earth. The species is man. And we have been
calmly told by author Vonnegut that the sole purpose of all
human history and evolution is to fulfill that one mission—deliver
the engine parts—after which humanity can sink back into
oblivion for all the sponsors of our evolution are concerned. The
scale on which they live and think is totally out of our league.

This is but one of the themes in the novel. There are lots more. Vonnegut's *Cat's Cradle* is possibly the equal of the *Sirens* in astonishing novelties. We get something of what may or may not be Vonnegut's philosophy in the religion called Bokononism introduced as part of the many elements of this cat's cradle of a novel. If the sayings of Bokonon have not gained the popularity accorded to Heinlein's water-sharing cult of *Stranger in a Strange Land* it is probably only because Bokonon is infinitely more cynical and yet far simpler. Youth is not yet that devoid of faith.

There is a quote from the First Book of Bokonon which is perhaps relevant to the purpose of mankind as given in *The Sirens of Titan*. Let me cite it:

> . . . God created every living creature that now moveth, and one was man. Mud as man alone could speak. God leaned close as mud as man sat up, looked around, and spoke. Man blinked. "What is the purpose of all this?" he asked politely.
>
> "Everything must have a purpose?" asked God.
>
> "Certainly," said man.
>
> "Then I leave it to you to think of one for all this," said God. And He went away.

This is, in a manner of speaking, Vonnegut's cosmic viewpoint. If existence has a purpose, he hasn't been able to determine it.

Vonnegut, who occasionally does not hesitate to intrude himself in his own novels, will sometimes repeat a character in two or more of his books. He has a science-fiction novelist named Kilgore Trout pop up in *God Bless You, Mr. Rosewater* (which is otherwise not one of his s-f books) and also in *Slaughterhouse Five*. Kilgore Trout has written some eighty-seven science-fiction space opera—and still has to hold a menial job in order to keep from starving to death. That may be a hint as to why Vonnegut prefers not to think of himself as being in the category. It is a bit rough, and things are really not at all that bad for professional s-f writers. But as Vonnegut himself would say, so it goes.

Similarly the American Nazi who shows up to lecture the American POWs in *Slaughterhouse Five* is the principal character of the novel *Mother Night*. A most complex character who may or may not be what he seems to be, this tall American is a man of easy speaking ability and considerable literary talent, a man of vigorous ingenuity, lots of originality, and spectacular frustrations. His name is Howard W. Campbell, Jr.

17

A Victorious Vernian

JOHN W. CAMPBELL, JR., is the editor and moving force behind the largest-selling s-f magazine, *Analog*. When Campbell, at that time one of the best writers of space opera of the thirties—his novels rivaled those of Edward E. Smith in style and popularity —became editor of *Astounding Stories* in 1937 it was an event which is generally credited as being the start of the change in the genre from the rather obvious pulp that had gone before to a far more sophisticated style of writing, more serious and complex plotting, and a generally more mature approach. Campbell's editing direction has always been hailed as the basis for this step upward in the whole field.

Let us examine this a bit more closely.

The one thing Campbell did do was to work a change of title away from the rather awful appellation "Astounding," which was an imitation of the original magazine title "Amazing" and in the worst tradition of the most garish days of the pulps. Campbell did not get his change through completely for some time, but he did get the title changed to *Astounding Science Fiction,* tried a few variations in relative sizes of the logo and eventually managed to signal a real maturation of the magazine with the title of *Analog.*

However, the question of whether it was Campbell personally who selected, chose, directed, and made authors revise until the field was upgraded is one of those "iffy" things which can never be resolved. For it seems to me that what happened is that the golden days of the forties, which are credited to Campbell's magazine, the days when a flood of really good writers began

to show up with style and skill and ingenuity, represented something a little different. They were actually the first generation of
writers who had grown up on science fiction, had been grounded
and, as it were, schooled in science fiction and hence were able
to utilize this in advancing further. Science fiction builds upon
science fiction—and in the fact that magazines had been publishing s-f under that label since 1926 lay the reason why this generation of writers reached their twenties in time to write for Campbell when he, who was also a first-generation writer raised in
the same school, was waiting and looking for better stuff. Campbell became an editor when the field itself came of age. Because
he himself had mastered the field as it stood and because he
himself, as an author, had fought to build upon what had been,
he was able to recognize and assist those of his own generation.

Before that, in the late twenties and through the thirties, the
men who wrote for the three or four science-fiction pulps—
Amazing, Wonder, Astounding—had had their grounding in the
general pulps. Their source of original foundations had been
such magazines as *Argosy, Blue Book,* or worse. Such new-
comers to s-f as began to show up in the pulps were very young
—high school students, college freshmen—I sold my first story to
Wonder Stories when I was eighteen. Very few of us had any
kind of real grounding in science. Campbell himself sold a group
of interstellar novels before he had his college diploma. And he
went into editing directly afterward.

So what he found was the first fresh flood of developed
science-fiction thinkers, men like Heinlein, Simak, and Asimov
who had not been tarred with the old pulp styles and who were
already sufficiently advanced in modern scientific study as to be
aware that mechanistic universes à la Ray Cummings, George
Allen England, and Homer Eon Flint were already passé.

However, let us not deny that Campbell was the right person
in the right place to give these writers recognition and to direct
them in advancing further. There were pulp magazines aplenty
in those days—the paperbacks had not yet begun to wash them
away, as they did after the war was over. These pulps were
edited by a breed of men who had learned what publishers of
pulps expected of their editors—breathless titles, lurid covers,

fast-action plots, and short easy-to-read paragraphs. John Campbell became a pulp editor too, but with one magazine to produce a month (as against the four, six, or eight that some of his colleagues had to contend with) he had the time to do a better job than usual, to give more attention to each story, to avoid the mistakes that the pulp-trained editors of *Wonder* and *Startling* and *Planet Stories* and *Amazing* were making. Campbell had the time and the understanding that they did not have.

I think, however, that the enigma of John W. Campbell today is partly answered by the role he now occupies in the paleontology of publishing. He is a living fossil; he is just about the last pulp editor still in business, still working on the same single title as when he started. He may hold the world's record for the longest continuous run on a single pulp magazine—1937 to date— well over thirty years. Though *Analog* is not printed on pulp paper, has a fine typographical setup (the best of any of the s-f periodicals), it is still technically the same genus of story magazine that all pulps were. It must be a frustrating thing for one man, so talented, to find himself in such a perpetual and isolated role. It is to that frustration that I place my own guess as to what makes Campbell tick.

To begin with, Campbell was aware, more so than most, of the dynamic era of science that was opening up after the war. He was aware of the potentials of science-fiction thinking for the working scientist when funds for research started to become virtually unlimited during the war and even more so afterward. He himself was a mine of new concepts—concepts which he gave freely to his writers and which sparkled and bounced through the pages of his magazine—he surely must have been charged with the need to join in that research, to partake of the wonders being discovered, to contribute his share and have his share of glory. But this was not to be. He was stuck where he was. He tried at one time to launch a general science magazine, even managed to get control of one for two or three numbers, but it proved a washout. So it was *Astounding* which had to be his workshop, his laboratory, his platform for glory.

You can't do much with a magazine outside of editorializing, and he began to do that. Then he made his first world-shaking offering—he "discovered" a scientific system which would shake the world and produce a new breed of supermen. Dianetics burst forth into the world's view in the pages of John W. Campbell, Jr.'s, *Astounding*.

Dianetics went its way, made a brief stir in America, gathered an assortment of honest but naïve experimenters and gullible guinea pigs and then quietly exited from the pages of Campbell's magazine. It represented one of Campbell's great blind spots—a mechanistic approach to psychology, sociology, and history. Campbell, grounded in physics and chemistry, has always approached humanity and the humanities with the supposition that the human mind and the human psyche can be handled in a laboratory with the techniques and impersonal methodology of the exact sciences. (Curiously, exactly the same approach that Karl Marx and Friedrich Engels attempted to use a century earlier, though they were in rebellion against the social order whereas Campbell seems to regard the social order of his time as the True Mathematical Fact not to be questioned any more than one would quarrel with an axiom of simple arithmetic.)

Dianetics went underground, emerged as the Church of Scientology, and may yet become the Neo-Mormonism of the twentieth century. Campbell may indeed have influenced his time more than he would like to know. Scientology is a movement of dangerous dimensions, great wealth, and sufficiently subversive mind-warping techniques to get it banned in many parts of the civilized world.

But Campbell seems to have realized that he had goofed with dianetics. He lay low for a while, then began playing around with a new series of discoveries. He discovered all by himself what the occultists and the psychic researchers had been dabbling with for a century. He discovered what he called "psi" powers, and for a number of years his magazine—and consequently the rest of the s-f literary world (for the highest paying market can set the tune and the overflow must run into the lower paying markets)—read like an educated and literary version of the bulletin of the Society for Psychic Research. Dowsing, telekinesis, telepathy, clairvoyance, pyromancy, and all the rest of the paraphernalia of the Victorian séances and mediums were paraded out in new forms, labeled "mutant" powers, and his readers were urged to look with an open mind upon these marvels of the psychic.

They did that. Because by then his readers were primarily men working in the engineering sciences, men who were as poorly grounded in psychology, history, theology, and sociology as Campbell himself.

The psi stories petered away too, and John Campbell turned to the affairs of the world. If he couldn't make a scientific discovery that would bear his mark, he'd at least advance his own original thinking about the affairs of humanity. Politics and social organization would be his oyster. What emerged from this was a series of glib, logical-sounding, very scientifically worded, and able literary lectures to his readers about how there really are superior and inferior people, about the idiocy of tampering with the profit motive, of the value of greed as a driving mechanism, of the inevitability and desirability of war as a natural outlet for a naturally aggressive race, of the superiority of the United States over all other countries and forms of government, well—the gamut.

Jules Verne was fascinated by the gimmicks and coming inventions of science, but he never quarreled with his class or his government. He was a French patriot, a French imperialist, a loyal supporter of his flag and country. No internationalist he.

John W. Campbell, Jr., a century later is also fascinated by the gimmicks and technological inventions of science, and he too is a patriot, an imperialist, a loyal supporter of his flag and country. No internationalist he.

Analog with Campbell represents the Vernian faction in science fiction today.

Yet Campbell is not in any way a fool. He is doing exactly the right thing for the readers of his magazine. He knows who they are, he caters to them, and they approve and support his magazine. For men who are making their living in scientific research today must be, in the majority, men working for corporations and industries operating on defense contracts. That's where the money is in research. To hold a job in such a laboratory you must have a security clearance. You must pass a series of intense investigations by any or all of several government and military agencies that must prove beyond a doubt that you have never entertained a single subversive thought in your life nor aided or abetted a single improper unpatriotic group or movement. If you want to make a living in research—chemistry, physics, astronautics, aviation, oceanography, etc.—you must be the kind of person who brainwashed yourself from your earliest days in high school right on through college, through postgraduate studies, to this very day.

But if you are also attracted by science, you will probably have passed through a phase of fascination for science fiction. You may, like a surprising number of scientific workers, still enjoy reading science fiction. If so, *Analog* is safe for you. Listing *Analog* as one of your regular reading habits will not get you in bad with any security agency. Campbell may or may not consciously know this, but certainly he is in accord with the Establishment. Upholding the idea of slavery as a practical proposition for the care and best utilization of naturally inferior races may be a shocking reversion that might startle even a John Bircher—but it will never get *Analog* a subversive rating. It is perfectly okay to advocate what *Analog* advocates.

So I must submit that John W. Campbell, Jr., is still the right person for the right magazine. *Analog* has a higher circulation than any of its competitors. Its readers must, to a large degree, be exclusive to it. For mighty few are the Hugos and Nebulas won by *Analog* entries. The highest awards of science fiction in literature and popular reader appeal go fairly consistently to novels and short stories from the pages of *Galaxy, Magazine of Fantasy and Science Fiction,* and the publishers of original novels in book form.

18

Wellsians in Crisis

WHEN I START out in this book saying that this is a world that science fiction made I am not taking either a Vernian or a Wellsian stand. If anything, it is a world that the Vernians made —only lately are we waking up to the rapidly approaching deadlines of pollution, overpopulation, and The Bomb to realize that we have too few Wellsians among the world's political leaders. Our gadgets and gimmicks, our televisions and airplanes and space ships, these are the things in which Verne would rejoice. But it will take more than gadget thinking to solve the equation of the next three decades.

I'd like to make it clear again that when I use the term "Wellsian" I do not mean what used to be called Wellsian socialism. I use it only in the sense that it follows the lead of H. G. Wells toward science fiction—that sociology and human relations merging with modern science are necessary ingredients of science fiction. Whereas I see the Vernian as essentially one accepting the status quo of the system in power, I see the Wellsian taking for granted that social relations will change with the application or lack of application of scientific development.

In the present science-fiction world it is mainly Wellsians who are in a crisis. Vernians go on as unthinkingly as before. It is the writers with social conscience who are increasingly disturbed by the three barriers of the twentieth century. Because we are living day by day among those three terrible challenges and because the Wellsians, aware of what they can mean, feel more and more the ineffectuality of protest and are imaginatively more sensitive to the ultimate disasters portending, it is Wellsians who reflect gloom and hysteria in their works.

In truth it *is* hard to see the forest for the trees. We have to fix our mental vision on a future which grows daily less and less visible. Our future—that of space-oriented humanity, of man bursting his planetary bonds and spreading out to infinity—was glimpsed more clearly in the thirties and forties. Now that we have actually reached the moon, moving across the threshold of that future, the three crises confronting the Terrestrial landscape becloud the view and in their darkening shadows the vision is lost to sight save in the mind's eye. All we can visualize on the day-to-day scene about us is the potential catastrophes of the immediate years to come.

The result has had its effect on science fiction. Many who would presumably be heralding glories to come have become ravens of doom. Cries of disaster are heard in their writings. One of the best expositions of this havoc-crying turned up on my desk just as I was working on this part of the book. It is from the editor's introduction to an anthology by Robert Silverberg of gloomy (mind you!) science fiction entitled *Dark Stars*. Let me quote:

> If the writer perhaps believes that human civilization is a can-
> cerous growth that has already consumed most of one planet and is
> about to spread to the others, he may not create fiction that sings
> hosannas to the valiant astronauts and cosmonauts. . . . If the
> writer thinks that man, for all his remarkable achievements, is
> nevertheless a flawed, turbulent, potentially dangerous character,
> as much demon as angel, then the writer will be cautious about
> applauding man's doings. . . .
>
> Once upon a time the bulk of science fiction was written by
> cheerful Rotarians eager to leap into the lovely future. That was
> in the 1930's, when the future still looked pretty good (especially
> in contrast with the present), and in the 1940's, when the defeat
> of the bestial Axis foe was supposed to open the gateway to
> Utopia. But a good chunk of that future has already unveiled it-
> self since those days of s-f's innocence, and what has appeared
> has not been so inspiring. . . . By measuring the fictional "1963"
> of 1938 against the real 1963, s-f writers have of necessity suffered
> a darkening of the vision. Hymns to the miracle that is color tele-
> vision become less meaningful when that screen is so often red-
> dened by the blood of those who were our best.

Utopians, in short, have given way to anti-Utopians. The purpose of Utopias has always been to hold before humanity the possibilities of our better sides. The anti-Utopians represent those who have come to deny that the better side can ever triumph. They hold before humanity the prospect of perpetual defeat.

Humanity is an obstinate and complex beast. I have but to remind myself that this aggressive, scheming, imaginative creature with all its faults has been around on this planet for many millions of years during which it has survived every known disaster of nature—famines, droughts, earthquakes, floods, ice ages, plagues, beasts, and the attacks of other members of its own species—and has still managed to dream of marvels, to create and keep new discoveries for the betterment of its descendants, to develop and cherish art, beauty and song, to work patiently day by dreary day toward the vision of Utopian concepts, each greater and more heavenly, and that this beast is not going to suddenly stop this millions-of-years ingrained drive just because of the shadows of the next thirty years. Utopia construction is part of our scene. Utopia downgrading has always represented the panicking of the fainthearted and the pretend-visionary. It is part of the marvelous complexity of a thinking beast that this is so. It is also a fact that the anti-Utopian image never achieves the power to move masses of men, whereas the Utopian concept usually can.

This being so, such downbeat visions as science fiction may choose to present—the world gone to pot—are taken as a warning rather than as a serious prediction. Watch out for this shoal and that—if we want to arrive safely at our spatial port.

Robert Silverberg chose to lead off his collection of downbeat tales with as black a novelette as has ever been written—one of the last stories of the late C. M. Kornbluth. Kornbluth, best remembered today as coauthor of *The Space Merchants* and *Gladiator-at-Law* with Frederik Pohl, died young and therefore the body of his work, signed by himself alone and not as a collaboration, is limited.

I do not think I can write objectively of Cyril Kornbluth and I will not try. He and I were good friends back in the days of the Futurian Society of New York, in years just before the war and the first year after Pearl Harbor too. The Futurians were a

special group of New York fans, most of us would-be writers or
writers in embryo, and we included a surprising number of
present-day "big names" among our members. But Cyril was
special, even for us. A very young man then—in fact, I believe
he was still in high school when he first made contact with us—
he rapidly built up close friendships with our group. Yet from
the start he had that deep streak of black humor, of alienation,
which was to come full bloom in his works after the end of the
war. It showed in the subtle touches of cruel comment he could
make about our rivals in fandom, it showed in occasional black
humor in the midst of conversations and social events, it showed
from the first in his earliest writings, his short stories and novelettes published under pen names in the science-fiction magazines
which came into existence under Fred Pohl, Bob Lowndes, and
myself back in those days.

Yet at that time he was not without his faith in the future—
his work was not that black—and he was able to write quite
funny pieces and even stories with a dream-desire quality sug-
gestive of the endless ideals that have always moved mankind—
the title of one, *The Golden Road,* is evidence of this.

Whatever was in Cyril Kornbluth's roots that embittered him
was never quite clear to me. Somehow he was always a little
apart from home, school, and society. It was to be the stresses of
marriage and war that eventually produced the C. M. Kornbluth
of maturity and total alienation. It was these same stresses that
severed our close association with him (we had even coauthored
several stories, even as Frederik Pohl was to do profitably and
extensively after the war). What transpired in the life and inner
personality of Cyril Kornbluth during the years 1942–1945 will
remain matters for speculation. What counts is that the Kornbluth who made his real mark on the world of science fiction was
a bitter, acid individual, a hermit by choice, dominated by an
alienation with the world as it existed and mankind as it is, and
plowing his vindictiveness into his short stories and novelettes.
His novels are models of sharp depiction, lucid writing, and they
have never had quite the despairing basis that he allowed his
shorter work to display. Unfortunately time has not dealt kindly
with the three novels he signed, which were presumably done

without collaboration. One of them dealt with the building of the first moon rocket, another with the Russian conquest of America (a popular item in the Joe McCarthy period), a third with the take-over of America by Mafia-type gangsters.

The third might seem to be timely until you consider that the Mafia at its alleged strongest is mighty small potatoes compared with the military-industrial complex about which the late President Eisenhower warned in his farewell address.

No, it is in his short stories that the pure poison exists. *Shark Ship*, an appalling story about the future, is indeed his blackest —and possibly one of the last stories he was to write. Anyone reading that tale and believing that this could be a true depiction of the future would be justified in declining to continue living. Could there be a society so vicious, so without "redeeming merit" as this? In the blackest period of human history—and there have been many—I do not think a philosophy as pervasively inhuman as this could exist.

There are others. There is *Two Dooms*, in which Kornbluth justifies the creation and use of the atomic bomb as the better alternative to what he described as the victory of the enemies in World War II. A hint here of his nonrecovery from the psychosis of military combat—it was written in 1958, a long time after that madness.

I remember especially *The Marching Morons*, based on the idea that, since low-intelligence people breed more children than better educated couples, the world will someday find a tiny hard-worked elite of normal 100 and 100 plus IQ people slaving away to keep a 99 percent majority of subnormals from starving to death. Kornbluth had one bit in there which struck me with more than usual impact: he described a car which was super-streamlined with a fake speedometer showing speeds of 200 miles an hour, while the car was only capable of really running a safe 25! Adding to the illusion for the moronic drivers of these cars was a device which created a dramatic *vroom* noise as if a gale were rushing past the car. This "got" to me when a recently purchased electric coffeepot turned out to have a noisemaker concealed in its base which made a boiling sound as soon as you plugged it in and obviously long before it really could have come to a perk!

Of course, considering the premises I have already stressed in this book, it is possible that the engineer who designed that percolator was a science-fiction reader and had got the idea from Kornbluth. The more I think of it, the more I think it probable.

The thing about Kornbluth's bitterest works is that he seems to have been ahead of the game by a dozen or more years. Some of the despair that shows up today in writers who contemplate the rest of this century was visible in Kornbluth way back then, long before anyone else. Whatever was the cause, it produced a mind and soul so embittered with the world around it and with its inhabitants that it is actually hard for me to conceive how he could have lasted much longer in it.

I recall having the reaction, after reading his final book of short stories, that this mind and the Earth simply could not coexist. One had to go. And since it is Nature that is infinitely the stronger, it was Kornbluth who had to exit. Which he did, dying suddenly of a heart attack at the age of thirty-five in 1958.

This sounds mystical, I know. Is it possible to become so alienated that life itself can no longer be an acceptable alternative? Viewing the subworld of drug addicts and LSD escapists and nut cultists, the drifting alienated psychotics of the so-called underground youth, I believe it possible. There is still among the majority of these that element of faith and hope—the flower children, the rebels, the commune organizers, and the poets still flourish, but the dark traces of the mind blowers streak the scene with the same sort of alienation.

On the other hand, a skepticism as to the merit of science and its future need not produce a sour viewpoint, as witness the satirical writings of Robert Sheckley.

19

The Darkest of Nights

ROBERT SHECKLEY a downbeat writer? Author of anti-Utopias? Yes, because one of the most effective ways of killing a thing is to laugh it to death, and this Sheckley does with vim and originality. His work is light, you could say frothy, and his view is, in its own way, as diabolically "anti" as anything Kornbluth would have dreamed up. But, whereas Kornbluth was sadistically agin' the future, Sheckley is amusingly agin' it. To him it is a potpourri of the same things most odious on Earth, drawn out in such a way as to seem less than real and laughable. The joke is always on us. This is what we value—see how silly it is on a cosmic scale.

Consider his novel *Dimension of Miracles*. Here is an average present-day man who awakens one night to learn he has been the winner of some sort of cosmic lottery—and is taken forthwith to some central depot in what is clearly a present-time existing galactic federative setup, and given his award. He has a hard time figuring out what is going on as naturally he's rather backward compared with all those advanced types, human and inhuman, but his award tries to help. It is a Prize, a living thing with a sarcastic tongue, a presumably wide knowledge, and a diabolical philosophy. As the poor man tries to get home with his Prize he finds that no one has made provision for that safe return. So away he goes in and out of an Alice in Wonderland cosmic madhouse, getting the facts of life in a thoroughly sardonic fashion. He meets a God, acquires a Nemesis, spends time in a perfect Utopian city (which proves to be quite a nightmare), and ends up in a museum of human waste whose motto is "Wastefulness in the defense of luxury is no vice; moderation in the dissemination of excess is no virtue."

We are told (I cannot resist quoting here) that the museum

"was designed by the architect Delvanuey, who also planned Death Trap 66, the famous New York toll road which no one has succeeded in driving from start to finish without accident. This same Delvanuey, you may recall, drew up the plans for Flash Point Towers, Chicago's newest slum, the only slum in the world in which form follows function; that is to say, the first slum which is proudly and avowedly designed *as* a slum."

On the little matter of overpopulation his novelette *The People Trap* says it all in much the same way as Brunner and Harrison do and manages to make it a mad farce. It all takes place on Land Race Day somewhere in the next century when the grand award of an actual acre of land and a house of one's own is given to the first ten men to reach Times Square from Hoboken, New Jersey, after they have passed an exhaustive elimination contest just to be entered in the race. The trip of our hero to his goal, a matter of 5.7 miles, takes him many many days and is a journey which makes Stanley's travels in Darkest Africa seem like a Sunday picnic. Going through the people-packed, jungle-savage streets of Darkest Manhattan is an experience that anyone else would have played as the most frightening of nightmares. But Sheckley does not permit the nightmare to be seen, save obliquely. He touches the surface aspects, he introduces with a light hand the sort of murder that would make a modern gang leader flinch, and he makes it stick. How can you argue with the scene? It is no more than an extension of things plainly in early growth form right now. When our hero wins—where's his acre? On the nearly vertical side of a barren Western desert mountain—that's all that's left of unoccupied land. Asimov spelled it out statistically—that's how it's going to be in only a century if we don't act. Sheckley painted the picture to the statistics.

Funny, yes. Anti-Utopian? To be sure. How else could you read it? Is this what the future is to be like? Is this what the galaxy is to be like? A further development of all our follies and mistakes?

The theme is carried further and more explicitly in a novel which I consider the most completely despairing in the whole of modern science fiction. This is the novel *Out of the Mouth of the Dragon,* the work of a young college graduate named Mark

Geston. It is Geston's second novel; his first was *Lords of the Starship*, the story of a future effort to rebuild civilization which ends in betrayal and world catastrophe.

Out of the Mouth of the Dragon starts a thousand or so years after that one left off. The place is Earth or a planet so similar as to make no difference. The time from our viewpoint must be several thousands of years in the future. The world is a place of ruins and memories and the records of endless failures. The population has diminished due to a series of recurring wars, a series of calls to Armageddon in each of which humanity is exhorted to go to battle in the sacred cause of destroying once and for all the Forces of Evil. Each successive Armageddon turns out to be a fraud, each is a disaster which sets humanity back further and further and saps the remaining strength of a near-licked and finished world.

The story is the account of the last such call to Holy Combat. Once again the last idealists, the last remaining young men who have faith, are roused from their half-empty cities and urged to go once more to the place of combat, to join the army that is to defeat that old enemy (who is never seen and never described). A young man follows such a prophet and once again the armies assemble—and are betrayed. Half-mad, the volunteer wanders over the world accompanied by a ghastly crew and as he wanders he sees that humanity has carried its last straw, it is finished, the world is finished, God is really now dead, and the universe is drying up and cracking up, and it is the absolute end of all hope.

A remarkable work, and especially potent when one considers that this is a novel that came from a member of the youngest generation, for Geston is in his early twenties. Is it possible that this is how an observant and sensitive young man of middle-class background, good education, and culture sees the future of the world he finds himself living in? The answer is obviously that it is.

Samuel R. Delany, at much the same age but with a widely different background, has turned out marvelous novels full of poetry and imagery which also envision a world of half ruins and mutated beings following the disasters of atomic war and cosmic tamperings. But Delany never loses his faith in the survival of art and song and beauty. Geston is capable of appreciating these things but sees no future for them any more than for the rest of the paraphernalia of civilization.

There is an unforgettable scene in *Out of the Mouth of the Dragon* when its half-crazed protagonist returns after seven years of wandering to the devastation of the last battlefield and in a moment of drunken inspiration sets up a banquet table amid the wreckage. About this he gathers twelve skeletons from the slaughter, dresses them in shreds of their old uniforms, props them up, and with himself as the thirteenth, makes a hideous parody of the Last Supper. Here, after nights of madness, the prosthetic voice box of one of the dead speaks to him of first causes and last responses:

> "And do you know what all this progressively more wretched Creation means? . . . It means that the thing which had given life to all of this in the first place and which had conceived of all the plans is a poor, stupid, fumbling idiot just like the rest of us!
>
> "Ah, that *is* beautiful! Think of it! The final basis for a million years of theology and a thousand years of philosophy—nothing more than a useless pile of shit! Noble minds striding the earth, putting their ascetic necks on the block in the name of something which didn't exist. Wars, evolutions, inquisitions, pain, pain: because it was part of the plan, the divinely inspired plan—so full of eternal wisdom that it sickens me now—and therefore how could it be bad?"

This is about as plain a statement of the most nihilistic view of the modern youngest generation as can be found. How representative is it?

I can recognize it in many facets of the so-called underground. It is there like a dark streak discoloring much that these flower children seem to be fighting for. But it is not the dominant view. There is still an overwhelming spirit that believes in a better future—and I will turn away from these spokesmen of negation and get on to the majority writers of science fiction.

20

Toward Galactic Maturity

AS THE CRISIS of the decade of the seventies continues—and continues to darken as surely it must—I have no doubt that the volume and percentage of pessimistic science fiction will increase. But I do not believe that it will ever overcome the immense lead that what I would call optimistic science fiction has. In fact, I am of the opinion that because of the very escapist nature of the science-fiction reader it could not. Too vast a volume of gloom would simply turn these sensitive readers away.

By optimistic science fiction I mean that which regards the future not with horror but as a place for the continuing exploits of humanity, singly or en masse, following the pattern I outlined in the eight phases of the future as unfolded through the medium of a thousand science-fiction fantasists.

Cyril Kornbluth, directly after returning from the war, spent three years with the Chicago bureau of a national press service. Anyone who knows that news-gathering field will realize that too close an acquaintance with the daily petty mishaps, villainies, and miseries of ordinary life could depress anyone—and the news medium is the place to become familiar with much more of it than anyone would reasonably wish to know. This familiarity may have been a factor in Kornbluth's implied resignation from the human race. Then consider the much greater news background of Clifford D. Simak.

Simak has been a journalist all his life and was for many years the news editor of a large metropolitan daily, during the course of which he must have been doused in all the daily human disasters possible. Yet for all that his writings reflect a positive and utterly compassionate sense of the joy of life, of man with nature, and of the infinity of the universe.

While his stories cover the entire scope of the field—from the immediate present to the days of galactic humanity—they seem always to reflect a fine touch for the essential humanness of things, for the small pleasures of daily living, for love and unity with nature. To be sure, Simak's audience, that audience of which we have been speaking all along, has responded with appreciation. Two of his books have won the highest awards of organized s-f fandom, *City* and *Way Station,* two books which incidentally are also among my own favorites.

City (an abominably misleading title, by the way) is a collection of eight episodes in the history of a family, ranging from the near future to ten thousand years from now. It is told as gathered together by man's inheritors and descendants on Earth, those whom we regard as our best friends today, namely, Dogs. The dogs, bred for intelligence, gradually take over our cities, our homes, as we human beings begin to spread into the universe, and *City* becomes in effect a sort of Doggy Bible—here is the legendry of our ancestry, and our makers scattered to the stars to take up life beyond our comprehension. A perfect presentation of the galactic infinite future but handled from a unique point of view.

Humanity develops and builds its robots and trains its canine friends. So the tale unfolds as robot servants, ever faithful, and dogs, ever reverent, remain behind to take the Earth for themselves. As for humanity, we have gone a-roving—to Jupiter, to the stars, changing forms for different planets, outward bound forever.

Here no atomic threat will blast our planet. Here the questions of overpopulation will solve themselves—to be honest, the book was mainly written before these things became manifest problems—but the book still sells well and is still a moving experience.

Way Station, written more than a dozen years later, is Simak's philosophical analysis of the situation of the world today and of the galactic future. A simpler story by far than *City,* it could almost have been compressed into a novelette save for the care and concern Simak takes in developing his personalities and calmly reviewing the situation.

There is, we learn, an already existing Inter-Galactic Council, a union of civilized planets numbering thousands. The Earth, in

its twentieth-century stage, is not ready for such acceptance—
our part of this galaxy is on an outlying and sparsely starred
arm of the Milky Way (which is true). But the needs of interstellar commerce require that a way station be planted on Earth
for the transshipment of travelers and products from one planet
to another in our sector. This is not done by space flight but by
some form of dimensional or supra-Einsteinian technique far
beyond our present scientific abilities. As at a relay station,
things are received at this building on Earth, rested up, then
rephased and sent off again.

A man is required to maintain this station—which exists unknown to human civilization. *Way Station* is the story of this
man, the manager of the Earth relay post, of his solitary life, of
his daily work, of the love in his life, of the crisis that comes to
him when eventually the government's secret agencies begin to
pry into the mysterious goings-on in his isolated Wisconsin
station.

Simak uses this as a platform to discuss the meaning of interstellar civilization, of the universality of life and hence the universality of tolerance, and of the particular provincial backward-
nesses that mark our present existence. The same problems that
defeated a Kornbluth, brought a Geston to despair, and reduced
a Sheckley to sarcastic laughter are shown to be simply factors
that every intelligent race, growing to maturity, must consider,
work out, and reduce to a proper historical perspective.

In the historical perspective of millions of years of evolution
upward and millions of years of cosmic maturity, perhaps we
are now going through no more than a series of minor tests. We
have overcome before—thousands of times before—and we have
the capacity to overcome now.

Which is not to say that the galactic civilizations are all
idealistic Utopias. Far from it; the travelers passing through
Earth's secret relay office tell of many crises, of political arguments, hint at trouble. No, Utopia is not in sight but there is the
unending conflict of intelligence against nature, which alone is
eternal and which alone is worth the game of life.

Such is Clifford Simak, as I read him, and this feel for the
galactic and for the strictly human is a combination hard to
match.

All of his novels and short stories are eminently readable, all are varied, some are facetious, some minor, and some strike moods and notes similar to the two I prize above the others.

21

Sailors of the Cosmic Seas

CONSIDER another writer of great consistency who has not won any awards, who is a lesser star in the heavens, but whose works in their own way remain true to the galactic future and to a belief in humanity. I refer to A. Bertram Chandler.

Chandler has been turning out good space opera for perhaps thirty years. He himself is a merchant seaman; we understand that these days he has achieved the status of ship's captain and commands a freight liner on the lonely route between Australia and New Zealand. This gives him two advantages over most writers of space-action adventure—he has the long hours of quiet and solitude necessary to dream out his tales of space captains and space explorers on the worlds of the galactic Rim off there in the future times of the Galactic Empire, and it also gives him the extra touch of authenticity that connects the sailors of the seas with those coming sailors of the cosmic oceans.

His space liners are sea liners transposed and transformed. His principal hero, one Grimes, rising from ensign to commander in the Rim Worlds Confederacy, must resemble his creator in more ways than one. No one could write so steadily of a single hero and not reflect himself in him—as indeed Chandler has the audacity to admit in one sequence wherein Grimes has a recession in time and meets up with his own writer!

Chandler's is the world of the Galactic Empire in full flow. Not one empire exactly—there are, we learn, several smaller autarchies, including the lone worlds at the very edge of the Milky Way, facing the vast gap of the cosmos whose other shores are the unattainable galaxies beyond. Here go the space liners, the naval ships of the Empire, the lone cutters of the small independent worlds, the far-faring freighters that journey from world to outlying world on trade. Here are people, colonized from old Earth, and beings born out there who partake of many alien things.

Here, too, is what must have often moved Chandler on his lonely routes across Earth's vastest ocean, where on the south lies the mysterious and mostly unexplored coast of the Last Continent, Antarctica, and on his north, the endless stretches of sea dotted here and there with tiny isles of wonder and mystery. And so we travel with Grimes as on one side lies the awful emptiness of intergalactic space and on the other lie the lost planets of far and isolated stars.

Chandler has worked out a fascinating gimmick to beat the speed-of-light limitation. His ships are equipped with a drive that moves the vessels back in time as they go forward in space. By thus moving along another dimension they make trips which might take many years into voyages of a few days or weeks. This gimmick also allows Chandler to delve into near-Fortean wonders of dimension and alternate worlds—for any such playing with the enigma of time-motion upsets the equilibrium of the universe we were born in—and accidents of the time drive account for many of Chandler's best space adventures.

Other writers have dealt with galactic travel and with colonized worlds, but none so consistently and thoroughly with one special range and segment of the imperial future. Yet of Chandler's dozens of novels and innumerable tales there is none I can single out above the others, and therefore none that has ever forced itself upon fandom as candidates for awards or for listing among the favorites. All his works are of a whole, yet all are individuals of equal interest. One reads Chandler to enjoy, not to cherish, and yet one cannot but get that sense of the infinite secrets of the sea as transposed to the celestial oceans of the sky.

The same is in a manner of speaking true of the work of Cordwainer Smith, the pen name used by the late Paul Linebarger for his books of the future. One cannot name any single Cordwainer Smith book as more outstanding and memorable than any other, and yet all are on a par. The secret is the same as

Chandler's—they are all part of a whole, but unlike Chandler's space opera the Cordwainer tales are not limited to the one factor of space travel. Rather they are a constantly shifting kaleidoscope of wonders in a galactic civilization that is truly of the future—it is no more a reflection of today than today would be a reflection of the Roman Empire. Everything is definitely of that future and part of it, advanced beyond ours by the evolution of time and society.

When I first started reading stories by Cordwainer Smith I wondered at the many loose-ended items he would slip into a story—odd references which seemed to be merely whimsical background bits. But as the stories continued to appear, as books were constructed from the various magazine parts, it became clear that nothing was without its significance. As with a gigantic jigsaw puzzle, every apparently meaningless segment belonged somewhere and referred to something.

I would dearly like to see the entire work of Cordwainer Smith gathered together in one single huge volume, put together in sequence. It would then develop as a unity. For what this amazingly talented man wrote was just that—one huge novel, potentially larger than the *Lord of the Rings* and even more complex. I fear, however, that what might have been the climax of the book was never written and what might then take shape might be a book leading up to something but never reaching it. Such is the danger of writing one connected cosmology when one's life span turns out to be shorter than one estimated.

When does this vast story take place? Sometime perhaps twenty thousand years from now—during the period of the Galactic Empire. Mankind has spread out onto dozens of worlds and the whole is held together by some sort of elite (hereditary? financial? this is not clear) known as The Instrumentality. Mankind has spread out in other ways too. Rather than robots, our ranks have been implemented by the surgical creation of *underpeople*, beasts transformed into human shapes and humanoid minds, yet kept on the servant level, counselors sometimes, slaves most of the time. Some of these underpeople, such as the marvelous cat-woman C'mell, are far from being "under."

And the worlds themselves—each different, each a jewel of

some fabulous sort, each logical in a weird intricate way. Old North Australia, a planet with a monopoly on a crop worth billions, a simple farming world, whose every citizen is wealthier than anyone could dream elsewhere, one of whose citizens wins enough money on the market in one night to go back to old Earth and simply *buy* it! But buying Earth turns out to be no simple transaction—the place is a Pandora's box of complexities and enigmas. *The Planet Buyer* and its sequel *The Underpeople* tell that story—they should be one book; instead they are two relatively undistinguished paperbacks.

Quest of the Three Worlds is another evidence of Cordwainer Smith's patterning. I published this book and I recall that when I had first read the four novelettes that combined to make it I had not realized they were all one novel. Yet they are. Each novel so attained only poses the problems of further works for none are without their unexplained minor mysteries—and with Cordwainer Smith, each is the seed of a new wonder growth.

The man who wrote under the name of Cordwainer Smith was a hardheaded diplomat, no left-winger, an adviser to the State Department, a supporter of Chiang Kai-shek. But despite this, there is nothing at all Vernian about his work. This is socially conscious, wonderfully alive writing. It achieves all this without being in any way of the Left. Such is the special talent of science fiction—that it alone can produce writers with vivid sparkling imaginations, a clearly visible love of the world and of its people, who have managed to be impervious to the lures of Utopian socialism.

Is this a good thing? I don't know. I cannot think of any other field of literature of which this could be said. In this day and age, when so much of the Left is bogged down in disillusion and so much of the Right smells of warmongering and defense hysteria, it is a rather remarkable thing that even those who firmly believe in the System as it is, in capitalism as it is supposed to be (free, opportunity-open, pioneering), can produce singing dreams of infinite mankind and the open cosmos.

22

"We'll make a star or die trying!"

CONSIDER one of the finest storytellers in the field, Poul Anderson. In the councils of the science-fiction writers he is of the Right. In the pages of his stories he sings of many futures, varied, near and far, galactic, and beyond the Galactic Empire, of exploration unending, of courage and of derring-do. One of his favorite heroes is a hardheaded entrepreneur of the old piratical variety, the Dutchman Nicholas van Rijn, who, living in the days of the early Galactic Empire, maneuvers his financial affairs with cunning and boldness on planets old and new. Here is an Astor or a Vanderbilt transformed into the far future—believable because such men have existed and do exist, and if the future is capitalist they will exist.

Another of his heroes is Dominic Flandry, a diplomat of the declining days of the Galactic Empire, of the times when corruption and decadence mark the coming end. Flandry himself, not unmarked by decadence, uses his wits and the weakening science of a corrupt empire to stave off the end, to confront inhuman aliens, and to keep the flag of humanity flying.

And after the Empire? Poul Anderson is intrigued by the ancient Vikings, being of Scandinavian ancestry, and in such a novel as *Star Ways* treats of raiders of space, nomad space ships living a free gypsy-Viking sort of life. In other works he deals with the new barbarians that may arise as the edges of civilized space crumble. We have a great variety in Poul Anderson, and he is a writer with color and skill, a tale-teller worthy of his saga-singing ancestry.

Arthur C. Clarke, who as far as I can tell is visibly neither of the Left nor of the Right, has become the best publicized science-fiction writer in the world. He has become the name one is most likely to hear when mainstream sources, unfamiliar with the field, choose an example of an s-f writer. Clarke is known today as the man who wrote *2001,* the movie that cost more and satisfied less than any other fantasy film yet produced. But to me Clarke means far more than this.

He is, for instance, credited with doing more than any other single writer to popularize and publicize space flight. He was active in the organization of rocket experimenter societies back in the days when it was unfashionable and in the public eye improbable. Some of his early novels dealt with that, novels I must confess I found not too interesting. For me Clarke was at his very best when he let his imagination wander far from the fields of real technology. One of his earliest books, a brilliant fantasy of the very far future, *Against the Fall of Night,* is virtually a prose poem of the last days of Earth and faith in man's immortality. A billion years from now, after man's empire has encompassed the universe, time has eroded it again, and there is but the one last city left where the last men dream and go their haunted way.

But the universe does not end here. For in this last city the last act is to send a message out into the universe where somewhere there must still be men to carry the word that Mankind would come back. A beautiful book, an act of faith for a science-fiction mind.

Childhood's End is Clarke's most famous novel. This tale of the new evolution of a generation of human children into something higher, managed and manipulated by peacemakers from outer space, has always seemed to me to be a novel of despair. Others may see it as offering hope, but this tampering with humanity always struck me as being synthetic, as being not of a par with Stapledon's new men, not to mention others who have attempted the theme.

Like most of the older generation of science-fiction writers and fans, I knew Clarke back when we were all just struggling fans, a tiny minority of beleaguered space voyagers. Fame and fortune came to him because of the technical faith he had in interplanetary flight first and because of the variety of his concepts in short tales of the immediate space adventures to come. Though he wrote of the period I have described as the Challenge to God, his fame came from the very first period, that of the first flights.

At this point it is imperative to mention Ray Bradbury, whose paperback editions now bear the quotation: "The world's greatest living science fiction writer." I can find no mention of the author of this quote, but no matter—it could be any of hundreds of reviewers from the mainstream press, taken by the skill and beauty of Bradbury's work, carried away by his intensely poetic fantasy and emotional impact, and entirely unaware that Ray Bradbury is not really a science-fiction writer at all.

Only a very small percentage of Bradbury's works can be classified as science fiction. Although his most "science-fictional" book, *The Martian Chronicles,* is a classic, its s-f plausibility is slight. Essentially (like almost all his books) a compilation of short stories (many of which originally appeared in s-f magazines) and roughly making a panorama of the next century, it has the form of science fiction but in content there is no effort to implement the factual backgrounds. His Mars bears no relation to the astronomical planet. His stories are stories of people —real and honest and true in their understanding of human nature—but for his purposes the trappings of science fiction are sufficient—mere stage settings.

Ray Bradbury is essentially a doomsman where the future is concerned. He distrusts science, distrusts technology, fears the complexity of a world deriving its substance from these things. He longs for the presumed simplicity of a past century and the innocence of boyhood. None of his work has impinged on the galactic cosmology of an Asimov or a Stapledon. He is outside the field—a mainstream fantasist of great brilliance, a literary warrior in an allied way against the three dooms of our century, an associate of the Wellsian concept, but certainly not "the world's greatest living science fiction writer."

If anyone could be said to have a claim to that sort of title, it could possibly be Robert A. Heinlein.

Like Poul Anderson, he is generally credited with being of the political Right, and he is also a storyteller of such talent that his novels outsell all others and his name remains fixed at the top of every list of favorites. Whether he is truly of the political

Right I am not so ready to say. It is an easy shibboleth, but dangerous. Heinlein himself has warned people not to judge his personal opinions by the attitudes and dialogues of the characters in his various stories. He may be right.

Farnham's Freehold may appear to be a firm bit of flag-waving fixed patriotism, but how can you square it with *Stranger in a Strange Land?* When the hippies and rebel youngsters of Haight-Ashbury and the other free communities of youth take the latter work as one of their Bibles, organize water-brotherhood societies, and pick up *grok* as a favored word, where can you say the author stands? When the latter work seems to present a case for free love, for free emotions, for standing aloof from the stiff formalized "civilization" of the stuffy older generations, can you call its author a rightist?

Maybe he is. I will not say that there isn't a case to be made for it. He is an Annapolis graduate, certainly a believer in free enterprise, and the bulk of his writings seem to reflect a viewpoint not too dissimilar to the economic-patriotic views of *Analog* magazine. But I can take it from Heinlein whereas I cannot take it from John Campbell. I know that Robert Heinlein did study the economic systems of the world, did investigate and see for himself the workings of many systems and the minds of advocates of all types of systems. In Bob Heinlein we have an extraordinarily sharp-eyed observer of the human world.

I would not advise being too quick to pin any label on Heinlein. I suspect that his views are always his own—that they parallel various viewpoints, usually right wing, but that they are not *of* the Right. Heinlein is first and foremost a free mind. It is as such that I read him. I do not necessarily like all that I read and I do not agree with a number of the viewpoints his characters express.

I found *Starship Troopers* militaristic and personally distasteful—but a good case can be made for the special rights of men who lay their lives on the line for their country, their people, their planet. When a book such as that also wins the Hugo for the best s-f novel of the year by the vote of readers and writers it would appear that Heinlein made his argument (as per that book) with the skill and wonder-creating ability which is his trademark.

To take an unpleasant proposition and make people like it, that is talent. Perhaps it might also be something that would make propagandists of the Left say such a man is to be feared and fought.

But then account for the whacky nihilism and hero-wrecking of *Glory Road* and the hippie-acceptance of *Stranger in a Strange Land.* Account for the faith in space of *The Man Who Sold the Moon* and for the exposure of religious fanaticism implicit in *Revolt in 2100* (a book which could be dynamite if Scientology or Jehovah's Witnesses ever had their way).

As far as I am concerned, Robert A. Heinlein is a universe maker who believes in the future of mankind and in the endless frontier of the galactic civilization that is to be. In this day of despair and crises, that faith is more of a true beacon than all the frightened philosophies of the panicked dystopians.

Look through the bulk of his novels and you will find that faith always shining through. Whatever the nature of the novel, whatever his message may be, this is the one constant that Heinlein will not surrender. Humanity, whatever its faults, is the best darned thing going and will never be pinned to the mat.

I riffle through his many juvenile novels—a collection that has influenced who knows how many minds that are now mature and working—and I recall a passage in one of the best, entitled *Have Space Suit—Will Travel.* A teen-ager acquires a space suit and then by a series of mischances and bold adventures goes out into the universe among aliens, eventually to find himself placed on trial, as spokesman for mankind before the Council of the Three Galaxies—a police body, not a government, whose concern is that humanity is a dangerous warmaking destructive race that ought to be exterminated before it becomes a menace to other intelligences on other worlds.

The outlook seems hopeless, for out of the boy's own mouth have been taped honest discussions of the black marks of our human past—wars and crusades and concentration camps. Desperate, the boy, considering the whole thing unfair, for he never sought to be the world's sole attorney at a trial, where all, the world itself, is in the balance, does his best. But at last, sensing that the trial is going against Earth:

> I looked around at the hall. . . . "Just this!" I said savagely. "It's not a defense, you don't *want* a defense. All right, take away our star—you will if you can and I guess you can. Go ahead! We'll *make* a star! Then, someday, we'll come back and hunt you down —all of you!"
>
> Nobody bawled me out. I suddenly felt like a kid who has made a horrible mistake at a party and doesn't know how to cover it up. But I meant it. Oh, I didn't think we could *do* it. Not yet. But we'd *try*. "Die trying" is the proudest human thing.

"We'll make a star or die trying," says Heinlein—and in their own way so say Simak and Chandler and Smith and Anderson and a myriad others who fill the pages of the real science-fiction magazines and the real science-fiction books that crowd the newsstands and bookstores of the world.

23

Après Nous le Déluge

DIAMETRICALLY OPPOSITE to this determined galactic optimism is the message that underlies the movement in science fiction known as the New Wave. Originating several years ago in London, and still mainly centered, as far as conscious editorial direction is concerned, around the British magazine *New Worlds,* it has aroused a great deal of controversy and discussion among science-fiction writers and readers.

New Worlds was originally a standard old-line science-fiction monthly that had appeared for many years edited by the distinguished science-fiction authority Edward John Carnell. But when Carnell stepped down as editor of the magazine, Michael Moorcock took the post and began to alter the policy of the magazine, as well as to redesign its entire appearance externally and internally.

Moorcock, himself a capable and talented writer, turned out to have some very different ideas about the future of science fiction, and these ideas rapidly made themselves known as the New Wave began to take shape and even to assume some of the aspects of a crusade.

Primarily we had once again the effort to merge science fiction into the mainstream of literature. This time the attempt was made in a much more organized and effective form. The charges brought against old-line science fiction were on the basis of both structure and content. Structurally the charge was made that too much of the writing retained the flavor of the pulps, that science-fiction writers were not keeping up with the experimental avant-garde of the literary world—the William Burroughs and Allen Ginsberg schools, for instance.

Internally the charge was made that science fiction actually was dead—because the future was no longer credible. The crises of the twentieth century—the Bomb, overpopulation, pollution—were obviously insurmountable. We would all never make it into the twenty-first century. This being so, these dreams of inter-planetary colonies, of technological things to come, of galactic empires, and so on were reduced to the status of pure fantasy—they could not be considered scientifically credible since they had been canceled out by the coming end of civilization and the world.

Hence science fiction as it had been during the forties and fifties had been swept aside by the facts of history of the sixties and seventies. *New Worlds* started to refer to "S-F" as meaning Speculative Fiction, a term they conceived to have more leeway and less "science."

Thus *New Worlds* and the writers associated with it began a campaign to change the nature of s-f. If you could not seriously believe in the future, all systems were no-go. Hence the realm of such literature was in that of the avant-garde—which is to say, let the readers and writers that used to dream of galactic futures now get their kicks out of experimental styles of writing, the free discussion of sex, the overthrow of all standards and morals (since, if the world is going to end, what merit had these things?).

Now, there was something to be said for improving the style of science fiction, of bringing it further away from its pulp origins, of adopting the best elements of the newest literary techniques if and when applicable. The best of the New Wave writers, J. G. Ballard, had never been in the pulp tradition, had always maintained some status with the British literary mainstream. But Ballard had, it must be noted, also always been a writer of doomed-world stories. None of his novels had ever fitted into the galactic tradition outlined in this study. All had been novels of the near future wherein the world faced total disaster of various types. Ballard needed no convincing to accept the full premise of the *New Worlds* message.

Brian Aldiss, a writer of the finest science-fiction talents, was the other major convert. He began a series of Joycean tales in *New Worlds,* which were eventually to collate into his book *Barefoot in the Head,* possibly his least comprehensible s-f work—a novel of hallucinatory passages, double images, Joycean constructions, and so on. After which, Aldiss went directly into the mainstream with a novel, *The Hand-Reared Boy,* which had no fantasy content whatever and made the best sellers on the basis of its sexual connotations.

The best—or perhaps it ought to be the worst—example of the New Wave is embodied in the novels and tales of a compound character called Jerry Cornelius—produced in a mélange of styles, chaotic plotting, and a chameleon of a protagonist who occasionally combines the characteristics of such as James Bond, Dr. Frankenstein, the Chevalier D'Eon, Jack the Ripper, and whatever else comes to mind. *The Final Programme* by Michael Moorcock was the first Jerry Cornelius novel to appear in book form—but other writers have been allowed to use the character in pieces of varying length and wild variety remarkably reminiscent of the sort of thing one finds in high school parodies.

The New Wave did some good—it did help to bring about an awareness of stylistic possibilities and thus to broaden the base of some of the more talented writers, such as Samuel R. Delany, Norman Spinrad, and possibly even John Brunner. But by and large it has begun to fade out due to its own negative outlook.

The *New Worlds* group certainly came from the Wellsian tradition, but they represent a group of socially sensitive writers who have decided that the battle for the future is a lost cause. In the tradition of *après nous le déluge* thinking, the sensual pleasures come to the fore as the only immediate real values left. Hence a great deal of the New Wave writing concerns itself with shock words and shock scenes, hallucinatory fantasies, and sex.

The New Wave represents a departure from the science-fiction directives for mankind, and its most devoted advocates have ceased to be universe makers.

24

Defy the Devil

BUT DO WE have any universe makers who seem to be of the New Wave? Some point to Harlan Ellison. In fact, on one of his books, *The New Yorker* is quoted as calling him "the chief prophet of the New Wave."

I think they are wrong, and as far as I know Harlan Ellison does not identify himself with the New Wave. He would be writing his kind of stories just the way he is writing them if there had never been a *New Worlds* magazine, or a Michael Moorcock or a Judith Merril, whose annual anthologies were the first heralds of the coming of the cult.

Harlan Ellison is one of those one-man phenomena who pop up in a field, follow their own rules, and have such a terrific charisma and personal drive that they get away with it. They break all the rules and make the rest like it. He is in an Asimovian sense a "mule," a unique sort of genius who can lead where others can never successfully follow, who can hold an audience enthralled yet never gain a convert, who can insult and have only the stupid offended.

New Wave—in the sense that Harlan Ellison's short stories have most certainly charted new paths in writing, in that he has indeed found new ultramodern ways of narration which yet manage to keep comprehension (compared with most of the New Wave pioneering which actually reverts back to antiquated experimental styles of the twenties and thirties without acknowledging it; a great deal of the New Wave material smacks of Dadaism, a 1919–1920 manifestation), in that he takes the downbeat view of the far future and therefore, by implication, seems to accept the view that there is no real hope for humanity and that we are not going to surmount the crises of this century.

In that sense Harlan Ellison is New Wave, and if so, is the best of them all.

Harlan, who started being noticed when he was but a kid fan, never stopped running. A bundle of incredible vitality, he has had more than twenty books published—collections of his over six hundred short stories—has carried off awards in whatever fields he has chosen to conquer, and is still turning out talented material at a great rate. I note that the novel is obviously not his form—he has but one s-f novel on his list of published works.

But the thing that concerns this discussion is Harlan Ellison as a prophet of doom. Ellison has never gone around saying that science fiction is dead and turning up his nose at s-f readers and fans—the implied viewpoint of the New Wavers. He has never proclaimed that his style of writing is the only modern one and everyone else should conform or go back to kindergarten. And he has never stopped defying the future to do its damnedest.

A Wellsian in the sense that I have defined it, he is always concerned with people and society, and anyone who could claim that he had hauled down his flag and was running into some somatic dugout would have to be totally unfamiliar with his work. Yet the fact remains that he is downbeat, that the great majority of his tales are downbeat, that they deal primarily with the next few decades, which are in no way pleasing to contemplate and which, as he depicts them, are quite gosh-darned nightmarish. But since Harlan Ellison is nothing if not exceedingly vocal, let me quote from a couple of places:

> "The world you were born into is going nuts. Just check around if you think I'm wrong. . . ."

> ". . . not Christ nor man nor governments of men will save you . . . writers about tomorrow must stop living in yesterday and work from their hearts and their guts and their courage to tell us about tomorrow, before all the tomorrows are stolen away from us . . . no one will come down from the mountain to save your lily-white hide or your black ass. God is within you. Save yourselves."

(The first is from the flyleaf of his first hard-cover book *Love Ain't Nothing but Sex Misspelled.* The second paragraph is from a paperback anthology, *The Beast That Shouted Love at the Heart of the World.*)

With the essence of that second statement I cannot disagree. It is what I have been saying here. It also defines the difference between Ellison and the Moorcock group—the latter clearly do not believe there will be a tomorrow to save or one that would be worth saving. And Ellison, who, from his stories, probably knows more and understands more about the hideous sides of the present and near future than they ever have, still thinks that there may be something over those stormy hills worth looking for.

25

Why Frodo Lives

STILL I QUESTION whether the constant depiction and reiteration of horrors, both mental and of the immediate future, are exactly the way to rally a fight for the cause of humanity. Considering the audience that science fiction reaches, the primary audience, that is, we have a readership of youth. It is youth in this day and age, we are told by newspapers and pedants, that is being alienated.

On the other hand, would a sort of Pollyanna Utopianism be of any greater merit? Equally unlikely—and the pure sort of idyllic Utopian tale is conspicuous by its absence in the strictly science-fiction output today.

But . . .

But there is something suspiciously like it around and thriving. And that is an allied field of fantasy which is being read by a large section of the science-fiction audience and an equally large section of youth who wouldn't be seen with a copy of *Analog.* I refer to what is called the literature of heroic fantasy, of which a dozen varieties are popping up in paperback books and which is elbowing its way onto the science-fiction racks on newsstands and into the columns of the magazines.

Most of it is scarcely worth looking at. Pulpy, quickly invented imitations of Edgar Rice Burroughs, Robert E. Howard, and J. R. R. Tolkien. Where did it come from? Why—from the popularity of the latter.

I spoke of *The Lord of the Rings* back at the start of this book, just to point out why that magnificent series of novels about Middle Earth cannot qualify for the designation science fiction. It is fantasy, wonderfully contrived, a world worked out in loving detail, a culture depicted with the depth of near-reality. This, however, does not explain why Tolkien's epic became so popular with youth, especially with college youth, and why it has sold in the millions of copies and is presumably still doing so.

It may not be science fiction but it is read and treasured by science-fiction readers. I myself as a member of the small committee of experts that first granted awards in the field, was instrumental in voting the Tolkien work the International Fantasy Award of its year (the Hugo awards came later and were a more popular-based outgrowth of this committee). As such I was guilty perhaps of being a premature Middle Earth enthusiast. In those days, the first year of its appearance in the United States, the Rings novels were available only in very high-priced hard-bound British imports.

I am also guilty of having lit the spark that started the explosion for Tolkien, in so far as it was the editions I initiated and edited that first put Tolkien on the newsstands in low-priced paperback editions.

Those pioneer paperback editions set off a controversy between publishers and fans that made headlines in newspapers and periodicals all over the country. I must admit that I was startled at the heat engendered. Those who felt that Tolkien had somehow been injured by the publishing competition rallied to his name with the ardor one would only expect from religious fanatics. It was clear that, while I, as an editor, could view Tolkien with a certain dispassion (after all, I had passed through my period of prime enthusiasm some years earlier), his newly found mass audience found in him something greater than mere entertainment reading, something you would almost suspect they were ready to die for.

It was a phenomenon one had to think about. Think about it I did, and observed too.

What did the *Lord of the Rings* signify? Why had it touched off such depths of support in its readers?

Looked at superficially, the *Lord of the Rings* novels might be supposed to be some sort of allegory about the rise of the Nazis and the defensive position in the face of that of Britain and France. But since we know that Tolkien started writing his epics long before Hitler, one could still suppose an allegory influencing its author's mind from World War I and the menace of the East against the comfortable shires and homes of Old England.

Tolkien himself has insistently denied this. At first I was inclined to take his denial as meaning that he himself simply wasn't aware of the allegorical significance. But I think now he is right. For what Tolkien did in his work was to write a modern fantasy in the style of the ancient epics of the founders of European civilization. *The Lord of the Rings* is not an allegory —it is of a style and form with Beowulf, the Nibelungen, the Eddas, the sagas of pre-medieval man.

In Middle Earth we have the ingredients of those works in that in the mind of the primitive saga storytellers such things as pure Good and pure Evil exist and are taken for granted. In those days a less sophisticated humanity could believe that there was in the universe an essence that was good and another essence that was evil. No psychological or economic analysis of one's opponents to shed light on their hidden motivations. No self-doubts, no seeking of the flaw in one's own soul, no anti-heroes or honorable villains, no room for weaklings or questioners.

So it is with Tolkien. Sauron is Evil, through and through, and his armies and minions are equally Evil. His motivation is all bad. His victory would be pure disaster, with no alleviating conversions.

Frodo is Good. His friends and companions are Good. Their motivations are unquestionably pure. Their victory is everyone's victory, because they are all that is Good and Sauron is all that is Bad.

Pure Good. Pure Evil. We had thought that in this twentieth-century world such concepts were taboo. Defunct. Compromise is the order of the day—if you can't lick 'em, join 'em.

But the men of a thousand years ago would never have understood that. They knew there was Good and that it had to be fought for.

So, then, what did it mean when thousands of college students, young people of our day and our age, suddenly started chalking on walls and penning on posters and putting on lapel buttons the slogan: "Frodo Lives."

What could it mean but that Good lives?

Good lives!

What does it mean when a thirst for novels wherein unmistakable heroes fight against unmistakable villains continues to show itself in fantasy writings, continues to force itself side by side with science fiction and compete for the same audience?

It means that there is hope for humanity and hope for youth. For it means that hundreds of thousands—possibly millions—of young intelligent people are not basically cynics and victims of despair. It means that the ancient belief in the rightness of innate Good—that belief which sustained all the armies of prehistory whose battles laid the foundations for all that we call civilization and culture—has not died from the human spirit. Youth recognized it when it came to them in its ancient pure form and rallied to it.

Let the New Wave sneer and snarl and cry that science fiction is dead and its vision of galactic futures dead; let them present their writings of despair filled with shock words and shock concepts; they have been defeated already by the cry *Frodo Lives!*

For, if Frodo lives, we shall not despair. However dark the clouds of the twentieth century, the shadow of Evil was equally dark—and, though it may take peril and pain, humanity shall overcome.

That is how I read the meaning of Tolkien.

26

Cosmotropism

I HAVE A THEORY. I think that space flight is not a whim that happened to arise in the minds of dreamers and became practical when rockets were invented for warfare and a lot of government money needed spending. I think that space flight is a condition of Nature that comes into effect when an intelligent species reaches the saturation point of its planetary habitat combined with a certain level of technological ability.

Since the human species had never previously fulfilled those conditions, we have never had occasion to note this outward-movement tropism before. But I think it is a built-in gene-directed drive for the spreading of the species and its continuation.

Let me give you an example of how this might be. If you have ever observed the growth of spore contamination in a Petri dish, you will be familiar with the experiment. Take a Petri dish—a flat dish of highly nutritive matter kept sterile—and expose it briefly to the air. Close it again, set it aside in a warm place, and watch it. Soon spots of dark green or brown or blue will appear on the surface of the nutriment. These are colonies of microscopic plant life, algae, fungi, mold, that have grown from spores which wafted down upon the surface of the culture during the brief period of its exposure to the atmosphere.

As you know, the air of Earth is contaminated with such spores, by the countless trillions of trillions, floating unseen by our eyes wherever there is air. The Petri dish experiment is a common one in elementary science which demonstrates exactly that point.

Let us watch what happens next. We have our re-covered dish with its several colonies of plant life. These grow as the growing vegetation (microscopic but vegetation just the same) pushes outward devouring the nutriment, turning it into new plant life (and also transforming some of it into waste). The several spots grow. They begin to touch each other's borders. There is a brief period of stasis, then they grow around and into each other. In time the Petri dish is one solid surface of mold life and no un-touched part of the nutriment can be seen. The mold flourishes. It grows dense. It grows tall. It then flowers—it begins to form spore balls.

Assume that the lid of the dish is taken off. The spore balls reach maturity—they burst and send out into the atmosphere millions and millions of new spore seeds to float away. After this flowering the mold forest begins to diminish. The nutriment of the dish is being exhausted. Some of the mold begins to dry up, to die away. Spots remain alive for a while, but unless new moisture comes, unless the nutriment is renewed, eventually the colony dies away.

Mold life, lichen, fungi—they are not intelligent species. What they do is all gene-programed, totally involuntary, automatic biochemical responses to given conditions. Of the millions of spores sent out from such colonies, how many will come to rest on surfaces conducive to new colonies? One? Two? Some will. Out of trillions whose numbers wander the airs of Earth from pole to pole and as far up as the limits of the stratosphere enough will come to rest to guarantee that the kinds of life that gave birth to them will be continued forever and forever.

But what of the original colonies—those of the Petri dish that sent these spores forth never to return? They vanish eventually. They can know nothing of their seedlings' success or failure. The reproduction of the mold species is an act of Nature that disregards the individual life of the parent plant.

Consider now the planet Earth. Upon its surface there arises an intelligent species which survives all natural disasters including its own various follies and manages to spread its colonies onto every inhabitable spot on Earth. Every continent, every island which can give adequate nutriment to a family of human beings, does so. The isolated colonies of human beings that existed on the planetary surface as of fifty thousand years ago— and the eons that preceded—made contact with each other in the past tens of thousands of years. They touched borders here and there, they clashed, they combined. Now, in this day and age, the earth is one inhabited surface—countries merge daily in commerce and interdependence, and the idea and necessity of merging all governments into a single supergovernment grows in the minds of men until it would seem that in the next century or so—other conditions set aside—there would be only one all-embracing worldwide government.

Consider also that the nutriment of the earth is rapidly being exhausted and that the numbers of humanity are growing to a danger point.

Now note that in the past half century the idea of space flight, which was a whimsy of past centuries, caught hold, became potent, powerful, and in the past three decades became an increasingly dominant factor in technology and social endeavors. A large section of the public funds of the two major powers of Earth is diverted to the development of means of getting into space—and there is strangely little protest from their populations.

What then? Science fiction, increasingly prominent in the concepts of the public and the projections of scientists, points continuously and insistently on exploring the neighboring planets, and on colonizing them if possible. The idea crops up of crossing the light years between our sun and the others around it in huge space ships, designed to carry a village-sized mass of men and women, designed as tiny man-made planets so that these men and women can propagate, raise children, raise the several generations that must live and die before the hundreds of years that it may take that vast ship to cross the gap between one sun and another at less than the speed of light. Such starships travel until they find a habitable planet, and settle thereon, ending their travel of many generations, discharging their cargo of human beings to establish homes on that distant world, to set up towns, to put a human culture there.

The thinking is present. It is now part of the general scene in science-fiction writing. It seems to have first made its appearance some time early in the 1930's—I recall a short story telling of the landing of such a starship with its hundreds of human colonists. I can't recall the title at the moment—it was not a distinguished tale otherwise, and I suspect that even earlier specimens might be found.

Some great novels have been written about such starships, about life aboard them, about the possible disasters that could confront them. Robert A. Heinlein wrote two great novellas *Universe* and *Common Sense* about such a starship—they are reprinted as one in his book *Orphans of the Sky*. Brian Aldiss' first really great s-f novel was such a book, called *Non-Stop* in its original edition, and simply *Star Ship* in its American edition. A recent Nebula winner, Alexei Panshin's *Rite of Passage,* is a particularly outstanding example. Dozens of other examples are available now in great variety and of varying quality.

The idea is accepted. It is part of the science-fiction roots of modern civilization. It will not be too long before the thought of constructing such vessels begins to slip into the halls of politics, first lightly, seemingly facetiously, then seriously. (Note how easily Vice-President Agnew slipped the idea of a manned expedition to Mars in the 1980's into the public eye with no particular gasps of astonishment or objections.)

We stop now to ask why. Starships will not alleviate the overcrowding of Earth. We cannot emigrate to the stars ourselves—only our children's children's children (who will never have known Earth)—and then only in minuscule numbers. What are a few thousand, or even a few tens of thousands of star migrants, when the Earth's population contains billions? Starships will be expensive—they will take a good chunk of any nation's economy. But they will be made. I have no doubt of that.

Because I think—and I think this argument will be used effectively by political leaders—they are humanity's guarantee of cosmic immortality. Once we have spread out beyond the now limited confines of this one habitable planet we—or human beings carrying our genes and our heritage—will become immortal. Let a thousand starships go out and we will be like the spores of the air—our species will go on forever and our memory, that of Earth, will be revered forever.

Because we are not mindless spores, do not forget. The analogy can go only so far. We are as far from the spores on the spectrum of life as we can get. Unlike those simple life forms, we are the only living species of Earth that can notice the stars, that can speculate upon them, that is conscious of past, present, and future, and that can project upon them. We can and we do direct our own fates. We can change nature—we are not totally dependent upon its bounty and doomed to die when we have used it all up. We know of what our Petri dish consists and we know how to conserve it, how to renew it, how to reconstruct it. True, we are bunglers and muddlers at this stage. But we do know how. Time and the pressure of numbers will force us to utilize our knowledge and our intelligent capacities to preserve ourselves here.

We do have this compulsion to go out. We have a conscious drive for immortality—if not of the individual, certainly of the nations and species. Our record is that of a fighting beast of herdlike nature yet of individuality. Our record, shown in a million ways, is that our individuals will sacrifice themselves for the common good—our young men have gone out in a thousand wars and a million tribal feuds before there were wars, and have given their lives in the belief they were fighting to save the lives and preserve the advantages of their kinsmen at home, of their fellow tribesmen, of their fellow countrymen. The man who sacrifices his life for his fellow men does not know whether he has died in vain. He cannot possibly gain personal advantage from his own death. He follows what must be a natural instinct, a human tropism, that programs him to be prepared to fight to the death for a cause he takes on faith to be necessary to his species' survival.

I think the drive to send out starships as spores of humanity is a tropism which, now that we have spread over all the Earth, is come to the fore in human affairs. I can foresee the day, which may be only in the next century or two, when it will be common practice to send up stargoing capsules, each with a dozen men and women, each directed at a star around which we will have cause to believe there are planets which may be habitable. Not blind, as with spores, but intelligently directed. If we can carry such men and women in suspended animation, so much the better. Robotic controls can do the work, automatic sensors can waken the cargo when the time comes.

Or mile-long self-contained starships, miniature worlds in which generations can live and die, may be the way. Whichever will prove most practical, that will humanity do. For it will be our ticket to immortality. It will be the birth of cosmic humanity, of that Galactic Empire which seems to be surely part of the future once we become truly the masters of space flight.

27

Shapers of the Future

NOW I COME TO THE END of this study of science fiction and its meaning in the world. The books and stories I have mentioned barely scratch the surface of the thousands and thousands of tales that have been amassed over the past half century and which compose the body of the field. These works represent in their way the visions of science-and-humanity-oriented minds of the way the world has gone and the ways in which we might go.

There is a rising tide of gloom and concern in the world today and it is reflected in modern science fiction. Yet it is but a tiny countercurrent to the vast movement of ideas that continue to fascinate and grip the minds of the most imaginative people of our day. It can never be otherwise.

Wherever science goes, in whatever direction a discovery seems to point, these are guidelines to the soaring speculations of the science-fiction writers. They seize upon, they examine, and they leap to conclusions that trained experimenters dare not. Their mirrors of the future shape the future. Such speculations, such visions, are not illusions to pass with the change of light, but affect that future. They make their mark, however faint at first, but a real mark nonetheless in the minds of men and the currents of the world.

When I say that science-fiction writing in the vast majority speaks of an infinite range that is about to open to humanity in the universe I say that that very thought reinforces the probability that this will be so. When I say that science-fiction writers believe we will survive whatever catastrophes nature or man may have in store for us, survive or bypass them, that too increases the chances for such survival.

Some anthropologists like to make the claim that humanity is but a very recent thing on this Earth—a mere newcomer whose tenure is measured in a few tens of thousands of years—which is like a second to the history of life on this planet. I say this is nonsense. We are the living descendants of ancestors whose roots go back to the very dawn of life. For the past eight or ten million years our ancestors have been living by their brain power, which has steadily increased as use and recurrent danger honed their wits. We ourselves, living today, are, each one of us, the descendants of the survivors of every disaster that has ever happened—the survivors, I repeat. We have a capacity for survival—by our wits—that should not ever be underrated.

The troubles that loom ahead may seem difficult to overcome, but science-fiction writers have already imagined various ways in which they could be met, by which they could be surmounted, or by means of which we could survive them. Once a thing can be imagined, it can be done—such is the lesson I draw from science fiction.

If we can conceive of it, then it is possible.

If it is possible, then eventually even the dullest among us will see the way when dire necessity compels.

The leaders of nations, the political rulers of the world, are a breed that often seems to be lacking in vivid imagination and not given to fantastic speculation. No matter. These politicians, whatever their philosophy or creed or allegiance, have one thing in common. They are not suicidal. When an issue comes up which threatens their power, their property, their glory, and their lives, they do act. Given the impetus of minds that have seen various ways forward, these leaders have a way of utilizing those programs.

This is the way it is and this is the way it is going to work out.

We live in a world shaped by science fiction and whose future has been charted by science fiction. I have spelled out something of that charting. The outlook is terrific. Whatever may be the personal fate of any specific individual in the years ahead, I have no doubt at all of the fate of the people of the Earth. Everything that has gone before is truly but prehistory.

Whatever may be, I am sure of one thing. There is a famous poem which has the constant refrain, "This is the way the world ends." Well . . .

We are not going to end with a bang.

We are not going to end with a whimper.

We are not going to end.

That's all.

INDEX